PEARSON

Larry DeBoer

MacroPolicy
Learning Macroeconomics
with Policy History

Ninth Edition

Pearson Education, Inc., 330 Hudson Street, New York, New York 10013
A Pearson Education Company
www.pearsoned.com

Printed in the United States of America

1   17

000200010272104035

KM

ISBN 10: 1-323-77776-8
ISBN 13: 978-1-323-77776-3

MacroPolicy
Learning Macroeconomics With Policy History
Ninth Edition

For Melody

Larry DeBoer
Department of Agricultural Economics
Purdue University
Krannert Building, Room 618
403 W. State Street
West Lafayette, Indiana   47907-9176
ldeboer@purdue.edu

What's on the Cover?

It's a collection of economic artifacts.

1. *A picture of a Federal Deposit Insurance Corporation sticker in a bank window. Chapter 5 examines the FDIC's purpose.*
2. *A 20 yuan bill from China. Chapter 8 considers China's current economic policy problems.*
3. *A 1000 yen bill from Japan. Chapter 11 covers Japan's economic troubles since the 1990's.*
4. *A one dollar Federal Reserve note. Chapter 4 starts the discussion of the Federal Reserve.*
5. *A postcard from the American Stock Exchange, c. 1960. Chapter 5 examines the stock market.*
6. *A ration book from World War II. Chapter 7 explains why rationing was needed during the war.*
7. *A one dollar Federal Reserve Note from 1918. Chapter 4 discusses how these paid for World War I.*
8. *A 50 baht note from Thailand. Chapter 10 covers the Asian crisis of 1997-98 that started in Thailand.*
9. *A postcard of the Mt. Washington Hotel in Bretton Woods, New Hampshire. Chapter 8 tells the story of how the world's international finance system was reorganized there in 1944.*
10. *A matchbook advertising war bonds from World War II. Chapter 7 explains their role in war finance.*
11. *A picture of a road sign from the American Recovery and Reinvestment Act. Chapter 11 considers its effect on recovery from the Great Recession of 2007-09.*
12. *A Social Security record book from the late 1930's. Chapter 6 looks at its origins and problems.*
13. *A button from the National Recovery Administration from the mid-1930's. Chapter 6 discusses the NRA and other New Deal programs.*
14. *A Whip Inflation Now button from 1974. Chapter 9 talks about the Great Inflation of the 1970's.*
15. *A 100 trillion dollar Zimbabwe note from 2008. Chapter 9 tells the story of hyperinflation.*

Table of Contents

Data Model Story

One goal of this book is to show you how you can use macroeconomic data and a model of the economy to analyze and understand economic events. We use the stories of the U.S. economy and policy since 1900 to demonstrate how this can be done.

The book assembles the model piece by piece as we tell the story of U.S. economic policy since 1900. If you want the whole model all at once, and a guide to its use, see the appendix starting on page 337. It's called "How to Use the Macroeconomic Model."

Here's a table showing where to find the 16 examples using the model to construct a story out of some macroeconomic data. The "data page" refers to the page that includes the table of macroeconomic data. Pages before and after show the model and tell the story.

You'll see that half of the analyses on this list are in Chapters 9, 10 and 11. That's because the macro model is completed in Chapter 8. These analyses use all the tools and data that we develop in the book. You'll also see that three of the analyses are about the Great Recession that started in 2007. We use that enormous event throughout the book, to relate history to current events. The analysis in Chapter 11 pulls it all together.

Event	Data Years	Chapter	Data Page
The Great Recession	2007-2009	3	72
The Panic of 1907	1906-1909	4	90
World War I and After	1918-1922	4	102
The Great Depression	1929-1933	5	120
The Roosevelt Recession	1936-1939	6	153
World War II	1940-1944	7	172
Korean War	1950-1954	7	185
The Great Recession Revisited	2007-2010	8	208
The Great Society and Vietnam	1964-1968	9	244
The First Stagflation	1969-1972	9	246
Oil Shock	1973-1975	9	251
Great Recession of 1981-82	1979-1983	9	258
Crowding Out	1983-1985	10	274
The Goldilocks Economy	1996-2000	10	284
The Great Recession Complete	2007-2009	11	313
The Long Slow Recovery	2010-2016	11	319

Chapter 1
The Big Picture

The recession that began in December 2007 and ended in June 2009 was the longest, and by some measures the deepest, since the 1930's. What made it so bad? The 1990's saw the longest economic expansion in United States history. Why did the economy do so well? Since 2009 the economy has grown slowly. It's been one of the slowest recoveries ever. Why did the long, long 1990's expansion have to end? Why was the 2007-2009 Great Recession so great? Why has the expansion since 2009 been so disappointing? And, is there another recession on the horizon?

These are the kinds of questions macroeconomics is meant to answer. We will develop models to explain and even predict changes in the economy. But before we can answer these questions, even before we can *ask* them, we have to know what happened. How do we know that there are expansions and recessions? How do we know that there was an expansion during the 1990's, and another between 2001 and 2007, and another since mid-2009? How do we know that 2008 and 2009 were recession years? How do we know that the recovery since the recession has been slow?

How do we know, as is so often said, that the 2007-09 recession was the worst since the Great Depression of the 1930's? Just how bad was the Great Depression, anyway?

People didn't need economists to tell them that the economy was doing badly in 2008 and 2009. People were losing their jobs and watching family members, friends and neighbors lose theirs. Businesses were going bankrupt. Banks were failing. Stock values were down. People were losing their homes. School districts were laying off teachers. Help-wanted signs were few and far between. But even in hard times, some people were being hired, some people were starting businesses, some banks were profitable, and some stocks were rising, and some people were buying homes.

Relying on the experiences of a few individuals is a haphazard way of knowing what is happening. Pick one group's experience and we'll get one view of the economy. Pick another's and we'll get a different view.

What's the solution to this problem? *Aggregation.* We'll add up the value of the things that businesses produce, and call it total output. We'll add up people's experiences finding and losing jobs, and call it total employment and unemployment. We'll average the prices that people paid for the things they bought, and call it the price level. We'll miss a lot of detail with aggregate measures. But we'll get a surer sense of what is happening to the economy as a whole.

Then we can ask why output rose, then fell, then rose and fell and rose again. Why were people employed yesterday but unemployed today? Why did prices rise so much in 2008, and why did they fall in 2009? We can create a macroeconomic model to answer these questions. The model will explain and predict changes in aggregate measures of the economy. That's what macroeconomics is: the economics of aggregates, the economics of the big picture.

We'll use four main measures of the economy to describe the big picture. They are: the output of goods and services, the prices of goods and services, the share of the labor force which is unemployed and the interest rates charged by lenders. The rest of this chapter will explain how each of these is measured and how each behaves in recessions and expansions. We'll discuss a tricky idea called purchasing power. We'll get to those questions about the Great Depression, too.

Output

Output is the result of production, cars, houses and hamburgers, roads and missiles, doctors', lawyers' and plumbers' services produced in a year. Output is measured by *gross domestic product*, known by its initials, GDP. GDP is defined as "the total value of final goods and services produced in a year."

> **Gross Domestic Product is the total value of final goods and services produced in a year.**

Gross domestic product is *product* because it measures production, the products the economy produces. It's *domestic* because it measures the products produced within the borders of the nation. And it's *gross* (make up your own joke here) because it doesn't subtract depreciation, the equipment and infrastructure that wears out when domestic product is produced.

The basic method for calculating GDP is simple. Take the number of things produced, multiply by the price at which those things sold, and add up the resulting dollar values. GDP is thus the dollar value of cars, hamburgers, doctors' services and everything else that people and businesses in the economy produced during the year. That's what we mean by *value*.

There would be a danger of double and triple-counting some production, though, if we didn't limit the value to *final* goods and services. These are the values of products sold to their final users. A car is a final good, sold to a consumer for transportation. The price of the car includes the price of the steel which the carmaker purchased during production. If we count the value of the steel, and the value of the car, we have counted the value of the steel twice. The steel used to make the car is not a final good. Only the sale of the car is counted in GDP. This does not mean that steel output is ignored. It is counted, as part of the value of the car.

Some sales of final goods are not counted in GDP, because they were not *produced during the year*. The biggest category of such goods is housing. The value of houses built in prior years but sold in the current year is not counted in current year GDP. Only newly constructed houses are included. A house built in 1997 and sold (again) in 2017 was counted in 1997's GDP, so it shouldn't be counted in 2017's GDP. The same logic applies to sales of used cars and "used" paintings by Picasso. The values of these things were included in the GDP of the year they were made. We don't want to count them again. The services of the real estate agent, auctioneer or broker are included in GDP, though. Bringing buyer and seller together this year is a service that counts as production.

GDP is not a perfect measure of the value of output. Some output is so hard to measure that it's ignored in the GDP accounts. Housewives and househusbands definitely produce services, but their output isn't sold so there's no receipt for prices and quantities. Clean air is valuable, and we make efforts to "produce" it, with smokestack scrubbers and other pollution control equipment, but air isn't bought or sold. You aren't charged every time you take a breath. The value of clean air isn't included in GDP.

Some products are sold for a price, but the transactions are hidden.   Illegal drugs are sold—they have prices and quantities—but the "sales people" take pains to hide the transactions. The GDP accountants don't know about them. These hidden transactions are known as the *underground economy*.   Less toxic activities like the unrecorded tips of servers in restaurants are also underground. Since the prices used to value restaurant meals don't include all the tips, their value in GDP probably is undercounted.

GDP is divided into five major categories: *consumption (C), investment (I), government purchases (G), exports (X) and imports (M)*. An identity that can help keep our thinking straight is

GDP = Q = C + I + G + X – M.

We'll use Q as the single letter symbol for output. It stands for "quantity," the quantity of all goods and services. The other letters stand for consumption, investment, government purchases, exports and imports, in that order.

Consumption is output purchased by households. We usually call them consumers. Some of this output is "non-durable", like food and clothing; some is "durable", like cars and appliances; and some are services, like haircuts, medical care and legal advice. Consumption is by far the largest category of GDP. Reporters are fond of writing that "consumers are more than two-thirds of the economy." They mean that consumption is always a bit more than two-thirds of the value of GDP.

> *GDP is the sum of consumption (C), investment (I), government purchases (G), exports (X), minus imports (M).*

Investment is output mostly purchased by businesses. It includes factories, equipment, office buildings, retail stores, warehouses, power lines, railroad tracks— in fact, anything used by businesses to produce other goods. In our model, investment does not mean financial investment. It is *not* stocks, bonds, land or gold.   It is the value of the tangible things which are purchased by businesses to produce other things. Housing is included as investment, even though it is purchased by consumers. This is because it lasts so long. Think of a house as a tangible investment that produces a service called "shelter." *Inventories* are also included as investment. Inventories are the products intended for sale to customers, but not yet sold. A product produced for sale in one year, but not sold until the next, is counted as inventory investment in the year it's produced.

Government purchases are resources or inputs purchased by government. We can't measure government output—the value of national defense or police protection or elementary education—because it is not sold at a price in a market. Even the quantity of government output is often hard to measure. How much "national defense" do the armed forces produce? Instead, we count the value of inputs: the wages of employees and the value of the buildings and equipment governments buy to produce output.   Employees, buildings and equipment are inputs used to produce government output. A local school district pays teachers, constructs classrooms and buys desks in order to produce education for pupils. We can't say for sure how much education is produced, and it isn't sold to pupils for a price, so we have to count the value of inputs instead.

Government purchases do not include *transfer payments*, which is revenue collected from taxpayers and distributed to retired people, disabled people, sick people, unemployed people or poor people. Examples are Social Security, Medicare and Medicaid, unemployment insurance, veterans' pensions, and welfare. These are not purchases by government. They are income for benefit recipients, and they are counted as consumption when the recipients spend the income. If we counted transfer payments as government purchases, and counted the consumer goods that beneficiaries buy with these payments, we'd be counting them twice.

Exports are sales of goods and services to people, businesses and governments of other countries. *Imports* are purchases of goods and services from people, businesses and governments of other countries. Since the value of exported goods and services are produced in the country during the year, we want to add them in with the nation's output. Since the value of imported goods is not produced in the country, we do not want to count them. We subtract M in the equation, rather than just ignoring imports, because imports are counted in C, I and G. Consumption, for example, includes cars made in Japan, shirts made in China, computer services delivered from India, coffee grown in Columbia. Imports are subtracted to remove the value of these items from total GDP. Exports minus imports, together, are called *net exports*. Net exports are a measure of the trade balance. If exports exceed imports, there is a trade surplus; if imports exceed exports, there is a trade deficit.

Real GDP. GDP in any year is the product of that year's output and that year's prices. When GDP changes from one year to the next, it's because output changes, and because prices change. This is unacceptable. We want changes in GDP to be a measure of changes in *production* from year to year. Price changes cloud this measure. *Nominal GDP* is output measured in current prices, the prices that existed in the year the output was produced. Even if output is the same from one year to the next, or if it declines, GDP may rise because of increases in the prices used to measure value. That makes it hard to identify recessions with nominal GDP.

We solve this problem by dividing nominal GDP by a *price index* to get real GDP. A price index measures the change in the prices of output, on average. Dividing nominal GDP by the price index gives *real* GDP, which is a measure of the change in output without the influence of price changes. This is called "deflating" GDP, which is why the price index is called the *GDP deflator*. Sometimes real GDP is called "GDP adjusted for inflation," sometimes "GDP at constant prices." In the macroeconomic model, and in this book, when we refer to GDP we usually mean *real* GDP.

Real GDP growth, or "economic growth," or just "growth", is much talked about in economic policy. These terms all mean the percentage change in real GDP from one year to the next. For example, nominal GDP in 2016 was $18,569 billion (about eighteen and a half trillion dollars). Nominal GDP in 2015 was $18,037 billion. The $533 billion increase between these years shows an increase in output. But since prices increased between 2015 and 2016,

> *Real Gross Domestic Product is Nominal GDP divided by a price index. Real GDP growth is the percentage change in real GDP from one year to the next.*

the true increase is masked. Part of the increase in output was just a rise in prices, not an increase in production.

A price index, the GDP deflator, is used to change nominal GDP to real GDP. The deflator in 2015 was 110.00. The deflator in 2016 was 111.45. The fact that the deflator increased means that the prices used to measure value increased from 2015 to 2016. The *base year* of the deflator is 2009, which means the deflator has been set to exactly 100 in that year. To measure real GDP, divide nominal GDP for each year by the deflator for that year:

2015: $18,037 / 1.1000 = $16,397
2016: $18,569 / 1.1145 = $16,661.

To use the GDP deflators this way we must shift their decimal points two places to the left; that is, dividing by 100. The results are real GDP for each year—GDP as it would be measured if prices had remained at their 2009 levels. It's called constant price GDP, or GDP at 2009 prices (since the deflator is 100 in the year 2009, nominal and real GDP are the same in that year).

GDP growth for 2016 is the percentage change in real GDP from 2015 to 2016:

$(16{,}661 - 16{,}397) / 16{,}397 = 264 / 16{,}397 = 0.016.$

Multiply by 100 to show the result in percentage terms, and GDP growth for 2016 is 1.6%. That's a positive number, so the quantity of goods and services increased between 2015 and 2016, though not by that much. Sometimes real GDP declines, as it did in 2008. Then the percentage change is negative. We refer to the measure as "growth" even when it's a decline. It's "negative growth." It makes sense to economists, anyway.

- *What happens to real gross domestic product in recessions and expansions?*

"The recession has (officially) ended" said a *New York Times* headline on September 20, 2010. Of course, the report said that the recession had ended in June, 2009, more than a year earlier. This just in!

The beginnings and ends of recessions are marked by a committee of ten economists on the Business Cycle Dating Committee at the National Bureau of Economic Research. The NBER is a nonprofit group based in Cambridge, Massachusetts. The NBER defines a recession as a significant decline in economic activity that spreads across the economy and can last from a few months to more than a year. "Troughs" mark the ends of recessions; "peaks" the ends of expansions. They use data on the production of goods and services, on employment, on incomes earned, and other indicators. The succession of expansions and recessions is called the *business cycle*. Since 1985 there have been three recessions, 1990-91, 2001 and 2007-2009.

Real GDP falls during recessions and rises during expansions. It's one of the main indicators of the "business cycle."

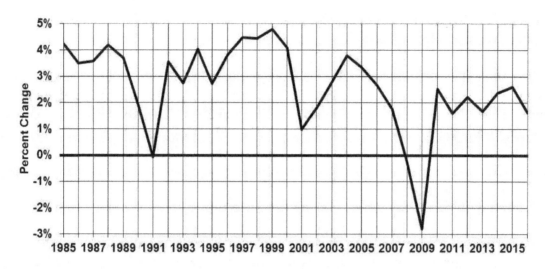

Figure 2-1. Real GDP Growth, 1985-2016. Calculated as the yearly percent change in real Gross Domestic Product. When the U.S. economy is expanding it tends to grow between 1.5% and 5% per year. "Negative growth" of real GDP means output fell from one year to the next. That's a recession. There was a recession in 1990-91, and another in 2001. The 2001 recession was mild. Real GDP fell during part of the year, but increased a little for the year as a whole. The 2007-09 recession began in December 2007. The 2.8% drop in real GDP in 2009 was the biggest decline since 1946. That's deep enough that we call it the "Great Recession." The economy began to recover in 2010, but growth has averaged only 2.1% since then, which is a very slow recovery.

What happens to real GDP during recessions? It goes down; unless it's going up. Real GDP increased in the middle quarter of the 2001 recession, and in the second quarter of 2008. That's one reason why the NBER takes so long to call peaks and troughs. What if the growth in 2009-10 had been followed by more declines? Would it be a new recession or a continuation of the old one? It took them more than a year to decide that there had been enough growth since mid-2009 to call the recession over. Any new declines in real GDP would indicate a new recession.

Some recessions are more serious than others. The 1990-91 recession had bigger drops in real GDP than the 2001 recession, but both are marked as lasting eight months. The 2007-2009 recession was 18 months long, longer than any recession since the Great Depression of 1929-1933. It had much bigger drops in real GDP than either of the previous two recessions.

The end of a recession does not mean that the economy is fully recovered. Far from it. Recession dates mark a period when the economy is getting worse. That's why the end of a recession is called a "trough." The last day of recession, and the first day of recovery, are the economy's two worst days.

Inflation Rate

We measure the level of prices with a price index. A price index is an average price of the goods and services produced in the economy. The GDP deflator is a price index. The products in the GDP deflator are "weighted" by the importance of each product in GDP. High value items (with high prices, big quantities, or both) are counted more; low value items are counted less. Increases in the price index imply that prices of goods and services have increased, on average. That's *inflation*. Decreases in the price index imply that prices of goods and services have decreased, on average. That's *deflation*.

There are two main price indexes used to measure inflation. One is the GDP deflator, which is the price index used to turn nominal GDP into real GDP. It measures the weighted-average price of all the goods and services included in GDP. The other is the *Consumer Price Index* (CPI) which is the weighted average price of goods and services that a typical household buys.

$1 in 1909 →in 1919?

$\dfrac{1919\ CPI}{1909\ CPI}$ × price in 1909

The GDP deflator includes the prices of more goods and services than the CPI. It averages the prices of the consumer goods and services that are in the CPI, but also investment goods like machinery and concrete, government goods and services like police officer wages and missile prices, and the prices of exports and imports. The CPI, though, is a better measure of the prices that households pay. It's also the inflation measure most often reported by the media. We'll use it as our inflation measure most of the time.

real price in 1983 in 2010

$\dfrac{price\ for\ year}{CPI}$ × 100

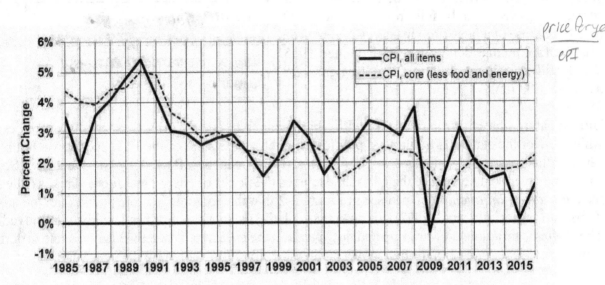

Figure 2-2. Inflation Rates, 1985-2016. Calculated as the yearly percent change in the Consumer Price Index, all items and core. The all items CPI inflation rate is affected by energy prices. When it's above the core inflation rate, oil prices were increasing. When it's below the core inflation rate, oil prices were decreasing. Oil prices surged in 2008 and collapsed in 2009, which explains the extremes in the CPI all items inflation rate. That collapse produced the deflation in 2009, a negative inflation rate. Oil prices fell in 2015, too, which is why the all items inflation rate was so much lower than the core inflation rate. Inflation tends to drop in recessions. This is especially evident in the core rate, without the "noise" from oil prices. Core inflation declined during and after the recessions of 1990-91, 2001 and 2007-2009. Likewise, the core rate tends to rise as expansions continue, as in 1986-90, 1999-2001, 2003-2006 and since 2014.

Price indexes are weighted averages, because they average the prices of goods and services based on their importance in GDP or in household spending. For example, if households spend twice as much on shoes as they do on shaving cream, the price of shoes will be twice as important as the price of shaving cream in the average price of consumer goods, as measured by the CPI.

An index takes the value of 100 in an arbitrary year. This means that the price index numbers are meaningless by themselves. They take on meaning only when compared over time, only when they are used to measure price changes: inflation and deflation. The GDP deflator equals 100 in the year 2009. The CPI equals 100 for the average of the years 1982-1984. We measure inflation or deflation as the percentage change in a price index over a period of time, usually a year. The inflation rate for 2014 is the percentage change in a price index from 2013 to 2014.

For example, the all items CPI for 2015 was 237.0 the CPI for 2016 was 240.0. The inflation rate for 2016 is

(240.0 – 237.0) / 233.0 = 3.0 / 237.0 = 0.013.

Multiply by 100 to show the result in percentage terms, and the inflation rate for 2016 is 1.3%. This is a positive number, so it represents inflation. Sometimes—very rarely—the inflation rate is negative. That's deflation. The average price of consumer goods actually fell from 2008 to 2009, mostly because of a huge drop in energy prices. This was the first annual deflation recorded since 1955. We'll still call it an inflation rate though. It's negative inflation.

> *An inflation rate is the percentage change in a price index from one year to the next.*

Unfortunately, the CPI often is distorted by big changes in energy prices, especially oil prices, which reflect the state of Middle East politics as much as the state of the U.S. economy. It also can be distorted by big changes in food prices, which can be affected by the weather. So, sometimes we use a version of the CPI that excludes the prices of energy and food. This is called the *core rate of inflation*. You can see in Figure 2-2 that the core rate is more stable than the all-items rate (especially since 1997), because two volatile categories of prices have been removed. The all-items inflation rate varies up and down around the core rate. When the all-items rate differs from the core rate one year, it often moves in the direction of the core rate the next year.

- *What happens to inflation in recessions and expansions?*

Inflation tends to fall after recessions start, and rise after expansions start. Inflation fell during and after the 1990-91 recession, and kept falling for years after that. But the end of the expansion it was rising, though. Inflation fell during and after the 2001 recession, but began rising in 2003. Inflation dropped a lot once the Great Recession turned really bad in 2009. It's begun to rise recently.

Sales decline during recessions, and businesses try to hold down price increases and even put their products on sale, trying to attract buyers. But why does inflation keep falling after the recession is over?

Remember that the end of the recession means the economy has stopped declining, not that it's suddenly just fine. The trough the economy's low point. The months after the trough are pretty close to that low point, too. The economy begins to expand, but full recovery takes years. Sales are still pretty bad in the first year or two of an expansion, so businesses hold off on price increases.

> *The inflation rate begins to fall after the recession is underway, and usually keeps falling for a few years after the recession ends.*

Unemployment Rate
The *unemployment rate* is the percentage of the labor force that is unemployed. The *labor force* is the number of people age 16 and over who are willing and able to work, whether they are

working or not. The labor force is the sum of the number of *employed* people and the number of *unemployed* people. There is also a large group classified as *not in the labor force*. Then there are people under age 16 (usually called "children") who are not classified in any of these categories.

> **The unemployment rate is the percentage of unemployed people in the labor force.**

The government surveys about 60,000 people each month to estimate the number of people who are employed, unemployed, and not in the labor force. People are classified as employed if they are working for pay, or working in a family business, on vacation, or otherwise absent from a job to which they expect to return. People are classified as unemployed if they are not working and are actively seeking work, or if they are laid off and expecting recall. People classified as not in the labor force are able to work but not working or looking for work, usually because they are retired, in school or keeping house. A special category of people not in the labor force are the *discouraged workers* who are not working and not seeking work because they do not think they will find a job. They are not counted as unemployed because they did not seek work in the past month, yet their numbers tend to rise in recessions. The rest of the population couldn't work even if they wanted to. They are mostly children under 16, but also adults in prison or in the hospital. The Bureau of Labor Statistics doesn't count these people.

For example, the average number of employed people each month in 2016 was 151,437,000, which we usually show as 151,437 thousand. The number of unemployed people was 7,749 thousand. The labor force is the sum of these two figures, 159,186 thousand. The number not in the labor force was 94,351 thousand. The unemployment rate is the number of unemployed as a percentage of the labor force,

$$\frac{UE}{E+UE} = \%$$

$$7{,}749 \,/\, 159{,}186 = 0.049.$$

Multiply by 100 to put this figure in percentage terms, and the unemployment rate for 2016 was 4.9%. The unemployment rate peaked at 9.6% in 2010, so it's dropped a lot since then. It's near the 4.6% rate in 2006-07, at the end of the expansion, just before the Great Recession.

- *Why are people unemployed?*

It is useful to divide the reasons for unemployment into three causes: cyclical, frictional and structural. Some unemployment is *cyclical*. When the economy falls into recession, workers are laid off or let go, and people entering the labor force have difficulty finding jobs. The unemployment rate goes up. When the economy moves back to expansion, workers are recalled to their jobs, firms increase their hiring, and people entering the labor force find it easier to get jobs. The unemployment rate goes down. Cyclical unemployment can drop to zero if the economy is operating at capacity, which simply means that all the economy's resources are in use. This is sometimes called *full employment*.

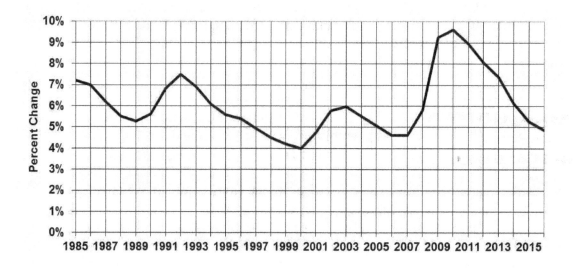

Figure 2-3. Unemployment Rate, 1985-2016. Calculated as the average yearly number of unemployed people as a percentage of the average yearly labor force. The unemployment rate falls in expansions, and rises during and just after recessions. The 1980's expansion brought the unemployment rate down to just above 5%, but after the 1990-91 recession it rose above 7%. The long 1990's expansion brought the unemployment rate down to 4% by 2000, the lowest rate in 30 years. The rate rose to 6% after the 2001 recession. The rate fell back under 5% in the 2000's expansion, but rose to 9.6% in 2010, as a result of the Great Recession of 2007-09. That was the highest rate since the early 1980's. Unemployment has fallen since then, finally dropping below 5% in 2016. Because of frictional and structural unemployment, the unemployment rate never hits zero.

Some unemployment is *frictional*. Frictional unemployment results from the fact that it takes time for workers to find jobs and for employers to find workers. People must search want ads, post resumes on the internet, and generally "pound the pavement." Employers must sift applications, schedule interviews, and decide who to hire. Frictional unemployment will exist even if the economy is at full employment, even if there is a job opening for every unemployed worker. Frictional unemployment is sometimes called *search* unemployment, because it simply takes time for employers and employees to find one another.

> **The three kinds of unemployment are cyclical, frictional and structural.**

Some unemployment is *structural*. There may be a million unemployed people and a million job openings, but if the jobs are for nurses and plumbers, while the unemployed people are programmers and steel workers, the jobs will not be filled and the workers will remain unemployed. Likewise, the job openings may be in Indiana but the unemployed people may be in California, or the job openings may be in the suburbs while the unemployed people are in the central city.

Technological change can cause structural unemployment. If factories install robots on their assembly lines, there will be job openings for robotics engineers, but unemployed factor workers.

Structural unemployment is sometimes called *mismatch* unemployment. The skills or locations of the unemployed and the job openings just don't match.

When cyclical unemployment is zero, the unemployment rate is still positive due to frictional and structural unemployment. This is sometimes called the *natural rate of unemployment*, and sometimes called (really!) the *NAIRU—the non-accelerating inflation rate of unemployment*. Less often it is called the "full employment rate of unemployment," perhaps because that sounds contradictory. Figuring out the level of the natural rate of unemployment is an important challenge. If the economy's unemployment is primarily cyclical, the actual unemployment rate is higher than the natural rate. Then policies to increase spending by consumers and businesses can bring unemployment down. If unemployment is mostly frictional and structural, these same policies may only cause inflation, with little effect on unemployment.

> **The natural rate of unemployment is about 5%.**

It's pretty clear in Figure 2-3, though, that once expansions get going the unemployment rate heads towards 5% or even lower. Check the ends of the expansions in 1987-90, 1997-2000 and 2005-07. Check the expansion we're in now. It looks like the natural rate of unemployment is between 4% and 6%. We'll use 5% as a rule of thumb natural rate through most of this book.

- What happens to the unemployment rate during recessions and expansions?

The unemployment rate goes up in recessions, and comes down during expansions. But not right away. Unemployment went up in 1992, after the end of the 1990-91 recession. It peaked in 2003, after the 2001 recession. And unemployment was highest in 2010, after the end of the Great Recession. Unemployment rates keep going up even when the economy begins to recover. The reason for this is that the labor force keeps expanding. Young people graduate from high school and college and enter the labor force looking for work. And, when the economy starts expanding, discouraged workers begin to re-enter the labor force, so it grows faster than usual. The number of jobs must increase to employ these added workers. That means the economy must grow, just to keep the unemployment rate from rising. If it doesn't grow fast enough, the unemployment rate will increase. That's where the phrase "jobless recovery" comes from.

> **The unemployment rate rises during recessions, and keeps rising in the early years of the following expansion.**

In the past real GDP had to grow about 3% per year to keep the unemployment rate from increasing. In the past ten years, labor force growth has slowed because the big baby boom generation has begun to retire. Now the unemployment rate will fall if real GDP grows by more than about 1.5%.

Interest Rates

An *interest rate* is an added percentage that a borrower must repay a lender in addition to the amount borrowed. Interest rates are usually measured on an annual basis—the percentage to be paid over a year—even if the loan is for less than or more than a year. Sometimes the interest rate is called "the cost of money" because it is the amount which a borrower must pay to use the lender's money.

There are a great many interest rates, because there are a great many kinds of loans. Here are a few of the important interest rates.

- *Federal funds rate.* This is the interest rate charged by banks when they lend to each other overnight. At the end of each day, some banks will have excess reserves—more money in the vault than they need—while others will be short of reserves. Those with excess will lend to those that are short, charging the federal funds rate. It is called "federal" even though it is set by banks in private markets. This is because this interest rate is very sensitive to policy decisions of the Federal Reserve. What is the Federal Reserve? It's the United States central bank. Don't worry, we'll get to that.

- *Treasury bond rates.* These are the interest rates paid by the U.S. Treasury when it borrows to finance a budget deficit. A bond is a promise to repay the lender plus interest. The Treasury borrows for shorter and longer periods, ranging from one month to thirty years. These bonds are sold to buyers in the bond market. The buyers are lending money to the government, on the promise of interest and eventual repayment. To buy a Treasury bond is to lend money to the Federal government. Short-term bonds are sometimes called "Treasury bills."

- *Prime rate.* This is the interest rate supposedly charged by banks to their best corporate customers. In fact the prime rate is more of a benchmark for many kinds of lending, including credit card debt and some mortgages. When the prime rate changes, lenders will often adjust these other interest rates too.

- *Commercial paper rates.* These are interest rates on short-term loans that lenders make to businesses for operations such as stocking inventories or meeting payrolls. The business repays after a few months out of their earnings from the sales of the inventories or the services provided by the employees.

- *Corporate bond rates.* These are the interest rates paid by corporations when they borrow for longer periods of time, usually for business expansion. When a corporation wants to expand its factories, offices, or stores, buy equipment, or buy another company, it will sell bonds in the bond market. Lenders will buy these bonds, the corporation will use the money it receives to expand, and the bond will be repaid from the corporations' added profits.

- *Municipal bond rates.* These are the interest rates that state and local governments pay when they borrow to build schools, jails, bridges, court houses and the other infrastructure they need to provide public services. Interest and principal are usually repaid out of tax revenues. Lenders like municipal bonds because the interest they earn is not subject to Federal taxes.

- *Mortgage rate.* This is the interest rate charged to people borrowing to finance a home purchase. It's the interest rate that often concerns consumers the most, because for most people a house is both the largest purchase they make and often represents a large share of their wealth. Home purchases and housing construction can be quite sensitive to variations in the mortgage interest rate. Mortgages vary in length, but a 30-year mortgage is common.

12

Lenders must take account of inflation when setting interest rates. If there is inflation, the money which a borrower pays back to the lender is worth less than the money that was originally lent. With prices higher, a particular amount of money can buy fewer goods and services. Lenders must set the interest rate at the rate of return they wish to receive, plus the inflation rate they expect. This implies that the *real interest rate* is the interest rate charged by the lender minus the annual inflation rate the lender expects during the length of the loan.

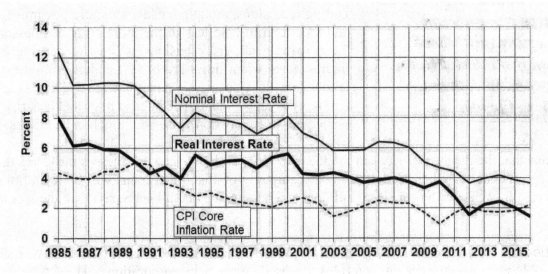

Figure 2-4. Real 30-year Mortgage Interest Rate, 1985-2016. Calculated as the nominal rate paid by homebuyers, less the CPI core inflation rate. The nominal interest rate has trended downward for the past two decades, from very high levels in the early 1980's. The Consumer Price Index core inflation rate is used to deflate the nominal interest rate because it's probably a better measure of the inflation rates that lenders expect. The fluctuations in energy prices are pretty unpredictable, so they aren't always reflected in lenders' rate decisions. Both the nominal and real mortgage interest rates have been near record lows since the end of the Great Recession.

For example, in 2016 the average interest rate on a 30-year mortgage was 4.17%. This is known as the nominal interest rate. The inflation rate for 2014, measured by the core CPI, was 1.75%. The real interest rate was

3.65% - 2.21% = 1.43%.

After the inflation of 2016, the money that a borrower is repaying is worth 2.21% less to the borrower because prices increased. The lender gained only 1.43% in added purchasing power by earning interest on the loan. Interest rates are set in advance based on the *expected inflation rate,* the rate that the lender expects over the length of the loan. Since measures of expected inflation are scarce, real interest rate calculations usually are made using the inflation rates that actually occurred. These are *ex-post* (after-the-fact), or *realized,* real interest rates—the rate of return that was actually earned during the year.

> **The real interest rate is the nominal interest rate charged by lenders minus the expected inflation rate.**

There's another way to use interest rates to measure what lenders are doing. An *interest rate spread* is the difference between two interest rates. Some business corporations are more risky, and some are less risky. A less risky corporation will certainly repay a loan. A more risky corporation may not. When the economy is doing well and lenders are confident, they are more willing to lend to risky businesses. More likely than not, in good times even a shaky company can earn enough to repay a loan.

> **An interest rate spread measures the difference between two interest rates, which can indicate the attitudes of lenders.**

During recessions, though, lenders are more pessimistic, and they tend to lend less to the more risky businesses. To borrow at all, risky businesses have to pay higher interest rates when times are bad. Lenders continue to lend to less-risky businesses, since even in bad times they are likely to repay loans. The interest rates that less-risky businesses must pay don't rise very much in bad times.

This means that the difference between the loans to more and less risky businesses measures the confidence of lenders. When lenders are confident and optimistic that loans will be repaid, the spread is small. When lenders are less confident and pessimistic about loan repayment, the spread is large.

Corporations are rated by bond rating agencies. Moody's and Standard and Poors are two such agencies. Moody's uses the designation BAA to classify more risky corporations. The AAA label is reserved for the less risky corporations. In 2016 the average interest rate on corporate bonds to BAA corporations was 4.72%, and the average interest rate on corporate bonds to AAA corporations was 3.67%. More risky corporations had to pay more to borrow money. The interest rate spread was

4.72% - 3.67% = 1.05%.

That's much lower than during the Great Recession, but higher than in 2013-14. The spread is usually above one percent when lenders are uncertain or pessimistic. As you can see in Figure 2-5, lenders were *very* pessimistic during the Great Recession, and with good reason. It wasn't clear which businesses would be able to repay loans, so lenders preferred corporations with the very lowest risk. Lenders regained confidence during the recovery, but the ups and downs of the interest rate spread show that lenders remained uncertain about business prospects.

- *What happens to the interest rate spread in recessions and expansions?*

> **The interest rate spread gets bigger during or after recessions.**

Remember that the spread between the interest rates charged to more- or less-risky business corporations is a measure of the optimism or pessimism of financial markets. Lenders shift their lending to less risky businesses when they are pessimistic. Interest rates paid by less risky businesses fall, and those on more risky businesses rise. The difference between them—the spread—gets bigger.

Lenders turned somewhat pessimistic in the recession of 1990-91. Lender pessimism resulted in a "credit crunch," which reduced borrowing and helped cause the recession. The spread began to drop quickly after the recession was over, and the 1990's were a very optimistic decade.

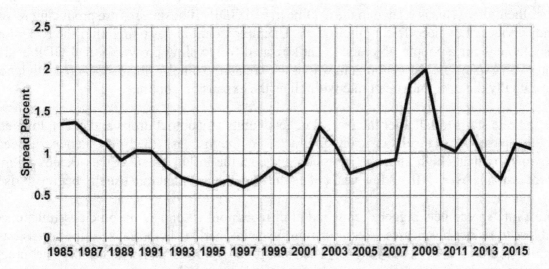

Figure 2-5. Spread between BAA and AAA corporation bond interest rates, 1985-2016. In good times, like the long expansion of the 1990's, the difference between the interest rates on loans to more risky corporations (rated BAA) and less risky corporations (rated AAA) tends to be less than one percentage point. The spread jumped during and after the recession of 2001. It dropped below one point again during the 2000's expansion, but then soared to two percentage points in 2008. Financial markets nearly collapsed during the Great Recession. For a while no one would lend to anyone. The spread dropped under on in 2013, but rose again in 2015. Lenders remained uncertain during the slow recovery.

In the 2001 recession financial markets were not pessimistic for the first eight months. The September 11 attacks came near the end of that recession. The World Trade Center was in the heart of the New York City financial district, and markets shut down for several days. The aftermath of uncertainty about terrorism and war kept lenders skittish for a few years. Lender pessimism was not a cause of the 2001 recession, but it probably slowed the recovery.

In 2008 and 2009 the spread exploded, hitting two percentage points. The panic in financial markets made a big contribution towards the Great Recession. When lenders don't lend, businesses can't borrow and spend. And they can't expand or hire either.

- *So, what happens during recessions and expansions?*

Every recession and expansion is different, but there are some patterns.

Real GDP declines during recessions, and grows during expansions. That's the main way we know there's a recession, when the production of goods and services shrinks. Real GDP won't necessarily decline in every quarter during a recession. Growth tends to be slow in the first few quarters after the recession ends, but after a while it usually tops 3%. But not always, as we've seen since 2009.

The unemployment rate rises during recessions. That's another sure indicator of recession, when people lose their jobs. This is related to the decline in real GDP. If businesses are producing fewer goods and services, they need fewer employees. Unemployment keeps rising after the recession trough, sometimes for a couple of years. That's related to the slow growth in real GDP at the beginning of an expansion. Not enough new jobs are created to employ the ever-increasing labor force. Eventually the unemployment rate will fall as the expansion continues.

The inflation rate starts to fall after the recession gets going. As output drops and unemployment increases, businesses can't sell as many products, so they're less likely to increase prices. Unemployment remains high after the recession ends, so the inflation rate usually keeps falling after the recession is over. After a few years of expansion, the inflation rate usually begins to rise.

The interest rate spread gets bigger during and after recessions. Lenders become pessimistic, so they lend less to riskier businesses. Pessimism in financial markets helps cause some recessions. In others, it's more of an effect of reduced sales and production. Expansions usually encourage lenders to lend, even to riskier businesses, and the spread gets smaller.

Purchasing Power: Bringing Home the Bacon

Three of the greatest hitters in the history of baseball were Babe Ruth, Hank Aaron and Barry Bonds. The Babe hit 714 homeruns. Hammering Hank broke that record with 755 homers. Barry Bonds broke Aaron's record with 762 homeruns (apply asterisk here).

Babe Ruth signed a contract with the New York Yankees in 1932 (for the 1933 season) for $80,000, by far the highest paid player of his era. When someone pointed out to Ruth that he was paid more than the President of the United States, he replied "Yeah, but I had a better year than he did." Since the President was Herbert Hoover, and it was during the Great Depression, the Babe was probably right.

Aaron and Bonds earned more than Ruth did. But prices were higher in Aaron and Bonds' time than they were in 1933. How much in goods and services could they actually buy with that higher pay? This is a question of *purchasing power*.

> *Purchasing power measures the amount of goods and services that an amount of money can buy.*

We'll use the consumer price index to measure purchasing power later. Let's start by measuring it with *bacon*. How much bacon could each hitter buy with his salary, at the price of bacon in his day?

The table has the data we need. The years and salaries actually paid to our three homerun hitters are shown in the first two columns. The next column shows the price of bacon per pound. Divide the salary by the price, and you see the number of pounds of bacon each player could buy with his salary that year.

	Year	Nominal Salary	Price of Bacon per Pound	Real Salary, Pounds of Bacon	Factor to 2014 Bacon Price ($5.43)	Salary to Match Bacon Purchasing Power in 2014
Babe Ruth	1933	$80,000	$0.41	195,122	13.2	$1,059,512
Hank Aaron	1973	$200,000	$1.34	149,309	4.1	$810,750
Barry Bonds	2003	$15,500,000	$2.94	5,272,109	1.8	$28,627,551

Babe Ruth could have bought 195,122 pounds of bacon with his $80,000. Sounds like something the Babe might like. Hank Aaron, though, could buy "only" 149,309 pounds of bacon, even though he was paid a lot more in dollars. Ruth's real pay, in bacon, was higher than Aaron's. Why? Because compared to Ruth, Aaron's salary did not keep up with the rising price of bacon. Aaron's salary was 2½ times Ruth's, but the price of bacon more than tripled. Aaron's salary was higher, but its purchasing power was lower.

There's no doubt that Barry Bonds' salary was higher in real bacon terms. He could buy 5.3 million pounds of bacon, even at the higher bacon price. His salary was more than 30-times higher than Aaron's. The price of bacon a bit more than doubled.

He Made Milwaukee Famous. Hank Aaron played baseball for the Milwaukee and Atlanta Braves and the Milwaukee Brewers. Here's his retired uniform number in the rafters of Milwaukee's Miller Park.

Here's another way to think about purchasing power. Babe Ruth could have purchased 195,122 pounds of bacon with his salary in 1933. How much money would he have needed in order to buy that much in 2016? The price of bacon in 2016 was $5.44 per pound, which was 13.3 times as high as the 41-cent price in 1933. To buy as much bacon, then, his salary would need to have been 13.3 times higher too. That's $1,061,480—195,122 pounds of bacon at $5.44 per pound. That's the salary that would bring home the bacon. To maintain purchasing power, pay must rise as fast as prices do.

But no one this side of Homer Simpson spends their whole paycheck on bacon. We need a way to measure purchasing power with the prices of all the goods and services that consumers typically buy. We need to use the Consumer Price Index (CPI).

The CPI is an index that measures changes in the prices of a market basket of goods and services that consumers buy. The next table replaces the price of bacon with the CPI and calculates the real salaries of Ruth, Aaron and Bonds. Real salaries are calculated by dividing salaries not by the price of a product, but by the CPI, after dividing the CPI by 100.

The result is measured in "1983 dollars." Babe Ruth would have needed $615,385 in 1983, to buy the same goods and services that his salary bought in 1933. Barry Bonds would have needed $8.4

million in 1983, to buy the same goods and services that his salary bought in 2003. Why the year 1983? For no reason other than the base year of the Consumer Price Index is 1982-84. The index nearly equals 100 in 1983.

The point is to compare the purchasing power of salaries over the years. It doesn't matter whether the base year is 1983, 1993 or 2013, as long as all the numbers are measured in the same year's dollars.

	Year	Nominal Salary	CPI	Real Salary, 1983 Dollars
Babe Ruth	1933	$80,000	13.0	$615,385
Hank Aaron	1973	$200,000	44.4	$450,197
Barry Bonds	2003	$15,500,000	184.0	$8,423,913

Finally, here's a table that looks at purchasing power the second way. How much must salaries increase in order to maintain their original purchasing power? The CPI in 2016 was 240.0. This was 5.4 times the CPI in 1973, when Hank Aaron earned his $200,000. Divide 240.0 by 44.4, and it rounds to 5.4. The prices of goods and services that Aaron could have been buying went up 5.4 times. To keep buying those same goods and services, his salary would need to rise by the same factor. Multiply $200,000 by 5.4, and get $1,081,081 (Remember that 5.4 is rounded. The actual multiplier is 5.4054.).

	Year	Nominal Salary	CPI	Factor to 2016 CPI (240.0)	Salary to Match Purchasing Power in 2016
Babe Ruth	1933	$80,000	13.0	18.5	1,476,923
Hank Aaron	1973	$200,000	44.4	5.4	1,081,081
Barry Bonds	2003	$15,500,000	184.0	1.3	20,217,391

So, in real terms, adjusted for inflation, in 1983 dollars (they all mean the same thing), Babe Ruth remained the highest paid baseball player for more than 40 years. Hank Aaron never matched him. But something happened later in the 1970's: free agency. Ruth's and Aaron's contracts tied them to their teams. They were not allowed to offer their services to the highest bidder. By the time Barry Bonds was playing, teams competed to sign the best players. Salaries exploded.

. . . Since the Great Depression

The phrase was everywhere after 2008. Here's a sample from the *New York Times* (italics added).

> September 19, 2008: "All week long, with Wall Street engulfed by what analysts are calling the worst financial crisis *since the Great Depression*, President Bush had mostly stayed out of sight, except when trying to maintain the façade of business as usual."

> November 7, 2009: With the release of the jobs report on Friday, the broadest measure of unemployment and underemployment tracked by the Labor Department has reached its highest level in decades. If statistics went back so far, the measure would almost certainly be at its highest level *since the Great Depression*.

> September 20, 2010: "The 2007-9 recession was the deepest on record *since the Great Depression*, at least in terms of job losses."

> May 30, 2011: The desire to own your own home, long a bedrock of the American Dream, is fast becoming a casualty of the worst housing downturn *since the Great Depression*.

> August 10, 2012: "Economists often assert that we are in the worst recovery *since the Great Depressio*n. Are we? Not technically, but it's still unusually bad."

"I'm thinking of creating a save-get key for 'since the Great Depression'" wrote reporter David Leonhardt on October 20, 2008. He would have used it for years.

- *How does the Great Recession compare to the Great Depression?*

We can compare this recent severe recession to the greatest of all depressions using the macroeconomic indicators. Figure 2-6 shows real GDP growth, the CPI inflation rate, the unemployment rate, and the corporate interest rate spread for the ten-year periods 1928-1937 and 2007-2016. The declining phase of the Great Depression is marked by the NBER from August 1929 to March 1933. The declining phase of the Great Recession is marked from December 2007 to June 2009. The 18 months of the Great Recession was the longest downturn since the Great Depression. But the economy declined for 43 months during the Great Depression.

The years 1928 and 2007 were the last full years of expansion before the downturns (or nearly so in 2007), so they are matched in Figure 2-6. There were similarities. The unemployment rates and interest rate spreads were practically identical. There had been a mild recession in 1927, so the 1928 economy showed slower real GDP growth and a negative inflation rate, which is deflation. The year 2007 was the sixth year of an expansion, and the economy had modest real GDP growth and somewhat elevated inflation.

Great Depression

	Real GDP Growth	CPI Inflation	Unemploy-ment Rate	Interest Rate Spread
1928	0.8%	-1.7%	4.7%	0.9%
1929	14.1%	0.0%	2.9%	1.2%
1930	-8.3%	-2.3%	8.9%	1.4%
1931	-6.8%	-9.0%	15.7%	3.0%
1932	-13.2%	-9.9%	22.9%	4.2%
1933	-1.2%	-5.1%	20.9%	3.3%
1934	11.3%	3.1%	16.2%	2.3%
1935	9.0%	2.2%	14.4%	2.2%
1936	12.9%	1.5%	10.0%	1.5%
1937	5.7%	3.6%	9.2%	1.8%

Great Recession and After

	Real GDP Growth	CPI Inflation	Unemploy-ment Rate	Interest Rate Spread
2007	1.8%	2.9%	4.6%	0.9%
2008	-0.3%	3.8%	5.8%	1.8%
2009	-2.8%	-0.3%	9.3%	2.0%
2010	2.5%	1.6%	9.6%	1.1%
2011	1.6%	3.1%	8.9%	1.0%
2012	2.2%	2.1%	8.1%	1.3%
2013	1.7%	1.5%	7.4%	0.9%
2014	2.4%	1.6%	6.2%	0.7%
2015	2.6%	0.1%	5.3%	1.1%
2016	1.6%	1.3%	4.9%	1.1%

Figure 2-6. Indicators in the Great Depression and Great Recession. The indicators are real GDP growth, inflation measured by the consumer price index (all-items), the unemployment rate and the spread between the Baa and Aaa corporate bond interest rates. The table matches the last full years of recovery, 1928 and 2007. The Great Depression began in 1929, the Great Recession in 2007. The Great Depression ended in 1933 (meaning the economy stopped declining). The Great Recession ended in 2009.

The downturns started in mid-1929 and at the very end of 2007. The 1929 data look fine, other than the rise in the interest rate spread (think stock market crash). The expanding economies earlier in the year more than offset the declines later. But 2008 was definitely a recession year, with falling real GDP and rising unemployment. The financial panic later in the year shows up in the high interest rate spread.

The years 1930 and 2009 were years of crisis. Real GDP plummeted by 2.8% in 2009, the worst showing since 1946. But 1930 was much worse, with an 8.4% drop. There was deflation in both years, though in 2009 it mainly was due to a collapse in oil prices.
Look at unemployment and the interest rate spread. *They are both worse in 2009 than they were in 1930.* By some measures, the crisis of 2009 was worse than the first full year of the Great Depression. Unemployment was slightly higher in 2009 than in 1930, and the interest rate spread was much higher. The financial crisis hit sooner during the Great Recession than it did during the Great Depression. The Great Depression's financial crisis was still to come.

After 2009 the similarity disappears. The year 2009 was the low point for the Great Recession. In mid-2009 the recovery began. Real GDP has been growing, unemployment has been falling ever since. Financial markets have calmed down. Inflation has remained low.

In 1930 the Great Depression was just getting started. There was with another huge drop in real GDP in 1931, and even bigger drop in 1932, and a fourth straight fall in 1933. Prices fell four years in a row, unemployment topped 20%, and there was an epic panic in financial markets. The panic became so severe that, by early 1933, the banking system shut down. All the country's banks closed.

The real GDP growth rates for 1934 and 1935 may confuse us, because we know that the Great Depression continued throughout the 1930's. Yet here is some of the fastest real GDP growth of the century. The unemployment rate tells the story. It remained above 9% until 1941. The economy was climbing fast—but out of a very deep hole.

The recovery from the Great Recession has been slower than we'd like. But after similar beginnings we recovered. They did not. We can be grateful for that.

- ***But Why?***

We need the macroeconomic indicators to describe what happened. We need a model of the economy to understand why. To build that model, we need to know about demand and supply. On to Chapter 2!

Terms in this Chapter, in order of appearance
Aggregation
Gross Domestic Product
Value
Final
Produced during the year
Underground economy
Consumption (C)
Investment (I)
Government purchases (G)
Exports (X)
Imports (M)
Inventories
Transfer Payments
Net Exports
Real GDP
Nominal GDP
Price index
GDP deflator
GDP growth
Business cycle
Inflation
Deflation
Consumer Price Index
Core rate of inflation
Unemployment rate
Labor force

Employed
Unemployed
Not in the labor force
Discouraged workers
Cyclical unemployment
Frictional unemployment (Search unemployment)
Structural unemployment (Mismatch unemployment)
Natural rate of unemployment
NAIRU--the non-accelerating inflation rate of unemployment
Interest rate
Real interest rate
Expected inflation rate
Ex-post or realized real interest rate
Federal funds rate
Treasury bond rates
Prime rate
Commercial paper rates
Corporate bond rates
Mortgage rate
Interest rate spread
Expansion
Recession
Peak (of an expansion)
Trough (of a recession)
Purchasing Power
Great Depression
Great Recession

Notes

Data for GDP, inflation, unemployment and interest rates come from the following websites, all of which I recommend to the interested reader:

GDP. U.S. Department of Commerce, Bureau of Economic Analysis.
www.bea.gov

Inflation (CPI). U.S. Department of Labor, Bureau of Labor Statistics.
stats.bls.gov/cpi/home.htm (no "www")

Unemployment. U.S. Department of Labor, Bureau of Labor Statistics.
stats.bls.gov/cps/home.htm (no "www")

Interest Rates. Federal Reserve Board.
www.federalreserve.gov/releases/h15/update

For one stop shopping, all of these data and (a lot) more are available at the St. Louis Federal Reserve's website.
research.stlouisfed.org/fred2/ (no "www")

Data on baseball salaries are available from Baseball Reference
www.baseball-reference.com

Bacon prices were derived from Information Please and the Bureau of Labor Statistics,
www.infoplease.com/ipa/A0873707.html
http://data.bls.gov/timeseries/APU0000704111?data_tool=XGtable

News Articles

Leonhardt, David. "Broader Measure of U.S. Unemployment Stands at 17.5%," *New York Times*, November 7, 2009.

Leonhardt, David. "The Recession Enters Its 2nd Year," *New York Times*, October 20, 2008.

National Bureau of Economic Research, Business Cycle Dating Committee. Press Release, September 20, 2010. [http://www.nber.org/cycles/sept2010.pdf]

Rampell, Catherine. "Is This Really the Worst Economic Recovery Since the Depression?" *New York Times*, August 10, 2012.

Rampell, Catherine. "Recession May Be Over, but Joblessness Remains," *New York Times*, September 20, 2010.

Rampell, Catherine. "The Recession Has (Officially) Ended," *New York Times*, September 20, 2010.

Stolberg, Sheryl Gay. "Bush Emerges After Days of Financial Crisis," *New York Times*, September 19, 2008.

Streitfeld, David. "Housing Index Is Expected to Show a New Low in Prices," *New York Times*, May 30, 2011.

Chapter 2
Demand and Supply

Gasoline prices rise. Gasoline prices fall. Prescription drug prices rise and rise some more. An increase in the minimum wage increases the incomes of less-skilled workers. Or it reduces their employment opportunities.

Why?

Economists try to understand what happens to the prices and quantities of goods and services in markets by using *demand and supply*. Consumers demand goods and services, businesses supply them. Over some time period, a quantity of goods or services are bought and sold in the market at a particular price.

With demand and supply we can figure out how much will be bought or sold, and at what price. We can understand and even predict how price and quantity will change if businesses or consumers change what they do.

Demand and Supply Schedules

Here's a made-up example: suppose in your community there are lots of consumers who want to buy pizza, and lots of restaurants that want to make and sell pizza. Suppose we, as economists, surveyed the consumers about how much pizza they would want to buy at several different pizza prices during a week. We'd ask each consumer how much he or she would buy at several different prices, and then add up the totals at each price. And, suppose we surveyed restaurants about how much pizza they would want to make and sell at these same prices during a week. Again, we'd add up the numbers of pizzas each restaurant would make and sell at each price.

The result would be a demand and supply *schedule*, and it might look like this.

Price per Pizza	Number of Pizzas Demanded	Number of Pizzas Supplied
$2	12,000	1,000
$6	8,000	2,000
$10	5,000	5,000
$12	3,000	8,000
$14	1,000	11,000

At low prices, people want to buy more pizzas. At higher prices, people want to buy fewer pizzas. Asking why seems a silly question. Of course people would rather pay less for a product than more. It is in their self-interest to spend less money to fill their bellies. They'll have more left over for other purchases.

Economists sometimes point to an idea called *diminishing marginal utility*. Diminishing means getting smaller. Marginal means the extra unit of anything. Utility is the satisfaction people get from the products they buy.   The satisfaction people get from each extra unit of anything they buy gets ever-smaller. That first slice of pizza tastes great. The second is almost as good. The third I can take or leave. The fourth—perhaps not. If I eat a fifth I'm going to be sick. Each extra slice brings less added satisfaction.

If I act in my own self-interest, doing the best I can for myself, I'll be willing to pay more for the first slice than the second. The price would have to be pretty low to get me to buy that fifth slice. I'm not interested in getting sick.

> **The Law of Demand says that people will buy less of a product if it costs more, and they'll buy more if it costs less.**

However it's described, we're so sure of the idea that people demand less of a product when its price goes up that we call it the *Law of Demand*.

Businesses set the prices of their products, but we assume they are *price takers*. That means businesses must set their prices in line with what the market will bear. Pizza restaurants can't charge just any price they want. They must set their prices based on what their competitors are doing, and on what people are willing to pay.

No firm wants to make pizza at a loss. We assume they are in business to make profits. They are *profit maximizers*. That's another way of saying that business owners act in their own self-interest (just like consumers).

Here's another important economic idea. As a business tries to increase its production of a good or service, the cost of each additional unit of output begins to rise. An additional pizza chef is hired, and more pizzas are produced. Then another, is hired, but two things happen. There's only so much space in the oven. And the second added chef isn't quite as fast as the first, because naturally the first chef hired was the best. The number of additional pizzas produced is smaller. Before long the added chefs are elbow-to-elbow and the pizzas are colliding as they're flipped in the air. Too many chefs actually could reduce production.

> **The Law of Diminishing Returns says that adding additional resources to production eventually produces fewer and fewer added products.**

Adding additional resources to production eventually produces a smaller and smaller added benefit. This idea pops up so often that it's sometimes called the *law of diminishing returns*.

When the price of pizza is high it will pay to hire an added chef even if he or she doesn't produce as many additional pizzas. Profits can be made with less efficient resources when prices are high. When prices are high, more is produced. When the price is low only highly efficient resources can be used profitably. When prices are low, less is produced. The quantity supplied increases with higher prices and decreases with lower prices.

Equilibrium Price and Quantity

We're not content with the schedules, though. So we plot demand and supply on a graph, like Figure 2-1. Put the price of pizza on the vertical axis, and the quantity of pizza demanded or supplied on the horizontal axis. Plot the points from the schedule and connect the dots. Label the demand curve with a "D" and the supply curve with an "S".

The demand curve slopes downward. That's because of the Law of Demand. When price is high, people want to buy less. When price is low, people want to buy more. The supply curve slopes upward. That's because businesses are profit maximizers. When price is low, it doesn't pay to supply much. When price is high, it pays to supply more.

There's only one point on this diagram where the amount people want to buy equals the amount businesses want to sell. That's where the two curves cross, at a price of $10 and a quantity of 5,000 pizzas. It's a nice point to be at. Everyone who wants to buy a pizza finds one to buy. Consumers aren't frustrated. Every pizza that a business wants to sell finds a buyer. No flour, tomato paste or pepperoni is wasted.

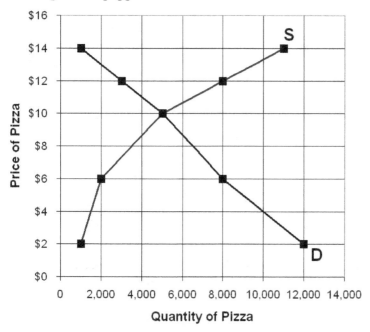

Figure 2-1. Connect the Dots. Each dot shows a pair of price and quantity numbers from the demand or supply schedule. The dot at the lower left, for example, shows that at a price of $2, restaurants will supply 1,000 pizzas. Demand slopes down and supply slopes up. The point where they cross is on both the demand and supply curves. That's the equilibrium price and quantity, $10 and 5,000 pizzas.

Is there any reason to think, though, that a market will end up at this point?

The answer is yes. Suppose the price was $14. According to the schedule and the curves, consumers want to buy 1,000 pizzas, but restaurants make 11,000 pizzas for sale. There is a *surplus* of pizza. In such a situation, desperate restaurant owners would try to attract customers by cutting the price of pizza. Some clever consumers might even offer a lower price to the owner to try to take advantage of the surplus. The price falls when there is a surplus, until the surplus is eliminated, at the *equilibrium* price and quantity. Once price equals equilibrium, there is no more surplus, so there's no more reason for price to fall.

> **At the equilibrium price the quantity that consumers demand equals the quantity that businesses supply.**

Suppose the price is $2. Now there's a *shortage*. Consumers want to buy 12,000 pizzas, but restaurants only make 1,000. Consumers are lined up around the block for a chance to buy pizza. Restaurant owners wouldn't take long to raise their prices in such a situation. Some hungry consumers at the back of the line might offer a higher price, to get into the restaurant.   The price rises when there is a shortage, until the shortage is eliminated, at the equilibrium price and quantity. Once price equals equilibrium, there is no more shortage, so there's no more reason for the price to rise.

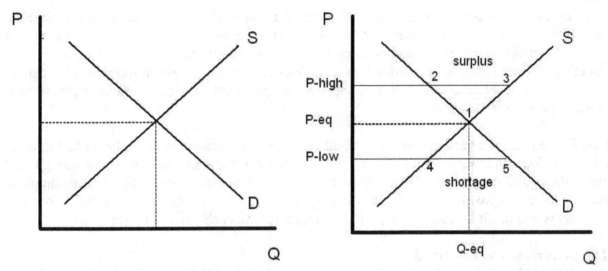

Figure 2-2. The Basics. This is the market for a particular product, like pizza or cars or widgets. P stands for the price of the product, Q for the quantity bought and sold. D stands for demand, S for supply. Demand slopes downward to the right, which means that at higher prices people want to buy less, at lower prices, more. Supply slopes upward to the right, which means that at higher prices businesses want to sell more, at lower prices, less. We call them "curves" even though they usually are drawn as straight lines. Where the demand and supply curves intersect is the "equilibrium" price and quantity, shown by the dotted line. This price and quantity is established by the way people and businesses behave, in a process called the "invisible hand." If price is higher than equilibrium, the amount people want to buy is at 2, the amount businesses want to sell is at 3. There is a surplus of goods on the shelves. Businesses respond by putting their products on sale, consumers by trying to bargain for a better deal. Price falls toward equilibrium at 1. When price is lower than equilibrium, the amount people want to buy is at 5, the amount businesses want to sell is at 4. There is a shortage of goods: the shelves are mostly empty. Businesses realize that they can raise their prices. Desperate consumers are willing to pay more. Price rises toward equilibrium. At the equilibrium price, 1, there is no incentive to raise or lower the price.

These ideas were put together first by an 18th century professor from Glasgow, Scotland, named Adam Smith.   Smith became famous throughout Europe teaching moral philosophy at the university there. (He was also famous as an absent-minded professor. He once brewed a beverage of bread and butter, and called it a terrible cup of tea.)

Adam Smith was interested in one question in particular: since people (being people) tend to pursue their self-interests before anything else, why does society not fall into anarchy? More than that, why do the tasks needed for society's survival get done?

In his great work, *The Wealth of Nations*, published in the easy-to-remember year 1776, Smith offered an answer. And offered, and offered—it was a nine hundred page book. *Self-interest* drove men and women to do the tasks that society was willing to pay for. "It is not from the benevolence of the butcher, the brewer, or the baker that we expect our dinner," he wrote, "but from their regard to their self-interest." If more people wanted dinner, they would bid up its price, and butchers, brewers and bakers who wanted that money would respond by making more.

Self-interested trades-people might charge Smith a very high price for his dinner, were it not for a second factor: *competition*. There were lots of people trying to sell dinners. It was in the interest of each to attract customers by undercutting the prices of the others, if they could. Prices would be cut right down to the cost of making the meal. Self-interest and competition combined to deliver the goods that people wanted. And it all happened automatically, in Smith's famous phrase, as if directed by an *"invisible hand."*

Usually we don't put numbers on our demand and supply diagrams, but draw them like Figure 2-2 instead. We can always point to the intersection of the demand and supply curves, though, and call it the equilibrium point. That's where the quantity demanded equals the quantity supplied, and the point where the market will wind up, through the actions of lots of self-interested consumers and profit maximizing suppliers, competing with each other to buy and sell.

The Determinants of Demand

Pointing out the equilibrium is just the start. Demand and supply are mainly used to figure out what happens to price and quantity when consumers or businesses change their behavior. When behavior changes, the numbers on the demand and supply schedules change. The quantities that consumers and businesses will buy or sell at every price are different. If demand or supply changes, the equilibrium price and quantity changes. This is shown on the graph as a shift in the demand or supply curve. A shift means that at each price, consumers will demand a different quantity of the product than before, or businesses will supply a different quantity than before.

What can change consumer demand? Here's a list:

- *Income.* If consumer income increases, consumers will demand more of most goods at any price. They can afford to buy more. If income decreases, consumers will demand less. These are called *normal* goods. There are a few *inferior* goods that consumers buy less of when income increases. With higher incomes they can afford better. Macaroni and cheese, ramen noodles and used cars are examples.

- *Prices of other goods.* Some goods are consumed together, like salsa and taco chips. Such goods are known as *complements*. If the price of salsa falls, more salsa will be purchased, and the demand for taco chips will rise too. Demand increases with a fall in the price of a complement, and rises with a rise in the price of a complement. Some goods are consumed instead of one another. Such goods are known as *substitutes*. Pizza and hamburgers are substitutes. If the price of pizza rises, consumers will shift their fast food purchases to hamburgers. Demand increases with a rise in the price of a substitute, and falls with the fall in the price of a substitute.

handwritten: price of good ↑ = demand of another good ↑

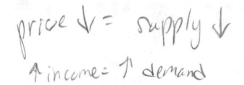
handwritten: price ↓ = supply ↓
handwritten: ↑ income = ↑ demand

- *Tastes and preferences.* Sometimes consumers decide that they like a good better than they used to. Fads and fashion or advertising can influence consumers to increase their demand for a good. Sometimes consumers decide that they like a good less. A health warning about a good can influence consumers to decrease their demand for a good.

- *Population.* Demand for a good will increase if there are more consumers in a market, and decrease if there are less.

- *Expectations.* If consumers expect the price to rise in the future, they'll demand more now. If they expect the price to fall, they'll delay their purchases, and demand less now. They'll buy more now if they expect a shortage in the future, too.

> ***An increase in demand causes a shift of the demand curve rightward, and increases equilibrium price and quantity. This is also an increase in <u>quantity</u> supplied.***

Changes in any of these factors will change demand, and that will change equilibrium price and quantity in the market. For example, suppose the price of gasoline increased and stayed high. Many drivers would sell their gas guzzlers and buy compact, fuel-efficient or even electric cars. Electric cars are substitutes for gasoline-powered cars. When the price of gasoline goes up, the cost of driving a gasoline-powered car increases compared to the cost of buying and driving an electric car. So some drivers buy electrics. A rise in the cost of gasoline increases the demand for a substitute, electric cars.

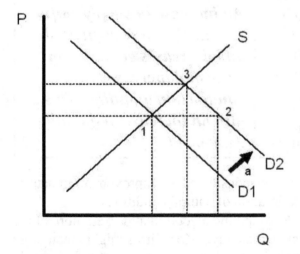

Figure 2-3. Pricey Substitute. Consumers in this market see an increase in the price of a substitute good. They are willing to buy more of the product on the Q axis at every price. Starting equilibrium price and quantity are at 1. Demand increases (a). Because the substitute is more expensive, at the original equilibrium price consumers want to buy more of the product, at 2. If price doesn't change, businesses still want to supply only amount 1. The quantity demanded at 2 is more than the quantity supplied at 1. That's a shortage. Businesses respond to the shortage by raising the price. In some markets consumers may bid up the price trying to buy what they want. The shortage is eliminated at 3, where the amount that consumers want to buy and businesses want to sell is again equal. The movement of the demand curve shown as "a" is an "increase in demand." The movement along the supply curve from 1 to 3 is an effect of the demand increase, and it's called an "increase in quantity supplied" (not an "increase in supply"). The change from equilibrium 1 to equilibrium 2 takes place because of Adam Smith's "invisible hand."

An increase in the price of a substitute increases demand. This creates a shortage at the original equilibrium price. Businesses respond by charging more, and consumers respond to offering more, for the scarce product. Price rises to a new equilibrium. Equilibrium quantity is higher too. This shows up on the graph as a rightward, upward shift in the demand curve, resulting in a new intersection at a new higher equilibrium price and quantity.

We call such a change a *shift in demand* because a change in consumer behavior caused the change in price and quantity. The cause of the change in equilibrium came from the demand side. Of course, the amount that businesses supplied also increased as they responded to the change in consumer behavior that increased the price. Businesses could make higher profits by producing and selling more. The increase in the amount businesses supplied was an effect of the demand increase. To give it a name, we call this a *shift in quantity supplied.*

The Determinants of Supply
Supply can change too. Here's a list of what can shift supply.

- *Costs of resources or inputs.* Businesses use employees, machines, land, energy and raw materials to produce goods. Changes in the costs or availability of these resources (also called inputs) will change supply by altering a businesses' profit calculation. If resources become more costly, less can be supplied profitably at every price. If resources become less costly, more can be supplied profitably at every price. This is shown on the graph as a shift in the supply curve. A rise in resource costs shifts the supply curve backwards to the left. That's a decrease in supply. A fall in resource costs shifts the supply curve forward to the right. That's an increase in supply.
- *Technology.* The methods businesses use to combine resources to make their goods is called technology. When technology improves, businesses can produce more goods with the same resources. This reduces the cost of production, and so increases the profitability of supplying the good at every price. Supply increases.

> *An increase in supply shifts the supply curve rightward, and decreases equilibrium price and increases equilibrium quantity. This is also an increase in __quantity__ demanded.*

- *Natural conditions.* Good weather increases the supply of crops; bad weather decreases supply. Natural disasters will reduce supply as well, by damaging and destroying resources. The discovery of new oil or natural gas reserves can be considered an improvement in natural conditions. Depleting those reserves is a deterioration of natural conditions.
- *Number of Firms.* If there are more businesses supplying a good in a market, more of the good will be supplied; fewer businesses mean less supply. More firms might mean more employees, machines, and other resources are being used to produce a good, which would increase supply. Of course, one big business could supply more than many small businesses, so there's another interpretation of this supply determinant. If a market has only a few firms, there is more likely to be collusion among them, an agreement to restrict supply in order to raise the price. If a market has many firms, collusion is more difficult to arrange, and supply is less likely to be restricted.
- *Expectations.* If businesses think the price of their product will rise, they may hold some of their product back from the market for later, decreasing supply now. If businesses think price will fall, they may try to supply more now.

Oil and Gasoline

Demand and supply is a nice story with a pretty picture. But what can it do?

The point of understanding demand and supply is to apply it to analyze daily life or the day's news. What is changing in your personal economy, or in the nation's economy? How will those changes affect the prices you pay or the quantity of products that are produced?

So let's apply demand and supply to analyze an issue that's always in the news: oil and gasoline prices.

The price of crude oil increased between 2009 and 2011, then bounced up and down between $80 and $120 per barrel for several years. Gasoline prices varied between $3 and $4. Suddenly, in the middle of 2014, crude oil prices began to fall, dropping from more than $100 to less than $50 per barrel. Gasoline fell too, and by early 2015 they dipped under $2, the lowest prices since 2009. One of the main reasons for this price drop was the increased production of oil in the United States. New horizontal drilling and "hydraulic fracking" technologies increased U.S. oil production by 80% from 2008 to 2014.

- *How would new oil production technologies affect the price and quantity of crude oil?*

Improved technology and increased productivity are determinants that increase supply. More product can profitably be supplied at each price. When supply increases there is a surplus at the original equilibrium price. To sell surplus output businesses must cut the price. This causes consumers to buy more. The equilibrium quantity increases, and the equilibrium price decreases, with the increase in supply. This shows up on the graph as a rightward, downward, outward shift in the supply curve. The new intersection is at a lower equilibrium price and a higher equilibrium quantity. We call such a change a *shift in supply* because a change in business behavior caused the change in price and quantity. It's also a *change in quantity demanded.* Consumers responded to the lower price by buying more.

How Low Can They Go? Gasoline Prices in December 2014 and January 2015, the result of supply increases and demand decreases.

This terminology will help us keep cause and effect straight. We reserve the phrase "change in supply" for a shift in the supply curve, caused by a change in business behavior. We reserve the phrase "shift in demand" for a shift in the demand curve, caused by a change in consumer behavior. Fracking was a new technology that increased the supply of oil. Supply increased, and price fell. The lower price moved consumers down their demand curve, towards a higher quantity. That was a increase in quantity demanded. The cause of the price and quantity change was a change in supply. The shift along the unchanged demand curve was an effect.

The economies of Japan and Europe struggled to recover after the Great Recession ended in mid-2009. We can tell from each country's real GDP growth rates. Japan had a second recession in 2011, and dipped into a third in mid-2014. Greece remained in recession through 2013, Italy entered a second recession in 2011, France in 2013, and from 2012 to 2014 even Germany saw near-zero growth. People drove their cars less to save money, and factories needed less energy since they were producing fewer goods. The demand for crude oil decreased. On the list of factors that can change demand, we could say that income has decreased, and crude oil is a normal good. Lower income means less oil is demanded

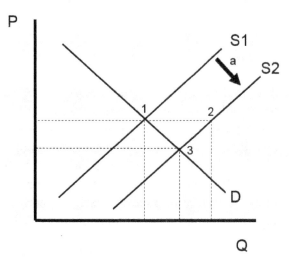

Figure 2-4. We're Fracking Here. Suppose this is the market for crude oil. The new oil production technologies increase the supply of oil in the world market. Crude oil supply increases (a). There is now a surplus at the old equilibrium price (1). The quantity demanded, where the old price intersects the demand curve (1), is less than the quantity supplied, where the price intersects the new supply curve (2). The price falls. Sellers must cut their prices to find buyers for all the new oil. Price falls until quantity demanded equals quantity supplied (3). The movement of the supply curve shown as "a" is an "increase in supply." The movement along the demand curve from 1 to 3 is an effect of the supply increase, and it's called an "increase in quantity demanded" (not an "increase in demand").

- *How would lower incomes in Europe and Japan affect the price and quantity of crude oil?*

When demand decreases there is a surplus at the original equilibrium price. Sellers cut the price trying to unload the excess supply. The equilibrium price decreases, and the equilibrium quantity decreases, with the decrease in demand. This shows up on the graph as an inward, downward, leftward shift in the demand curve. The new intersection is at a lower equilibrium price and a lower equilibrium quantity.

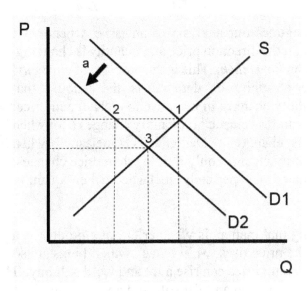

Figure 2-5. Not so much. Again, suppose this is the market for crude oil. Recession in Japan and Europe decreases incomes, and oil is a normal good. Crude oil demand decreases (a). There is now a surplus at the old equilibrium price (1). The quantity supplied, where the old price intersects the demand curve (1), is more than the quantity demanded, where the price intersects the new demand curve (2). The price is bid downward. Price falls until quantity demanded equals quantity supplied (3). The movement of the demand curve shown as "a" is a "decrease in demand." The movement along the supply curve from 1 to 3 is an effect of the demand decrease, and it's called a "decrease in quantity supplied" (not a "decrease in supply").

We call such a change a *shift in demand* because a change in consumer behavior caused the change in price and quantity. It's also a change in quantity supplied. The lower price moved producers down their supply curve, towards a lower quantity. The cause of the price and quantity change was a change in demand. The shift along the unchanged supply curve was an effect.

So there were (at least) two reasons for the drop in the price of crude oil: increased supply in the United States, and decreased demand in Japan and Europe. Both cause equilibrium price to fall, but one increases equilibrium quantity (Figure 2-4), and one decreases equilibrium quantity (Figure 2-5). The only way to tell which effect is bigger is to check on total sales and purchases of crude oil. Sales were up in 2014 and 2015. The increase in supply was bigger than the decrease in demand.

I don't buy crude oil. You don't buy crude oil. We're more concerned with the price of gasoline.

Crude oil is an input in the production of gasoline. Refineries must have crude oil to produce gasoline. A decrease in the cost of an input, crude oil, makes the production of gasoline more profitable. Refiners find that they can use their less efficient inputs profitably. The result is an increase in the supply of a gasoline.

- *How would lower crude oil prices affect the price and quantity of gasoline?*

If we let figure 2-4 apply to the gasoline market, rather than the crude oil market, it shows what happens. Gasoline supply increases with the falling cost of crude oil. The equilibrium price is bid downward. Equilibrium quantity increases. It's an increase in supply and an increase in quantity demanded.

This is why the prices of oil and gasoline tend to rise and fall together. When the price of crude oil decreases, production costs for gasoline fall, gasoline supply increases, and the price of gasoline decreases.

> *Elasticity measures the size of the response of one variable to another, like the response of quantity demanded to a change in price. If quantity changes a lot, demand is elastic; if it changes only a little, it's inelastic.*

Sometimes our analysis of an issue depends not just on the direction price and quantity is changing, but on *how much*. This is the problem of *elasticity*. The elasticity of demand is the amount that quantity changes in response to a change in price. Demand is "elastic" if quantity changes a lot when price changes. Demand is "inelastic" when quantity changes only a little when price changes. Demand is "perfectly inelastic" when quantity doesn't change at all with a price change.

What makes demand elastic or inelastic? One thing that matters is whether or not a product is a necessity. Some things we can take or leave, so if the price rises, we'll leave. Other things are so essential that we'll move heaven and earth to have them. Price can rise a lot and we'll still buy. I may need a medication to survive. Its price can go up and up and I'll still find a way to buy it. I don't need tacos to survive. If taco prices go up, I'll buy burgers instead. Necessities tend to have inelastic demand.

One definition of a necessity is something that has no substitutes. If there is no substitute for a good, we'll often swallow hard and pay a high price. If there are substitutes, we have the satisfaction of walking out on the seller and buying something else. Products with more substitutes have more elastic demand. My medication may have no substitutes. It's a necessity, and my demand for it is inelastic. But there are many kinds of fast food. My demand for tacos is elastic.

Here's an example. Gasoline prices increased back in 2011. The average price of a gallon of unleaded regular rose from $2.94 in January to $3.76 in May. The *New York Times* reported that in San Francisco "the daily number of cars driving across the Golden Gate Bridge has dropped while passengers on the buses and ferries have risen." When gasoline prices went up in San Francisco the number of cars crossing the Golden Gate Bridge decreased. In a big city, drivers had the option of taking buses and ferries instead. The purchases of gasoline for cars decreased.

The availability of substitutes matters for elasticity. The availability of a substitute meant a bigger decrease in quantity demanded with the rise in price. The demand for gasoline is more elastic in San Francisco because buses are available as a substitute for driving. Where there is no bus service, drivers must continue to buy gasoline, even as the price rises.

Time matters for elasticity. Again during the gasoline price increase in 2011, the *New York Times* interviewed Loraine Greene, a customer relations manager in New York's Hudson Valley. She "spent the weekend packing up to move to a rental house much closer to work. At $4 a gallon, gas is too expensive to justify the 50-mile round-trip commute." Ms. Greene said that "the option was either to sell my truck and get something smaller, or to try to get closer to work." When the price of a product rises we may pay at first, but if the price hike lasts we'll somehow adjust our lives to buy less. That's what Loraine Greene did.

Income matters for elasticity. People with high incomes tend to have lower demand elasticities for everything. For them, price is no object. When price goes up, rich people keep buying. Likewise, demand is less elastic when the price of the good is small compared to income. A rise in the price of bubble gum isn't going to change behavior very much, because the price of gum is such a small share of consumers' incomes.

> ***Demand is more elastic when a good is not a necessity, when there are more substitutes for the good, when there is more time for people to adjust their purchases, and when price is small compared to income.***

It's convenient to represent demand elasticity with the slope of the demand curve. If the demand curve is flatter, a small change in price will produce a big change in quantity. That's elastic demand. If the demand curve is steep, a big change in price will produce a small change in quantity. That's inelastic demand. Perfectly inelastic demand requires a vertical demand curve—price can vary up and down, but quantity never changes.

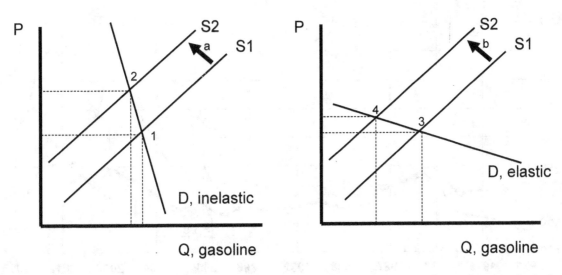

Figure 2-6. Steep or Flat? Suppose the supply of gasoline decreases, shown by a in the left market and b in the right market. In the market on the left, there is no mass transit, so drivers have no choice but to buy gasoline. The quantity of gasoline demanded does not drop very much as price rises, just from 1 to 2. Demand is inelastic. In the market on the right, drivers have the option of taking the bus to work. When the price of gasoline goes up, lots of drivers quit driving, and the quantity of gasoline demanded goes down a lot, from 3 to 4. The decrease in supply is the same, but in a market with inelastic demand price must rise a lot to reach equilibrium. In a market with elastic demand, price only rises a little.

There are supply elasticities too, of course. If price rises a little and businesses supply a lot more, supply is elastic. The supply curve is flatter. If price rises and businesses supply only a little bit more, supply is inelastic. The supply curve is steeper. If price rises and nothing happens to the quantity supplied, supply is perfectly inelastic. The supply curve is vertical.

The Real Price of Gasoline

If we really want to know how the price of gasoline has changed, we need to compare it to the prices of other things we buy. We need to look at the real price of gasoline. That requires a price index, specifically, the consumer price index (CPI). We looked at the CPI in Chapter 1.

Here's how to use the CPI to get a better measure of the changes in oil prices since the 1970's. Divide the CPI by 100, to move the decimal place two places to the left. Now the index equals one in 1982-84. Next, divide the price of gasoline in each year by the CPI (divided by 100) for that year. The result is the *real price of gasoline*, the price of gasoline relative to the average price of everything that consumers buy.

The price of gasoline actually paid each year is known as the *nominal price*. The price of gasoline *deflated* by a price index is known as the *real price*.

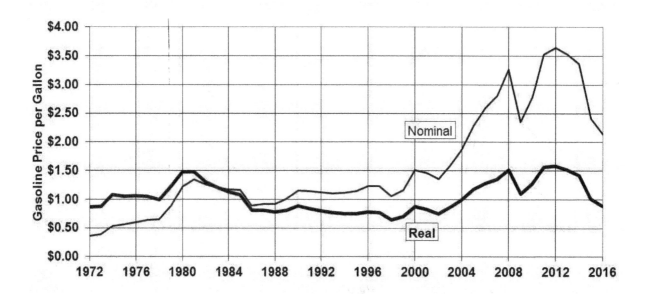

Figure 2-7. Nominal and Real Gasoline Price per Gallon, 1972-2016. The nominal price of gasoline is divided by the Consumer Price Index (see Chapter 1) to get the real price of gasoline. The real price rose from 1972 to 1981, creating havoc for drivers and the economy. The real price fell and remained low in most years from 1981 to 1998. The real price increased after that, with both the real and nominal price peaking in 2012. That's what people were responding to in 2011. But in late 2014 the price began to drop. In 2015 and 2016 the real price dropped back to where it was in 2003.

Let's try deflating a few gasoline prices.

Year	Nominal Price	CPI	Real Price
1972	$0.36	41.8	$0.86
1980	$1.22	82.3	$1.48
1998	$1.06	163.0	$0.65
2003	$1.59	184.0	$0.86
2012	$3.66	229.6	$1.60
2016	$2.14	240.0	$0.89

In 1972 the gasoline price was $0.36 (36 cents) and the CPI was 41.8. Divide the CPI by 100 to get 0.418. Then,

$0.36 / 0.418 = $0.86.

Relative to the average level of prices in 1972, the price of gasoline was $0.86. Another name for the real price when deflated by the CPI is $0.86 *in 1983 prices*. A way to think about that real price is this. Suppose the level of consumer prices had stayed the same over the whole period, at the level they had in 1983. Then the price of gasoline would have been $0.86 in 1972, and $1.60 in 2012.

The real price of gasoline was cheapest in 1998. How can that be, when the price consumers actually paid was $1.06, about triple the actual price in 1972? Because, while gasoline prices rose three-fold, the prices of all consumer goods and services *increased four-fold*. The CPI increased from 41.8 to 163.0 from 1972 to 1998. Gasoline prices didn't increase nearly as much as the prices of everything else. Relative to everything else, gasoline was pretty cheap.

- *Why did purchases of gas-guzzling minivans and SUV's increase in the 1980's and 1990's, and why did purchases decrease after that?*

As you can see in Figure 2-7, real gasoline prices peaked in 1980-81. That's why drivers were so upset. The real price fell most years through 1998. Gasoline became cheaper and cheaper for almost thirty years.

The real price of gasoline affected the cars people bought. In January 2015 the *New York Times* reported,

> Low gas prices, for years on end, persuaded many drivers to give up their small cars. When the era of cheap gas began, in the mid-1980s, the Honda Accord, the Ford Escort, the Ford Tempo and the Chevrolet Celebrity — all modest-size — were among the country's 10 best-selling vehicles. When the era ended, in 2002, the Ford Explorer, the Chevrolet Trailblazer, the Chevrolet Silverado and the Dodge Ram — all trucks — were among the best-selling.

Drivers preferred fuel-efficient small cars in the mid-1980's. Figure 2-7 shows why. The real price of gasoline had been above a dollar since 1973. Then the real price of gasoline decreased, and gasoline is a complementary good to big vehicles. Minivans, SUV's and trucks became popular. The demand for gas-guzzlers increased. Gasoline prices rose in most years since 1998, except for a downward spike in 2009. In 2011 and 2012 real gasoline prices just topped the real prices from 1980-81. Gas-guzzlers are became less popular.

Gasoline prices fell a lot in 2015 and 2016. You'd expect the demand for big cars and trucks to increase as a result. And they did. The *Times* reported in January 2017

> Sales of trucks and S.U.V.s accounted for nearly two-thirds of the sales volume during December as consumers continue to turn to the larger vehicles over cars. Analysts expect the trend toward larger vehicles to continue as long as gas prices remain low.

Prescription Drugs

EpiPen is the brand name for a device that injects adrenaline to save the lives of people who have severe allergic reactions to bee stings, peanuts and other allergens. Between 2009 and 2016 the price of package of two EpiPens rose from $104 to $609. The *New York Times* interviewed Naomi Shulman, who buys EpiPens because her 12-year-old daughter is allergic to cashews.

> "I called the insurance company and asked why it was so high and was told that, actually, it's $700 total, and my co-pay is $400," she said. For the first time in 10 years, Ms. Shulman said she briefly considered forgoing the purchase, but didn't want to risk it. "It's very wrong," she said. "It's gouging parents about their children's lives. It's not like letting them sniffle. It's life or death."

The demand for life-saving drugs is inelastic. Price may rise substantially, but people will keep buying if their lives depend on it. It's easy to understand why the demand for life-saving drugs and other medical treatments would be inelastic. But *how* inelastic is demand? We need a way to measure elasticity.

Measuring Elasticity. We measure the elasticity of demand for a product by gathering data on prices and quantities. When a business increases the price of its product, what happens to sales? When a product's price is slashed, how much more is sold? If we could gather a lot of data about such events, we could calculate an elasticity. We could take the percentage change in quantity that price changes cause and divide by the percentage change in price. Like this.

Elasticity = (Percentage change in Q) / (Percentage change in P)

If the data we collect show that a 10% rise in price tends to cause a 5% drop in quantity, then the elasticity is -0.5. That's -5% divided by +10%. If the data show that a 20% drop in price causes a 50% rise in quantity, the elasticity is -2.5. Demand elasticities that are more negative than -1 (like -2.5) are called elastic, because the response of quantity to price is big. Elasticities between zero and -1 (like -0.5) are called inelastic, because the response of quantity to price is small. An elasticity of exactly -1 is called a "unitary elasticity." It's neither elastic nor inelastic.

Knowing the elasticity of a product can be pretty useful to a business. Suppose a shoe store knows from long experience that the elasticity of demand for shoes is -2. The annual sale is coming up, when prices will be cut by 20%. Sales will increase, of course, but how many more shoes should the store have in stock? The answer is 40% more, because

-20% x -2 = +40%.

The 20% price cut times the -2 elasticity equals a quantity increase of 40%.

Research on the elasticity of demand for prescription drugs shows elasticities near -0.2. This is inelastic. A 10% increase in the price of a drug would cause only a 2% reduction in purchases. But even that elasticity must be too negative (that is, too far from zero) in the case of the EpiPen. Price increased by almost 500% between

> *An elasticity is measured as the percentage change in quantity divided by the percentage change in price.*

2009 and 2016, which would imply a change in purchases of -100% (+500% x -0.2). A 100% drop means people stopped buying it altogether. Of course, Ms. Shulman and millions like her kept buying. The EpiPen elasticity must be even closer to zero.

Why did the price go up so much? The supplier of EpiPens is the Mylan company, which is a *monopoly*, the only supplier of EpiPens. One of the determinants of supply is the number of firms. Fewer firms may supply less because there are fewer factories or retailers. It's also possible that just a few firms could negotiate an agreement to restrict production, to raise price and profits.

When there is a monopoly, there is just one firm, so no negotiation is needed. The firm can simply restrict its own production of the product and raise its price. That means a monopoly is a *price-setter*, not a price-taker.

We can use a demand and supply diagram (like Figure 2-8) to measure the amount of revenue a business earns. We measure the original equilibrium price with the distance from the origin (where the two axes meet) and P1. The quantity of goods sold is measured by the distance from the origin to Q1. The price times the quantity sold is the total revenue the firm earned from its sales. Multiply two line segments at right angles together and what do you get? The area of a rectangle! The shaded boxes in Figure 2-8 represent the total revenue at the first and second equilibria.

When the demand for a product is inelastic, setting a higher price can be very profitable. Figure 2-8 shows why. At first the price is P1, and the monopoly earns revenue equal to the price of the product, times the number sold. In the diagram, that's the area of the box, P1 x Q1. The monopoly then raises the price and reduces supply. That's the same decision for a monopoly. Reducing supply raises the price a lot, but reduces quantity only a little. Now revenue is shown by the box P2 x Q2. Because price has increased more than quantity has decreased, the box is bigger. Revenue has increased. And because output is smaller, costs have probably decreased, so profits have increased. Higher revenue and lower costs will increase profits.

If demand were elastic, the same reduction in supply would cause quantity to fall more and price to rise less. Revenue would decrease. Profits might still rise, depending on how much costs decreased, but not as much as when demand is inelastic.

Selling EpiPens is really profitable. So why don't other firms get in on the deal, and start supplying adrenaline injectors?

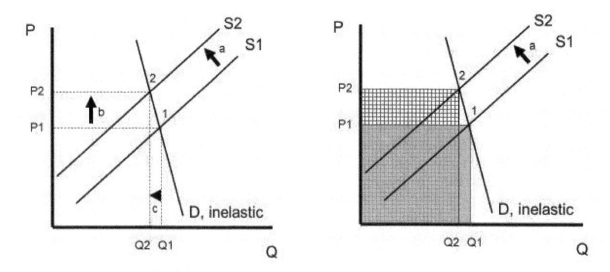

Figure 2-8. It's no game. The left market shows a good with inelastic demand. The demand curve is steep. A monopoly supplier decreases supply (a) and sets a higher price (P2). That's the same decision for a monopoly. Price increases a lot (b), but quantity falls just a little (c). The right market shows the same diagram, with two shaded boxes. The revenue earned by the monopoly before the price rise is P1 x Q1, the area of the grey box. Revenue after the price rise is P2 x Q2,the area of the cross-hatched box. Revenue goes up. Since the firm is producing fewer goods, costs probably go down, so profits increase. If demand were elastic, profits would not rise as much, or maybe not at all, because quantity would fall more than price increased.

The answer is *barriers to entry*. Other firms don't enter because they can't.

New prescription drugs are patented. The U.S. Patent and Trademark Office gives the developer of a new drug exclusive rights for 20 years. Other businesses aren't allowed to produce it. This is meant to encourage innovation. Research and development of new drugs is extremely expensive. Twenty years of monopoly profits provide an incentive to bring new and better products to market. Patent protection is a legal barrier to entry. Only after twenty years are competitors allowed to produce generic versions of new drugs.

But the EpiPen has been around since 1977. At the *New York Times* reported, "research and development costs were recouped long ago." Still, Mylan was the only supplier.

The very large investment required to produce new drugs is itself a barrier to entry. Enormous expenditures in buildings, equipment and expertise are required to manufacture even well-known drugs or devices. Few firms can afford it. We pay special attention to the quality of drugs. New versions of a product must be judged to be safe by the Food and Drug Administration. A competitor to Mylan introduced a device called Auvi-Q, but it was found to give improper doses and was discontinued.

The original producer of a new drug often has an advantage. Patients, doctors, insurance companies, and even local schools are used to buying and prescribing EpiPens. It's hard for a firm with a new version of an established product to get a foothold in the market. A competitor sells an injector called Adrenaclick, but insurance companies don't always cover it, and many people won't trust a life-or-death choice to a product they don't know.

Perhaps Mylan's monopoly will fade, if substitutes like Adrenaclick or some new device from another manufacturer are approved for use. Until then, the combination of monopoly supply and inelastic demand will keep the price high.

Health Insurance

Suppose we want to provide health insurance to a population with two groups, a large group of low-risk people, and a smaller group of high-risk people. Low-risk people are less likely to get sick and need medical care. High-risk people are more likely to get sick and need medical care. The population of low-and high-risk people to be insured is called the *risk pool*.

Suppose everyone buys health insurance at a particular price per year, called the *premium*. The insurer collects the premiums, then pays for health care when people get sick and make claims for benefit payments. The insurer must set premiums so that the total premium revenue is enough to meet the total claims.

What happens, though, if total premiums paid fall short of total claims? Maybe the high-risk people had more claims than usual. Maybe some of the low-risk people turned out to be high-risk people. Maybe the costs of health care procedures went up unexpectedly. The insurer will experience losses. If the insurer is a private company it would go bankrupt if it had too many losses for too many years.

So, the insurer raises the premiums for the whole risk pool, enough so that the total premiums collected are enough to pay all those claims. That could work, except for a problem called *adverse selection*. Low-risk people have more elastic demand for health insurance. Since they aren't very likely to get sick, they are more likely to give up their insurance if the premiums are too high. High-risk people have less elastic or more inelastic demand for health insurance. Since they are more likely to get sick, they resist giving up their insurance even if premiums increase (Figure 2-9).

> ***Adverse selection occurs when less-healthy people form a large share of the risk pool, which is the total number of people who are insured.***

As premiums increase the insurer suffers adverse selection. Low-risk people drop out, high-risk people remain. The risk pool now includes a greater share of high-risk people who make lots of claims. The insurance company finds that despite higher premiums, their revenue has decreased, because fewer people are insured. But their claims have not decreased very much, because the high-risk people are still in the pool. The company sees more losses.

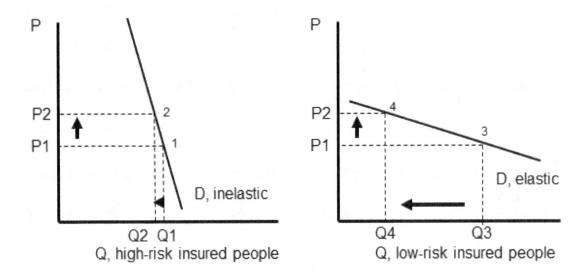

Figure 2-9. Adverse Selection. These two diagrams show the demand for health insurance policies by high-risk and low-risk people. No supply curve is needed). The insurer raises the premium for health insurance from P1 to P2. High-risk people who are more likely to get sick and make claims have inelastic demand for health insurance policies. Most keep their coverage (1 to 2). Low-risk people are less likely to get sick, so many drop their insurance rather than pay the higher premium (3 to 4). Revenue collected from low-risk people (the right diagram) declines. At the lower premium revenue is measured by the price times quantity box P1-3-Q3. At the higher premium revenue is measure by the box P2-4-Q4. The risk pool now has a higher share of high-risk people. Revenue has decreased, but claims have not decreased much. The insurer is in danger of a death spiral.

If the insurance company tries to remedy this problem by raising premiums again, more low-risk people drop out, high-risk people remain, and losses continue. This is called an *insurance death-spiral*. Higher premiums lead to adverse selection, which leads to losses, which lead to higher premiums again. With ever climbing premiums fewer and fewer people are insured. Eventually the insurer fails.

How can adverse selection, insurer losses and the death spiral be avoided? Here are three possibilities.

1. *Charge high-risk people higher premiums.* The insurer also may limit the coverage provided to high-risk people, excluding certain medical conditions. Lower risk people would be charged lower premiums, which would keep them in the risk pool. But, high-risk people may be charged premiums so high that they cannot afford insurance. That's an advantage to the low-risk people, because with fewer high-risk people in the pool there are fewer claims, so premiums can be lower. It means, though, the people with dire health care needs will be unable to buy insurance. This is a problem for people with pre-existing conditions. It can also lead to higher premiums for particular classes of people. Charging different premiums based on the peoples' characteristics is called *underwriting*. For example, older people are more likely to get sick, so the insurer might charge higher

premiums based on age. Young women might be charged higher premiums because they are at risk of undergoing that expensive medical procedure called "giving birth". The former is known as "age rating," the latter as "gender rating."

2. *Require low-risk people to buy insurance.* Establish a penalty for low-risk people if they refuse to buy insurance, perhaps an additional tax. This will make their demand for health insurance less elastic. Low-risk people will join the risk pool if the tax penalty is high enough. But, many low-risk people will object to this requirement, since they are not likely to make claims and would rather use their premium money for other expenses. Lower income people may not be able to afford even low premiums, so government must offer subsidies to keep their premiums low. This requires an income test for receiving subsidies. The subsidies cost the government money, which must come from higher taxes, reduced spending on other government functions, or borrowing. Low-risk people may decide that the tax penalty is cheaper than the insurance premiums, and refuse to buy insurance. Insurers may decide not to offer insurance in markets where too few low-risk people buy insurance.

3. *Tax everyone to provide insurance coverage to everyone.* Have government provide insurance instead of private companies. Establish a tax as a percentage of each person's income. Use the tax revenue to subsidize the health care costs of each person. This keeps everyone in the risk pool. But, no one likes an added tax. The cost of health care for hundreds of millions of people will add hundreds of billions to the government's budget. And private insurance companies will object to the loss of their lucrative health insurance business.

Possibility #1 describes the private insurance market in the United States prior to the Affordable Care Act ("Obamacare"). Insurance companies made profits and avoided death spirals, but insurance was not available to many people, especially those with pre-existing conditions. Insurance companies charged older people and women higher premiums. Possibility #2 describes the Affordable Care Act. Many more people were insured. However, tax penalties were not high enough and subsidies were too low to encourage participation by enough low-risk people in many localities. Insurers dropped out of many markets. Possibility #3 is known as "single payer." The Medicare program for people age 65 or over works this way—and it is expensive.

The Minimum Wage
The minimum wage is the lowest hourly wage the employers are legally allowed to pay workers in most industries. It was first enacted in 1938, when the minimum was set at 25 cents per hour. As of 2017 the Federal minimum wage is $7.25 per hour. The most recent increase occurred in mid-2009, when the wage rose from $6.85 per hour.

Proponents of raising the minimum wage point out that rising prices continually erode its purchasing power. If the prices of goods and services rise, but the minimum wage stays the same, the quantity of goods and services that the wage can buy decreases.

- *How high is the minimum wage, adjusted for consumer prices?*

We can use the consumer price index to measure the purchasing power of the minimum wage. Just as we did with gasoline prices, we divide the CPI by 100, and then divide the minimum wage by the result, to get the real minimum wage. This is the minimum wage relative to the price level, if the price level had remained where it was in 1983. It's the minimum wage in 1983 dollars.

Let's compare increases in the minimum wage since 1960 to increases in prices since then. We'll measure the price increases with the CPI. If prices have risen faster than the wage, then the wage can buy less now than it could then. The *real minimum wage* is lower.

Here are the data for a few years.

Year	Minimum Wage	CPI	Real Minimum Wage
1968	$1.60 / hour	34.8	$4.60
1983	$3.35 / hour	99.6	$3.36
1989	$3.35 / hour	123.9	$2.70
1998	$5.15 / hour	163.0	$3.16
2006	$5.15 / hour	201.6	$2.56
2009	$7.25 / hour	214.6	$3.38
2016	$7.25 / hour	240.0	$3.02

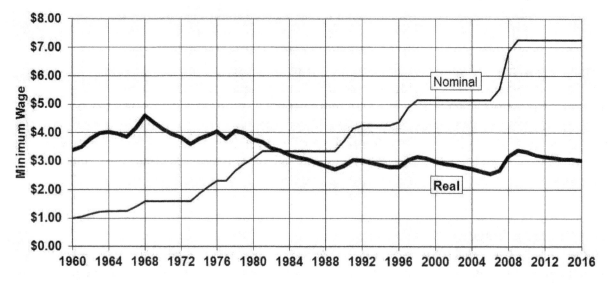

Figure 2-10. Nominal and Real Minimum Wage, 1960-2016. The nominal minimum wage has increased from $1.00 a hour in 1960 to $7.25 an hour in 2016. The real minimum wage has decreased during these years. In 1983 dollars, the real wage varied around $4.00 an hour from the mid-1960's to 1980. Then the nominal wage was held at $3.35 from 1983 to 1989 while prices rose, and the real wage dropped under $3.00. The real minimum wage has varied around $3.00 ever since.

Back in 1968, when Lyndon Johnson was president, the minimum wage was $1.60 an hour (no kidding!). But prices were a lot lower back then, too. We can tell how much lower from the CPI. The index in 1968 was 34.8. In 2016 it was 240.0. Prices have increased almost seven times since 1968.

To compare the minimum wage and prices we can divide the wage by the CPI (after dividing the CPI by 100).

1968: $1.60 / 0.348 = $4.60
2016: $7.25 / 2.400 = $3.02.

The result is the real minimum wage. This number is the amount needed at 1982-84 prices to buy what $1.60 bought in 1968, or $7.25 bought in 2016. If you had $4.60 in 1983, you could buy the same stuff you bought with $1.60 in 1968. If you had $3.02 in 1983, you could buy the same stuff you bought with $7.25 in 2016. If we convert wages for all the years to *1983 dollars,* we can compare the purchasing power of the minimum wage over time.

The real minimum wage in 1983 is a special case. Drop that calculation into the above sentence, and it reads, "In 1983 you would have needed $3.36 to buy what $3.35 bought in 1983." The *base year* of the CPI is centered on 1983. So, it's already in 1983 dollars, and it changes hardly at all when it's deflated. Of course that must be true, because in its base year a price index equals 100, so you're dividing the nominal figure by one when you deflate.
You can see in Figure 2-10 that the minimum wage sometimes has been held constant for long periods of time. It was $3.35 from 1983 to 1989, and $5.15 from 1998 to 2006. Now it's been $7.25 since 2009. During these periods prices continued to increase, so the real minimum wage fell. As prices rose the wage could buy less and less. Its purchasing power declined.

It turns out that the purchasing power of the minimum wage was highest in 1968. In 1983 you would have needed $4.60 to buy what $1.60 bought in 1968. The purchasing power of the minimum wage was lowest in 2006. In 1983 you would have needed only $2.56 to buy what $5.15 bought in 2006.

So, it's no mystery why advocates of increasing the minimum wage often compare the purchasing power of the wage now to what it was in 1968. That's the year when its real value was highest.

- *How high would the minimum wage need to be in 2016 to match its purchasing power in 1968?*

This kind of question is often asked by policy analysts when the minimum wage is debated. We can provide policy guidance with the CPI. Prices increased 6.9 times between 1968 and 2016. You get that by dividing the 2016 CPI by the 1968 CPI. So, for the minimum wage to buy now what it bought then, it must rise 6.9 times, too. Here's the calculation.

Price Increase, 1968 to 2016: divide the 2014 index, 240.0, by the 1968 index, 34.8
240.0 / 34.8 = 6.9.

Minimum Wage in 2016 to Match 1968 Purchasing Power: multiply the 1968 nominal
minimum wage by the price increase factor to 2016, $1.60 x 6.9 = $11.04.

To match its 1968 purchasing power in 2016, Congress would have had to increase the minimum wage to $11.04. That's 52% higher than the $7.25 minimum now.

Twenty-nine states have increased their state minimum wages above the Federal $7.25. There seems to be a lot of support for raising the minimum wage. About 3.3 million people earn the minimum wage, and another 25 million make less than $10 an hour. Raising the wage will help low-income working people, so surely the best thing to do is raise it.

Not so fast.

Increases in the minimum wage always cause vigorous debate—and the debate is always the same. Consider the following.

December 2014: As 20 states increased their minimum wages for the New Year, Advocates say the wage is too low compared to what it takes people to get by. Jack Mozloom of the National Federation of Independent Businesses says "The likeliest scenario won't be layoffs, it'll be employers on a broad scale finding ways to avoid creating new jobs." A higher minimum wage would lead to fewer jobs and hours, he claims.

May 2007: Congress passes an increase in the minimum wage. Many businesses groups oppose the increase, arguing that it would cause businesses to postpone hiring and reduce the number of jobs. Supporters claim that in the first year that it would provide a family of three with money to buy an additional 15 months of groceries.

May 1996: Congress approves an increase in the minimum wage. Supporters assert that higher pay will get people off welfare. Opposing legislators argue that "we have these perverse employment effects where that entry level job for the most needy worker in America just goes away" when the minimum is raised.

July 1973: Congress votes to raise the minimum wage. Opponents say it will increase unemployment among low-skilled workers. When the President vetoes the increase two months later, supporters accuse him of holding back added pay for the poorest workers in America.

It's the same argument every time. Supporters of raising the minimum wage claim it will increase the incomes of less-skilled workers. Opponents claim that it will reduce employment opportunities for less-skilled workers.

- *Does a higher minimum wage create a tradeoff between higher incomes and lower employment for less-skilled workers?*

We can use demand and supply analysis to answer this question, but we'll need to redefine the demand, supply and the price and quantity axes so we can analyze the labor market. And we'll need to figure out what happens when price is not allowed to move to equilibrium. What if the "invisible hand" is "hand-cuffed"?

The Labor Market and Opportunity Cost. So far we've looked at markets for goods and services that businesses sell to households. In the labor market, buyer and seller are reversed. Households sell labor time, businesses buy it. In the labor market the price is the wage paid to employees. The quantity is the number of hours worked or the number of employees hired and working. Demand shows how many workers that firms will hire at each wage. Supply shows how many workers want to work at each wage. At the equilibrium wage, the number of people seeking jobs equals the number of workers that businesses want to hire.

Businesses demand labor because they want to produce products to sell for a profit. When wages are higher, labor is more expensive, production is less profitable, and businesses will either find a way to produce with fewer employees, or produce fewer products. A higher wage causes a decline in the quantity of labor demanded. The labor demand curve slopes downward.

Households (that's you and me) supply labor to earn a living. But wait: if the wage is high, people don't have to work as much in order to eat and pay the rent. Why wouldn't a higher wage *reduce* the amount of labor supplied?

One explanation is a very old idea in economics: *opportunity cost*. Opportunity cost is the next best use of resources we give up when we make a choice. One resource is our time. We all possess a limited amount of time. We can use it for leisure, like sleeping, watching screens, or going out with friends. Or we can use it to work for pay. The opportunity cost of time used for leisure activities is the amount of pay given up by not working. When the wage is higher, the opportunity cost of leisure is greater. We give up more money by goofing off.

> **Opportunity cost is the next best use of resources we give up when we make a choice.**

Here's another use of the law of demand! When something is more expensive, people do less of it. If the wage is high, leisure is more expensive, so people do less of it. If they're not using their time for leisure, they're using it for work. And that means that higher wages increase the quantity of labor supplied. The labor supply curve slopes upward.

When you choose to attend college, you give up other uses of your (or your parents') tuition money. But opportunity cost tells us that you are also spending your time, and (to "coin" a phrase) time is money. You could be working, full-time, at a job. Perhaps some of your friends from high school made this choice. While you live the life of the impoverished student, your employed friends are buying cars and clothes and kitchen appliances with the money they earn. The opportunity cost of going to college is the tuition plus the wages you give up. (Sounds like an expensive choice. It's likely to pay off, though. Probably you'll recoup that cost, and then some, within a few years of graduation. The pay of college graduates is about double the pay of high school graduates, on average. College graduate unemployment rates are about half those of high school graduates too.)

Opportunity cost has many more applications. If I choose to spend my time taking a nap, I give up spending my time perfecting my lecture notes. If you choose to spend your money on a new hat, you give up spending it on a pizza supreme. If a farmer uses her land to grow corn, she gives up what could be earned growing beans. If a retailer uses his shelf space to stock corn flakes, he gives up what could be earned stocking raisin bran.

The choices are how to spend or use resources like time, money, land, or retail space. Choosing to use resources in one way means giving up the opportunity to use them in another. The benefits you could have had using your time for lecture preparation or your money for pizza measure the cost of your choice. That hat cost you one very tasty pizza supreme.

The definition measures opportunity cost with the "next best" use of resources given up. Presumably, everyone devotes their resources to their best possible use. There are usually many other possibilities. Which one is *the* opportunity cost? It's the second best use of resources.

A Price Floor. So far we've looked at markets where price is free to find the market's equilibrium. The invisible hand pushes high prices down toward equilibrium and low prices up toward equilibrium. In some markets, though, there are reasons why prices can't adjust. One such reason exists in the labor market. There is a legal minimum wage. It is illegal to pay employees the equilibrium wage if it is below the minimum. At the equilibrium wage, the quantity of labor supplied and the quantity of labor demanded will be equal. If the wage can't fall to equilibrium, the quantity supplied will exceed the quantity demanded. More people will be seeking jobs than businesses want to hire. That's a labor surplus, also known as unemployment.

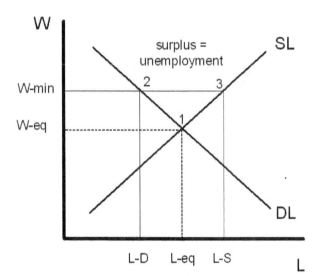

Figure 2-11. The Floor of the Market. This is a diagram of the labor market. The price is the wage paid to labor. The quantity is the number of people working or the number of hours worked. Labor is demanded by business firms—employers. Labor is supplied by households—employees. Equilibrium is at 1, where the quantity of labor demanded equals the quantity of labor supplied. All jobs are filled; all workers find jobs. A legal minimum wage above equilibrium creates a surplus of labor. The quantity of labor demanded is L-D at 2, while the quantity of labor supplied is L-S at 3. The surplus is point 3 less point 2, and it's called unemployment. Households are trying to supply labor that businesses don't want to buy. But those who are working are paid more.

Figure 2-11 illustrates the problem. Less-skilled workers are earning more at the minimum wage W-min, if they still have their jobs. That's because W-min is above the equilibrium wage, W-eq. *But fewer less-skilled workers have jobs.* With the lower equilibrium wage, the number of jobs businesses offer is L-eq. With the minimum wage, it's only L-D. Those workers who keep their jobs earn more. Those who lose their jobs earn nothing.

We can compare the effect of the lost jobs to the effect of the higher pay with demand and supply. We just need those price times quantity boxes, like we used in Figure 2-8.

How do businesses figure out their payrolls? By multiplying the wage they pay their workers by the number of workers they employ. In the left market in

> *The minimum wage is a price floor which keeps the price of labor from falling to equilibrium. Some workers are paid more, but some lose their jobs.*

diagram 2-12 the equilibrium wage is measured by the W-eq, and the number of employees is L-eq. The wage times the number of employees is the total earnings of the workers in this market. That's the area of a rectangle. The shaded boxes in Figure 2-12 represent the total earnings of all the employed workers

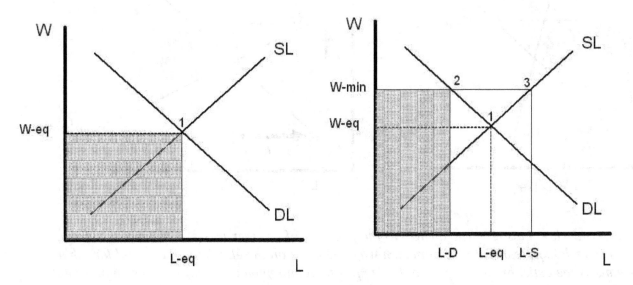

Figure 2-12. Does It Pay? With no minimum wage, the equilibrium is at 1. The wage is W-eq and the number of people employed is L-eq. The wage times the number of people employed is total wages earned. W-eq makes one side of a box, L-eq makes another side, so their product is the area of the box, which is shaded. With a minimum wage, the quantity of labor demanded is at 2, the quantity supplied is at 3. The difference is the surplus of labor, unemployment. The minimum wage (W-min) is higher than the equilibrium wage, so the vertical side of the earnings box is longer. But the horizontal side is shorter, because the number of people that firms hire (L-D) is less than equilibrium employment (L-eq). Less-skilled workers get a higher wage, but fewer are employed. In these two diagrams it's not clear whether less-skilled workers end up earning more or less, in total. Which shaded box is bigger?

The change in earnings—in the size of the boxes—caused by the minimum wage depends on the *elasticity of demand for labor*. Remember that the elasticity tells us how much quantity changes with a change in price. When the wage increases, how much does the quantity of labor demanded decrease? How many jobs are lost?

When the minimum wage is imposed, the number of workers drops to L-D, but the wage they earn rises to W-min. There's a new shaded box. We can compare the earnings of the workers in this market by comparing the sizes of the boxes. It's hard to tell which is bigger in Figure 2-12.

Figure 2-13 shows why the demand elasticity matters. On the left, the demand for labor is inelastic. The curve is steep, and that means that a change in the wage causes just a small decrease in the quantity of labor demanded. Lots more workers earn a higher wage, but only a few lose their jobs. Total earnings increase. The shaded box gets bigger when the minimum wage is imposed.

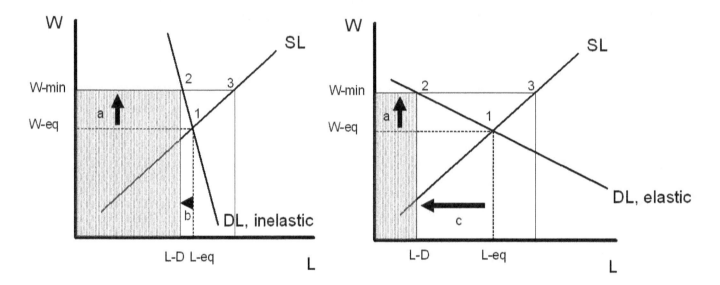

Figure 2-13. How Elastic? The answer to the question of whether less-skilled workers in total earn more or less in total with the minimum wage depends on the elasticity of demand for labor. If demand is inelastic, in the diagram at left, imposing a minimum wage (a) reduces employment only a little (b). The added earnings from the higher wage are greater than the lost earnings from fewer jobs. If demand is elastic, in the diagram at right, imposing a minimum wage (a) reduces employment a lot (c). The added earnings from the higher wage are less than the lost earnings from fewer jobs.

On the right is an elastic demand for labor. The demand curve is flat, which means that a wage increase causes a big drop in the quantity of labor demanded. Lots of jobs are lost, and only a few workers remain employed to earn the higher wage. Total earnings decrease.

- *How much does employment of less-skilled workers fall when the minimum wage increases?*

The minimum wage debate turns on the tradeoff between pay and jobs, and the tradeoff depends on the elasticity of demand for labor. So, is the demand for labor elastic or inelastic? Let's measure another elasticity!

Lots of research has been done on the demand for less-skilled labor. The research has produced lots of different results because researchers use different methods on different sets of data. But most studies find the demand to be inelastic. The elasticity appears to be in the range of -0.1 to -0.3. A ten percent rise in the minimum results in a 1% to 3% drop in employment. (Many studies find an elasticity near zero, meaning demand for less-skilled labor is almost perfectly inelastic.)

This means the inelastic demand curve on the left in figure 2-13 is the better picture of what actually happens. A minimum wage increase increases the total earnings of less-skilled workers.

- *Does economic analysis support an increase in the minimum wage?*

Again, not necessarily.

It's very likely that an increase in the minimum wage increases the earnings of most less-skilled workers. But even if only a few workers lose their jobs to a higher minimum wage, they pay a very high cost to provide somewhat higher earnings for everyone else. Less-skilled workers who are still employed will have more purchasing power. Those who lose their jobs have no purchasing power at all.

The increase in the price of less-skilled labor raises input costs for the businesses that employ them. This will decrease supply and increase the price of the products they produce. Higher wage workers don't get a pay increase, but they do pay those higher prices. Higher prices mean that the purchasing power of their wages will fall.

The minimum wage redistributes income. Those who keep their jobs gain; those who become unemployed lose. Those who get no wage increase but pay higher prices lose. An increase in the minimum wage shifts real income from more-skilled, higher wage workers to less-skilled, minimum wage workers.

Economics provides a lot of information about the consequences of this policy change. But the question of who deserves to earn more and who deserves to earn less requires value judgments. Economists are no more qualified to make those value judgments than are plumbers, lawyers, convenience store workers, or even college students. Economics lays out the issue, and (we hope) raises the quality of the debate. The decision is up to the policymakers, and the public.

Terms in this Chapter, in order of appearance

Demand
Supply
Demand and supply schedule
Diminishing marginal utility
Law of Demand
Price takers
Profit maximizers
Law of Diminishing Returns
Surplus
Shortage
Equilibrium
The Wealth of Nations
Self-interest
Competition
Invisible hand
Income
Normal goods
Inferior goods
Prices of other goods
Complements
Substitutes
Tastes and preferences
Population
Expectations
Shift in demand
Shift in quantity supplied
Costs of resources or inputs
Technology
Natural conditions
Number of firms
Expectations
Shift in supply
Shift in quantity demanded
Elasticity
Monopoly
Price setters
Barriers to entry
Risk pool
Premium
Adverse selection
Underwriting
Consumer Price Index (CPI)
Nominal figures
Real figures

Deflate
Real minimum wage
Labor market
Price Floor
Wage times employment equals earnings
Elasticity of demand for labor
Measuring elasticity
Perfectly inelastic

Notes
The first economics book I ever read—and still one of the best—is Robert Heilbroner's *The Worldly Philosophers*. He makes the lives of the great economists exciting, which is no mean feat. There are now later editions, but I used the one I got as a freshman economics student in 1974, the 4th edition. Chapter 3 is about Adam Smith.

Sources

Congressional Research Service. 2015. *Health Insurance: A Primer.* Washington, D.C.: CRS (January 8).

Doucouliagos, Hristos and T. D. Stanley. 2009. "Publication Selection Bias in Minimum-Wage Research? A Meta-Regression Analysis." *British Journal of Industrial Relations,* 47 (2): 406-428.

Heilbroner, Robert L. 1972. *The Worldly Philosophers.* (4th Edition) New York: Simon and Schuster.

Kaiser Family Foundation, The. 2008. *How Private Health Coverage Works: A Primer, 2008 Update.* Menlo Park, California: Kaiser Family Foundation (April).

Liu, Su and Deborah Cholet. 2006. *Price and Income Elasticity of the Demand of Health Insurance and Health Care Services: A Critical Review of the Literature.* Mathematic Policy Research, Inc. (March 24).

Rattinger, Gail B., Rahul Jain, Jing Ju and C. Daniel Mullins. 2008. "Principles of Economics Crucial to Pharmacy Students' Understanding of the Prescription Drug Market." *American Journal of Pharmaceutical Education* 72 (3): 1-5.

News Articles
Carroll, Aaron E. "The EpiPen, a Case Study in Health System Dysfunction," *New York Times*, August 23, 2016.

Clymer, Adam. "House Approves Increase to $5.15 in Minimum Wage," *New York Times*, May 24, 1996.

Labaton, Stephen. "Congress Passes Increase in the Minimum Wage," *New York Times*, May 25, 2007.

Leonhardt, David. "Gas, Still Not as Cheap as It Used to Be," *New York Times*, January 27, 2015

Madden, Richard. "Senate Votes Bill to Raise Minimum Wage to $2.20," *New York Times*, July 20, 1973.

Mouawad, Jad and Nick Bunkley. "U.S. Economy Is Better Prepared for Rising Gas Costs," *New York Times*, March 8, 2011.

Norris, Floyd. "Oil Supply Is Rising, but Demand Keeps Pace and Then Some," *New York Times*, November 23, 2012.

Parker-Pope, Tara and Rachel Rabkin Peachman. "EpiPen Price Rise Sparks Concern for Allergy Sufferers," *New York Times*, August 22, 2016.

Rich, Motoko and Stephanie Clifford. "In Consumer Behavior, Signs of Gas Price Pinch," *New York Times*, May 17, 2011.

Shabekoff, Phillip. "Labor and the Minimum Wage," *New York Times*, September 16, 1973.

Yergin, Daniel. "Who Will Rule the Oil Market?" *New York Times*, January 23, 2015.

Chapter 3
A Macroeconomic Model

So far we have measures of the aggregate economy, and we have demand and supply. We can combine the two to come up with a *macroeconomic model* to help us understand the macroeconomy. What causes recessions and expansions? What are the likely results of "shocks" to the economy? What policies might be used to improve the economy's performance, and what might be the consequences of these policies?

We'll start with two markets. Each market stands for a part of the economy that we can measure. Each uses demand and supply to show what makes each measure change. Here's an overview.

The Goods Market. This is the demand for and supply of the economy's output. We measure output with real Gross Domestic Product, and the price with a price index like the Consumer Price Index or the GDP deflator. Demand is called *aggregate demand*; it depends on spending by households on consumption, by businesses on investment on plant and equipment, by governments for its employees and equipment, by Americans on imports, and by the world on American exports. Supply is called *aggregate supply*; it depends on the production of goods and services by businesses. The equilibrium is the intersection of aggregate demand and aggregate supply, and it determines the price level and the level of output—real GDP. When aggregate demand or aggregate supply change, the equilibrium changes. The resulting increases in real GDP are expansions and decreases in real GDP are recessions. Increases in the price level are inflation and decreases in the price level are deflation.

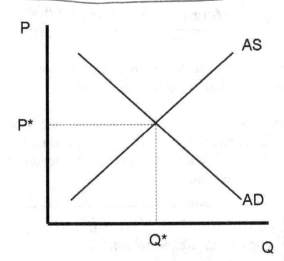

Figure 3-1. The Goods Market. That's output (Q) on the horizontal axis, measured by real Gross Domestic Product, and the price level (P) on the vertical axis, measured by a price index like the Consumer Price Index or the GDP deflator. The demand curve is aggregate demand (AD), which depends on spending, and the supply curve is aggregate supply (AS), which depends on production. The intersection is the equilibrium, where spending equals production. P* shows the price level and Q* shows the level of real GDP.

The Money Market. This is the *demand for money* and the *supply of money*. The important indicator in this market is the real interest rate, which is the price of money. The quantity of money is the amount of cash in circulation plus deposits and reserves in banks. Demand is the demand for money by households and businesses. It is related to income and the price level. Supply is the supply of money, determined by the behavior of private lenders like banks and bond buyers, and by the monetary policy of the Federal Reserve. The equilibrium is the intersection of money demand and money supply. It determines the quantity of money, but more important, it determines the real interest rate. When money demand or money supply changes, the real interest rate changes.

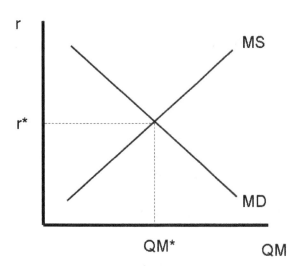

Figure 3-2. The Money Market. The quantity of money in circulation—including cash and reserves and deposits in banks—is on the horizontal axis (QM). The real interest rate (r) is on the vertical axis. That's the price of money. The demand for money (MD) depends on the price level and income, while the supply of money (MS) depends on monetary policy and on bank behavior. The intersection shows the equilibrium quantity of money (QM*) and real interest rate (r*).

We'll spend this chapter explaining the goods and money markets. Later we'll introduce an exchange market. Throughout the book we'll add whistles and bells so the model can analyze all sorts of events and policies. If you want it all at once, though, the Appendix is called "How to Use the Macroeconomic Model."

> *If you want to see the full macroeconomic model in action, see the Appendix, "How to Use the Macroeconomic Model."*

The Goods Market

The goods market is the most important. It's the one that shows us the main things we want to know: what causes recessions and expansions, inflation and deflation, and unemployment?

The goods market looks at what determines spending and production, known as aggregate demand and aggregate supply. The equilibrium shows the price level and real output. When spending or production change, aggregate demand or supply shift. The result is a change in the price level—inflation or deflation—and a change in output—expansion or recession.

Aggregate demand is the sum of spending on consumption, investment, government purchases, and net exports, which are exports minus imports. That's our old friend, C+I+G+X-M. In the following chapters we'll look at what lies behind each kind of spending, but for now, just think of consumers, businesses, governments and the rest of the world making decisions on how much to spend on the nation's output of goods and services.

> *In the goods market, shifts in aggregate demand and aggregate supply cause changes in output and the price level. That explains recession and expansion, and inflation and deflation.*

Aggregate supply is the production of goods and services, mostly by businesses. Its determinants are familiar—the costs of inputs such as labor, capital and land, the level of technology, and natural conditions. These are the same as supply in a single market, discussed in Chapter 2.

We use the goods market to understand why output and prices change. Consumer spending decreased in 2008 and 2009 for lots of reasons. Home values declined. So did the stock market. People were less wealthy. The unemployment rate went up, so peoples' jobs were less secure. Consumption declined, and so did aggregate demand.

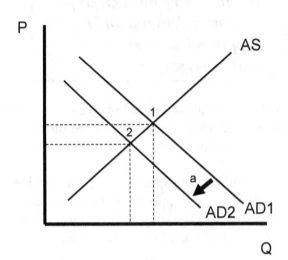

Figure 3-3. Consumers quit spending. In the goods market, start with aggregate demand (AD) and aggregate supply (AS) in equilibrium at 1. The falling value of homes, and the threat of unemployment, causes consumers to cut back on their spending. Consumption declines. Consumption is the most important part of aggregate demand, and the drop in consumption causes aggregate demand to decline (a). The new equilibrium at 2 has lower output and a lower price level. The decline in output is a recession, and the decline in the price level is deflation.

Businesses sell less, so they decide to produce less. Output declines. They lay off workers, who spend less too. That's a recession. Prices of goods and services fall as businesses cut prices to try to unload unsold goods. The price level falls, which is deflation.

Investment Spending in the Goods Market

Like consumption, investment spending by businesses is part of aggregate demand in the goods market. Investment spending is determined in part by the real interest rate. A higher real interest rate reduces investment spending; a lower real interest rate increases it.

Investment spending depends on the real interest rate because money for business investments is often borrowed from banks or from financial investors by selling corporate bonds. Investment decisions are made by comparing the cost of borrowing, which is the real interest rate, to the real expected earnings from the project. A business will make an investment if the project is expected to earn enough to repay the loan with profits left over.

When the real interest rate rises, borrowing becomes more expensive. An investment project must earn more in order to be profitable after the loan is repaid. A rise in the interest rate can make some investment projects unprofitable, causing businesses to cancel them. A higher interest rate reduces business investment in buildings and equipment. When the interest rate falls, borrowing is less expensive, more investment projects look profitable, and investment in buildings and equipment increase.

The Money Market
The real interest rate helps determine investment spending. The real interest rate itself is determined in the money market. Like the goods market, the money market has a demand curve and a supply curve. Equilibrium shows the price of money, which is the real interest rate, and the quantity of money in circulation. Shifts in money demand and money supply change the equilibrium real interest rate and the equilibrium quantity of money.

People need money to pay for their purchases of goods and services. Money is demanded because households, businesses, and governments need it to use for *transactions*. The quantity of money in the money market includes cash and coin, but also checking accounts and savings accounts. People keep cash in their pockets to buy lunch. They keep

> *In the money market, shifts in money demand and money supply cause changes in the real interest rate.*

money in their checking accounts to write checks for doctor visits and small appliances. They keep money in savings to buy a car or to guard against emergencies. And people need money in checking and savings to pay off the credit card bill every month (or at least pay the interest!).

People who have more income make more transactions. That's because most goods and services are normal, meaning the amount purchased increases with income. So, people with more income must keep more cash in their pockets, and bigger balances in checking and savings. When aggregate income rises, lots of people have more income, so the demand for money rises.

Likewise, when prices are higher, people need more cash and bank balances to pay them. Each transaction requires more money. People who face higher prices must keep more cash in their pockets, and bigger balances in checking and savings. When prices rise, so does the demand for money.

> *The Federal Reserve is the U.S. central bank. It conducts monetary policy, which influences the money supply and real interest rates.*

Money supply depends on the banking system. When the real interest rate is higher, banks lend more money; when the rate is lower, they lend less. Since the act of lending creates more money (we'll discuss that in Chapter 5), that means the quantity of money is greater when the real interest rate is higher. The money supply curve slopes upward.

The money supply depends on the *Federal Reserve* too. "The Fed" is the United States' central bank. One of the Fed's important functions is *monetary policy*. Monetary policy is the effort to manipulate the money supply and interest rates to achieve stable prices, high real growth, and low unemployment. How the Fed does this is a topic for later chapters.

When the Fed wishes to raise interest rates, it decreases the money supply. With less money to lend, banks respond by raising interest rates to discourage borrowers. The Federal Reserve can't set bank interest rates, but it can influence interest rates and bank lending.

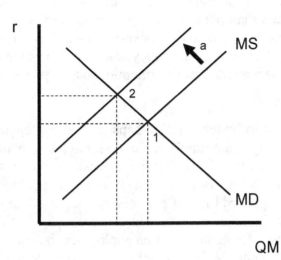

Figure 3-4. It makes the world go around—and stop going around. The money market starts in equilibrium at 1, which defines the equilibrium real interest rate and quantity of money. The Fed decides to decrease the money supply (a). The equilibrium shifts to 2, at a higher interest rate and smaller quantity of money.

Potential Output

Can we spend our way to wealth? So far the goods market says yes. Increase consumption spending, investment spending, government purchases, export spending (or decrease import spending), and aggregate demand will increase. Output will rise. And rise. The more spending rises, the more output rises. Prices rise too, of course, but according to the goods market graph any amount of goods and services can be produced, if only we're willing to spend.

This is wrong.

It's wrong because resources are limited. There's only so much labor, land and capital available at any time, and these resources can only produce so much output with the technology available. We call it *potential output*. It's the amount of output the economy can produce when resources are employed as they normally are. On the goods market diagram it's drawn as a vertical line and labeled Qp, the "quantity" of output that can "potentially" be produced.

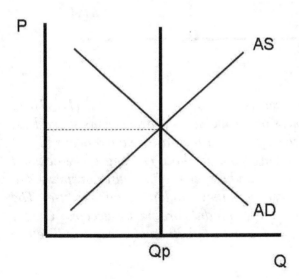

Figure 3-5. Spending won't make it so. Qp is potential output, drawn as a vertical line at a particular output level. Here, it crosses the equilibrium point, where the AD and AS curves intersect. There's a reason for that. Read on.

When the aggregate demand and aggregate supply curves intersect to the left of potential output, there are unemployed resources. Actual output is less than potential because some workers are unemployed, some factories are shut down, and a pile of raw materials is sitting unused in some warehouses. Aggregate demand or aggregate supply has decreased. Policymakers will be called upon to try to increase output back to potential. This is how our macroeconomic model represents increases in cyclical unemployment.

> **Potential output is the amount that can be produced when resources are normally employed.**

More difficult to understand, perhaps, is that aggregate demand and aggregate supply can intersect to the *right* of potential output, too. That implies that all the nation's resources are being used, and then some, to produce beyond the supposed limit of potential output.

How can this be? Consider one of the resources: labor. Remember that unemployment has three causes: cyclical, frictional and structural. Potential output is the amount that will be produced when cyclical unemployment is zero. People are still unemployed, because it takes time to find work, or because their skills don't match the open jobs, or because the job openings are in a different place. But not because there are no job openings for all the people who want to work.

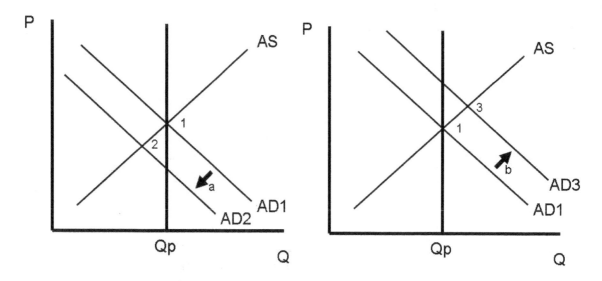

Figure 3-6. A temporary thing. The goods market starts with output at potential (1). Then, perhaps, aggregate demand decreases (a). Consumers or businesses or governments spend less, fewer resources are required to meet this demand, unemployment increases, output drops (2). A recession has pushed output below potential. Or, starting from potential (1), aggregate demand may increase (b). The lure of higher prices, bigger sales, and larger profits causes businesses to hire workers they wouldn't ordinarily hire, and use resources they wouldn't ordinarily use. The lure of higher wages causes workers to accept jobs they wouldn't ordinarily accept. Output increases beyond potential (3). Neither situation (2 nor 3) can last. Ultimately, output will return to potential. We'll see why in coming pages.

The unemployment rate when cyclical unemployment is zero is known as the *natural rate of unemployment*. Suppose, though, that business conditions really improve. Suppose businesses think they can sell all they can produce and more for a high price. They'll want to expand their operations and hire more workers. After a while cyclical unemployment is zero. So many workers have been hired that unemployed workers are hard to find. The businesses raise their wage and benefit offers, trying to attract employees.

Frictional unemployment declines. Workers are excited by these higher-than-usual wages, so they intensify their job searches. Businesses want to hire workers fast, so they accelerate their hiring procedures.

Structural unemployment declines. Workers become willing to move out-of-state to take higher paying jobs. Or they decide to make long commutes out of the central city to the suburbs. Businesses offer to pay moving expenses and provide temporary housing. They charter transportation from city to suburb. Workers search out training opportunities at community colleges or technical schools. Businesses offer to pay for training, or decide to hire less-skilled employees and train them on-the-job.

Similar stories can be told about other resources. Farmers plant "fence row to fence row" when they expect corn prices to rise. Manufacturers may keep technically obsolete factories open longer because product prices are high. The unemployment rate drops below the natural rate, more workers and other resources are employed, and output rises above potential.

That's why we define potential output as the amount produced when resources are employed as they normally are. At potential output businesses and employees are not doing anything extraordinary to connect people to jobs. Above potential, resources are employed with extraordinary intensity.

Output can be above potential. This seems to fly in the face of the potential output idea. What is limiting about potential output, if resources can be used more intensively, pushing output beyond potential? The answer: output above potential can't last.

Second Shifts

We measure four main economic indicators in these two macroeconomic markets: real output, the price level, the unemployment rate, and the real interest rate. Understanding how the economy works means we want to know about the relationships among these indicators. When output rises, what happens to the real interest rate? When the real interest rate or the price level changes, what happens to the unemployment rate? When the price level falls, what happens to the real interest rate?

In the macroeconomic model, it's useful to see what happens in one market when one curve shifts. But the model is most useful when it shows what happens when one shift causes another. We'll call these *"second shifts."*

Football coaches and choreographers break down plays or dances into a series of smaller moves that can be learned and practiced one by one. That's what we'll do here. Learn the "second shifts", and when they come up in the "macro policy ballet" you'll understand what's going on.

Second shifts show how a change of one demand or supply curve affects other demand or supply curves in the same market or in other markets. For example, suppose money supply decreases, increasing the real interest rate. In the goods market, the real interest rate helps determine investment spending. A higher real interest rate reduces investment spending, and that reduces aggregate demand. Output and the price level decline. The change in money supply in the money market caused a change in aggregate demand in the goods market. That's a second shift.

This second shift tells us about the relationship between the real interest rate, real output, and the price level. When the real interest rate goes up, real output and the price level tend to go down. The second shift shows the relationships and tells us why it happens.

We'll number the second shifts to help you keep track of them. When second shifts pop up in future chapters, you can refer back to Chapter 3 to remember how they work. The numbers aren't very important, though. It's the relationships among markets and indicators that matter.

Second Shift #1: Aggregate Demand to Aggregate Supply

Suppose output is equal to potential, and then spending increases. Aggregate demand rises. Firms bring resources into use that would not ordinarily be used. They raise wages to attract workers. Output moves above potential.

But the price level has increased, too. This has eroded the real value of the higher wages. Eventually workers and other resource suppliers discover this fact, and start to demand higher pay and higher prices to compensate. Perhaps it took them a while to demand pay hikes because the price level is made up of hundreds of prices, changing at different times, even in different directions. After a while, though, the trend becomes clear. Or, perhaps labor or supplier contracts had kept wages and costs fixed. Those contracts expire. New contracts are negotiated at higher wages. Input costs increase.

The increase in aggregate demand was the first shift. Now comes the second shift. Increases in input costs cause a decrease in aggregate supply. Output begins to decrease and continues to decrease until it's back at potential output. The price level increases even more.

In the end, the increase in aggregate demand only temporarily increased output. It may take time—months or years—but output eventually returns to potential. The only permanent result is a higher price level. This is why potential output is a limit on equilibrium output. In the short run, before contracts are rewritten or expectations adjust, equilibrium output can be above potential output. But this can't last. Aggregate supply will shift back and equilibrium will return to potential. Potential output limits equilibrium output in the long run.

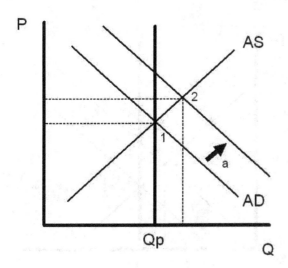
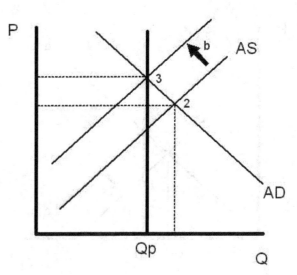

Figure 3-7. Loop. Start with equilibrium at potential output (1). Aggregate demand increases (a). Employees accept wage increases and work more. Product prices have risen even more, so employers want to hire. Output increases (1 to 2). Eventually, workers and other resource suppliers realize that prices have risen, and their real pay is down. They demand higher pay. Contracts are rewritten. Resource costs rise, which decreases aggregate supply (b). Output returns to potential (2 to 3). This is second shift #1.

Second Shift #1: In the goods market, when aggregate demand shifts and equilibrium output differs from potential output, aggregate supply will shift to bring output back to potential.

Second shift #1 works the other way, too. Starting at potential, aggregate demand falls. Businesses cut their prices. Their contracts with their employees fix the wages they must pay so they can't cut wages. Profits are squeezed, and businesses reduce output and lay off workers instead. Or, if there are no contracts, businesses offer lower wages to their employees to stay on, but employees refuse. They haven't adjusted their price expectations; they haven't realized that the price level has fallen. They quit instead. Output declines.

After a while, contracts expire. New contracts are written at new lower wages. After a while unemployed workers learn that they cannot get jobs at the old higher wages. They adjust their price expectations downward and decide that the lower wage offers are acceptable. Wages and other input costs decrease.

Here comes the second shift: lower input costs increase aggregate supply. With resources less costly, firms increase output. Output rises back to potential.

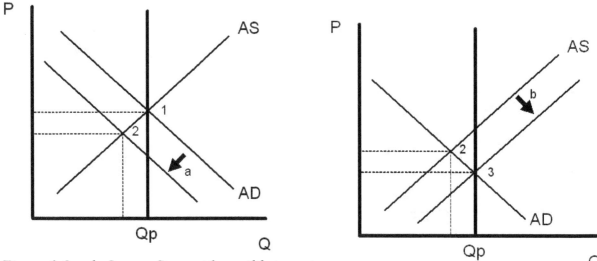

Figure 3-8. de Loop. Start with equilibrium at potential output (1). Aggregate demand decreases (a). Contracts keep wages from falling and employees resist wage cuts, so as prices fall business profits shrink. Output is reduced (1 to 2). Eventually, contracts expire, and workers realize that they must accept lower wages. Resource costs fall, which increases aggregate supply (b). Output returns to potential (2 to 3). This is also second shift #1.

Did you catch the theoretical problem in all this? Think about the demand and supply analysis in Chapter 2. How long did we say it took for prices to adjust to a new equilibrium, after demand or supply shifted?

The answer: no time at all! It's in the interests of both producers and consumers to adjust to the new price as quickly as possible. Yet here in the macroeconomic model, we're saying the price adjustment takes time. "After a while," contracts expire, expectations adjust, and the price level moves.

In fact, if prices adjust to equilibrium instantly, the aggregate supply curve is effectively vertical at the potential output level. Aggregate demand drops and the aggregate supply rises simultaneously, so output never differs from potential. Decreases in aggregate demand could not cause recessions.

This was the view of most economists during the Great Depression, and as a result they had no explanation for why output remained low and unemployment remained high for so long. A British economist named *John Maynard Keynes* came up with an answer in his book *The General Theory of Employment, Interest and Money*, published in 1936. It was perhaps the most influential book about economics in the 20th century.

The problem, Keynes said, was consumption, saving and investment. Households would prudently consume less than they earned, saving the rest. Sometimes, businesses would decide that the level of consumption did not justify investment in new plant and equipment. In the economy as a whole, one person's spending is another person's income. If everyone tries to spend less, everyone's income will fall.

With consumption and investment spending down, output and incomes would fall. In the long run prices might adjust downward to encourage more spending. But, Keynes said, "in the long run we are all dead." People are still talking about the meaning of this phrase.

Keynes was making fun of the old "classical" economists, as he called them. In the long run the economy will adjust to equilibrium, they said, so there was no point in trying to understand why there was temporary unemployment in the short run. But, Keynes said, human beings adjust to equilibrium in the long run too—the very long, very still, very stable equilibrium called death. Does that imply that we should ignore what happens when we're alive, which is, after all, just the short run? Of course not. Life is what happens in the short run. Keynes wanted economists and policymakers to pay attention to the short run, before prices adjusted, when recessions and depressions happened.

By 1965 the economics of John Maynard Keynes reigned supreme. Keynesian economists dominated policymaking in Washington. In December, *Time* magazine put Keynes on its cover, though he had been dead for almost twenty years.

Keynesian economists had decided that there was a tradeoff between inflation and unemployment, which could be used for policy. Engineer an increase in aggregate demand, and a nation could have lower unemployment, but at the cost of higher inflation. You can see that tradeoff in shift "a" in Figure 3-7. Aggregate demand increases, output goes up, unemployment goes down, but the price level goes up. Engineer a decrease in aggregate demand, and a nation could have the opposite. That's shift "a" in Figure 3-8. Economists in the Kennedy and Johnson administrations in the 1960's engineered an income tax cut to increase consumer spending and bring down unemployment, and that's exactly what happened. At first.

Then inflation started rising, and unemployment increased, too. Where was the tradeoff?

University of Chicago economist *Milton Friedman* offered an explanation in a speech to the American Economic Association in 1967. "There is always a temporary tradeoff between inflation and unemployment," Friedman said. But "there is no permanent tradeoff." Why not? Because prices will rise, and "employees will start to reckon on rising prices of the things they buy and to demand higher nominal wages for the future." Higher wages would eat into employer profits, output would be reduced, and employees would be laid off. That's shown in the aggregate supply shift "b" in Figure 3-7.

In our macroeconomic model, when output moves beyond potential, prices rise, input costs rise, and eventually aggregate supply decreases. Output returns to potential, and all that results is a higher price level. Inflation is higher, and unemployment is right back where it started. There is no permanent tradeoff.

In a sense, John Maynard Keynes discovered the goods market first shift, the drop in aggregate demand. Milton Friedman discovered the goods market second shift, the increase in aggregate supply. That's Figure 3-8 shift "a" (Keynes) and "b" (Friendman).

In 1969, Friedman himself made the cover of *Time*. In 1976 he won the Nobel Prize for Economics. But perhaps his most important legacy is in the macroeconomic model that most economists use every day. The macroeconomic model could be called the Keynes-Friedman model.

Second Shift #2: Money Market to Goods Market
Second shift #1 takes place entirely in the goods market. The other second shifts occur across markets. The two markets interact. A shift of demand or supply in one market can cause another shift in another market. The next two "second shifts" involve the interaction of the goods and money markets.

The real interest rate is determined in the money market. The interest rate determines investment spending in the goods market. The interest rate changes when the demand for money or the supply of money changes. That changes aggregate demand in the goods market, which changes output and the price level.

> *Second Shift #2: In the money market, money demand or supply shifts and the equilibrium real interest rate changes. This affects investment in the goods market, causing a shift in aggregate demand.*

Suppose the Federal Reserve changes the money supply. If the money supply decreases, the interest rate rises. The higher interest rate reduces investment spending, which reduces aggregate demand. Output falls and so does the price level.

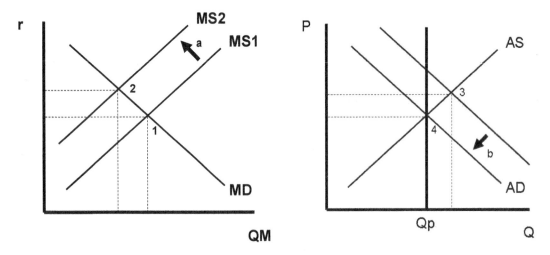

Figure 3-9. Stop inflation before it starts. The Federal Reserve sees output above potential (3), and realizes that inflation is a threat. It decreases the money supply (a), raising the real interest rate (1 to 2). This reduces investment spending, and decreases aggregate demand (b). Output drops back to potential, and the price level does not rise (3 to 4). This is second shift #2.

The Fed might make such a move when it expects output to rise above potential, or after output has risen above potential. Output can remain above potential only temporarily. Sooner or later, second shift #1 will set in, aggregate supply will fall, and output will drop back to potential. The price level will rise, and that's inflation. To prevent inflation, the Fed might decrease the money supply, raise the interest rate, cut aggregate demand, keep output at potential, and stop inflation before it starts.

Second shift #2 works the other way, too. If the money supply increases, the interest rate falls. The lower interest rate increases investment spending, which increases aggregate demand. Output rises, and so does the price level.

The Fed might make such a move when it expects output to fall below potential, or after it has fallen below potential. Aggregate demand falls, output drops, unemployment increases, and the economy is in a recession. Of course, the Fed could wait for second shift #1 to work, reducing input costs, increasing aggregate supply, and returning output to potential-ending the recession. That's usually too painful because it takes too long. Too many people have to remain unemployed for too long a time.

Instead, the Fed cuts interest rates to increase aggregate demand. The price level and output rise back to potential. The recession is avoided, or it's shorter and milder than it could have been.

These two Fed moves make up the core of *monetary policy*. That's the effort to manipulate the money supply and interest rates to achieve stable prices, high real growth and low unemployment. The Fed cuts the interest rate when it expects recession, and raises the interest rate when it expects inflation. It aims to keep output at potential, with an unchanged price level.

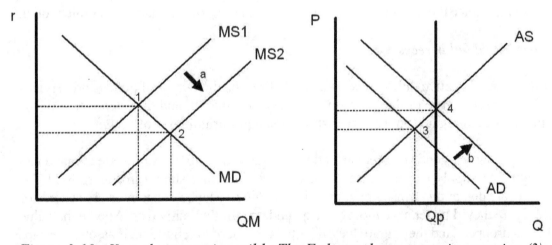

Figure 3-10. Keep that recession mild. The Fed sees the economy in recession (3), with output less than potential. In response, the Fed increases the money supply (a), which reduces the real interest rate (1 to 2). Investment spending increases, which increases aggregate demand (b). Output rises back to potential, and the original price level is restored (3 to 4). This is also second shift #2.

Second Shift #3: Goods Market to Money Market

Money demand depends on income and the price level. And income and the price level are determined in the goods market. The price level is right there on the vertical axis. Output is on the horizontal axis, but in the aggregate, output and income are the same thing. That's because businesses sell their products for a price, and the resulting revenue is divided up as income among workers, lenders, landlords and business owners. Workers receive wages, lenders get interest, landlords receive rents, and business owners get profits. Those are the main forms of income. Add up the value of output sold, and you've got the value of income received.

> *Second Shift #3: In the goods market, aggregate demand or supply shifts and equilibrium price and income changes. This affects money demand in the money market, causing the real interest rate to change.*

When prices and incomes are higher, people need more cash and checking deposits for their transactions. Money demand goes up. That leads to the third "second shift." Suppose spending increases in the goods market. Aggregate demand increases, and this increases output (income) and the price level. A higher price level and income increase money demand in the money market. The interest rate rises.

This explains why interest rates tend to rise during expansions, even without action by the Federal Reserve. People spend more, aggregate demand increases, and income and prices rise. Money demand increases and the real interest rate goes up.

Recession and the Macroeconomic Model

In Chapter 1 we looked at real GDP growth, inflation measured by the consumer price index, the unemployment rate, and the spread between the Baa and Aaa corporate bond interest rates. We used these four indicators to show how each indicator behaves in recession and recovery. Now, let's see if we can reproduce those tendencies using the two markets of our macroeconomic model.

- *Why does output fall in recessions?*

Real GDP growth turns negative during recessions. That means the output of goods and services goes down. The horizontal axis of the goods market measures output, and the intersection of the aggregate demand and aggregate supply curves shows the equilibrium level of output.

There are two ways that the goods market can show a decrease in output. Aggregate demand can decrease, or aggregate supply can decrease. These possibilities are shown in Figure 3-11. A decrease in aggregate demand is caused by a drop in spending. Maybe consumers are scared for their jobs, and figure they'd better save more (and spend less) for that rainy day. Maybe the value of their stocks has dropped, and they figure they'd better save more to rebuild their assets. Perhaps businesses find that they've over-invested in plant, equipment or inventories, and they're producing more than they can sell. They cut back on investment spending. Perhaps a war has ended, and the government cuts back on its military spending. Maybe there's a recession in Europe or Asia, and exports to foreign buyers drop off. These are the sorts of things that can reduce consumption (C), investment (I), government purchases (G) or net exports (X-M). They all could reduce aggregate demand.

Now businesses find that they can't sell all their output at the prices they expected. Inventories of goods accumulate. There are unsold cars on dealer lots, unsold houses in newly built neighborhoods, and unsold lawnmowers in the garden departments of big box stores. There may be unsold steel beams for office buildings that won't be built, or even cancelled contracts for fighter jets.

So businesses cut their output. They lay off employees and cancel their purchases of raw materials and parts, of trucks and machine tools. The laid off employees cut their spending. The raw material, parts, truck and machine tool companies see their inventories accumulate, and they cut their production and lay off some of their employees. The decrease in aggregate demand ripples through the economy. Output decreases.

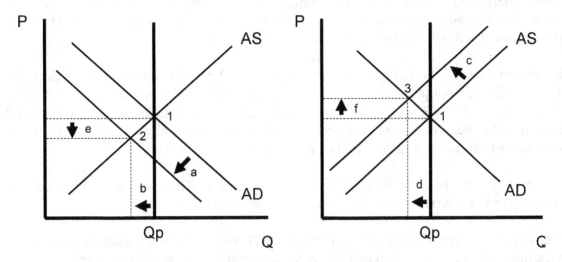

Figure 3-11. Two Goods Market Recessions. Both goods markets start at an equilibrium with output equal to potential (1). On the left, aggregate demand decreases (a), moving the equilibrium from 1 to 2. Equilibrium output decreases (b), and the equilibrium price level declines (e). On the right, aggregate supply decreases (c), moving the equilibrium from 1 to 3. Equilibrium output decreases (d), and the equilibrium price level rises (f).

Or, aggregate supply can decrease. Remember, that's a shift upward and to the left. Producer costs have increased. Perhaps oil prices increased suddenly, due to a war in the Middle East, or a political action by oil producers, or a hurricane in the Gulf of Mexico. Maybe a drought increased corn and soybean prices, or a freeze did the same for the prices of citrus fruit. Maybe a union action raised wages in major industries, or the government passed a big hike in the minimum wage. All these could cause a decrease in aggregate supply, though in reality in the United States only the oil price increases have had a big enough effect to produce a recession.

With costs up, businesses find it less profitable to produce. They reduce their output of goods and services by laying off their least efficient employees, closing their least efficient factories, or abandoning their most distant markets. The decrease in aggregate supply causes output to fall.

The decline in real GDP is shown by the decline along the output axis, labeled b and d in Figure 3-11. But which change caused the recession? Was it a decrease in aggregate demand or aggregate supply? To figure that out, we have to look at prices.

- *Why does inflation decrease during and after recessions?*

We observed that the inflation rate begins to decline a few months after a recession begins, and continues to decline for a couple of years after the recession is over. This is most consistent with the story told by the decrease in aggregate demand. In Figure 3-11 a drop in aggregate demand causes a fall in the price level.

Here we need a little finesse. The inflation rate falls during recessions, but most of the time it's still inflation. The price level is still rising. Only once since the 1950's has the consumer price index recorded deflation. It was the result of a huge oil price drop in 2009. In the 1950's and before recessions did cause decreases in the price level, which is deflation. We saw the huge deflation rates associated with the Great Depression in Chapter 1.

Our goods market diagram shows that decreases in aggregate demand result in a drop in the price level—actual *deflation*—not just a drop in the rate that the price level is rising—lower inflation. There are reasons for this. Government policy usually doesn't let deflation develop during and after recessions anymore. We'll see how in later chapters. For now, though, we'll treat a drop in the inflation rate as equivalent to a drop in the price level in the goods market.

Economists have given a name to falling inflation: *disinflation*. That's when the inflation rate falls from one year to the next. Prices are still rising. Just more slowly.

In the recessions we looked at in Chapter 1, 1990-91, 2001 and 2007-09, inflation decreased. We suspect, then, that the causes of these three recessions were decreases in spending. Aggregate demand decreased.

If we found a recession when inflation increased, we'd suspect a decrease in aggregate supply. This has happened. Recall the data on real gasoline prices from Chapter 2. Prices jumped in 1974. Higher energy prices increased business costs, which caused a decrease in aggregate supply. The inflation rate increased from 6.3% in 1973 to 11.0% in 1974, while real GDP was declining and the unemployment rate was increasing. They called it *stagflation*, simultaneous stagnation in output and inflation in prices.

The inflation rate fell in 1975 and 1976, as in all recessions. But when you see a burst of inflation at the beginning of a recession, at the same time that output is falling and unemployment is rising, probably there's been a decrease in aggregate supply.

The inflation rate continues to fall even after output stops falling. That's because of second shift #1. Equilibrium output is less than potential. Costs decline and aggregate supply begins to increase, moving towards potential output. This can reduce the price level, or the inflation rate, even as output begins to increase. Eventually equilibrium output approaches potential. The inflation rate stops falling.

- *Why does the unemployment rate increase during and after recessions?*

A simple answer: equilibrium output is less than potential. Potential output shows the level of output when resources are normally employed. Output less than that means resources are unemployed. Labor is a resource, so the unemployment rate rises when output drops below potential. In Figure 3-11, the amounts "b" and "d" represent unemployed resources, the difference between equilibrium output and potential output.

Spending drops. Businesses can't sell all they were producing before, so they cut back. If they're producing less, they don't need as many employees, so they lay them off, and reduce their new hiring. Cyclical unemployment increases.

Or, costs rise. Businesses find production more expensive and less profitable. They reduce their output by reducing their use of less efficient resources. Among those resources are employees. Again, cyclical unemployment increases.

Unemployment often keeps rising at the beginning of the recovery. The unemployment rate peaked at 9.6% in 2010, the year after the Great Recession ended. This happens because potential output is always increasing. The labor force is growing, technology is improving, we accumulate more buildings and machinery. If equilibrium output is growing slowly at the beginning of the recovery, and potential output is growing faster, the gap between equilibrium output and potential output could increase. That would indicate higher unemployment. We won't usually show potential output rising on our goods market diagrams, simply because it make the diagrams too cluttered and confusing.

Remember, throughout most of this book we'll estimate the natural rate of unemployment at 5%. That's the unemployment rate when output equals potential. When the unemployment rate is less than 5%, resources are employed with extraordinary intensity. Output is above potential. When the unemployment rate is more than 5%, there is cyclical unemployment. Output is less than potential.

- *Why does the interest rate spread increase during recessions?*

We haven't used the money market yet. Here's our chance. Figure 3-12 shows the money market. There's a panic in financial markets. Lenders turn pessimistic and are unwilling to lend to riskier businesses. The money supply decreases because less money is available for lending (we'll see exactly why this happens later). The real interest rate rises, especially for riskier borrowers. The interest rate spread increases.

Now comes second shift #2. The higher real interest rate (especially for riskier businesses) causes a reduction in borrowing for investment. Investment spending decreases, aggregate demand falls, and equilibrium output drops below potential. The economy enters recession.

In other cases lender pessimism is an effect of a recession, not a cause. Aggregate demand falls and output decreases. As their sales decrease some riskier businesses face bankruptcy. Lenders see this and cut back on their lending to riskier businesses.

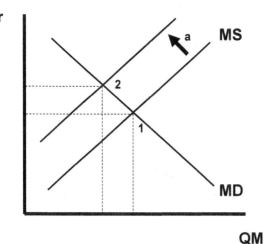

Figure 3-12. The Money Market in Recession. Pessimism in financial markets has reduced lending, causing the money supply to decrease (a). The real interest rate rises (1 to 2). In the goods markets (see Figure 3-11) this causes a decline in investment spending, due to second shift #2. Aggregate demand falls and output is reduced, causing a recession.

Data, Model, Story: The Great Recession

Three chapters into the book, and we've got enough to tell the story of the Great Recession of 2007-09. We'll be adding more as we go, but here's the outline.

This is an opportunity to piece together the data, model and story. Let's look at the data, and figure out what must have happened in the goods and money markets. Then we'll try to tell a story about what happened. The analysis from the data and model should make sense of the events of the Great Recession. Here's a table with real GDP growth, CPI all-items inflation, the unemployment rate, and the corporate bond interest rate spread. The recession began in December 2007 and ended in June 2009.

The Great Recession

Year	Real GDP Growth	CPI Inflation	Unemploy- ment Rate	Interest Rate Spread
2007	1.8%	2.9%	4.6%	0.9%
2008	-0.3%	3.8%	5.8%	1.8%
2009	-2.8%	-0.3%	9.3%	2.0%

- *What happened in the 2007-09 Great Recession?*

The table shows our four indicators, real GDP growth rates, inflation rates, unemployment rates and the interest rate spreads. All four are represented on the horizontal or vertical axes of the goods and money market. Let's start with the horizontal axis of the goods market.

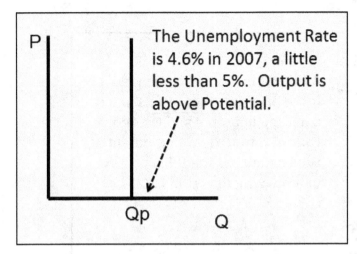

Figure 3-13. Equilibrium and Potential Output on the Goods Market horizontal axis.

The unemployment rate shows us where to start. It's 4.6% in 2007, which is less than 5%, which is the unemployment rate when output equals potential. That means resources are being employed with extra intensity. Cyclical unemployment is zero, and frictional and structural unemployment are being reduced through extra efforts by businesses and job seekers. Equilibrium output in 2007 must be just to the right of potential output. That's shown in Figure 3-13.

So we start with aggregate demand and supply crossing at equilibrium output to the right of potential, in Figure 3-14. Real GDP falls in 2008, and drops a lot more in 2009. Real GDP growth is negative. That means output is moving to the left on the horizontal goods market axis. The unemployment rate rises above 5% in 2008, then rises way above 5% in 2009. That means equilibrium output must be well below potential output in 2009.

The inflation rate actually increases in 2008. Then it falls to -0.3% in 2009. This is both disinflation and deflation: the inflation rate fell from 2008 to 2009, and the price level actually decreased in 2009. Both disinflation and deflation are shown with a downward move on the vertical axis in the goods market

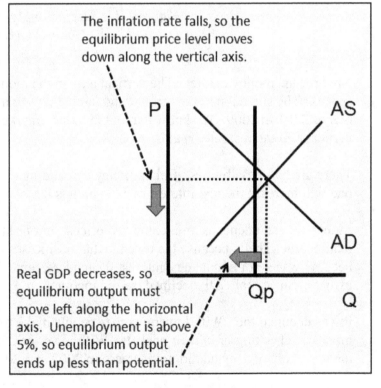

Figure 3-14. Output and the Price Level in the Goods Market.

There's only one shift that can reduce output on the horizontal axis, move equilibrium output from above potential to below potential, and reduce the inflation rate. That's a decrease in aggregate demand, shown in Figure 3-15. Spending by consumers and businesses must have decreased. If people are buying less, businesses have less reason to produce goods and services. They cut back on output, lay off workers, and stop increasing their prices (as much).

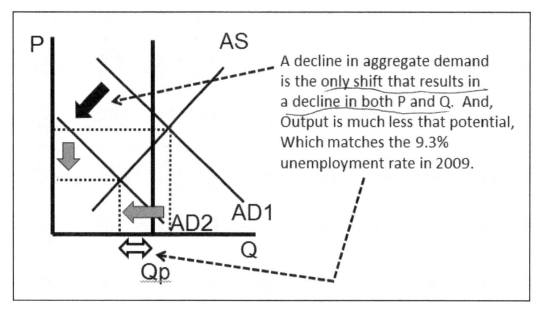

*Figure 3-15. Decline in Aggregate
Demand in the Goods Market.*

Now for the money market. The vertical axis in the money market represents the interest rate spread. The spread increased from a moderate 0.9% to a very high 1.8% in 2008 and an even higher 2.0% in 2009. We know that in the money market there must be a move upward on the vertical real interest rate (r) axis.

There are two possibilities. Either money demand increased, or money supply decreased. Either one will increase the real interest rate. Which is it?

Money demand depends on income and prices. In our aggregate model, real GDP is the same as real income. That's because the revenue that businesses receive from the sales of their products become wages for employees, interest for lenders, rents for landlords, or profits for business owners. Since real GDP declined, so did income.

Prices declined too. With lower incomes people make fewer transactions, so they need less money in checking or in their pockets. With lower prices, the transactions don't require as much money. Money demand did not increase in 2008 and 2009. It probably decreased.

An increase in money demand could not have caused the rise in the interest rate spread. It must have been a decrease in money supply. Money supply decreased and the interest rate spread increased, as shown in Figure 3-16.

Starting with the four macroeconomic indicators, we've plotted goods and money market diagrams showing what must have happened in the U.S. economy during the Great Recession, 2007-09.

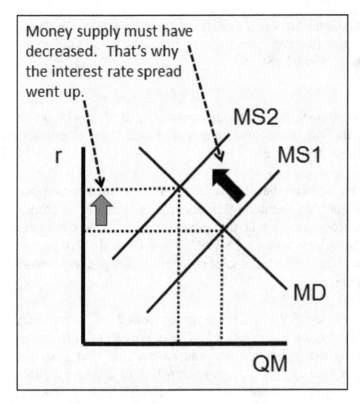

Money supply must have decreased. That's why the interest rate spread went up.

MS2

MS1

r

MD

QM

Figure 3-16. Decline in Money Supply in the Money Market.

Let's tell a story to match.

It started with a housing boom. In the first half of the 2000's the prices of houses exploded, especially on the coasts and in bigger cities. Income growth during the long expansion of the 1990's and low mortgage interest rates after the recession of 2001 increased housing demand, which helped cause the boom. Demand increased even more as people began to expect house prices to rise.

Construction companies built a record number of new houses, until finally the increase in supply began to reduce the price. People who had bought houses because they expected prices to rise now sold their houses before prices dropped further. That added to supply, and caused house prices to collapse.

With so many houses for sale, there was no need to build more. Housing construction dropped. Construction workers and real estate agents found themselves unemployed. They cut back on their consumption spending. Falling home values reduced the wealth of home owners. No more home equity loans to finance new consumption spending! Spending by homeowners fell too. Spending decreased, aggregate demand decreased, as in Figure 3-15.

The crisis came in the second half of 2008. It turned out that a very large share of the world's financial institutions were involved, directly or indirectly, with lending for mortgages in the booming housing markets. As home values declined, more and more homeowners defaulted on their loans. In mid-September a major investment bank failed (Lehman Brothers) and a huge insurance company became insolvent (AIG). Financial markets panicked.

Financial panic reduced the money supply and increased real interest rates and the interest rate spread, as in Figure 3-16. Second shift #2 kicked in. With real interest rates higher businesses found it hard to get loans. So did homeowners and college students. Borrowing decreased, and investment and consumption spending dropped, businesses cut production, output fell further below potential, and unemployment increased a lot. That made 2009 a lot worse than 2008. The inflation rate fell, partly a result of oil price decreases in 2009, partly the result of declining aggregate demand.

There it is, the story of the Great Recession. Combine a few macroeconomic indicators, models of two macroeconomic markets, and knowledge of news events during the period, and you've got an explanation of what went wrong. Data. Model. Story.

Potential Output Growth
Most of the time we'll analyze economic events with potential output unchanged. It works, and it keeps the diagrams simpler. Sometimes, though, an issue requires us to consider changes in potential output. Here are two instances where that's true.

A Jobless Recovery. In the goods market, we've seen that increases in output always correspond to decreases in the unemployment rate. Both are represented by rightward shifts on the horizontal Q axis. But sometimes output and unemployment rise at the same time. This has happens frequently in the first years of recovery from recessions. In 1992, 2002-03 and 2010 output increased, and so did the unemployment rate. Unemployment kept rising after the recovery began. These years are often called *jobless recoveries.*

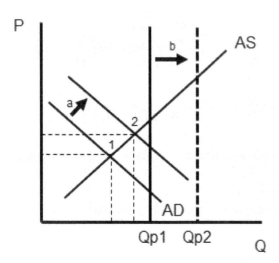

Figure 3-17. A paradox explained. The economy starts in recession at 1. Unemployment is illustrated by the difference between output at 1 and potential output at Qp1. Aggregate demand increases (a) and output increases to 2. If potential output remains unchanged, unemployment is defined as the difference between output at 2 and Qp1. Output has increased and unemployment has decreased. But if potential output grows (b) to Qp2—perhaps because the labor force increased—unemployment will be defined as the difference between 2 and Qp2. That's a bigger distance than 1 to Qp1. Output has increased, but so has unemployment. Growth as not fast enough to provide jobs for the expanding labor force.

At first the economy struggled to recover after the 1990-91 recession. In July 1993 Louis Uchitelle of the *New York Times* wrote

> Americans are being bombarded with explanations of why the nation cannot generate enough jobs . . . . The biggest problem is simply a lack of robust economic growth -- the most basic source of job creation. Until the national economy kicks into higher gear, they say, faster job growth will be hard to come by.

In the goods market, unemployment is shown by the difference between equilibrium output and potential output. If equilibrium output grows, but potential output stays put, unemployment must fall. But if potential output grows more than equilibrium output, unemployment increases. Real GDP isn't growing enough to generate new jobs for the growing labor force. Figure 3-17 demonstrates this possibility with a goods market diagram.

Output Growth at Potential. Suppose a recession reduces aggregate demand, and output falls below potential. Many people, buildings, machinery and other resources are unemployed. Then spending resumes and aggregate demand begins to increase. Output rises back towards potential. Unemployed people, buildings, machinery and other resources are called back into use.

Output can rise quickly because there are unemployed resources to employ. The economy is closing the gap between equilibrium and potential output by using inputs that already exist. Real GDP growth averaged more than 5% in the first years of recovery after the 1973-75 and 1981-82 recessions. Growth averaged more than 3.3% while recovering from the 1990-91 and 2001 recessions—after a short period of jobless recovery.

But what happens when equilibrium output reaches potential output? Inputs are fully employed. There are no more unemployed inputs waiting to be hired. The economy can expand only as fast as the increase in available inputs and improvements in technology.

Of course, it's possible for output to move beyond potential. But then the costs of scarce inputs will rise, aggregate supply will decrease, and output will return to potential (remember second shift #1). The economy can't sustain output beyond potential. The growth of potential output limits the growth of equilibrium output.

The labor force is the main input that we can measure. People are employed to produce output. Added buildings and machinery and improving technology will increase the amount that each employee can produce. Added output per worker is called *productivity growth*. Once the economy reaches potential, output growth will limited by the growth of employment plus the growth in productivity.

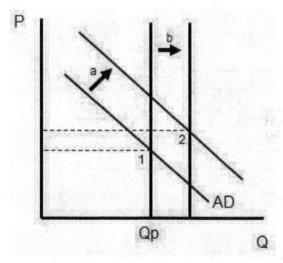

Figure 3-18. Decluttering the graph. Second shift #1 assures that equilibrium output will return to potential, because of shifts in aggregate supply (see Figures 3-7 and 3-8). In the long run, once second shift #1 is complete, we can treat the vertical potential output line as long run aggregate supply, and leave the AS curves out. Increases in potential output determine the growth of real GDP (b). Increases in aggregate demand determine the level of prices (a). Most of the time, aggregate demand grows faster, and real GDP growth is accompanied by inflation (1 to 2)

Output above potential is temporary. Eventually aggregate supply will shift to bring output back to potential. If we want to look at this long run—a time period long enough for aggregate supply to adjust—we can remove the aggregate supply curve from the goods market diagram (Figure 3-18). The potential output line becomes the *long-run aggregate supply curve*. The intersection of aggregate demand and the potential output line shows the level of output and the price level.

This implies that potential output determines equilibrium output. The increases in the labor force and productivity determine output growth. Increases in aggregate demand will determine the inflation rate. If potential output is rising faster than aggregate demand, the price level will fall. There will be deflation. This describes what happened in the United States from 1865 to 1896, when there was a long period of deflation. If aggregate demand rises faster than potential output, the price level will rise, which is inflation. This describes what has happened throughout most of the decades since 1900.

Growth, Productivity and the Labor Force
The unemployment rate dropped below 5% in 2016. We must be at or very near potential output. Over the next few years real GDP growth will be limited by the growth in potential output. How fast is that? Can we measure potential output?

Let's use our goods market model to estimate potential output. Each year's real GDP is equilibrium output, where the value of aggregate demand equals the value of aggregate supply. Most of the time equilibrium output is different from potential output. The aggregate demand and supply curves don't cross at Qp. But sometimes they do—and we know when! When equilibrium output equals potential output, the unemployment rate is near 5%. So, let's pick out the real GDP figures in the years of 5% unemployment, and we'll have an estimate—for those years—of potential output. Connect the points, and we'll have an idea of how potential output has grown.

The dots in Figure 3-19 show real GDP when the unemployment rate was between 4.5% and 5.5%. (Except 1941. The unemployment rate was 6% that year, but we need a real GDP figure just before World War II. That year's estimate of potential output is a little low.) The line connects the dots, and gives estimates of potential when unemployment is not near 5%.

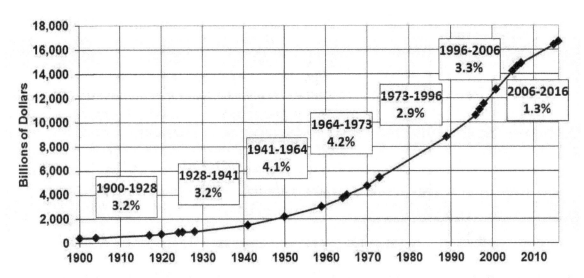

Figure 3-19. Estimated Potential Output, 1900-2016. When equilibrium output equals potential output, the unemployment rate is about 5%. So, when the unemployment rate has been near 5% since 1900, actual real GDP must be near potential real GDP. The points show real GDP when unemployment was near 5%. The percentage changes show how potential output has grown during seven interesting periods since 1900.

Potential output always increases, but sometimes faster and sometimes slower. The boxes in Figure 3-19 show seven time periods marked by the years when unemployment was near 5% (plus 1941). The average growth in real GDP was 3.2% over the 1900-2016 century plus. That's how fast output grew from 1900 to 1941. Notice that the Great Depression of the 1930's had no effect on potential output growth. Equilibrium output was far below potential during the Depression.

Growth accelerated from 1941 to 1973, then dropped substantially in 1973-1996. The difference between 4.2% annual growth and 2.9% growth may not seem substantial. But if growth had continued at 4.2% during 1973-1996, at the end of this period output would have been 33% higher. An employee earning $50,000 a year by 1996 would have earned $66,000 with faster growth.

There was a decade's acceleration from 1996 to 2006. But in the most recent decade potential output has grown more slowly than at any time in the long century. We're wondering if slow growth is the "new normal."

We can get some clues about the reasons for the variation in potential output growth. People produce output in fields, factories and office buildings, using their labor with tools and technology. We can divide real GDP by total employment to get output per employee. Changes in output per employee represent the growth of productivity. *Productivity growth* is how much added output the average employee produces each year. It's a rough measure of the effect of the increase in the capital stock (the tools) and the improvement of the technology used in production.

The sum of productivity growth and employment growth equals the growth of real GDP. Output increases because more people are working with more and better tools. Let's use the growth of the labor force instead of employment, so that recessions and expansions don't have so big an effect on the number of people available to work. We can use productivity growth between years when unemployment was 5%, so recessions and expansions don't affect our productivity measure very much.

Figure 3-20 shows the result. On average, the labor force increased 1.5% per year and productivity rose 1.8% per year over the whole 117 year period. That sums to 3.3%, pretty close to average real GDP growth of 3.2%.

The labor force grew rapidly from 1900 to 1928. The United States was still permitting a large amount of immigration during that period, and it added to employment. Birth rates had been higher in the nineteenth century too. Labor force growth dropped with new immigration restrictions in 1928-41, but this was offset by more rapid productivity growth. New technologies like electrification and more and better motor vehicles added to growth. So potential output increased 3.2% per year in both periods, because of rapid labor force growth early, and rapid productivity increases later.

Productivity growth exploded in the 1941-64 period, and continued above average in 1964-73. These were the peak years of the United States industrial economy. Labor force growth was slow through 1964, partly because the Great Depression had reduced birth rates. There were fewer people growing to working age. This ended with a "boom" in the early 1960's, as the first of the baby boomers entered the labor force. Women entered the labor force in large numbers during 1946-96 as well. Rapid growth in potential output from 1941 to 1973 is due to booming productivity, then booming labor force growth.

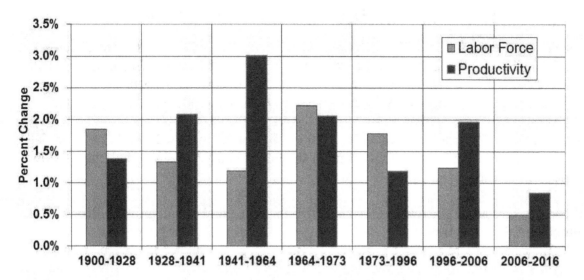

Figure 3-20. Labor Force and Productivity Growth, 1900-2016. The grey bars show the average percentage increase in the number of people in the labor force. The black bars show the average growth in real GDP per employee, also known as productivity. The sum of the two figures is an estimate of potential output growth.

But in 1973-96 productivity growth fell substantially. At first the new baby boomer work force lacked experience, which made them less productive. Energy costs increased suddenly in 1973, which made much energy-intensive machinery obsolete. High interest rates in the 1980's may have reduced investment in new machinery. Government regulations may have shifted investment to worker safety and pollution control, rather than added productivity. Labor force growth slowed after all the boomers grew up, but it was mainly slower productivity growth that reduced the growth of potential output.

Productivity recovered in 1996-2006, due to the wave of new information technology. Personal computers, the internet, email and many other innovations added to output per worker. Labor force growth continued to slow. Women were full participants in the labor force by then. But added productivity growth caused an increase in potential output growth.

More rapid productivity growth didn't last. Since 2006 it has been slower than at any time since 1900. The reasons are still a mystery. Not so mysterious is the drop in labor force growth. The baby boomers have started to retire.

We're adding fewer workers, and our tools and technology are not adding to productivity as fast as before. The result is slower growth in potential output. Perhaps productivity growth will revive, but demographics virtually guarantee slower labor force growth. Potential output is likely to grow more slowly for the foreseeable future. Potential output growth of less than 2% may be the new normal.

Terms in this Chapter, in order of appearance
Macroeconomic Model
The goods market
Aggregate demand
Aggregate supply
The money market
Demand for money; money demand
Supply of money; money supply
The Federal Reserve
Monetary policy
Potential output
Natural rate of unemployment
Second shifts
Second shift #1: aggregate demand to aggregate supply
John Maynard Keynes
Milton Friedman
Second shift #2: money market to goods market
Second shift #3: goods market to money market
Deflation
Disinflation
Jobless recovery
Productivity growth
Long-run aggregate supply curve

Notes
The story of John Maynard Keynes is told by Heilbroner in chapter 9 of his wonderful book.

John Maynard Keynes' first bestselling book was *The Economic Consequences of the Peace,* a vigorous criticism of the Versailles treaty after World War I. The economic conditions imposed on Germany were unworkable, he wrote. The European economy would not recover from the war. People would starve. And worse. "For starvation, which brings to some lethargy and a helpless despair, drives other temperaments to the nervous instability of hysteria and to a mad despair. And these in their distress may overturn the remnants of organization, and submerge civilization itself. . . ." It was published in December 1919. Corporal Hitler had joined the German Workers Party just three months before.

In the cover story of the issue with Keynes on the cover, *Time* quoted Milton Friedman saying "We are all Keynesians now." Friedman dashed off a letter to the editor in protest. The rest of the quote (which *Time* left out) was ". . . and none of us are Keynesians." He meant that in thirty years macroeconomics had built ideas on the foundation of the *General Theory* which had never occurred to Keynes. Fifty years of macroeconomics since then has added more.

Milton Friedman's speech to the American Economic Association was printed in the *American Economic Review* in 1968. Like Keynes, Friedman anticipated an awful lot of bad stuff that eventually came to pass, in the 1970's.

It took some time, but macroeconomics came to accept Friedman's ideas. We can see it in the textbooks. Paul Samuelson was the leading Keynesian economist of the day, and in some ways Friedman's great rival. Samuelson's introductory textbook was a best seller. The 1967 edition says that there is a tradeoff between inflation and unemployment that policymakers can use. The 1980 edition says that the tradeoff is less pronounced in the long run. The 1985 edition says there is no permanent tradeoff. Friedman's idea had won.

Ben Bernanke offers an appreciation of Friedman's contributions in a speech he gave in 2003. That's before he became chairman of the Federal Reserve—though he was a leading candidate, even then.

Sources
Bernanke, Ben S. 2003. "The influence of Milton Friedman's Monetary Framework on Contemporary Monetary Theory and Practice." Remarks at the Federal Reserve Bank of Dallas Conference on the Legacy of Milton and Rose Friedman's Free to Choose, Dallas, Texas, October 24.

Friedman, Milton. 1968. "The Role of Monetary Policy" *American Economic Review* 58 (March): 1-17.

Heilbroner, Robert L. 1972. *The Worldly Philosophers.* (4th Edition) New York: Simon and Schuster.

News Articles
Uchitelle, Louis. "A Recovery That's Too Weak Results in Too Few New Jobs," New York Times, July 17, 1993.

Chapter 4
Panic and the Fed

We've seen how to measure economic events with economic indicators. We've seen how to organize our thinking about these data using the goods and money market models. What we need now is practice, and what better practice than to apply the data and the model to actual events from United States policy history?

This is not a history book, though, so we'll look for ways that our analysis of the past helps us understand the present. As Mark Twain (supposedly) said, "History does not repeat itself, but it rhymes." We'll find some current issues that rhyme with our policy past.

Let's start at the beginning of the twentieth century, in 1906. The nation was prosperous. Output was growing, unemployment was down. The economic thinkers of the day called the decade between the mid-1890s and the mid-19-aughts "the most unexampled prosperity in our history."

All good things must come to an end. A financial market collapse in October 1907—the Panic of 1907—sent the economy into a sharp recession. Some of the causes of the panic were spectacular, like a huge natural disaster and a failed stock market maneuver. Some causes were mundane, like the normal operation of the banking system and the annual fall harvest. To really understand what happened, though, we need to know more about the money market. Let's start with money demand.

Money Demand: Liquidity vs. Earnings

Events in the money market can affect the goods market. A financial panic or a change in the money supply affects the real interest rate, which affects investment spending, aggregate demand, and ultimately prices and output. We call that second shift #2.

So far we've drawn the money demand curve sloping downward, just because, well, demand curves slope downward. But money demand slopes downward because of a particular tradeoff, between liquidity and earnings.

When we say money we mean mostly the cash and checking accounts that people use for transactions. You might use the cash in your pocket to buy lunch. Maybe you visit the ATM machine before lunch so you've got the cash. You might write a check to buy a microwave. You might use a debit card for the same purpose. Or you might charge the tickets, and then write a check to pay off the monthly credit card bill.

- *Why do people keep some of their wealth in cash or checking accounts? Why do they keep some in interest-earning assets?*

People keep part of their total wealth or assets in the form of money to use for transactions. If you kept all your money in non-money assets, like stocks or bonds or land or gold, it would be tough to buy lunch or pay bills. That's because stocks, bonds, land and gold are not *liquid assets*. A liquid asset is one that can be converted into cash quickly and easily, so it can be used for transactions. Cash is liquid by definition. A checking account is liquid because you can withdraw balances in cash on demand. Land is not a liquid asset. Converting it to cash means selling it, and this requires real estate brokers and time to link up buyer and seller.

Since liquid assets are so convenient for transactions, why don't people keep all their wealth in cash or checking accounts? Because cash and checking accounts don't earn interest. Cash earns nothing. Some checking accounts earn a small interest rate, but other assets earn more.

> **Liquidity means how quickly and easily an asset can be converted to cash, to be used for transactions.**

Money demand is also known as *liquidity preference*, which really is a more descriptive name for it. How much of your wealth do you prefer to keep in liquid form? Money demand shows how much of peoples' assets they want to keep in liquid form at each real interest rate.

Now here's why money demand slopes downward. Holding wealth in cash or checking creates an *opportunity cost*. You give up the income you could earn from holding an interest-bearing asset. If I keep a thousand dollars in cash, I don't own a $1,000 certificate of deposit (a CD), so I don't earn the interest return that the CD might bring.

When the real interest rate is high, the opportunity cost of holding assets in liquid form is high. If the interest rate on a CD is high, maybe 5%, the opportunity cost of holding cash is high. I'll try to economize on what's in my checking account or in my pocket. But if the interest rate is low, say 1%, then it doesn't much matter (that's more realistic in 2017!). The opportunity cost is low, so I might as well keep cash, for its convenience. Notice that this is yet another application of the Law of Demand. When something is more costly, people do less of it. When the real interest rate is high, people demand a smaller quantity of money.

This adds to our story about the money market. Suppose the money supply decreases. Why do people reduce the amount of money they wish to hold, to match the new lower quantity available? Because, a smaller quantity of money means a higher real interest rate. People want those earnings, so they economize on cash and checking. The quantity of money demanded drops to match the quantity of money supplied.

That's why money demand slopes down. Just as important, though, is the question, why does it shift?

We've hinted at the answer before. Money demand depends on incomes and prices. People use money to pay for *transactions*. You need money to buy a sandwich or a computer, or (if you're a business) a backhoe or an inventory of apples, or (if you're the government) a school building or a guided missile. That's true even if you're buying on credit. People need money in checking to pay the interest and principle on those loans.

If you want to buy more, you need more money in cash or in your checking account. Since most goods and services are normal, people with higher incomes buy more. They make more transactions. That means people with more income must keep more cash in their pockets, and bigger balances in their checking accounts.

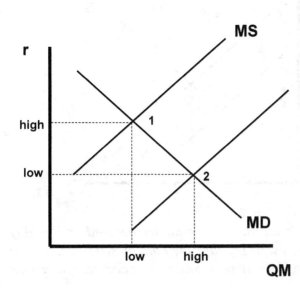

Figure 4-1. Demand slopes down (again). When the real interest rate is high (1), the quantity of money demanded is low. It is costly to hold wealth in cash or checking accounts because lost interest earnings are so high. When the real interest rate is low (2), the quantity of money demanded is high. Cash and checking are convenient for transactions, so people hold more when lost interest earnings are low.

In the macroeconomy output and income are the same thing. Businesses sell their output, and the revenue they receive becomes income for their workers, creditors, landlords and owners. So when real GDP increases, income increases, people want to make more transactions, so money demand increases. When real GDP decreases, so does income, transactions are fewer, and money demand falls.

Likewise, when prices are higher, people need to keep more in cash and checking accounts to pay them. Transactions require more money. When prices rise, each purchase is more expensive, so more money is needed. The demand for money goes up. An increase in the price level, or the inflation rate, will increase the demand for money.

There are other determinants of money demand that sometimes are important. Money demand can be seasonal. During the holiday season people need more money for gifts and travel. They'll take money out of savings or even sell some stock for these transactions. Money demand increases in December, and in January too as credit card bills come due.

Back in the day, money demand increased in October, too, during the harvest season. That was important in 1907.

Remember what's happening in the money market when people demand more money. They are increasing their liquidity preference, which means they are converting more of their wealth from interest-earning assets like stocks, bonds or CDs, to liquid assets like checking accounts and cash. Their total wealth may or may not be changing. They're changing the form in which their wealth is held.

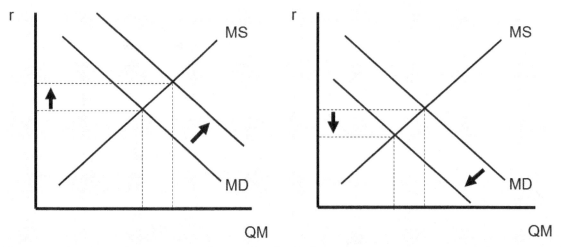

Figure 4-2. Liquidity, more or less. On the left is an increase in money demand or liquidity preference, caused by an increase in income, or prices, or perhaps the holiday season. The real interest rate goes up. On the right is a decrease in money demand, caused by a decrease in income or prices (or holiday season exhaustion!).

Money Supply: The Banking System

We keep our money in banks. Banks hold money. It turns out, though, that the banking system creates money too. To understand, we need to know about two ideas: *fractional reserve banking*, and the *multiple expansion of bank deposits*.

Every bank has a huge vault with a ridiculously heavy door, often round. The bank keeps cash in there, and perhaps other valuables in safety deposit boxes. We might think that the main purpose of a bank is to keep our money safe.

We might think that. We'd be wrong.

Banks keep only a tiny fraction of our money in the vault. Most of the money we deposit is lent to borrowers. The bank takes my deposits, and yours, and the deposits of many others, combines them and offers loans for home construction, business expansion, or even to cover government deficits. Each interest rate listed in Chapter 1 is tied to a particular kind of loan.

Banks are sometimes called *financial intermediaries*, because they stand between people with money to lend, and people who want to borrow. The money we're not using for daily transactions is deposited in savings or certificates of deposit. That's money we want to lend. People who want to borrow go to the bank and make their case. The bank uses its expertise to decide which loans are good risks, and what interest rate to charge. In a sense, we hire the bank to lend our money and collect our interest payments on those loans. Of course, the bank keeps some of the interest on those loans, before they pay us. Those are the bank's profits.

Banks reserve some of our deposits, as cash in the vault, or (more likely) in very liquid assets that can be had at a moment's notice (like overnight loans to other banks). They keep *reserves* because sometimes their depositors show up to withdraw their money. If the day's *withdrawals* are greater than the day's deposits, the bank had better have some money in reserve. The fraction that banks reserve is usually 10% or less of total deposits. That's fractional reserve banking.

> *Fractional reserve banking means that banks lend most of their deposits, and reserve a small fraction.*

To see fractional reserve banking in action, consider Figure 4-3. Suppose $1,000 in cash is deposited in a bank. Suppose that it is the bank's policy to keep 20% of deposits in reserve—to handle withdrawals—and to lend 80% in mortgage loans or business loans. Of that $1,000 deposit, the bank will reserve $200 and lend $800.

Who borrowed the $800? In 1907, perhaps a shopkeeper wanting to buy one of those new-fangled Model T automobiles. He pays the Ford dealer, and the dealer deposits the $800 in his own bank. That's a new deposit for his bank, which now reserves 20%, and lends 80%. The bank keeps $160 in new reserves and lends $640. The borrower spends the $640, perhaps on a trip to Chicago to watch the Cubs in the World Series (see them now or wait a long long time!), and the ticket seller deposits the $640 in his bank. The process continues. The total deposits created are much more than the initial deposit. That's multiple expansion of bank deposits.

> *Multiple expansion of bank deposits means that bank lending expands the quantity of money beyond initial deposits.*

How much more? As the table shows, if the process continued down to fractions of pennies, the total added deposits would be $5,000. We know this because the *money multiplier* shows the total new deposits generated by added reserves. The money multiplier is calculated as

Money multiplier = 1 / rr

where "rr" is the *reserve ratio*. The reserve ratio is the percentage of deposits that banks keep as reserves. When the reserve ratio is 0.2 (20%), the money multiplier is 5, and an initial $1,000 deposit creates $5,000 in total deposits. That's the process shown in Figure 4-3.

Bank reserves plus money in circulation outside of banks are known as the *monetary base*. The money multiplier times the monetary base is the total quantity of money. So the quantity of money has two components: the monetary base, made up of bank reserves and circulating cash, and the money multiplier, which depends on the share of deposits that banks reserve. The money multiplier depends on the banks' willingness to lend. The total quantity of money is made up of circulating cash, bank reserves and all those deposits that the reserves support.

> *The monetary base is reserves in banks plus currency in circulation. The money multiplier depends on banks' willingness to lend. The product of the two is the quantity of money.*

Deposits	Reserves (20%)	Loans (80%)
$1,000	$200	$800
$800	$160	$640
$640	$128	$512
$512	$102	$410
$410	$82	$328
. . .		
Eventual Totals		
$5,000	$1,000	$4,000

Figure 4-3. Fractional Reserve Banking and Multiple Expansion of Bank Deposits. Banks accept deposits, reserve a fraction and lend the rest. Those loans are deposited in the banking system, which creates more reserves and loans. In the end, the $1,000 initial deposit created $5,000 in total bank balances. The money multiplier is 5, because the reserve ratio is 20%.

Deposits	Reserves (50%)	Loans (50%)
$1,000	$500	$500
$500	$250	$250
$250	$125	$125
$125	$63	$63
$63	$31	$31
. . .		
Eventual Totals		
$2,000	$1,000	$1,000

Figure 4-4. More Reserves, Less Expansion. If banks reserve more of their deposits (here they reserve half) less money is loaned. The multiple expansion of bank deposits produces a smaller eventual total bank balance. With the reserve ratio at 50%, the money multiplier is 2, and the $1,000 initial deposit supports $2,000 in total money.

The reserve ratio helps determine the quantity of money. If banks reserve more, the quantity of money will be less. If banks reserve less, the quantity of money will be more. Another way to think of the money multiplier is the relationship between the monetary base and the quantity of money. The money multiplier shows the quantity of money supported by each dollar of the monetary base.

Figure 4-4 shows what happens when banks increase their reserve ratio. At a 50% reserve ratio more is reserved and less is lent. If less is lent, less is deposited in the next round. The money multiplier is 2 (= 1 / .50). The quantity of money is smaller than when the reserve ratio was 20%, as in Figure 4-3.

We can use these ideas to explain why the money supply curve slopes upward. If the real interest rate is high, the opportunity cost of holding deposits as reserves is greater. Banks want to hold

88

fewer reserves and make more loans. There's always a risk that borrowers won't repay, but it's worth the risk if the interest return is high enough. More lending and fewer reserves increases the money multiplier, and the quantity of money supplied goes up.

When the real interest rate is low, the opportunity cost of keeping reserves is low, especially compared to the risk that lenders won't repay their loans, or that depositors will show up to withdraw their money. Banks won't be too sorry if they keep their funds safe, so they reserve more and lend less. That reduces the money multiplier and the quantity of money supplied.

When the real interest rate is lower, the quantity of money supplied is lower. When the real interest rate is higher, the quantity of money supplied is higher. The money supply curve slopes upward.

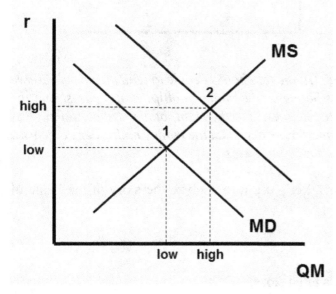

Figure 4-5. Supply slopes skyward (but why?). When the real interest rate is low (1), the quantity of money supplied is low. There's not much return to lending, so banks keep higher reserves. The money multiplier is lower. When the real interest rate is high (2), loans are more profitable, and banks reserve less. The money multiplier is higher.

We can also explain one reason behind shifts in money supply. Suppose banks become optimistic about the economy. People are earning good incomes. Businesses are making profits. There are lots of loans that look like they'll be repaid, and little chance that depositors will panic and withdraw their money. So banks increase their lending and decrease their reserves. The money multiplier increases, and the money supply does too. The real interest rate decreases. That's shown in Figure 4-6.

Figure 4-6 also shows the result of bank pessimism. If the economy is in trouble, loans might not be repaid and depositors might decide to withdraw their money. Banks keep higher reserves and lend less. The money multiplier gets smaller, the money supply decreases, and the real interest rate increases.

Notice how this differs from the explanation of the upward slope of the supply curve. The upward slope results from a rise in money demand, which increases the real interest rate and encourages lending. The shifts in money supply results from changes in bank expectations about the risks of lending. The result is a change in the real interest rate.

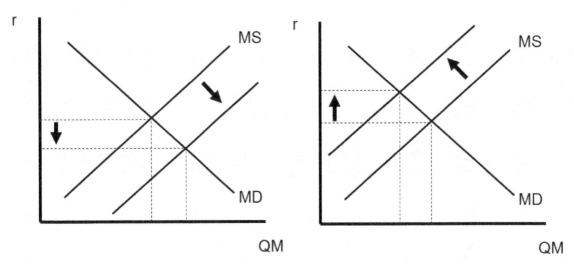

Figure 4-6. Multiple expansion or contraction. On the left, banks decide to lend more and reserve less. The multiple expansion of bank deposits happens, the money multiplier increases, and the money supply increases. The real interest rate declines. On the right, banks decide to lend less and reserve more. There is multiple contraction of bank deposits, the money multiplier decreases, and so does the money supply. The real interest rate increases.

Now we've got a model of the money market. Let's use it to analyze the story of the Panic of 1907.

The Panic of 1907
We've got a model. Here are some data. Let's tell a story.

Start with the money market. The interest rate spread in the table is not the BAA-AAA corporate spread, because that's not available before 1919. Instead it's the difference between an interest rate on short-term business loans and the interest rate on long term government bonds. Governments can repay loans by raising taxes. Businesses can't. So government loans tend to be less risky than business loans. The spread still represents the difference between interest rates on more risky loans and less risky loans.

The interest rate spread jumped in 1907. The real interest rate rises on the vertical axis of the money market when money demand increases or money supply decreases. Which is it?

Panic of 1907

Year	Real GDP Growth	CPI Inflation	Unemploy- ment Rate	Interest Rate Spread
1906	13.8%	1.9%	2.5%	1.5%
1907	-1.9%	4.6%	3.1%	3.0%
1908	-13.2%	-1.8%	7.5%	1.6%
1909	16.6%	-1.8%	5.7%	1.3%

Income and prices determine money demand. Real income fell in 1907, because real GDP fell. They're the same in the aggregate. Inflation was high enough, though, that it may have offset the drop in income. Money demand may have increased, or it may have decreased. Since we're not sure money demand increased, we can say that the big jump in the interest rate spread must have been due to a decrease in money supply. That's what's shown in Figure 4-7, as money supply shift a.

Now check out the unemployment rates in 1906 and 1907. They were well below 5%. The economy was booming, and resources were being used with extraordinary intensity. Equilibrium output must have been above potential output. That's point c in Figure 4-7.

Now to real GDP, on the horizontal axis of the goods market. It was growing very rapidly in 1906, but output declined in 1907 and declined a lot in 1908. This was a severe recession. Output decreased in the goods market. The shift from c to d shows the drop in output.

The unemployment rate rose above 5% in 1908. Now there were unemployed resources. Output was less than potential. That's shown by an output level to the left of potential output (Qp, point d).

The price level is measured on the vertical axis of the goods market. Inflation had increased in 1907, perhaps because output was above potential, input costs rose and aggregate supply decreased (that's second shift #1). But in 1908 the inflation rate declined into deflation. The price level fell.

The goods market equilibrium fell from point 3 to point 4. There's only one shift that can cause both a drop in output and a decline in prices: a decrease in aggregate demand. That's shown in Figure 4-7 too.

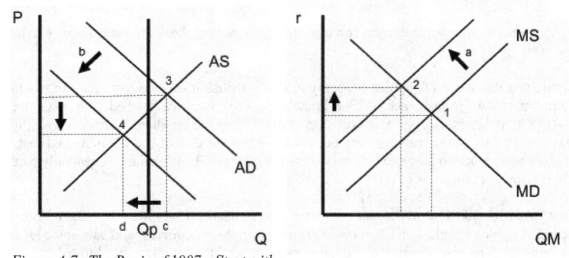

Figure 4-7. The Panic of 1907. Start with   *the money market on the right. Money supply decreased with the panic in financial markets (a). The real interest rate increased (1 to 2). Now the goods market, on the left. Equilibrium output was above potential at the beginning of 1907 (c). Higher real interest rates caused a drop in investment spending, which decreased aggregate demand (second shift #2, b). Output and the price level declined (3 to 4). Output dropped below potential (d).*

The data from 1906 to 1908 imply a decrease in money supply in the money market, a decrease in aggregate demand in the goods market, and a drop in output from above potential to below potential. So we must look for reasons why money supply dropped, and why aggregate demand dropped.

Here's the story.

The economy was booming in 1906, and San Francisco shared in the boom. With its superb natural harbor and easy access to inland farms and mines, its population was 350,000 and growing in 1900. It had grown ten-fold in the previous half-century, and was the ninth largest city in the country, by far the largest west of the Mississippi River.

Then, at 5:13 a.m. on Wednesday, April 18, 1906, a shift in a three hundred mile section of the San Andreas Fault in northern California caused a devastating earthquake. Recent estimates put the earthquake's magnitude at just less than eight on the Richter scale. The ground shook violently for almost a minute. When it was done, thousands of buildings had been damaged and 800 people were dead.

Then the fire started. The city was built of wood—lumber was the cheapest, most plentiful building material—and the quake had destroyed the water mains. The chief engineer of the fire department had been mortally injured in the quake, leaving the department without experienced leadership. The fire burned for four days and destroyed almost five square miles of the city. More than 2,000 people died in the fire, and more than half the city's population was left homeless. Damage was estimated at half a billion dollars, which was nearly two percent of United States Gross Domestic Product.

Seismographs around the world felt the force of the 1906 earthquake. The world also felt its economic effects.

Great Britain was the world's dominant economy in 1906. British insurance companies provided a large amount of the fire insurance for San Francisco. They were avalanched with insurance claims. At first the insurance companies resisted, claiming that the buildings were destroyed by the quake, not the fire, so the insurers were not liable. The prospects of bad publicity and legal actions before San Francisco juries convinced the insurers to pay. British insurers eventually paid about $50 million in claims.

Both Great Britain and the United States were on the gold standard. That meant that paper money was "backed" by gold. People with paper could exchange it for gold coins or gold bars at the local Treasury branch. That also meant that the amount of paper in circulation was limited by the amount of gold that a county had in the vault. If too much paper money was printed, there might not be enough gold if people demanded it.

All those insurance payments required that gold be shipped to the U.S. So much gold left Britain that its central bank, the Bank of England, became concerned about the effect on the nation's money supply. So, in the fall of 1906 they increased interest rates to encourage banks and wealthy people to lend in Great Britain, rather than in U.S. It worked. Gold began to flow out of the United States to Great Britain. The U.S. gold stock decreased by ten percent.

The United States had no central bank to counter this gold flow, so the U.S. money supply began to shrink. U.S. interest rates increased. Higher interest rates reduced investment spending. Real GDP growth slowed to a stop by mid-1907. The nation was edging into recession by the autumn of 1907.

Agriculture was once much more important in the United States economy than it is today. The Census of 1900 reported that 36% of Americans workers were employed on farms (it's less than 1% today). Each fall when the grain was harvested it would be transported from the west where it was grown, to the east where most people lived, and where it could be exported to Europe. Buyers of grain would withdraw their funds from banks to pay farmers. Shippers would withdraw their funds from banks to pay railroads. Railroads would withdraw their funds from banks to pay employees. Banks had to build their reserves in order to pay all these withdrawals.

This meant that each fall, money was "tight." Loans from banks were hard to come by, because banks needed all their reserves and then some for the harvest-time withdrawals. With less money available for lending, interest rates would increase. Interest rates usually increased in October. (That may be one reason why so many of our historic financial panics seem to take place in October.) With fewer loans, home or factory construction declined, and construction workers would be laid off. Most years the economy muddled through this seasonal lending drop.

In the fall of 1907, though, money was already tight. The money supply was dropping as gold flowed to Britain. British lenders were still refusing to lend to Americans. The usual harvest season money supply drop was in full swing. In normal years, what happened next might not have been a problem. In 1907, it was.

F. Augustus Heinze was a millionaire copper magnate from Montana. In October 1907 Heinze and a partner tried to corner the stock of a large copper company. Cornering the stock of a company meant buying so much of it that one could charge anyone who wanted to buy its stock a very high price. On October 16, 1907, Heinze's attempt to corner the copper stock failed. He had paid high prices to acquire a great deal of copper stock, but couldn't buy enough to dictate the price himself. He now had a huge number of shares, most worth less than he had paid for them. He would not be able to repay his loans.

Some of the money for Heinze's venture came from a lender called the Knickerbocker Trust. Trusts were new in 1907. They had grown to be important lenders only in the previous decade, and bank regulations had not yet caught up with them. They kept smaller reserves than banks, paid higher interest rates on deposits, and made loans that were more risky.

The Knickerbocker Trust Company's depositors saw Heinze's failure, and realized that a lot of his lost money was in fact their money loaned to him by Knickerbocker. They began to worry. After the losses on Heinze's loans, did the Trust have enough funds to pay back their deposits? They began showing up at the door demanding to withdraw their funds. When lots of depositors try to withdraw their money all at once, it's called a *bank run*. A run on the Knickerbocker Trust began on October 18.

The nation's most important banker, J. Pierpont Morgan, recognized the danger and organized a fund to lend to troubled trusts. The trusts would use the loans to pay their depositors. Depositors would find that they could withdraw their money with no problem, their panic would subside and the run would end. But which trusts deserved to be saved? Not the Knickerbocker, Morgan decided. They'd made too many bad loans. On the morning of October 22 the trust paid out its remaining $8 million in reserves, then closed its doors. It had failed.

Banks all over New York—and all over the country—watched with apprehension. Panics like this could spread nationwide.

And sure enough, the panic didn't end with Knickerbocker. Attention turned to the Trust Company of America, another trust whose directors were associated with Heinze. A newspaper article in the *New York Times* comparing the two Trusts may have created anxiety.

The Trust Company faced its own run on Tuesday, October 22. Morgan sent Ben Strong, a young up-and-coming banker, to examine the company's books. He worked through the night, and in the morning he reported to Morgan. The old man had just one question. "Are they solvent?" Strong said their reserves were almost gone, but their assets were intact, more or less. Most of the loans they'd made were good; they just couldn't be sold for cash fast enough.

"Should we see them through?" Morgan asked.   Strong said yes. "This is the place to stop the trouble, then," J. Pierpont Morgan said.

When they opened Wednesday morning Trust Company directors found a line of their depositors snaking out into Wall Street. Every last one wanted to withdraw funds. It was clear that the Trust would fail without help. By 2:15 in the afternoon the trust's reserves were down to $180,000. Receiving word from Morgan, Trust Company officers carried boxes of securities to his office, as collateral for a loan. Morgan deposited three million dollars in cash with the Trust. The Trust met the demands of its depositors. Besides, if J.P. Morgan was willing to lend to the Trust Company, it must be all right. Depositors lost their fear, and the Trust Company of America survived.

Probably the panic would have been worse had Morgan not acted. But the damage was done. Trusts and banks lend each other money, and have deposits with each other. People do business with more than one bank. If one bank fails, other banks may lose their deposits or not have their loans repaid. If borrowers have their loans called by one bank in trouble, they may withdraw their funds from another bank. Financial difficulties and bank runs can spread like a disease. So economists call it *contagion*.

Seeing the problems in New York, banks around the country began building up their reserves. Many of them had deposits with the New York banks, and tried to withdraw them. Depositors around the country began withdrawing funds, too. Finally banks "suspended payments", meaning they refused to pay out cash to depositors, while continuing to clear checks and accept deposits.

How do we know that trouble in the money market reduced spending in the goods market? The data doesn't necessarily reveal in which market the *shock* occurred. That's why we need the story to go along with the data and the model.

Stories like this. Here are some brief news items from the *New York Times*, October 29, 1907, just *one week* after the failure of the Knickerbocker Trust.

> Wilmington, Del. It was learned here to-day that the construction work on the new dynamite mill of the Du Pont Powder Company, at Tacoma, Washington, has been stopped because of the present condition of the money market.

> Railway Work Stops. Suspension of Construction on South and Western Affects 10,000 Men. Bristol, Tenn. President George L. Carter of the South & Western Railway to-day issued an order suspending practically all construction on that road. The announcement followed the return of the President from New York, where he spent several days in consultation with associates.

> Money Tied Up, Stop Work. A Pennsylvanian Has $800,000 in Knickerbocker Trust. Lancaster, Penn. The failure of the Knickerbocker Trust Company of New York has caused the McCalls Ferry Company to lay off 300 men who were at work on the dam over the Susquehanna River. At the time it closed its doors, the trust company is said to have had on deposit about $800,000 belonging to the McCalls Company.

The last item is especially telling. The McCalls Ferry Company had its money in the failed Trust. Prices have risen about 25 times since 1907, so that $800,000 is equivalent to $20 million today. Where did the money go? Partly, the Trust had lent it to Augustus Heinze, who lost it in his stock speculation. The loan was never repaid.

Eventually McCalls may have recovered some of their money, after court proceedings had worked out how much of the Trust's remaining assets each depositor would get. By then, though, the company was in bankruptcy itself.

All of these projects count as investment spending—construction of a dynamite mill, a railroad and a dam. When the projects were halted, investment spending declined, and workers were laid off. The shock was in the money market. The effect halted construction project, bankrupted businesses, and threw people out of work.

Let's flesh out the story in Figure 4-7. The failed stock speculation made banks pessimistic. They increased reserves and cut back on lending, especially to private businesses. The money multiplier decreased and so did the money supply. The earthquake and the harvest season added to the money supply drop.

Panic in the money market caused recession in the goods market. Wall Street's trouble found its way to Main Street. Higher real interest rates reduce investment spending, which reduces aggregate demand. This is second shift #2, where a change in the money market affects the goods market. Construction activity slows, less equipment is purchased, workers get laid off. The decline in spending by businesses and unemployed people reduce business sales, so they cut production, lay off more employees and cut prices. Lower output, higher unemployment and deflation are the result.

The Federal Reserve
The nation had been prosperous. Within two years it was prosperous again. It seemed that the panic and recession had been unnecessary, caused by a one-time disaster out west, the actions of the British central bank, and the ambitions of a few New York speculators. It spread because of contagion in the banking system, made worse because it was harvest time and money was tight. If the consequences of those actions had been nipped in the bud—as Morgan tried to do—and if the banking system had been less vulnerable to panic, perhaps the recession could have been avoided. Congress began to consider reform.

The outlines of what was needed were clear. The banking system needed a source of emergency reserves. Some agency needed to do what J.P. Morgan had done, lend emergency cash to banks with good loans as collateral, only on a bigger scale and in the public interest. The banking system needed a *lender of last resort*, to lend to banks when no one else was lending.

In addition, the money supply had to be made *elastic*. This meant that when the demand for currency increased, as it did during disasters and during harvest every fall, additional currency could be supplied without forcing banks to build reserves, stop lending and restrict investment. (Note that this is a second use of the term "elastic." We don't mean a response of quantity to price here.)

There may have been consensus on what to accomplish, but *how* to accomplish it was another matter. Bankers, and many of their Republican allies, had long advocated the creation of a central bank. They looked to the tradition of Alexander Hamilton, who had created a central bank in the nation's early days. A central bank would be a "banker's bank," one which could increase and decrease the supply of money when needed, and provide banks with reserves in emergencies. There would be one big bank in New York or Washington, like the Bank of England in London. Only a big bank would have reserves enough for the nation's whole banking system. It would be owned and controlled by bankers, because only they had the expertise. It would *not* be controlled by political leaders, for fear that interest rates would become the tool of the political parties in every election year.

Most Democrats opposed the creation of a central bank. This also was a long party tradition, dating back to Andrew Jackson in the 1830s. Jackson had engineered the destruction of the early U.S. central bank. It was a newer party tradition, too. Democrats had favored a policy called "bimetallism" during the later 1800's. It would have expanded the money supply by adding silver to the gold standard, to the benefit of borrowers. Bankers opposed bimetallism. Democrats also feared that a central bank would be run as a monopoly for the benefit of bankers. The central bank would cooperate with bankers to keep interest rates high, and sometimes even *cause* panics. Many thought that panics were profitable for bankers. They earned high interest on the emergency loans they issued. J.P. Morgan probably did make a profit with his actions to stop the panic in 1907.

On May 30, 1908, the Congress passed and President Teddy Roosevelt signed the Aldrich-Vreeland Act, named after Nelson Aldrich from the Senate and Edward Vreeland from the House. The new law included some temporary measures to try to halt panics, and it set up a National Monetary Commission to study the issue of currency reform and banking regulation. The Commission worked for four years and issued a report in 1912. The report became the basis for a reform debate in 1913. The debate resulted in legislation that established the *Federal Reserve*.

The debate took place under political conditions that had not existed for more than half a century. The Democrats had gained power in the 1912 elections. Democrat Woodrow Wilson had been elected President, and both houses of Congress had Democratic majorities. The Democrats would write the reform legislation, and they were not going to create a central bank if they could help it.

Legislators proposed a solution for keeping monopoly power out of the hands of a central bank: create not one bank, but many. How many? Democrats wanted a lot, perhaps one in each state, while Republicans wanted not more than three or four. Eventually Congress compromised at 12 regional banks. The thought was that with 12, every banker in the country would be a night's train ride from a regional bank. If he needed cash, he could carry a bundle of securities on a train ride to his regional bank, get a loan, and send a telegram before his bank opened the next day telling his depositors that they need not panic.

> **The Federal Reserve became the U.S. central bank, with the power to influence interest rates using monetary policy. It was established in 1913.**

Even the Democrats thought that the 12 regional banks needed some central coordination. Sometimes, for example, the reserves of one regional bank might not be enough to stop a panic, and a central body could direct other regional banks to help. Supporters of a central bank hoped this body would become a central bank, opponents feared that it would. The compromise was a board in Washington, known as the Federal Reserve Board, with limited power over the actions of the regional banks. The Secretary of the Treasury was made chair of the Reserve Board, so someone directly responsible to the President would have a say in policy decisions.

Since legislators thought they were creating something that was *not* a central bank, little attention was given to the goals of Federal Reserve *monetary policy*. What criteria should the Fed use in setting interest rates, influencing the quantity of money, or deciding which banks deserved loans? Questions that would concern the Fed in coming years were not the subject of much debate.

There was another reason for the lack of policy guidance. Many on all sides of the debate thought that monetary policy would be automatic. The nation would remain on the gold standard. The Federal Reserve Act said explicitly that the gold standard was not to be repealed, even though the Act established a new institution with money-creating powers. Gold would provide a ceiling on the amount of money the Fed could issue. There had to be a gold reserve of 40%, meaning that the Treasury had to have in its vaults 40 cents in gold for every one Federal Reserve note. The Fed's new currency would be elastic underneath this ceiling.

The Fed would act as a lender of last resort. Banks could borrow from the Fed if they faced bank runs. The money wasn't free. The Fed would charge an interest rate for their lending, known as the *discount rate*. The banks would borrow from the Fed, using as collateral the expected repayment of the loans they had made to businesses.

The discount rate could be used as a tool of monetary policy. If the Fed raised its discount rate, banks would be discouraged from borrowing. They would have less to lend to their customers and would raise their own interest rates. If the Fed cut its discount rate, banks would be encouraged to borrow more. They would have more to lend and would reduce their own interest rates. But the discount rate was not viewed as a policy tool at first.

> *The discount rate is the interest rate the Fed charges when it lends money to banks. It was the Fed's first monetary policy tool. The discount rate influences the interest rates that banks charge their customers.*

The bill passed Congress, and President Woodrow Wilson signed the Federal Reserve Act on December 23, 1913. Within a year, the world for which the Federal Reserve was created was gone.

World War I

The Great War that we now call World War I began in Europe in August, 1914. The United States was determined to stay neutral. Neutral, but not out of it. As a rapidly growing industrial power with close trade ties to the combatants, the United States had to be affected by a big war. England and France looked to the United States for war material and food. Other countries looked to the U.S. for the goods they had been importing from England, France and Germany. U.S. exports increased.

The United States declared war on Germany on April 6, 1917. Now the United States needed to build its own army. The army had fewer than 100,000 soldiers in 1913. By the end of World War I about a million were in service in Europe. Soldiers had to be trained, equipped and fed. That meant moving people and production from civilian uses to military uses. Farmhands would become soldiers. Plowshares would be converted to guns.

- *How can resources be shifted from civilians to the military during wartime?*

Government has three ways to shift resources from civilian to government goods. It can impose *taxes*. Civilian taxpayers are required to turn over resources to the government, so it can provide government services. Government income increases and civilian income decreases. Government buys what civilians cannot. Civilian consumption spending declines.

Government can *borrow*. It can sell Treasury bonds to lenders on the promise to repay plus interest in the future. The government spends the borrowed funds. With so much lent to the government, civilian businesses find it harder to borrow for their needs.

Businesses must forego the buildings and equipment which they would have acquired, had they been able to borrow. Civilian investment spending declines.

And government can *print money.* It uses the new money to offer producers higher prices for their goods than civilians can afford. This is sometimes called an *inflation tax.* The government shifts resources from the public to itself by creating money, which raises prices beyond what the public can pay.

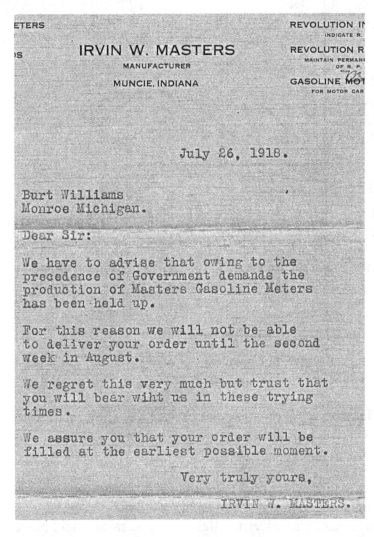

Don't you know there's a war on? A July 1918 letter from the Masters Manufacturing Company of Muncie, Indiana, informing a customer that production of his gasoline meter has been held up. The reason was "owing to the precedence of Government demands." "We regret this very much but trust that you will bear with us in these trying times." Military production replaces civilian production in wartime.

The U.S. government built an army and a navy, and spending on soldiers' and sailors' pay and on military equipment increased a lot. Federal revenues and spending were small before the war, a bit more than $700 million raised and spent each year. By 1919 Federal spending was $17 billion, 24 times higher.

The income tax had been invented only a few years before, and it was a major source of added revenue. Federal revenues increased by $4.5 billion by 1919. That was a very large increase, but it was only one-quarter of what was needed. The government spent much more than it raised in taxes. The Federal budget deficit was more than $13 billion in 1919, which was about 17.5% of GDP.

> **To shift resources from the private sector to the public sector, governments can tax, borrow or print money.**

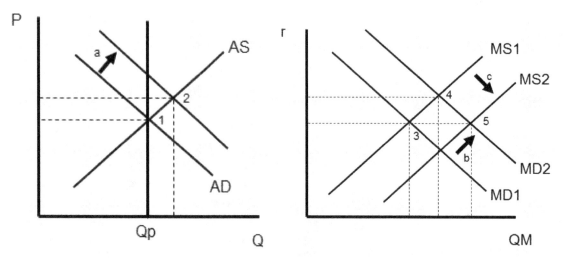

Figure 4-8. The large Federal budget deficit increased aggregate demand (a). Output and prices increased (1 to 2), and output moved above potential. Higher incomes and prices caused money demand to increase (b, Second shift #3). The real interest rate would have increased (3 to 4). But the Treasury told the Federal Reserve to hold interest rates steady, so the Fed increased the money supply (c). Interest rates did not increase (3 to 5).

The large Federal deficit added to aggregate demand. The increase in spending on military purchases was not offset by a decrease in consumer and business spending, which would have occurred if taxes had increased enough. This increased prices and output (Figure 4-8).

The deficit was a problem for the U.S. Treasury. Taxes would not finance the whole war effort, so borrowing would be necessary. But the deficit caused rising prices and incomes, and that would increase money demand (second shift #3). Rising money demand would increase interest rates, including Treasury bond interest rates.

Higher interest rates would reduce investment spending, which would hold down the increase in aggregate demand. But that was not the Treasury's concern. Higher interest rates would make borrowing for the war more expensive. Money that could have been spent on ammunition would be paid to lenders instead.

Something had to be done to keep interest rates low. The Treasury looked to the newly created Federal Reserve. To keep interest rates low with rising money demand, the Fed had to increase the money supply. Federal Reserve notes made their first appearance as circulating currency. From 1915 to 1919 the amount of currency in circulation doubled.

The Treasury borrowed from the public to pay for war expenses, by selling war bonds. The Federal Reserve would lend money to banks so they could lend for bond purchases, and to buy them themselves. To make this pay, the Treasury had to pay an interest rate on its borrowing that was higher than the Fed's discount rate. So the Treasury pressured the Fed to keep the discount rate low, so it would cost the Treasury less to borrow all that money for the war effort. From 1916 to

1918, the average Treasury bond interest rate was 4.3%, and the average discount rate was 3.7%. It paid to borrow from the Fed and lend to the Treasury.

They paid for World War I. This is a Federal Reserve Note from 1918, which the Fed issued to help pay for the war effort. Each regional Federal Reserve branch bank issued currency with its name prominently displayed.

From the Treasury's point of view, the whole war was paid for with taxes and borrowing. But much of the money it borrowed was created by the Federal Reserve, lent to banks at the discount rate. The money supply increased a lot. And Federal Reserve notes were here to stay.

- *Why do wars so often create inflation?*

The American Civil War created inflation. So did World War I, World War II and the Vietnam War. Wars seem to create inflation—but they don't have to. If the big increases in government military spending are paid for with equal increases in taxes, aggregate demand will not change very much. Civilian consumption spending will decrease by about as much as military spending increases. In Figure 4-8, aggregate demand would remain unchanged, and the price level would remain at point 1.

Suppose the government does not raise taxes enough, and instead runs a budget deficit, spending more than it collects in revenue. This still won't produce much inflation. If the big increases in military spending are paid for with borrowing, aggregate demand also will not change much. Government will borrow all it needs, and civilian businesses will have to borrow less. Think of *crowding out* from Chapter 3.

Suppose, though, that the big increases in government military spending are paid for with big increases in the quantity of money. The government does not raise taxes enough, so it runs a budget deficit. It doesn't finance the whole deficit with borrowing. Instead, it covers the deficit by creating money and spending it.

> **Inflation can be caused by "too much money chasing too few goods."**

"Too much money chasing too few goods" is a fine description of the source of inflation. The nation's output is limited by its resources and technology. When all the nation's labor, land and capital are in use, only so much food, clothing, guns and ships can be produced. That's potential output, the maximum amount that can be produced when all resources are employed as they usually are. The government prints money and uses it to "outbid" civilians for those resources. You can't outbid the government, since the government prints the money. The quantity of money can grow and grow, but the nation's production has a limit. Too much money will chase too few goods. Inflation is the result.

Wars often create inflation because government spends more than it collects in taxes, then pays for the deficit by printing money.

After the War

Let's use the data to follow the economy from the end of the war through 1922. The unemployment rate in 1918 was 1.2%, and in 1919 it was 2.3%. These rates are way less than 5%, so output was way above potential. That's shown in Figure 4-8. The war effort employed resources that would not ordinarily been used. Since the war ended late in 1918, this effort continued into early 1919.

World War I and After

Year	Real GDP Growth	CPI Inflation	Unemploy-ment Rate	Interest Rate Spread
1918	9.3%	18.0%	1.2%	
1919	0.4%	14.6%	2.3%	1.8%
1920	-1.5%	15.6%	5.2%	2.1%
1921	-2.4%	-10.5%	11.3%	2.4%
1922	6.0%	-6.1%	8.6%	2.0%

Output grew rapidly in 1918, and continued to increase slowly in 1919. Then it decreased for two years, in 1920 and 1921, before rising again in 1922. Inflation was in the high double-digits from 1918 to 1920, then came two years of rapid price decreases—deflation. The 18% inflation rate was the highest of the 20th century. The 10.5% deflation rate was the lowest (the most negative) of the 20th century. The unemployment rate was very low in 1918 and 1919, but rose to high levels in 1921 and 1922. The BAA-AAA corporate bond interest rate spread (first available in 1919) increased in 1920 and 1921.

Let's make sense of these macroeconomic indicators with our goods and money market models. The unemployment rate was 5.2% in 1917 (not shown in the table). Figure 4-8 shows what happened in the goods and money markets in 1918 and 1919. The unemployment rate in 1917 was near 5%, so the goods market starts at potential output. Government military spending increased, while taxes did not. The rising budget deficit increased aggregate demand, which increased output and prices. Real GDP grew, and the positive inflation rate shows the big price increase. In the money market, we know that the Fed increased the money supply to hold interest rates stable, though we don't have the data for 1917 and 1918.

The war was won and the Armistice signed in November 1918. In 1919 government spending on soldiers and equipment fell drastically. There was a brief downturn, but then the economy boomed. Consumers wanted to spend their war-time savings on consumer goods. Businesses wanted to meet these demands, and export goods to the war-damaged nations of Europe. Businesses financed production by borrowing from banks, and the banks borrowed (and borrowed and borrowed) from the Federal Reserve.

Now look at output, inflation and unemployment in 1920. The unemployment rate rose to 5.2%, very near potential output. Inflation continued in double-digits, but output fell. There's only one possible shift in the goods market consistent with these data. Aggregate supply must have decreased. The result is a fall in output and a rise in the price level.

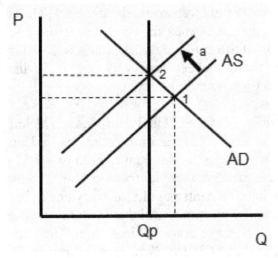

Figure 4-9. 1919-1920. Output is above potential as a result of government spending on the war (as in Figure 4-8). The scarcity of labor and other inputs causes business costs to rise, which reduced aggregate supply (a). Output decreases while inflation continues in double digits (1 to 2). Output returns to potential, with an unemployment rate near 5%.

Well, we should have expected that. Business costs rise when output is above potential, due to competition for scarce resources. Eventually this decreases aggregate supply. We call that second shift #1. Output falls towards potential, but the price level continues to rise. That's a fall in real GDP, rising unemployment and high inflation. That's what happened in 1920.

It's easy to find examples in the news of the time. On December 12, 1920, for example, the *New York Times* reported that the average cost of operating a train had increased by 50 cents per mile over the previous year. Wages and coal costs were higher. The cost of repairing engines was higher too. This explained why the increase in freight rates—the prices charged by railroads to their business customers—had not resulted in an increase in railroad profits, the *Times* said.

What happened next was the first monetary policy debate that included the new Federal Reserve. Some regional bank leaders saw the double-digit inflation as the result of the borrowing and the increasing quantity of money. They advocated an increase in the discount rate. A higher discount rate would make borrowing from the Fed more expensive, so banks would borrow less.

In the early days of the Fed the Secretary of the Treasury was also chair of the Federal Reserve Board. Carter Glass was the Treasury Secretary, and he opposed an increase in the discount rate.

The last "Victory Loan" war bond drive had ended in May 1919. But the Treasury had to refinance the war debt when those loans came due, so Glass still wanted low interest rates.

Ben Strong, J.P. Morgan's old protégé and now the head of the New York Federal Reserve Bank, began to worry about inflation early in 1919. By August he was praying to be "released from this government borrowing bondage [to be] able to deal with money rates on sound lines." He wanted the discount rate ("money rates") raised to battle inflation, not limited by the needs of the Treasury to borrow.

Strong threatened to raise the New York Fed's discount rate without the approval of Washington. Glass threatened to have President Wilson dismiss him from his post. Throughout most of 1919, Carter Glass got his way. Interest rates remained low, and inflation continued.

This was an argument about policy, but also about power. Strong represented New York, Glass represented Washington. Strong was, to his supporters, the spokesman for banker expertise and sound money. To his detractors, he was the tool of the Wall Street money trust. Glass was, to his supporters, the spokesman of the people and a patriot trying to keep war costs down. To his detractors, he was the symbol of crass political influence on economic policy.

Strong had contracted tuberculosis in 1916 and never really recovered. On doctor's orders he left on a world-wide rest tour in December 1919. The New York Fed's interim leaders carried on Strong's fight. In January 1920 they recommended an increase in the discount rate, from 4 3/4% to 5 1/2%. They were astonished when Secretary Glass demanded a rate increase to 6%! A new problem had appeared. The government was required to have 40 cents in gold for every one dollar in paper notes. This was the gold standard ceiling on the Fed's actions. All that bank borrowing at the discount rate was increasing the number of Federal Reserve notes in circulation. The ratio of notes to gold had been near 50 cents per dollar at the start of 1919. Now it was down to 43 cents, and falling.

Glass knew that a rise in the discount rate would stop bank borrowing, so new Federal Reserve note issues would stop. The discount rate was raised the next day. The 1 1/4 percent increase remains the biggest single-day discount rate hike in Fed history.

One day it was profitable to borrow from the Fed and lend at a higher interest rate. The next day, with the higher discount rate, it was not. Banks stopped borrowing from the Fed and stopped lending to businesses and consumers. Consumption and investment spending dropped. A recession began, and it became one of the sharpest downturns in U.S. history.

We can see it in the data, and in Figure 4-10. The interest rate spread increased in 1920, and again in 1921 (the Fed increased the discount rate again in 1921). The Fed influences money supply, so the interest rate increase in the money market must have been caused by a decrease in money supply. By 1921 falling incomes and prices would have decreased money demand, which would have decreased the interest rate spread. That didn't happen.

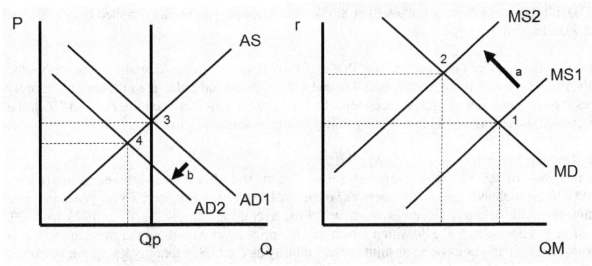

Figure 4-10. 1920-21. In the money market in 1920 and 1921, the Fed increased the discount rate. This discouraged borrowing from the Fed, so the money supply decreased (a). Higher interest rates (2) discouraged investment spending (second shift #2), which decreased aggregate demand (b). Output fell below potential, prices fell, and unemployment increased (3 to 4).

Higher interest rates starting in 1920 discouraged investment spending. Again the money market caused trouble in the goods market, through second shift #2. Construction projects were canceled and equipment went unpurchased. Businesses cut production and dismissed workers, and (eventually) cut their prices. Real GDP fell in 1921, and 1921 saw the only double-digit deflation rate of the 20th century.

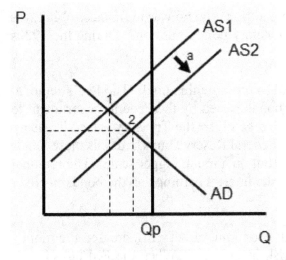

Figure 4-11. 1921-22. Output is less than potential at 1. Inputs costs fall as unemployed workers accept lower wages and other input suppliers accept lower prices. Falling input costs increase aggregate supply (a). Prices fall and output rises, but not all the way to potential output (1 to 2).

Again we should be able to guess what would happen next in the goods market. With output less than potential, unemployment was high. Workers were willing to work for lower wages. Suppliers of other inputs were willing to take lower prices. Business costs fell, and aggregate supply increased. This is second shift #1, from the other direction (compared to 1920). That explains the 1922 combination of deflation (falling prices) and output growth. Output didn't reach potential in

1922, with the unemployment rate still at 8.6%. The unemployment rate dropped below 5% the next year, though.

Ironically, the diagram that describes the Panic of 1907 is similar to the diagram that describes the Fed's 1920-21 policy (compare Figures 4-7 and 4-10). A dramatic decline in the money supply raises interest rates and triggers a recession. In 1907 the recession created the Fed. In 1920, the Fed created the recession. This monetary policy business was going to be tricky.

The Roaring Twenties

The recession of 1920-21 was severe. But it was short, and after it ended the economy roared. Real GDP grew an average of 5.0% per year from 1921 to 1929, the highest 8-year peacetime rate in the twentieth century. Unemployment was low, averaging only 4.1% from 1923 to 1929. Inflation was near zero at 0.3%, which meant that the price level was about the same in 1929 as it was in 1922. That's as close to absolute price stability as the U.S. economy got in the twentieth century. After 1921, the decade saw only two mild recessions.

Technological improvements increased productivity, and improved people's lives. Automobiles became commonplace. A Ford Model T cost the average worker two years' pay before the War; by the end of the '20's a Model A cost only three months' pay. With the new installment buying plans, owning a car was even easier. Electricity brought light to cities (though not to most rural areas). By the end of the decade 70% of factories were powered by electricity. Families gathered around that technological marvel, radio, to listen to their favorite network programs. Radio had barely existed before 1920. Movies provided another new form of entertainment, and by the end of the decade they talked. Charles Lindberg flew the Atlantic to point out the possibilities of air travel.

Open Market Operations. There was no financial panic to fight and no war to finance. What was the Federal Reserve supposed to do? What was its monetary policy mission? During the 1920s they worked one out: stabilize the domestic economy.

The Federal Reserve had discovered a new policy tool to promote this goal. The Fed's regional banks would sometimes buy Treasury securities, the bonds issued by the Federal government to borrow when spending was more than tax revenues. To be clear, the Treasury issued Treasury bonds when it borrows to pay for a budget deficit. The Federal Reserve buys and sells these bonds in the bond market, just like all the other bond traders (but on a much bigger scale). The regional Federal Reserve banks would buy these assets and use the interest earnings on the bonds to cover their expenses like employee payrolls.

The Fed soon noticed that buying these bonds had an economic effect. It increased the money supply. Banks often own Treasury bonds as a low-risk investment. When the Fed buys bonds from banks it creates new money to pay for them. Banks receive payment for their bonds and use the money to make loans. Added lending means more investment in buildings and equipment by businesses, more purchases of homes and cars by families. Banks attract new borrowers by reducing interest rates. On the other hand, when the Fed sells bonds, banks pay with money that they could have used for loans. Less money is available for lending. The banks raise interest rates, and this reduces investment and purchases.

The Fed conducts *open market operations* by buying and selling Treasury bonds in the bond market. By 1923, the Fed had learned that these open market operations could influence interest rates, the money supply, and ultimately economic activity. The Federal Reserve Board in Washington established an Open Market Investment Committee, made up of board members and regional bank officials, to coordinate bond sales and purchases among the regional banks.

In 1913, just ten years before, the Fed had been created to be anything but a central bank. It was to be an association of regional banks to provide for harvest-time increases in the money supply, and to be an emergency lender of last resort. Its operations were to be virtually automatic under the gold standard. Now it had a national policy mission, with policy established by a committee in Washington, and the tools to influence economic activity as it saw fit. This was a central bank.

> *Open market operations are a monetary policy tool of the Federal Reserve. Buying and selling Treasury bonds influences the money available for lending, which influences interest rates.*

- *How did the Fed use open market operations during the 1920's?*

The Fed's first opportunity to use its new open market tool came in 1923. The economy had grown very rapidly for two years. Now inflation appeared to be a threat. The Fed responded by selling government securities. The banks used their reserves to buy these securities, and so had less to lend to businesses and consumers. They raised interest rates. Businesses invested less, consumers spent less, and the economy slowed. Growth dropped from 13% per year in 1923 to 2.5% in 1924. A mild recession began in May 1923 and lasted into 1924, so the Fed reversed course and bought Treasury bonds. The money created to buy the bonds gave banks more funds to lend. Investment spending increased and growth resumed at a more moderate pace. The inflation rate dropped from 1.8% in 1923 to zero percent in 1924. Mission accomplished. Domestic growth and prices were stabilized.

What the Fed did in 1923 and 1924 was *counter-cyclical monetary policy*. The Fed saw a problem, rising inflation, and acted to bring inflation down. They increased interest rates. Then, the Fed saw another problem, recession, and acted to make the recession shorter and milder. They decreased interest rates. It's called monetary policy because it involves changes in the money supply and interest rates. The policy is counter-cyclical because it "counters" the "business cycle." The *business cycle* is the succession of recessions and expansions, low inflation (or deflation) and high inflation, one after another, that characterizes the economy. The Fed tries to smooth these fluctuations, to stabilize the economic ups and downs, to counter the cycle. Counter-cyclical policy is also known as *stabilization policy*.

The Panics of 1907 and 2008

In 2008 and 2009 we became used to the phrase, "since the Great Depression." But the Panic of 2008 had a lot in common with the Panic of 1907, too. Consider the parallels.

In 1907 a stock speculator named Augustus Heinze borrowed lots of money from some trust companies, which were largely unregulated financial institutions, but lost his speculative gamble. His assets were worth less than he owed.

In the 2000's the Lehman Brothers investment bank, and many, many other financial institutions, made enormous investments in "mortgage derivatives," which were largely unregulated assets based on risky home mortgages. When the housing market crashed, these assets were worth less.

In 1907, Heinze's main creditor, the Knickerbocker Trust, was insolvent as a result of its bad loans for his stock speculation. It owed more to its depositors and creditors than its assets were worth. When word got out a bank run developed, and the Trust could not pay its depositors what they were owed. The Trust failed. Contagion developed, as fear of default spread from one institution to another.

In 2008, Lehman Brothers became insolvent, as its investments in mortgage derivatives were worth less than it owed its depositors. Lehman Brothers failed. The Reserve Primary Fund, a money market fund, lost money it had lent to Lehman Brothers. It "broke the buck," paying out less than the full amount its customers had deposited. Contagion developed. Many money market funds experienced on-line bank runs.

In 1907, banks all over the country held on to their deposits and refused to make loans. Interest rates increased, investment dropped, and the nation fell into recession.

In 2008, money market funds and then many more lenders held on to their money, and refused to make loans. Businesses that depended on short-term business loans couldn't get them, and some went bankrupt. What had been a mild recession turned into a steep decline.

Even some of the names were the same in the two panics. In 1907 J.P. Morgan, the man, stepped in to rescue the Trust Company of America, and then supported the stock market. In 2008 J.P. Morgan-Chase, the bank, purchased the troubled investment bank Bear Stearns, rescuing its depositors and creditors. But in 1907 J.P. himself had refused to rescue the Knickerbocker Trust. In 2008 J.P. Morgan-Chase asked Lehman Brothers to put up more collateral for money it had borrowed, which Lehman couldn't do. That pushed the bank closer to bankruptcy.

What was the main difference between the Panic of 1907 and the Panic of 2008? Probably, the Federal Reserve. We had a central bank to rescue the banking system; they did not. Of course, they had a central bank during the Great Depression too. Spoiler alert: it didn't help.

Terms in this Chapter, in order of appearance
Liquid assets
Opportunity cost
Liquidity preference
Transactions
Fractional Reserve Banking

Deposits
Multiple expansion of bank deposits
Multiple contraction of bank deposits
Financial intermediaries
Withdrawals
Reserves
Money multiplier
Reserve ratio
Monetary base
Bank run
Contagion
Lender of last resort
Elastic currency
Federal Reserve
Monetary policy
Discount rate
Tax
Borrow
Print money
Inflation tax
Treasury bonds
Crowding Out
Open market operations
Counter-cyclical monetary policy
Stabilization policy

Notes

The description of the scene in J. P. Morgan's office in October 1907 is from Strouse's biography of Morgan (1999, p. 574-578). Columbia University economist R.A. Seligman called the decade up to 1907 a time of "unexampled prosperity" (quoted in Degen, 1987, p.15).

Odell and Weidenmeir (2002) tell the story of the international economic effects of the San Francisco earthquake. Earthquake details come from the U.S. Geological Survey website, and the Virtual Museum of the City of San Francisco websites.

The Panic of 1907 is probably the second most important U.S. economic crisis of the 20th Century, after the Great Depression of the 1930s, because it led directly to the creation of the Federal Reserve system. Perhaps for this reason there is more written about the panic than about most downturns. Bruner and Carr (2007) devoted an entire book to the panic on its hundredth anniversary. Tallman and Moen (1990) and Moen and Tallman (1992), focus on the role of the Trusts. Morgan's part is told in Strouse's biography (1999, pp. 573-596). Friedman and Schwartz (1963, pp. 156-168) and Degen (1987, pp. 11-16) provide overviews of economic events.

Timberlake (1993, pp. 214-234) discusses the debate over the Federal Reserve Act in detail.

Friedman and Schwartz (1963, pp. 196-221) describe the situation before and after the U.S. declaration of war. Chandler's biography of Benjamin Strong (1958, pp. 99-134) is also useful, as is Degen (1987, pp. 30-36).

The boom and bust of 1919-1921 are described in Friedman and Schwartz (1960, pp. 221-239), Degen (1960, pp. 36-40) and Chandler (1958, pp. 134-187). The story of the struggle between Strong and Carter Glass is told in Chandler (1958), especially in a letter Glass wrote a decade later (pp. 164-65) describing the events. A true politician, Glass describes Strong as "then a stranger but since my warm friend." Friedman and Schwartz, and Degen, conclude that the discount rate should have been raised sooner and cut sooner in 1919-1921. They speculate that the recession would have been milder *without* the existence of the Fed.

Sources
Ahamed, Liaquat. *Lords of Finance: The Bankers Who Broke the World.* New York: Penguin Books, 2009.

Bruner, Robert F. and Sean D. Carr. 2007. *The Panic of 1907.* Hoboken, New Jersey: John Wiley and Sons.

Chandler, Lester V. 1958. *Benjamin Strong, Central Banker.* Washington, D.C.: The Brookings Institution.

Crabbe, Leland. 1989. The International Gold Standard and U.S. Monetary Policy from World War I to the New Deal. *Federal Reserve Bulletin* 75 (6) (June): 423-440.

Degen, Robert A. 1987. *The American Monetary System.* Lexington, Massachusetts: D.C. Heath and Company, Lexington Books.

Eichengreen, Barry. 1992. *Golden Fetters: The Gold Standard and the Great Depression 1919-1939.* New York: Oxford University Press.

Friedman, Milton and Anna Jacobson Schwartz. 1963. *A Monetary History of the United States, 1867-1960.* Princeton, New Jersey: Princeton University Press.

Manchester, William. 1974. *The Glory and the Dream.* New York: Bantam Books.
Moen, Jon and Ellis W. Tallman. 1992. "The Bank Panic of 1907: The Role of Trust Companies." *Journal of Economic History* 52:3 (September): 611-630.

Odell, Kerry A. and Marc D. Weidenmier. 2002. Real Shock, Monetary Aftershock: The San Francisco Earthquake and the Panic of 1907. National Bureau of Economic Research Working Paper 9176 (September).

Strouse, Jean. 1999. *Morgan.* New York: Random House.

Tallman, Ellis W. and Jon R. Moen. 1990. Lessons from the Panic of 1907. *Atlanta Federal Reserve Bank Economic Review* (May/June): 2-13.

Timberlake, Richard H. 1993. *Monetary Policy in the United States: An Intellectual and Institutional History.* Chicago: University of Chicago Press.

United States Geological Survey. 2006. the Great 1906 San Francisco Earthquake. Website: http://quake.wr.usgs.gov/info/1906.

Virtual Museum of the City of San Francisco. 2006. The Great Fire and Earthquake. Website: http://www.sfmuseum.org/1906/06.html.

Wheelock, David C. 1992. "Monetary Policy in the Great Depression: What the Fed Did, and Why." *Federal Reserve Bank of St. Louis Review* 74 (2) (March/April): 3-28.

News Articles
de la Merced, Michael J. "Companies Under Pressure," *New York Times*, September 26, 2008.

New York Times, October 29,1907. Various brief articles about the panic.

New York Times, December 12, 1920. "Operating Costs Absorb Rate Rise."

Nocera, Joe. "As Credit Crisis Spiraled, Alarm Led to Action," *New York Times*, October 2, 2008.

Story, Louise and Ben White. "The Road to Lehman's Failure Was Littered with Lost Chances," *New York Times,* October 6, 2008.

Chapter 5
Money and the Great Depression

The 1920s roared, and people were excited and optimistic about business prospects. "The man who builds a factory builds a temple," said President Calvin Coolidge. "The man who works there worships there." "Everybody ought to be rich," said John Raskob of General Motors in the *Ladies Home Journal*.

The Stock Market

Perhaps it was the optimism of the day (everybody ought to be rich!). Perhaps it was the excitement over new technologies like radio, or the new mass consumer market that installment credit was creating. Perhaps it was the Fed's low interest rates in 1927 (the result of an effort to counter another mild recession). But whatever the reason, more and more people began to buy stock, and values on the New York Stock Exchange began to rise.

A share of *stock* is a share of ownership in a company. It entitles the owner to vote for company directors. It also entitles the owner to a share in the company's profits, which are called *dividends*. If you own a share of Microsoft stock, you are a part-owner of Microsoft, just like Bill Gates (though he owns a tad more of the company than you do). If Microsoft earns profits, they may pay a dividend, which is a dollar amount per share. That way some of the company's profits are paid to stockholders.

> *A share of stock is a share in the ownership of a company. It entitles the owner to a share of the company's profits. If a company is expected to be more profitable, more people demand its shares, and the stock's price rises.*

If people expect a company to become more profitable, they'll want to own shares of the company's stock, to share in those higher profits. The demand for shares increases and the price of the stock rises. That means that people can earn income from the dividends paid on their shares, and profits from the rise in the value of the company's shares, if they decide to sell. If a company is expected to become more profitable, the value of its stock will rise. That's why stock values are thought to be measures of the prospects of a company.

Companies often start out owned by its founders. "Taking the company public" means to sell off a portion of the company to stock buyers in order to raise money for new investment in facilities, equipment or technology (or to turn the value of the company into more liquid wealth for its founders). An *initial public offering* (IPO) is the original sale of stock by a company to raise such funds.

Most sales of stock are not IPO's, though. Shares are bought and sold among secondary buyers, who are looking for a share of the company's profits or hoping to benefit from a rise in the stock's value. The secondary buying and selling helps companies raise money with their IPO's, though. An investor is more likely to buy a share of a company if he knows that the share can be sold in the stock market at any time. The investor's money is not tied up forever.

When the economy is doing well, lots of companies become more profitable, and lots of stock values will rise. We measure changes in stock market prices with *stock price indexes*, the most famous of which is the *Dow Jones Industrial Average*. It's actually just an index of the stock prices of thirty important industrial companies. That means it's like the Consumer Price Index, only it measures the prices of stocks instead of consumer goods and services. Back in January 1929, the Dow Jones Industrial Average included General Motors, Sears, Nash Motors, Radio Corporation of America (that's RCA), Woolworth, and General Electric. The list of thirty changes now and then as the fortunes of companies rise and fall. These days the Index includes the stock prices of Microsoft, Exxon-Mobil, Wal-Mart, Apple, McDonalds, Disney and (still) General Electric. There are other stock price indexes that include more companies, such as the Standard and Poor's 500 and the Wilshire 5,000, but the Dow Jones Industrial Average is the most famous.

That's a lot of bull. There's a statue of a bull on Wall Street in New York City, because a "bull market" means that stock values are rising.

If enough people expect stock values to rise and demand shares for that reason, stock values *will* rise. It can be a self-fulfilling prophesy. Sometimes investors get so excited about a booming economy and the rising stock values that they pay little attention to the potential profitability of the companies. Stock values can rise beyond any reasonable expectations for future profits. The stock market experiences a *speculative bubble*. This is what happened on the stock market at the end of the 1920's. The Dow Jones Industrial Average increased by 50% in 1928. That means an investment of $1,000 in the 30 stocks on January 1 would be worth $1,500 by December 31.

A large part of the demand for stocks was financed by borrowed money. Banks, and then other companies, began lending their reserves to people who wanted to buy stocks. Borrowing to buy assets like stocks can multiply profits. That's known as *leverage*. Suppose, for example, that an investor has $1,000 of her own money, which is called *equity*. She could invest it in the stock market, and if the market rises by, say, 10% over a year, she could sell for $1,100. She's made $100, a 10% return on her equity. Nice, but not too exciting.

Suppose instead that she borrows $9,000, and uses the loan and her $1,000 in equity to buy $10,000 in stock. Again, the stock market rises by 10%. Now her stock is worth $11,000. She still owes $9,000, but the value of her equity has doubled from $1,000 to $2,000. That's a 100% return on equity. She's doubled her money in a year. That's exciting. And if she'd borrowed $99,000, and bought $100,000 in stock, a 10% market rise would increase her equity to $11,000. That's a 1000% return on equity. That's very, very exciting.

Fueled by leverage, stock prices were running, then leaping and galloping upward in 1928. When lots of stock prices rise all at once, it's called a *bull market*. That's why there's a statue of a bull on Wall Street. A market with falling values is a *bear market*. Somehow, there is no statue of a bear on Wall Street.

- *How did the Federal Reserve respond to the Stock Market boom in the late 1920's?*

The Federal Reserve had begun out of the financial panic of 1907. Now in 1928 many at the Fed saw the great bull market as a speculative bubble. They feared that stock prices would be bid upward beyond what company profits would justify. The inevitable crash would bankrupt people, companies and banks, and, perhaps, send the economy into sharp recession, just as in 1907. The speculation had to be stopped.

Power at the Fed was divided between the Federal Reserve Board in Washington and the regional banks, principally the New York Regional Bank still headed by Benjamin Strong. Strong wanted to stop speculation by raising the discount rate. With interest rates higher, banks would borrow less from the Fed, interest rates would rise, speculators would borrow less from the banks, the demand for stocks would diminish, and stock prices would fall. Strong favored a sharp rise in the discount rate that would be sure to prick the speculative bubble before it inflated too much.

The Reserve Board in Washington opposed Strong's idea. They worried that higher interest rates might reduce productive investment. The debate continued throughout 1928 and into 1929, and in the end the discount rate was increased, but not sharply. It did not stop speculation. Stock prices rose another 18% from January to August 1929.

But the interest rate increases did slow down the economy. Higher interest rates caused consumers to buy fewer houses and cars, and caused businesses to invest less in plant and equipment. The diversion of funds into the stock market also reduced funds available for investment in factories and equipment.

The excitement about the growing economy had affected businesses, too. They had invested in new buildings and equipment, stocked more inventories, and built more houses, expecting that consumers would buy them out of their growing incomes. They overdid it. Unsold inventories began to accumulate, so businesses cancelled orders for new goods until they were sold. Factories laid off workers. This is known as an *inventory recession*, and it's a common reason that recessions start. A recession did begin. The National Bureau of Economic Research marks the economy's peak in August 1929.

The Stock Market Crash
The stock boom continued until the end of the summer. Then, in September, stock prices stopped their steep climb. One day they would be down, another day up, then down again. Was the market simply "taking a breather," making ready for another climb, as it had in June and July the year before? Or was this the end of the boom? The answer came in October.

With the perfect knowledge of hindsight, we know that the high point of the Dow Jones Industrial Average came on September 3, 1929, at 381 (oh for a time machine!). It fell, gradually, through September and into October.

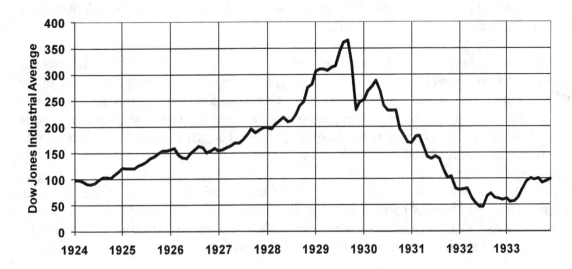

Figure 5-1. The Dow Jones Industrial Average, monthly, 1924-1933. The Dow Jones Industrial Average is a price index of the stocks of 30 important companies. Its value doubled from 1924 to 1928, then rose from 200 to 300—50%--in 1928 alone. Its monthly value peaked in September 1929. The crash in October and November 1929 cut the Average by about a third. By mid-1932 the Average was less than 50, a decline of almost 90%.

To this day no one knows what in particular caused the crash. We now know that stocks were overvalued. The Dow Jones Industrial Average would not reach its 1929 peak again until *1954*. We know that the economy had turned to recession, that business profits were declining, and that the Fed's monetary policy was contractionary. All of these factors could cause a fall in stock prices. But we don't know why thousands of optimistic buyers so suddenly turned into pessimistic sellers, and why it happened in the last two weeks of October.

But it did. On October 24, Black Thursday, the panic began. People feared that the value of their stocks would fall, so they sold them. All that selling increased the supply of stocks, and that reduced their prices. The expectation that prices would fall caused them to fall. And the stock value fall confirmed expectations, and caused more people to sell.

Bankers offered "organized support," again operating out of J.P. Morgan's office (he was the son of old J.P. of 1907). Markets calmed somewhat on Friday and the half-day session on Saturday. But on Monday the market dropped again, and on October 29, Black Tuesday, it collapsed. That day sixteen million shares were sold, an enormous volume in the days of pen and paper, not to be reached again for decades. The stock ticker was overwhelmed, falling two hours behind, leaving investors around the country uninformed about prices, but fearing the worst. This added to the panic. The Dow Jones Industrial Average lost 30% of its value in just one week.

Now leverage worked in reverse. Invest $1,000 in equity in stocks, and a 10% decline loses $100. Our investor has $900 in equity left. Borrow $9,000 to buy $10,000 in stock, and a 10% decline leaves the investor with $9,000. That's what she owes to the lender. Her equity is wiped out, a 100% loss. And the investor that borrowed $99,000 now has stocks worth only $90,000. She owes more than her assets are worth. Now the bank that made the loan is in trouble. It now has a loan worth less than what it owes its depositors.

The value of the stocks served as collateral for the loan. If the bank loaned $99,000, and the stocks were worth $100,000, the bank felt secure. If necessary, the borrower could sell the stocks, or the bank could sell them, and recoup the loan. When stock values fell, though, a bank would feel insecure. It would demand that the borrower put up more collateral. This is known as a *margin call*. Buying on the margin was buying with borrowed money. The "call" was a note a bank would send to a borrower, asking for more collateral.

When margin calls went out, somehow the borrowers had to get cash or stocks for more collateral. This might mean trying to borrow more money somewhere else, but who would lend? Probably it meant selling stocks to raise cash, and using the cash as collateral. The additional selling increased the supply of stocks some more, and values fell even faster.

The crash and continuing volatility of stock prices challenged peoples' assumptions about the future. Increasingly through the roaring '20's people decided that the economy had entered a new era. Irving Fisher, the most respected American economist of the day, had said (three days before the crash!) that "stock prices have reached what looks like a permanently high plateau." Now the upward march had stopped. What did it mean? Economic forecasts were all over the map. Some predicted resumed growth, others continued decline. Many admitted to uncertainty.

Not knowing what to expect, businesses postponed investment. Why build a new factory now if it was not clear whether the new output could be sold to consumers? Why not wait and see what happens? Investment projects were postponed. Construction workers weren't hired. Factories that would have manufactured new equipment shut down instead. *Expectations* turned pessimistic, and this reduced investment spending.

> **The stock market crash caused uncertainty and reduced household wealth. Both caused consumers and businesses to reduce spending, which reduced equilibrium output.**

Not knowing what to expect, consumers postponed big purchases. Don't borrow to buy that new car, that new house, when you might soon be laid off from your job. Make do with the old for a few months to see what would happen.

Peoples' willingness to buy consumer goods depends in part on how wealthy they are. With a big portfolio of stocks, people buy more and bigger cars and houses. Their savings goals for retirement or education have been met by rising stock prices, so they can increase their spending for car or house payments. If they lose a job for a time, the wealth will support their payments. With the crash, much wealth disappeared. Within three years the Dow Jones Industrial Average lost 87% of its value. A thousand dollars invested in September 1929 was worth about $100 by mid-1932.

Now people needed to save more to regain financial security. Saving more meant spending less. The decline in wealth helped cause a decline in consumer spending. This is known (not too cleverly) as the *wealth effect*.

With greater uncertainty and lower wealth, the end of 1929 saw a big drop in consumer spending and in business investment spending. The recession that had begun in mid-1929 took a turn for the worse. The unemployment rate rose from 2.9% in 1929 to 8.9% in 1930. By mid-1930 the recession looked to be as bad as the severe downturns in 1907-08 and 1920-21.

Firms continued to expect growing sales for a time, but saw unsold inventories accumulate. They cut back on inventory investment in response. The decline in investment spending reduced aggregate demand.

The stock market crashed. Now consumers had less wealth and had to start saving more. Consumption spending fell. Both consumers and businesses became uncertain or pessimistic about the future of the economy. They cut back on spending until prospects became clear. This also reduced aggregate demand, and this dropped output below potential.

The Banking System Collapse

Farmers had not shared in the prosperity in the roaring twenties. The agricultural economy had been in recession through most of the decade. The reason was easy to see. During the Great War the farms of Europe could not export, so consumers everywhere looked to American farmers to fill the gap. Commodity prices rose, and farmers increased output. After the war European farms were back in business. Especially after the recession of 1920-21, commodity prices fell and stayed low.

Agriculture's problems in the 1920's had a more serious result for the economy. Most banks in the United States were small. National branch banking was prohibited, so each bank was an institution on its own, lending to local borrowers. Banks in rural areas, of course, lent mostly to farmers. During the prosperous war years, farmers expanded their operations, borrowing to buy more land and pay for new equipment. When farm prices dropped in the 1920's farmers were hard put to keep up with their loan payments. Many small, rural banks saw too many of their borrowers default on their loans. These defaults were not offset by good loans in other industries because virtually all of the rural banks' loans were to farmers. While the 1920's roared in the cities, hundreds of rural banks failed each year.

In the Fall of 1930, with business conditions even worse, rural banks started failing in greater numbers. Fear became contagious. Depositors listened for the slightest rumor that their bank was in trouble, then rushed to withdraw their funds. This time fear spread from the country to the city, and on December 11, 1930 a large commercial bank in New York City succumbed to a bank run and closed its doors. The bank's name, unfortunately, was "Bank of the United States." It was just a privately-owned bank, but with a name like that it sounded like an agency of the government. News that the Bank of the United States had failed caused a further blow to confidence.

What was a bank run like? Consider the story of the First National Bank of Ogden, Utah, owned by a banker named Marriner Eccles. The First National was a small bank. The big bank in town was the Ogden State Bank. By mid-summer 1931 this old, respected bank had seen so many loan defaults that it was insolvent. It owed its depositors more than its loans were worth. Rumor spread among Ogden's other bankers one weekend that the Ogden State Bank would not open its doors on Monday.

That worried Marriner Eccles. His bank's assets were sound. That didn't matter. If Ogden's leading bank went under, depositors all over town would panic. They would rush to withdraw their funds from Eccles' bank too. Eccles had reserves enough to meet normal withdrawals, even heavier than normal withdrawals. But there weren't enough to handle an all-out bank run.

He called his employees in early that Monday morning and told them they would face a panicked crowd. "If you want to keep this bank open," he said, "you must do your part. Go about your business as though nothing unusual was happening. Smile, talk about the weather, be pleasant, show no signs of panic." No teller should step away from his window, not even for lunch. Sandwiches would be brought in. "If any teller's or clerk's window in this bank closes even for a short time, that will stir up more panic."

But cheerfulness was not Eccles' only strategy. All withdrawals would be paid, but he told his tellers, "you are going to pay them very slowly." Check the signatures of even the most familiar customers. Pay out in small bills. Count slowly. "Our object is to pay out a minimum today."

The bank's doors opened and the crowd rushed in. People were tense, afraid that when they reached the front of the line, there would be no money left.

Despite his tellers' efforts, Eccles could see that his reserves wouldn't last the day. So he called the Salt Lake City Federal Reserve Bank and asked to borrow some cash, using his good loans as collateral. Soon an armored car arrived. The crowd parted to allow the guards to carry sacks of cash to the vault. Eccles spotted Morgan Craft, deputy manager of the Federal Reserve Bank, who had come along for the ride. Eccles grabbed his arm and pulled him through the crowd. He leapt onto the counter.

"Just a minute!" he cried, to quiet the crowd. "It appears we are having some difficulty handling our depositors with the speed to which you are accustomed. . . . I just wanted to tell you that instead of closing at the usual hour of three o'clock, we have decided to stay open just as long as there is anyone who wants to withdraw his deposit or to make one.
. . . We have just brought up from Salt Lake City a large amount of currency that will take care of all your requirements. There is plenty more where that came from. And if you don't believe me, I have here Mr. Morgan Craft, one of the officers of the Federal Reserve Bank." Eccles pulled Craft up onto the counter.

Craft came through. "I just want to verify what Mr. Eccles has told you," he shouted. "I want to assure you that we have brought up a lot of currency and there is plenty more where that came from." There was—though it didn't necessarily belong to Eccles' bank. Craft wisely omitted that detail. Payments continued into the evening.

Finally the last customer left the bank and Eccles closed the doors. He gathered his exhausted workers in the lobby. "Now listen," he told them, "Tomorrow there will be the makings of another crush, and we are going to meet it by doing the opposite of what we did today. Instead of opening at ten, we are going to open at eight. Nobody is going to have to wait outside of the bank to start any sort of line. When people come in here, pay them very fast. . . . Don't let any line form. It will mean a continuation of the panic."

It worked. Lots of money was paid out on Tuesday, but no lines formed. Customers walking by the bank saw business as usual, and kept on walking. Eccles' bank had survived the run.

- *How did bank runs and bank failures help cause the decline in output and employment during the Great Depression?*

In 1931 banks everywhere were in trouble. Incomes were falling, unemployment was rising. Business sales dried up, farm prices fell. Farmers and business people who had been prosperous and reliable during the 1920's were now unable to repay their bank loans. Such loans had to be "written off." They were no longer paying assets of the banks, so they were removed from the books. Many banks found that they didn't have enough assets to meet the demands of their depositors. They were insolvent. They shut their doors.

> *When a bank failed, households lost their checking and savings deposits, or saw them tied up in court. Households cut their spending. Businesses had to find new lenders for business loans. This was hard to do with business conditions so bad, and many businesses failed for lack of loans.*

As always during banking crises, banks tried to build up reserves and people became reluctant to make deposits. Both actions reduce the availability of loans and cause interest rates to rise. Investment and durable goods purchases fall. With bank failures this widespread, there are other effects. Pessimism replaced uncertainty, causing people and firms to permanently cancel spending.

When a bank failed people lost their savings, or their savings were tied up in court for months or years, while a judge decided who would be paid how much out of the bank's remaining assets. This caused another wealth effect reduction in spending.

When a bank failed, its small business borrowers had to look elsewhere. This meant reestablishing relationships with new bankers. Business was bad, so it might be tough to convince a new banker that your firm was a good risk. That meant delays in getting new loans, if loans could be had at all. Small businesses needed loans for inventories and payrolls. Without loans businesses would have to close, and their employees would be out of work.

That's the story. Now for the data and model. The unemployment rate in 1929 was 2.9%, less than 5%, so equilibrium output must have been above potential. In 1930 and after it was above 5% (and then some!), so output dropped way below potential. Real GDP declined for four years in a row. By 1933 the production of goods and services was 25% smaller than it had been in 1929. The inflation rate is negative, so there was deflation for four years too. The price level also fell about 25%. The BAA-AAA corporate interest rate spread rose to 3.0% in 1931, then to 4.2% in 1932, the highest spread ever recorded.

The Great Depression

	Real GDP Growth	CPI Inflation	Unemploy-ment Rate	Interest Rate Spread
1929	5.6%	0.0%	2.9%	1.2%
1930	-8.4%	-2.3%	8.9%	1.4%
1931	-6.9%	-9.0%	15.7%	3.0%
1932	-13.4%	-9.9%	22.9%	4.2%
1933	-1.3%	-5.1%	20.9%	3.3%

Let's use the model to make sense of these numbers. Figure 5-2 shows a familiar picture, a lot like Figure 4-7, which analyzed the Panic of 1907. The very low unemployment rate in 1929 means that output in the goods market starts above potential. Businesses stock inventories that they can't sell, so they reduce investment spending. The Federal Reserve raises interest rates, to slow stock market speculation, but discourages business investment instead. Then the stock market crashes, creating business pessimism and reducing household wealth. Aggregate demand falls. Businesses have less reason to produce output, so they lay off workers and cut prices. Output falls, unemployment increases and deflation results. Output falls below potential.

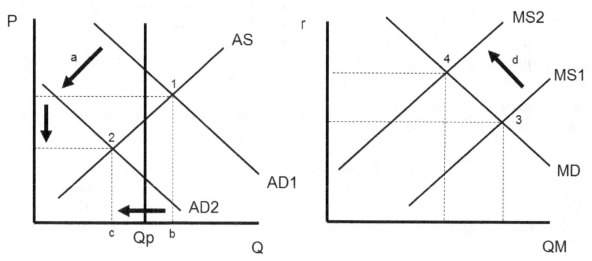

Figure 5-2. 1929-33. Output is above potential in the goods market in mid-1929 (b). The accumulating inventories, higher interest rates and the stock market crash reduce business and consumer spending, and aggregate demand falls (a). Deflation and recession result (2), and output drops below potential (c). In the money market, loan defaults and bank runs cause bank failures. Banks increase reserves, and the money multiplier falls. Money supply decreases (d), and the real interest rate rises. (3 to 4). Second shift #2 causes another reduction in investment, and aggregate demand falls more. The recession turns into a depression, and the depression becomes great.

Now the bank runs and bank failures start. These really got going in 1931, which is when the interest rate spread jumped. People and businesses can't repay their loans. Bank runs threaten even well-run banks. Banks increase reserves and the money multiplier falls. This decreases the money supply. Real interest rates and the interest rate spread increase.

Investment projects that might still have been profitable now are not, because borrowing is so expensive. Investment spending declines some more through second shift #2. Aggregate demand drops more, and the recession turns into the Great Depression.

- *Why didn't wages and resource costs fall, increasing aggregate supply and eliminating the recession?*

That would be second shift #1. With output below potential for so long, declining wages and costs would have increased aggregate supply, and returned output to potential at a lower price level. Many economists of the day expected this to happen. They recommended that the government not take any action to fight the gathering Depression, but to simply wait for price and wage adjustment to bring recovery. But wages and prices did fall, a lot, and the Depression got worse.

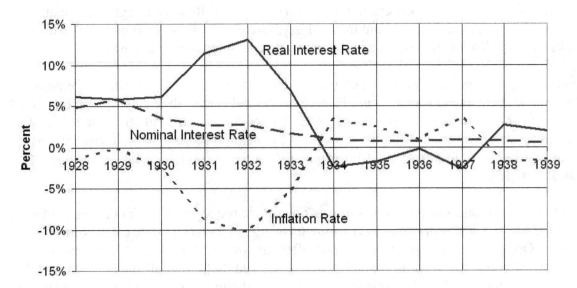

Figure 5-4. Real Interest Rate, 1928-1939. The nominal interest rate is the one year commercial rate charged by banks. The real interest rate can be calculated as the nominal interest rate less the inflation rate. In 1931 and 1932, the nominal rate had fallen, but prices were falling faster. Subtracting the negative price change from the nominal rate gives double-digit real interest rates in 1931 and 1932. The real interest rate has not been higher since.

One reason is that really severe deflation creates a problem for lending. Consider 1932, when prices fell 9.9%. Even a zero nominal interest rate made for a real interest rate of 9.9%. So lenders could "earn" a return on their money by holding it. Lock it in the vault or stuff it in the mattress on January 1, 1932, and by December 31 it would be worth 9.9% more in purchasing power. For many banks that seemed to be a better idea than actually lending the money to a risky borrower who might or might not pay it back. Deflation itself raised real interest rates, and reduced lending.

121

Investment spending fell. While deflation may have been increasing aggregate supply, it was simultaneously reducing aggregate demand some more.

The Fed's (Non-) Response
What did the Federal Reserve do? What did the nation's lender of last resort, the institution designed to prevent bank failures, the hand at the tiller of monetary policy, do about the worst economic disaster in American history?

Not nearly enough.

Occasionally an alert Fed official like Mr. Craft in Ogden would loan a bank some money. But for the most part the Fed stood by. It reduced the discount rate slowly. It refused to buy bonds in open market operations in substantial amounts. It denied loans to banks seeking to calm bank runs by paying depositors. The Fed stood by as one-third of all banks failed. The Fed watched the money supply fall month after month, year after year. It did not use counter-cyclical policy, to counter the worst downward cycle in history.

- *Why didn't the Fed use countercyclical policy during the Great Depression?*

Immediately after the stock market crash, the New York Federal Reserve bought a large amount of government bonds, injecting cash into the banking system. The Reserve Board in Washington didn't like the New York Fed's independence and made them stop their purchases.

Why could the powerful New York branch not persuade the Board of its position? Perhaps the main reason: Benjamin Strong was dead. Strong had been the most powerful, most knowledgeable, most articulate central banker in the United States. He died on October 16, 1928, of complications from tuberculosis. His death left the Federal Reserve without leadership. Some think that had he lived, the Fed would have pursued more appropriate policies, and the Great Depression avoided.

Strong's former assistant, George Harrison, was now in charge at the New York Fed. Often in 1930 and 1931 he would take the train to Washington to argue for discount rate cuts or open market purchases. Occasionally he succeeded; more often he was voted down. Harrison had the disadvantage of being new, and as Strong's protégé, he had "inherited all the antagonisms that poor Ben left behind him," said an observer. The regional banks weren't going to let the New York Fed dominate policy anymore.

Some Fed officials supported the theory that the Federal Reserve was like an electric utility. A utility supplied as much electricity as was needed. When the demand for loans increased, banks would borrow from the Fed and the money supply would rise. When demand was down, they borrow less, and repay old loans, and the money supply would fall. In 1931 the demand for loans was very, very low. So, the theory said, there was no need for the Fed to increase the money supply.

Others argued that a downturn was necessary for the future health of the economy. A recession was needed to *liquidate* the assets of speculators and poorly managed businesses. Let them sell their assets to those who could manage them better, at lower, more reasonable prices, and the economy could begin to grow again. To delay the liquidation with open market purchases was to delay recovery.

The most famous "liquidationist" was Treasury Secretary Andrew Mellon. President Herbert

> *The Fed failed to protect the banking system from bank runs. Banks increased reserves as a result, which reduced the money multiplier. The Fed failed to increase the monetary base enough to compensate, so the money supply fell and real interest rates rose.*

Hoover recalled Mellon's advice: "liquidate labor, liquidate stocks, liquidate farmers, liquidate real estate.... it will purge the rottenness out of the system. High costs of living and high living will come down. People will work harder, live a more moral life. Values will be adjusted and enterprising people will pick up from less competent people." Less successful managers would sell to more successful managers, and businesses would be run better. The trouble was, in the Great Depression even well-run businesses were failing.

Harrison failed to persuade his colleagues to expand the money supply. Most economists now think that he was right and they were wrong.

Fear Itself: The Last Bank Run, 1933

Had the Fed supported the banking system as the lender of last resort, bank runs might not have been so severe, and banks might not have increased reserves as much. The money multiplier would not have fallen as much as it did. Had the Fed increased the monetary base to offset the money multiplier drop, the money supply might not have fallen. The quantity of money would not have decreased as much as it did, and real interest rates would have been lower. The Great Depression might not have been so great.

In 1932, after three years of worsening Depression, the nation held an election. Franklin Roosevelt defeated Herbert Hoover in a landslide. Rightly or wrongly, the voters blamed Hoover for the economic disaster. Unfortunately, in 1933 the new president would not be inaugurated until March. The 20th Amendment to the Constitution had passed, making January 20 inauguration day, but it would not take effect until 1936. This one last time, there would be four months with a lame duck president. This time, it mattered.

The last bank run began in February, 1933. People in big cities and small towns all over the nation lined up with bags and suitcases to cart their money away. One by one, then by dozens and hundreds, banks closed, their reserves gone. The governor of Michigan declared a bank holiday, closing all the banks in his state. By the end of the month governors in 31 more states had done the same. The economic life of the nation slowed to a crawl.

President Hoover pleaded with the Federal Reserve for action. The Fed offered excuses. Hoover pleaded with Roosevelt, the President-elect, to bolster confidence by revealing his intentions, or joining with Hoover in joint policy statements. Roosevelt refused. He would not be tarred with

Hoover's unpopularity, nor drawn in as a supporter of Hoover's policies. Roosevelt waited, and so did the nation.

On inauguration day, Saturday, March 4, 1933, the new President Franklin Roosevelt finally took the oath of office and declared that "the only thing we have to fear is fear itself." He was right—fear had caused the banks' collapse. People were afraid that their banks would fail, and they would lose their checking and savings deposits. So they tried to withdraw their money, in such large numbers that this caused thousands of banks to close. Fear was itself dangerous.

After the speech, in the White House and the Treasury, members of the old Hoover administration and new Roosevelt administration worked desperately to craft a solution to the banking crisis. On Sunday Roosevelt used war-time powers to order all banks in the country officially closed—they called it a *bank holiday*—then called for a special session of Congress.

By the morning of Thursday, March 9, the administration had cobbled together an Emergency Banking Act. There was no time to print copies for the House of Representatives to consider, so at one o'clock that afternoon, House Banking Chairman Henry Steagall rolled up a newspaper, waved it over his head and shouted "Here's the bill. Let's pass it!" After 38 minutes of debate they did. The Senate passed it later that day. At 8:36 in the evening, President Roosevelt signed it into law.

Listen to the Radio. At the Roosevelt Memorial in Washington D.C., a statue of a man listening to the radio. President Franklin Roosevelt explained the bank holiday and the legislation to deal with banking problems in his first "fireside chat" radio broadcast in March 1933.

On Sunday night Roosevelt spoke directly to Americans on the radio, in his first "fireside chat." He explained what his government had been doing over the previous week. He said, "It needs no prophet to tell you that when the people find that they can get their money—that they can get it when they want it for all legitimate purposes—the phantom of fear will soon be laid. People will again be glad to have their money where it will be safely taken care of and where they can use it conveniently at any time. I can assure you, my friends, that it is safer to keep your money in a reopened bank than under the mattress."

It was. The first banks reopened on Monday, March 13. When the banks reopened, deposits exceeded withdrawals. The banking system revived. The last run was over.

The Functions of Money
For almost two weeks the nation lived without banks. Money became scarce. Some of the nation's currency was locked in bank vaults, unavailable with the banks closed. Many people hoarded what cash they had, for emergencies. That took it out of circulation. It was hard to cash a check, because merchants didn't know when or if banks would reopen. People with charge accounts at stores were in luck, but almost no one had credit cards. Without dollars and cents to make purchases, people had to improvise. They called it a "bank holiday," and, somehow, it put many people in a holiday mood.

- *What is money for?*

We take money for granted. It's something we live with without thinking much about it, like air or gravity. If money disappeared, though, perhaps we'd start to consider just what money is for.

> Salt Lake City, Utah, March 7. Two pairs of silk hose, two tubes of tooth paste, a man's hat and a pair of trousers were among the "fare" accepted by a local transportation company from passengers who lacked cash. The trousers, the manager hastens to assure those viewing the exhibit, were the extra pair.

Sometimes we think of money as the same thing as wealth or income. It's not. Suppose people owned wealth, and earned income, but there was no money with which to store the wealth or exchange the income. People would resort to *barter*, the direct exchange of goods for goods. That's what happened in March 1933.

> Oklahoma City, Oklahoma, March 7. Pigs, chickens, eggs and vegetables will be accepted as payment during the bank holiday, a hotel here announced today. "We'll take anything we can use in the coffee shop," said the manager. A pig was accepted in the first barter.

What makes barter difficult? It requires a *double coincidence of wants*. To make an exchange, each person must have what the other wants. A farmer has a pig, and wants to stay at a hotel. The hotel has a vacancy, and needs bacon for the coffee shop. An exchange is made. But suppose the potential customer was an encyclopedia salesman. The hotel would not likely accept World Book volume Aardvark to Aztec in exchange for a room. No exchange is made, even if the book is worth as much as the pig.

This is not a problem with money, because money is universally wanted. The salesman has money, the hotel wants it. The coffee shop has money, the hog farmer wants it. The salesman pays money for the room; the hotel pays money for the pig. In effect, a room has been exchanged for a pig, but with money in between. That's why money is called a *medium of exchange*. It comes between goods for goods transactions, and makes them easier.

- *Why is money universally wanted?*

    Chicago, March 10. Scrip in the form of "company checks" and "pay roll drafts" was the most prevalent medium of exchange as Chicago business firms prepared yesterday to meet their second weekly pay roll under the continued bank moratorium. Confidence in the security of the individual firm is the basis on which merchants are honoring the scrip, which has no legal foundation.

    The Western Electric company established a scrip system by allowing employees to deposit their pay checks in a department created for the bank holiday emergency. Here the checks are broken up into $5 and $10 pay roll drafts on the company. Neighborhood merchants are honoring the drafts for the 9,500 employees, and are giving merchandise certificates as change.

Scrip was paper money printed by anyone but the Federal government. A big employer like Western Electric could pay its workers with printed paper, and the workers would accept it in exchange for their labor. Why? Because they knew that the local merchants would accept the scrip in exchange for merchandise. And why would the merchants accept this scrip? Because they knew that Western Electric was a reliable business that would honor its scrip, exchanging it for money when it became available (or exchanging it for telephones, which Western Electric manufactured).

> *Money acts as a medium of exchange, a unit of account, and a store of value. It allows people to specialize in what they do best, so it's a technology that increases the output of goods and services.*

Money works because of this *network of trust*. Everyone who accepts money does so because he or she believes that everyone else will accept money. Workers would not accept scrip as wages if they found that local stores rejected it as payment for merchandise. Workers who tried to shop outside the neighborhood where Western Electric was trusted would find that their scrip was mere paper.

Consider the problem of Francis Saitta, a lawyer from Brooklyn.

    New York, March 4. When he learned of the bank holiday he congratulated himself on having taken two $100 bills as a fee on Friday evening. He attempted to cash the bills at the Fulton Savings Bank, the County Treasurer's office and a leading Brooklyn restaurant. There were no takers. Finally he obtained two $50 bills for one of the notes at a postal savings bank. Going to a cigar store where he is known, he ordered $1 worth of cigars and proffered a $50 bill.

"Just give us an I.O.U., Mr. Saitta," said the clerk. Mr. Saitta has the cigars—which he did not want—and the $200.

Merchants were hoarding their small bills and change. Mr. Saitta's hundred dollar bills had effectively ceased to be money. No one would accept them in exchange for merchandise. Had he known, he most likely would not have accepted them himself. Ironically, these hundred dollar bills, with all the "legal foundation" one could ask, did not act as money. Western Electric scrip, with no legal foundation at all, did act as money. Legal standing helps build a network of trust. But it doesn't guarantee it.

There's another problem with barter. The Golden Gloves boxing tournament in New York City hired an appraiser to stand at the gate. The ticket price was fifty cents, but anything worth that amount was accepted: hot dogs, noodles, spark plugs, canned goods, potatoes, and foot balm were all accepted in exchange for a ticket.

> Lewiston, Montana, March 7. The Lewiston Democrat-News announced that, until April 1, the following subscription rates will be in effect: One year, ten bushels of wheat; two years, 18 bushels; three years, 26 bushels.

> North St. Paul, Minnesota, March 7. Foodstuffs of a value of 50 cents were accepted tonight as admission prices for a high school basketball tournament.

How many hot dogs is a boxing ticket worth? How many pigs does it take for a week's stay at a hotel? Is a pair of pants good for a one way bus ride, or a round trip? With barter, people must keep in mind the values of every good or service in terms of every other good or service. If there are two goods, there is one rate of exchange to know (two hot dogs = one ticket). If there are three goods, there are three rates of exchange (hot dogs and tickets, tickets and noodles, noodles and hot dogs). If there are 100 goods, there are 4,950 rates of exchange. There are thousands of goods.

One way to solve this problem is to hire an expert. The boxing promoter hired an appraiser to judge the value of everything patrons offered. That slowed down the process of selling tickets, though, making for long lines, probably cutting down on attendance. The newspaper thought of another solution in Montana. If everyone has access to the same product, like wheat, prices can be quoted in that product. That simplifies matters, unless the subscriber raises corn.

Money solves this problem, because it is a *unit of account*. The prices of all products are measured in money. The number of prices merely equals the number of products. People know the relative value of goods and services by comparing their prices, measured in money. That's what they did in North St. Paul. They measured the value of foodstuffs in money, to determine how much was needed for a ticket. Money was used to measure value, even when the money itself wasn't used in the exchange.

Some people have an advantage in barter.

> Miami Florida, March 5. The Brooklyn Dodgers, training here in this winter playground, today found their official till totaled exactly $5.85. Manager Max Carey shot 18 holes of golf on the Miami-Biltmore course today and paid off his caddy with an autographed baseball.

> New York, March 4. Take the plight of Irving Leibowitz, president of a watch company, who had an engagement to go horseback riding. He had the horse and the crop, but no riding boots and no money. He resorted to barter, finally exchanging a watch for a pair of boots.

Some goods are almost universally wanted. Doctors and farmers do alright with barter, because medical care and food are almost as universally wanted as money. (If money disappeared today, computer experts could probably be added to the list of fortunate occupations. Everyone needs tech support!) There's always a baseball fan wanting an autograph from the Dodger manager. Everyone can use a watch. But barter is time consuming. Mr. Leibowitz *finally* made a barter deal. With money, he could have spent more time on his horse.

A watch manufacturer has another advantage. His product can be a *store of value*. If he has a thousand watches in his warehouse, he knows that he can buy food, pay the rent, and go horseback riding in the future. Even if the stable owner already has a watch, he or she might take another because it will hold its value. A watch is a way to save wealth for future purchases. The Dodger manager is less fortunate. Fame is fleeting, and if the Dodgers have a losing season, perhaps even a baseball fan won't want his autograph. The manager can't be too sure that his closet full of signed baseballs will buy anything in the future.

Money solves this problem, too. Money is a store of value. It can be kept and exchanged for products in the future. Barring too much inflation, it holds its value.

Back in 1933, economic activity began to shrink without money. Broadway theaters were among the first to feel the pinch. People still wanted to see shows, and they had enough income to do so. They just had no way to pay for the tickets. The presence of money increases economic activity. Its absence decreases it. In a sense, money is a technology that facilitates exchanges, just like eBay on the web.

Money facilitates exchanges, and that facilitates *specialization*. The need for a double coincidence of wants makes barter a risky business. If Mr. Saitta, the lawyer, can't find someone who needs legal advice in exchange for lunch, he goes hungry. So he dare not specialize exclusively in legal work, even if that is the very best thing he does. He must be part farmer, to make sure he is fed, part tailor, to make sure he is clothed, part carpenter, to make sure he is housed. He must do these things even if he is not very good at them. He gives up doing what he does best to do things he doesn't do well. Society gives up high quality legal services and gets low quality carpentry. In general, with barter society would move its resources from their best uses to lesser uses. Fewer goods and services would be produced.

Money is a universally wanted medium of exchange. People can specialize in the things they do best. Good lawyers produce more legal advice, good farmers produce more food, and good carpenters produce more houses. Money allows more output to be produced from a nation's resources. Money not only facilitates more exchanges, it facilitates more production.

Measuring Money

Money can be a slippery thing to measure. Sometimes it's useful to measure the quantity of money in circulation and in banks, as when we want to decide whether a change in money demand or money supply caused a real interest rate change. A measure of the quantity of money known as "*M-1*" includes just circulating cash, deposits in checking accounts, and bank reserves (since this money could be used for transactions if banks would lend it).

In recent decades, though, other assets have become more liquid. At one time banks restricted the amount that could be withdrawn from a savings account without prior notice, for example. Now many banks allow unlimited transfers between savings and checking. That means savings accounts are almost as liquid as checking accounts, so perhaps our measure of the quantity of money should include savings accounts too.   "*M-2*" money includes everything in M-1, plus savings accounts and other interest-earning liquid accounts, such as money market funds.

M-1 and M-2 are the most frequently used measures of money. There are others, defined by the ever-less liquid assets that are included. Different countries used different definitions. In the United States, the Federal Reserve discontinued measuring M-3 in 2006, for example, because (they said) "M-3 does not appear to convey any additional information about economic activity that is not already embodied in M-2 and has not played a role in the monetary policy process for many years."

Deposit Insurance

Banks began to reopen on March 13. Bank runs did not resume. People seemed to have lost their fear. Deposits exceeded withdrawals.

The banking bill was just the first of a flurry of acts during what is now called "The Hundred Days." Some were temporary measures. Others had their time upon the policy scene, then disappeared. But some permanently changed the way the nation did business.

> *Deposit insurance means bank failures do not cost people their checking and savings accounts. It eliminates the reason for bank runs. This allows banks to keep lower reserves and charge lower interest rates.*

Closing banks was a temporary, and unsatisfactory, solution to the bank run problem. Policymakers now looked for a more permanent solution. They found it in *deposit insurance*. Banks would pay insurance premiums based on the amount of deposits they had. If the bank failed, the insurance fund would pay, and the bank's depositors would not lose the money in their checking or savings accounts. They would be repaid from the insurance fund, created by contributions from all insured banks.

Between 1896 and 1933, 150 bills had been introduced to insure or guarantee bank deposits. The measures had always been defeated at the Federal level, but eight states had adopted such plans (the Great Plains states from Texas to North Dakota, plus Washington State). Under the stress of the bank failures of the 1920s and the banking panics of the Great Depression, all of these plans had failed. Their insurance funds had run out of money.

In 1933 Congressman Henry Steagall of Alabama again proposed deposit insurance. The Depression bank runs had given Steagall and his supporters powerful arguments. They pointed out that the fear of bank runs caused bankers to restrict lending, in an attempt to build reserves. This reduced investment. They pointed out that bank failures caused people to lose their savings, which reduced consumption. And, they pointed out the sheer injustice of a family losing the savings of years due to a bank failure. Deposit insurance would solve these problems, they declared. Bank runs would not occur, because depositors would not fear losing their money if a bank closed. This would free banks to keep lower reserves and lend more. Bank failures would not reduce consumption, because the insurance fund would repay depositor losses. Justice would be served because families would not lose their savings when their bank closed.

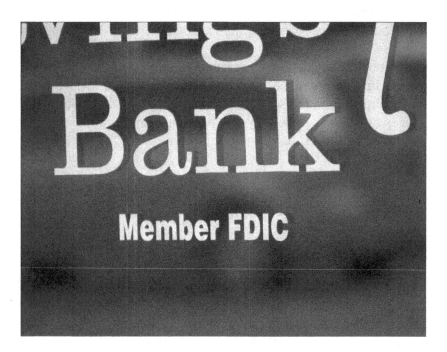

Posted in the window. Banks post the phrase "Member FDIC" in their windows to assure their depositors that their money is protected by the Federal Deposit Insurance Corporation. Should the bank face financial troubles, there's no reason to withdraw deposits. Deposit insurance means customers will be paid by the insurance fund if the bank fails.

Opponents of deposit insurance were ready with their arguments. If contributions to the insurance fund were based on a percentage of deposits, most of the fund would come from big city banks in the Northeast and Midwest. Most of the failures since the war had been in small rural banks in the south and west. Under an insurance scheme, these failed banks would receive the payments from the fund. It wasn't fair to force big banks to subsidize small banks, city banks to subsidize country banks, the northeast and midwest to subsidize the south and west. Especially, they said, it wasn't fair for successful banks to be forced to subsidize failed banks.

Deposit insurance also would promote bad banking practices, opponents claimed. Banks that took big risks sometimes made big profits. They might offer high interest rates on deposits, hoping to attract depositors from their competitors. They might lend to speculative real estate or mining ventures, hoping for big returns. Often enough, big risks made for big losses. Banks didn't operate this way because people would not deposit their money in a bank that took big risks. Depositors had to monitor the practices of their banks, for fear that the bank would fail and they'd lose their money, and this prevented risky practices. If deposits were insured, this incentive for people to monitor their banks would disappear. Banks could take risks without fear of losing depositors. Prudent banking practice would become impossible, because customers would flock to the banks that offered outrageously high interest rates. Deposit insurance, its opponents said, would ruin bank management, create even more bank failures, and ultimately cost depositors and taxpayers very large sums in insurance payments.

This is an argument known to economists as *moral hazard*. Sometimes, adopting policies to reduce the consequences of risk causes people to take more risks. Well-paved roads may make people drive too fast. Flood insurance may encourage people to build on the flood plain. A well-run fire department may cause people to be

> *Moral hazard occurs when protecting people from risk causes them to take more risks.*

careless about fire. Health insurance may encourage more people to try sky-diving. Here, deposit insurance may make bank customers ignore risky bank practices. The result of moral hazard could be more accidents, more flooded homes, more fires, more people falling from the sky—and more bank failures.

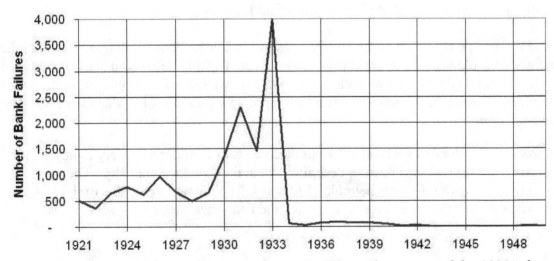

Figure 5-5. Number of bank failures, 1921-1950. Throughout most of the 1920's between 500 and 1000 banks failed every year. The figure topped 2,000 in 1931 and peaked at 4,000 in 1933. With the introduction of deposit insurance in 1934, the number of failures dropped to near zero.

Supporters of insurance responded to this problem by placing an upper limit on the amount of deposits to be insured. The original ceiling was $2,500—an individual's deposits up to this amount were guaranteed, but deposits beyond this amount were not. Because most depositors had small amounts of money, under this ceiling 97% of all *depositors* were fully insured. But because big depositors made up a large share of total bank deposits, only 27% of total bank *deposits* would be insured. This meant that large depositors would still have an incentive to monitor bank management. Supporters argued that only big depositors were able to do such monitoring anyway.

Deposit insurance passed. The *Federal Deposit Insurance Corporation* began operations in 1934. It was instantly successful. More than one thousand banks had failed in each year from 1930 to 1933. A total of 4,000 had failed in 1933 alone. In 1934, *nine* banks failed. For the next 50 years, the annual number of failures was less than 100; in most of those years, less than ten. By 1935, even the bankers had come around to support the idea.

We Won't Do It Again

When Ben Bernanke was a graduate student at the Massachusetts Institute of Technology, reported the *New York Times* in May 2010, his advisor urged him to read "The Great Contraction, 1929-1933." In that book Milton Friedman and Anna Schwartz blamed Depression's severity and duration on the Federal Reserve's failure to expand the money supply. The book ignited a passion. "I guess I am a Depression buff, the way some people are Civil War buffs," Bernanke said.

Later, in 2002, at a party to honor the 90th birthday of Professor Friedman, Bernanke, by then a governor of the Federal Reserve, brought up the mistakes the Fed made that helped cause the Depression. He said, "You're right, we did it. We're very sorry. But thanks to you, we won't do it again."

As a Princeton economics professor Ben Bernanke made a career studying Federal Reserve policy during the Great Depression. He concluded, as have many others, that the mistakes in Fed policy turned a nasty recession into a full blown ten-year Great Depression.

Then Bernanke became chairman of the Federal Reserve in 2006. Perhaps Bernanke thought he was joking when he told Milton Friedman that "we won't do it again." How could he have guessed that he would be the Fed Chair who would have to decide what the Fed would do in the worst banking crisis since the Great Depression? But he was, so now we must ask: what did he do? Did he "do it again" or not?

Every six weeks the Federal Open Market Committee meets to consider monetary policy. They make a decision and issue a press release, describing what they've done and why. The statements have a reputation for impenetrable "Fed-speak." With our knowledge of the Fed, the economic indicators and the macroeconomic model, the Fed's statements may speak to us.

Here's part of the statement from October 29, 2008, in the midst of the Panic of 2008.

> The Federal Open Market Committee decided today to lower its target for the federal funds rate 50 basis points to 1 percent.
>
> The pace of economic activity appears to have slowed markedly, owing importantly to a decline in consumer expenditures. Business equipment spending and industrial production have weakened in recent months, and slowing economic activity in many foreign economies is damping the prospects for U.S. exports. Moreover, the intensification of financial market turmoil is likely to exert additional restraint on spending, partly by further reducing the ability of households and businesses to obtain credit.

The press release doesn't leave readers in suspense (spoiler alert!). The first sentence tells what they decided. A *basis point* is financial-speak for one-one hundredth of a percentage point. Fifty basis points, then, is one-half of one percent (0.5%). The Fed reduced the *federal funds rate* from 1.5% to 1.0%. Half-a-point is usually the biggest change the Fed makes at any one time. So this was a big policy response.

Recall that the federal funds rate is the interest rate charged by banks when they lend to each other overnight. Banks with excess reserves will lend to those that are short, charging the federal funds rate. This rate shows the effects of Fed policy first. When the Fed buys bonds, banks sell them and receive money. They won't be able to lend to businesses or home buyers right away, so they have excess reserves at the end of the day. They lend to other banks overnight. Since there are more excess reserves after the Fed's bond purchases, the supply of funds to lend will increase, and the federal funds interest rate will fall.

The next paragraph is the Fed's analysis of the state of the economy. It could have been taken directly from our macroeconomic model. Slowing economic activity means declining output and rising unemployment. The reasons were declines in consumer spending and business investments in equipment. Export declined too, because of recessions in other countries. "Financial turmoil" means that banks were increasing reserves and cutting back on lending, so that the money multiplier fell. Consumers and businesses couldn't get loans, so they cut their spending even more.

A reduction in the federal funds rate indicates open market bond purchases by the Fed. The Fed was increasing the money supply, trying to decrease interest rates. By the end of 2008 they had reduced to federal funds rate to near zero, as low as it can go.

Figure 5-6 compares the two main policy interest rates during the Great Depression and the Great Recession. That's the discount rate in the earlier period, and the federal funds rate in the later period. It's monthly data. The two series are lined up so that 1929 matches 2007. Those were the years that the downturns began, in August 1929 and in December 2007. So the 12 months labeled "1929-2007" show the interest rates for January to December in 1929 and in 2007.

The rates are similar before the downturns started, 5% in 1929 and 5.25% in 1930. The rates are still not very different 18 months later, 2.5% in mid-1930, 2% in mid-2008. But by the end of the second year, the latter-day Fed had cut the federal funds rate to near-zero, as low as it could go. The discount rate in December 1930 was still 2%.

Some minor reductions were made in the first half of 1931, but then, in October and November 1931, the Fed *increased* the discount rate. They did it again in March 1933, at the very low point of the Depression. They had their reasons—we'll look at the 1931 change in Chapter 8—but we now see these increases as *pro-cyclical monetary policy*.

Pro-cyclical monetary policy means the Fed looked at the economy's main problem, high unemployment, falling output, deflation, and adopted a policy *to make those problems worse.* Higher interest rates would discourage borrowing and investment spending, reduce aggregate demand, and cause more declines in output, higher unemployment, and further deflation. It's the opposite of counter-cyclical policy. We call it "pro-cyclical" because the Fed is *promoting* the business cycle. Pro-cyclical policy destabilizes the economy.

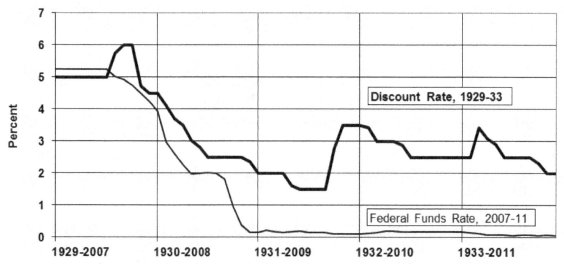

Figure 5-6. They didn't do it again. Here's a comparison of the Fed's discount rate monthly from 1929 to 1933, and the Fed's federal funds rate monthly from 2007 to 2011. The rates were nearly the same at the beginning of 1929 and 2007. Decreases were similar through mid-1930 and mid-2008, but the latter-day Fed cut the federal funds rate to near-zero by the end of 2008, and left it there. Three times during the crisis, the Depression-era Fed increased the discount rate, in late 1929, late 1931 and early 1933. That's pro-cyclical monetary policy.

From 1929 to 1933 the quantity of money fell by 25% (measured by M-1). From 2007 to 2011 the quantity of money increased by 46%. That's pro-cyclical policy during the Great Depression and counter-cyclical policy during the Great Recession.

The Fed did not "do it again."

Terms in this Chapter, in order of appearance

Open market operations
Counter-cyclical monetary policy
Business cycle
Stabilization policy
Stock
Dividends
Initial public offering
Stock price index
Dow Jones Industrial Average
Speculative bubble
Leverage
Equity
Bull market
Bear market
Inventory Recession
Stock market crash
Margin call
Expectations
Wealth effect
Liquidate
Bank holiday
Barter
Double coincidence of wants
Medium of exchange
Scrip
Network of trust
Unit of account
Store of value
Specialization
M-1
M-2
Deposit Insurance
Moral hazard
Federal Deposit Insurance Corporation

Notes
Good descriptions of the Roaring '20s can be found in Galbraith (1954), Schlesinger (1956), and Kennedy (1999). Calvin Coolidge is quoted in Schlesinger (p. 57), John Raskob in Galbraith (p. 57), Irving Fisher in Galbraith (p. 75), who notes correctly that Fisher made a great many lasting contributions to economics. His reputation should not rest on his infamous stock market prediction.

The Fed's discovery and use of open market operations are covered in Timberlake (1993, pp. 261-63), Friedman and Schwartz (1963, pp. 240-98) and Degen (1987, pp. 41-60).

You still can't beat Galbraith's (1954) description of the stock market crash for sheer drama.

Romer (1993) offers a good overview of the Depression, and takes the view that declines in consumption and investment were a major cause.

The description of Marriner Eccles heading off a bank run, doing Jimmy Stewart for real (in *It's a Wonderful Life*) is from Hyman (pp. 78-81).

The classic analysis of the Fed's (lack of) actions during the Great Depression is by Friedman and Schwartz (Chapter 7, "The Great Contraction"). Especially useful are the details of the arguments between George Harrison and his opponents (pp. 363-380). It was these authors who nailed down the fact that the Fed's policy in 1929-33 was contractionary. Degen, Romer, and just about everyone since 1963 has something to say about the Fed's culpability. Wheelock (1992) discusses several explanations for why the Fed acted as it did. The "antagonisms" quote about Harrison is from Ahamed (p. 319).

Eichengreen (1992), Temin (1989) and Bernanke (1994) are excellent sources showing how the gold standard contributed to the Depression. Stein (1996, pp. 26-38) tells the story of President Hoover's 1932 tax increase. The Tax Foundation (1994, pp. 98-109) provides data on federal tax rates before and after 1932.

There are a great many descriptions of Franklin Roosevelt's inaugural and Henry Steagall's famous rolled up newspaper. from the description here is based on Kennedy (1999, pp. 131-137).

Humor writer Dave Barry got it exactly right when he explained money in his book, *Dave Barry's Money Secrets* (2006, pp. 10-11).

> If our money is just pieces of paper, backed by nothing, why is it valuable? The answer is: *Because we all believe it's valuable*.
>
> Really, that's pretty much it. Remember the part in *Peter Pan* where we clap to prove that we believe in fairies, and we save Tinker Bell? That's our monetary system! It's the Tinker Bell system! We see everybody *else* running around after these pieces of paper, and we figure, *Hey, these pieces of paper must be valuable*. That's why if you exchanged your house for, say, a pile of acorns, everybody would think you're insane; whereas if you exchange your house for a pile of dollars, everybody thinks you're rational, because you get . . . pieces of paper! The special kind, with the big hovering eyeball!

The Federal Reserve's press release about discontinuing the M-3 money measure can be found on their website at www.federalreserve.gov/releases/h6/discm3.htm .

Manchester (1974, p. 78) provides examples of how people dealt with the bank holiday.

The Federal Deposit Insurance Corporation has published a nice history of itself (1998). Flood (1992) and Friedman and Schwartz (pp. 434-442) offer the details of the debate on deposit insurance.

Eichengreen (2015) compares the causes and policy responses in the Great Depression and the Great Recession.

Sources

Ahamed, Liaquat. *Lords of Finance: The Bankers Who Broke the World*. New York: Penguin Books, 2009.

Barry, Dave. 2006. *Dave Barry's Money Secrets*. New York: Three Rivers Press.

Bernanke, Ben S. 1994. "The Macroeconomics of the Great Depression: A Comparative Approach." NBER Working Paper No. 4814. Cambridge, Massachusetts: National Bureau of Economic Research.

Degen, Robert A. 1987. *The American Monetary System*. Lexington, Massachusetts: D.C. Heath and Company, Lexington Books.

Eichengreen, Barry. 1992. *Golden Fetters: The Gold Standard and the Great Depression 1919-1939*. New York: Oxford University Press.

Eichengreen, Barry. 2015. Hall of Mirrors: The Great Depression, the Great Recession and the Uses—and Misuses—of History. New York: Oxford University Press.

Federal Deposit Insurance Corporation. 1998. *A Brief History of Deposit Insurance in the United States*. Washington, D.C.: FDIC.
Flood, Mark D. 1992. The Great Deposit Insurance Debate. *Federal Reserve Bank of St. Louis Review* 74 (4) (July/August): 51-77.

Friedman, Milton and Anna Jacobson Schwartz. 1963. *A Monetary History of the United States, 1867-1960*. Princeton, New Jersey: Princeton University Press.

Galbraith, John Kenneth. 1954. *The Great Crash 1929*. Boston: Houghton Mifflin Company (3rd edition, 1972).

Hyman, Sidney. 1976. *Marriner S. Eccles: Private Entrepreneur and Public Servant*. Stanford, California: Stanford University Press.

Kennedy, David M. 1999. *Freedom From Fear: The American People in Depression and War, 1929-1945*. New York: Oxford University Press.

Manchester, William. 1974. *The Glory and the Dream*. New York: Bantam Books.

Romer, Christina. 1993. "The Nation in Depression." *Journal of Economic Perspectives* 7 (2) (Spring): 19-40.

Schlesinger, Arthur M., Jr. 1956. *The Crisis of the Old Order.* Boston: Houghton Mifflin Company.

Stein, Herbert. 1996. *The Fiscal Revolution in America.* (2nd Revised Edition) Washington, D.C.: AEI Press.

Tax Foundation. 1994. *Facts and Figures on Government Finance.* Washington, D.C.: Tax Foundation.

Temin, Peter. 1989. *Lessons from the Great Depression.* Cambridge, Massachusetts: MIT Press.

Timberlake, Richard H. 1993. *Monetary Policy in the United States: An Intellectual and Institutional History.* Chicago: University of Chicago Press.

Wheelock, David C. 1992. "Monetary Policy in the Great Depression: What the Fed Did, and Why." *Federal Reserve Bank of St. Louis Review* 74 (2) (March/April): 3-28.

News Articles
Andrews, Edmund L. "Obama to Nominate Bernanke to Continue Role as Fed Chief ," *New York Times*, August 25, 2009.

Baker, Peter. "A Professor and a Banker Bury Old Dogma on Markets," *New York Times*, September 21, 2008.

Chan, Sewell. "Is Ben Bernanke Having Fun Yet?" *New York Times*, May 14, 2010.

Chapter 6
Fiscal Policy

On that desperate day in March 1933, when President Roosevelt took the oath of office and said there was nothing to fear but fear, many people must have thought, "yes, but what will you *do*?" Roosevelt hadn't really said during the campaign, and he wasn't saying now. He was elected, not so much for a set of policies, but for an *attitude*. He'd said it in a speech in the spring of the campaign, at Oglethorpe University in Georgia:

> The country needs and, unless I mistake its temper, the country demands bold, persistent experimentation. It is common sense to take a method and try it: If it fails, admit it frankly and try another. But above all, try something. The millions who are in want will not stand by silently forever while the things to satisfy their needs are within easy reach.

"Bold, persistent experimentation" is the phrase most remembered from this speech, but another phrase, "above all, try something," may have been a better gauge of his thinking.

The country may not have known what Roosevelt's policies would be, but those policies had a name: the *New Deal*. In a speech accepting the Democratic nomination for president in July 1932, Roosevelt declared, "I pledge you, I pledge myself to a new deal for the American people". The press picked up the phrase "new deal," and that's what they called the collection of policies that the administration hoped would end the Depression. The members of the administration were called "New Dealers." Eventually even Roosevelt began using the term.

No one knew for sure what had caused the Great Depression, or why it was lasting so long, or what to do about it. Economic theory seemed to have nothing to contribute. According to demand and supply analysis, the Depression would solve itself. Were people unemployed? Then wages would fall until the number of workers demanded equaled the number wanting work. Were businesses having trouble selling goods? Then prices would fall until the amount of goods for sale equaled the amount people wanted to buy. Were businesses refusing to invest in new plant and equipment? Then interest rates would fall until money was cheap enough to encourage borrowing for investment.

Traditional economic theory had one message for government: hands off! The market mechanism would correct the problem, through changes in prices, wages and interest rates. The *liquidationists* thought that a recession might even do the economy some good, by making people work harder and save more, and by bankrupting inefficient businesses, so their resources would pass to more efficient hands.

But wages had fallen, and still unemployment rose. Prices had fallen, and still goods remained on the shelves. Interest rates had fallen (in nominal terms, not in real terms), and still businesses would not invest. Economics still had no message other than "wait."

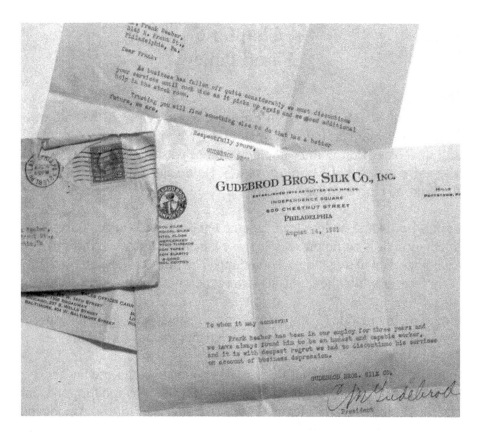

A Great Depression story. A letter to Mr. Frank Beaber, from his employer, Gudebrod Bros. Silk Co., dated August 14, 1931. "Dear Frank," it reads. "As business has fallen off quite considerably we must discontinue your services until such time as it picks up again and we need additional help in the stock room. Trusting you will find something else to do that has a better future, we are Respectfully yours." They enclosed a letter of recommendation. It reads, "Frank Beaber has been in our employ for three years and we have always found him to be an honest and capable worker, and it is with deepest regret we had to discontinue his services on account of business depression."

What about monetary policy? The policy failures of the Fed in 1929-33 had a curious side effect. Many inside and outside of the Federal Reserve thought that Fed policy had been expansionary. Hadn't they reduced the discount rate? Hadn't they made some open market bond purchases, including a really big one in 1932? They decided that since the Fed had tried but failed to stop the Depression, monetary policy was ineffective. Reducing interest rates could not stop an economic downturn. Only in the 1950s and 1960s did researchers look again to find that the Fed had allowed the money supply to fall by about a quarter. Most now think that expansionary monetary policy could have been effective, if only the Fed had tried it. The effects of the Fed's counter-cyclical policies during the Great Recession of 2007-09 support this conclusion.

Maybe it wasn't tried, or maybe it didn't work, but one way or another monetary policy wasn't doing the job. There was another possibility: *fiscal policy*. Fiscal is an adjective meaning "having to do with government taxes and budgets." The problem during a recession or depression is lack of demand. Businesses can produce more goods and services and employ more workers doing it, but consumers do not have the means or the desire to buy these products. With fiscal policy, government steps in and fills the void.

Government can cut *taxes*. This would give consumers greater *after-tax income*, which they could use to buy more goods and services. Businesses would then have reason to produce. They would open their factories and hire more workers. With sales rising, they would have greater reason to invest in plant and equipment, anticipating greater demand in the future.

> **Fiscal policy tries to stabilize the economy with changes in the Federal government's budget. Changes in government spending and taxes influence total spending, and so change aggregate demand.**

Government can increase *transfer payments*. Transfers are payments of income by the government to households. Examples are unemployment insurance, social security, welfare, health care subsidies and veterans' pensions. Again, with more income, people would buy more goods and firms would produce more goods, hiring more workers and increasing investment.

Government can increase its *purchases*, buying directly the goods and services produced by businesses. Government can hire more employees to do useful things (or not-so-useful things). The employees can build dams, roads, post offices, aircraft carriers, pyramids. They can rake leaves. They can dig holes and fill them in again. The businesses that supply the materials like bricks, steel, lumber or asphalt would have a reason to produce, hire workers, and make investments. So would the businesses that supply equipment, like earth movers and cranes, shovels and rakes, furniture and appliances.

Of course, during a recession or depression government tax revenue goes down. People pay a share of their incomes to income taxes, but with wages falling and all that unemployment there is less income to tax. Federal government budget deficits usually get bigger during a recessions (or surpluses turn into deficits), which means that the revenue the government collects is not enough to pay for its spending. During a recession, revenues drop and spending does not. The government borrows the difference by selling *Treasury bonds*. Investors lend the government money in exchange for bonds, which are promises to repay plus interest after a period of time. These are the very bonds that the Federal Reserve buys and sells in open market operations.

To use fiscal policy to fight a recession or depression, then, the government must be willing to make its deficit bigger. Raise spending on transfers and purchases, cut taxes, and government will be spending that much more than it takes in. This is called *deficit spending*. That was controversial during the Great Depression. (It still is.)

Keynes and the Consumption Function

"Above all, try something." But what? Deficit spending? Many economists inside and outside the administration were against the idea. Even Roosevelt was skeptical—he had criticized the Hoover administration's deficits during the campaign. What was missing was guidance from an economic theory that explained what was wrong and what could be done about it. So, the administration tried lots of different ideas, some at cross-purposes.

An new economic theory was at hand. John Maynard Keynes supplied the theory in a book he published in 1936, *The General Theory of Employment, Interest and Money*. It was probably the most influential book about economics written in the twentieth century, and it became the basis for what we now call "macroeconomics." This book is a distant descendant of the *General Theory*.

Keynes was an economist at Cambridge University in England. He was well-known among British policymakers (though he was out of favor at the time). He was respected on Wall Street as the head of an insurance company and as a successful currency speculator. He was a friend of the English literary elite and was married to a Russian ballerina.

Keynes was an advocate of fiscal policy, and of deficit spending. To introduce these possibilities into his model, he devoted an entire section of the

> *Economist John Maynard Keynes published the General Theory of Employment, Interest and Money in 1936. The book marked the beginning of what we now call macroeconomics.*

General Theory to describe how changes in income affect consumption. We can capture his ideas in an equation, called the *consumption function*, which is

$$C = A + b (Y - T + R).$$

The "C" stands for consumption spending—spending by households on food, clothing, washing machines, plumber's, doctor's and lawyer's services and the like. The terms to the right of the equals sign show what determines consumption spending. It's an equation in three parts.

In parentheses is "$Y - T + R$." Y stands for income. When people have more income, they consume more goods and services. Most goods and services are "normal," after all, meaning the demand for them increases with income. An increase in income increases consumption. But the equation recognizes that people can't spend the income listed at the top of their pay checks. First they must pay taxes. That's what "T" stands for, the taxes paid out of income. Taxes are subtracted from income, and the result is (surprise!) after-tax income. That leaves "R", which stands for transfer payments (since we've already used "T" for taxes). Transfer payments are income taxed away from one group and paid to another, like social security, Medicare and Medicaid, welfare, unemployment insurance and veteran's benefits. That gets added to the income people earn. The result is "after-tax-and-transfer-income," which is a mouthful, so we call it *disposable income*.

Disposable income can be disposed of in two ways: it can be spent on consumption, or it can be saved. The coefficient "b" shows how much of each extra dollar of disposable income is consumed. It's called the *marginal propensity to consume (MPC)*, and its value is between zero and one. It's "marginal" because it measures how *changes* in one thing affect changes in the other (we say it's the effect "at the margin"). An

> *The consumption function shows how added income affects consumer spending. The income multiplier shows how much added output is created by additional spending.*

MPC of 0.5, for example, means that someone with an extra $1,000 in disposable income spends an extra $500 and saves the rest. An MPC of 0.8 means $800 of an extra $1,000 is consumed.

What if income was zero? Would people stop consuming everything? Not if they could help it—spending on food, clothing, and shelter would continue, somehow. That's what the "A" represents. It's called *autonomous consumption* because it is independent of current disposable income. People manage to consume even when income is zero by drawing on savings or wealth, borrowing, or relying on family or charity (we've already included options like welfare or unemployment insurance in transfers, R). People with more wealth or savings, or with a greater ability to borrow, have larger autonomous consumption.

With the consumption function in hand, we can figure out how to measure the *income multiplier*. Start with our old friend,

$$Q = C + I + G + X - M,$$

and recall that output and income are the same for the whole economy. Revenue from sales of output by businesses are distributed to employees as wages, to lenders as interest, to landlords as rent, and to business owners as profit. Wages, interest, rent and profit are four kinds of income. Call income "Y", since we already use "I" for investment. Now substitute the consumption function for "C" to get

$$Y = [A + b(Y - T + R)] + I + G + X - M.$$

Use a little algebra (remember algebra?) to group the "Y" terms on the left, factor out the Y and divide both sides by what's left, and you'll get

$$Y = [1 / (1 - b)] \times [A - bT + bR + I + G + X - M].$$

The bracketed term to the right is the sum of things that add to or subtract from spending—autonomous consumption, taxes and transfers, investment, government purchases, exports and imports. The bracketed term on the left is the income multiplier. When investment or government purchases or autonomous consumption change, the effect on income (and output) is that spending change times the multiplier,

$$1 / (1 - b).$$

The multiplier depends on the marginal propensity to consume. The bigger the MPC, the bigger the multiplier. If consumers spend 75 cents of each extra dollar, the multiplier is $1 / (1 - 0.75) = 1 / 0.25 = 4$. With this multiplier, an increase in government purchases (G) of $1,000 increases income or output (Y) by $4,000. A thousand dollars spent on public works becomes income for a construction worker. The worker spends $750 on groceries, and that $750 becomes income for the grocer. The grocer spends 75 cents of each extra dollar, too, which is $562.50, which becomes someone else's income. This process continues until we're down to fractions of pennies. The total of the initial $1,000, and all the subsequent income, will be $4,000. When the whole economy is aggregated, output and income are the same, so the income multiplier is also an output multiplier. It shows how much GDP will increase with an initial increase in spending.

Now we've got the government's budget in our goods market model. Government taxes (T) are in the consumption function. Raise taxes and consumers spend less. Aggregate demand declines. Cut taxes and consumers spend more. Aggregate demand increases.

> **The government's budget balance is the difference between tax revenues and spending, which includes purchases and transfer payments.**

Transfer payments (R) also are in the consumption function. Raise payments to the unemployed, the sick, the retired or the poor and they will consume more. Cut those payments and they will consume less. Aggregate demand will rise with higher payments and fall with lower payments.

And government purchases (G) have been part of spending and aggregate demand since Chapter 3. Increase purchases and aggregate demand increases; decrease purchases and it decreases.

Those three terms make up the government's budget. The *budget balance* is

Budget Balance = T − (G + R).

Government revenue less government spending is the budget balance. If revenue exceeds spending, there's a surplus. If spending exceeds revenue, there's a deficit. Surpluses tend to decrease aggregate demand, and deficits tend to increase aggregate demand.

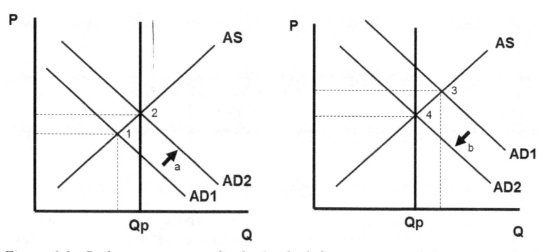

Figure 6-1. Both are counter-cyclical. On the left, output starts below potential (1). Counter-cyclical fiscal policy cuts taxes, increases transfers and increases government purchases. All these increase spending, and aggregate demand (a). Output increases and unemployment declines (2). On the right, output starts above potential (3). Inflation is a threat, if second shift #1 decreases aggregate supply. Instead, taxes are increased, transfers are reduced, and government purchases are reduced. Aggregate demand declines (b) so that output is back at potential (4) and inflation is not a threat.

Now *counter-cyclical fiscal policy* is possible. If output is less than potential, aggregate demand can be increased with tax cuts, transfer payment increases, or higher government purchases. Deficit spending when output is less than potential is counter-cyclical. That's because it counters or offsets the problems of low output, high unemployment and deflation. A *government budget surplus* would be counter-cyclical fiscal policy when output is greater than potential and inflation is a problem. Higher taxes, lower transfers and lower government purchases reduce aggregate demand, which could head off inflation. Whether a particular fiscal policy is counter-cyclical or not depends on what's wrong with the economy.

Keynes and Roosevelt

Though the Roosevelt administration's policies have been called *Keynesian*, Keynes never had much direct influence on the President. Several of Roosevelt's advisors had heard of Keynes, and a few knew him. They introduced the economist to the President on May 28, 1934. John Maynard Keynes talked for an hour with President Franklin Roosevelt.

We have a good idea about what Keynes must have said. He had addressed an open letter to the President five months before, on December 31, 1933, offering his views on what Roosevelt should do:

> An increase of output cannot occur unless by the operation of one or other of three factors. Individuals must be induced to spend more out of their existing incomes, or the business world must be induced, either by increased confidence in the prospects or by a lower rate of interest, to create additional current incomes in the hands of their employees, which is what happens when [investment] is being increased; or public authority must be called in aid to create additional current incomes through the expenditure of borrowed or printed money.

In bad times, he said, individuals and businesses can't be counted on. Only government expenditures will help. The administration had failed to increase deficit spending enough. The continuing Depression was the predictable result. He couldn't blame the administration "for being cautious and careful" with its spending. "But the risks of less speed must be weighed against those of more haste." What was needed was a large increase in deficit spending, with "preference given to those which can be made to mature quickly on a large scale. . . . The object is to start the ball rolling."

After the meeting Keynes told a friend "I had a grand talk and liked him immensely." But he also said he had "supposed the President was more literate, economically speaking." Roosevelt hadn't appeared to follow all that Keynes had said. The President told Labor Secretary Frances Perkins, "I saw your friend Keynes. He left a whole rigmarole of figures. He must be a mathematician rather than a political economist."

Keynes dropped by Perkins' office after the meeting and explained the multiplier effect. He said that a dollar spent on relief by the government was a dollar given to the grocer, by the grocer to the wholesaler, and by the wholesaler to the farmer. With one dollar paid out for relief or public works or anything else, you have created four dollars' worth of national income. Perkins wished he had been as concrete when talking to the President, instead of "treating him as though he belonged to the higher echelons of economic knowledge."

Keynes' ideas began to make inroads once the *General Theory* was published. To the some, it was a revelation. Young economists, who had grown up during the Depression, chafed under what they saw as their elders' stale old ideas, and embraced Keynes' revolutionary theory. Paul Samuelson, who would later be the first American to win the Nobel Prize in economics, described the reaction of young graduate students: "Bliss was it in that dawn to be alive, but to be young was very heaven!" Now the Depression could be explained. Now the battle of ideas could be joined. The theory recommending "do nothing" was met with an equally sophisticated theory that said "do something."

The Tax Increase of 1932

Now we can use our macroeconomic model to analyze fiscal policy. President Herbert Hoover, Roosevelt's predecessor, was not willing to make the Federal budget deficit bigger. In fact, he saw the deficit as part of the problem. In his December 1931 state of the union address he called "credit paralysis" one of the "outstanding obstacles to recovery." And he had an idea about what to do about the problem.

> Our first step toward recovery is to reestablish confidence and thus restore the flow of credit which is the very basis of our economic life. The first requirement of confidence and of economy recovery is financial stability of the United States Government.

So he proposed a tax increase.

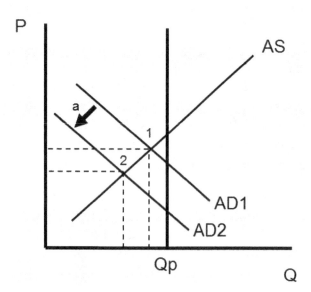

Figure 6-2. The economy starts with output less than potential (1). Taxes increase, which reduces disposable income, and so reduces consumption spending. Aggregate demand decreases (a). Output falls further below potential, so unemployment increases. The price level falls, causing more deflation. The Depression gets worse. This is pro-cyclical fiscal policy.

The government was running a large deficit. Income tax revenue had dropped with falling incomes and rising unemployment. The government had to borrow to fill the gap between revenues and spending. The money the government borrowed, Hoover thought, was money that was denied to private industry. To allow businesses to increase investment spending, the government's budget had to be balanced, and that meant taxes had to be increased.

Congress was persuaded, despite the fact that 1932 was an election year. President Hoover signed the tax increase into law on June 6, 1932. It was a truly enormous tax hike. The top tax rate increased from 25% to 63% of income. For taxpayers with incomes under $8,000—which was most of them—the rate increase from one and a half percent to 4%. That's a 167% increase in tax bills. The deduction for a married couple was reduced from $3,500 to $2,500, which meant that millions of lower income people had to start paying. The tax on corporations was increased from 12% to 13.75% of profits. Estate and gift taxes were raised as well. Revenues jumped in 1933 and the deficit got smaller, but the budget was still not balanced.

President Hoover pushed for higher taxes to balance the budget and encourage investment spending. He got little argument from either politicians or economists about his reasoning. But the tax hike is now seen as a big mistake. The consumption function is $C = A + b (Y - T + R)$. An increase in taxes, T, caused a reduction in disposable income (you can think of it as "after-tax income" too). Households had to cut their consumption spending. This decreased aggregate demand. Businesses had even less reason to produce goods and services, so they cut production and dismissed workers. Now these workers had less income, so they spent less. The income multiplier went to work in reverse. The effect of the tax increase multiplied through the economy, and the Depression got worse.

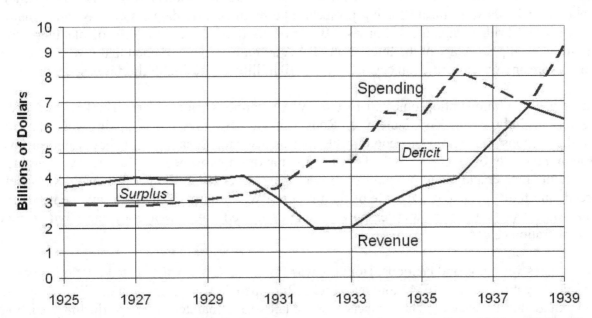

Figure 6-3. The Federal Budget. Federal revenue exceeded spending from 1925 to 1930. That's a budget surplus. Then revenue dropped with the Depression, causing a budget deficit. Revenue didn't drop from 1932 to 1933, probably because of the Hoover tax hike. Revenue began to recover after 1933, but by then the Roosevelt administration was increasing spending. The spending cuts in 1937 and 1938 nearly balanced the budget, but also helped cause a recession within the Depression.

President Hoover's 1932 tax increase is the classic example of *pro-cyclical fiscal policy*. Falling output, falling prices and rising unemployment were the problem. A tax increase made those problems worse. It's fiscal policy because it changed the government's budget, taxes in this case. It's pro-cyclical because it promoted the economy's problems, rather than countering them.

Employment Programs
Some members of the Roosevelt administration strongly favored balanced budgets. Budget Director Lewis Douglas knew that big deficits would mean lots of borrowing, which meant of Treasury bonds to sell. The banks and the public couldn't buy them all, so the Federal Reserve would buy them. The Fed would create money to do that, and all that added money would cause inflation.

Inflation was Douglas' worst nightmare. He contended that the Communists in Russia and the Nazis in Germany had come to power after inflation had ruined their economies. It would happen in the United States, too. "Great inflations have been followed by revolutions," he said, "The sheer weight of the economic and social forces will compel a dictatorship." Inflationary policies, he once said, would mean "the end of western civilization."

With the Great Depression at its worst, the pressure to "try something" soon overwhelmed any effort to avoid deficits. Congress pushed President Roosevelt to increase spending on construction projects, and he signed a bill creating the Public Works Administration (PWA). The $3.3 billion in borrowed funds were meant for big projects, like hydroelectric dams, sewer systems, major highways and bridges, apartment houses. Big projects required a great deal of planning, and Harold Ickes, the Secretary of the Interior and PWA administrator, cautioned that it would be two years before any real construction began. Only $110 million of the $3.3 billion was spent in 1933.

Others in the administration objected to the PWA's cautious pace. Harry Hopkins had been director of relief for New York State when Roosevelt had been governor. Hopkins worried about how the millions of unemployed people would live and eat, and especially how they would survive through the winter of 1933-34. In the fall of 1933 Hopkins approached the President with an idea for a temporary employment program to provide paychecks for millions of people. Roosevelt agreed, and they decided to use some of the unspent PWA funds. Even Ickes saw the need and didn't object (as long as it was temporary). They named the new agency the Civil Works Administration (CWA).

Where Ickes was slow and cautious, Hopkins was fast. The CWA was created on November 9, 1933, and by mid-January 1934 more than four million people were employed on CWA projects. How could this be done? The projects were small—road maintenance, refurbishing existing schools and hospitals, even installing outhouses for farm families—but that meant that they could be started quickly. Hopkins got tools from army warehouses and used the Veterans Administration to distribute paychecks. In its five month existence, the CWA spent more than $800 million on work-relief, completing 180,000 projects.

In the mid-term Congressional elections (when the President's party usually loses seats), the Democrats won nine new seats in the House and ten in the Senate. They now had enormous majorities in both houses of Congress.

The voters seemed to have put a seal of approval on the administration's policies. Harry Hopkins saw his chance. "Boys—this is our hour!" he declared to his staff. "We've got to get everything we want—a works program, social security, wages and hours, everything—now or never. Get your minds at work on developing a complete ticket to provide security for all the folks of this country up and down and across the board."

Hopkins' had in mind a public works program much bigger and longer lasting than the CWA. His staff worked up a plan, the President agreed, and on April 5, 1935 the Emergency Relief Appropriation Act had passed Congress and was on the President's desk. (But the President wasn't at his desk. He was vacationing on Vincent Astor's yacht. The bill was brought to Florida and he signed it when the boat docked.)

> **Big government construction projects may take years to plan, so they won't add to spending right away. Small projects add to spending faster, but may not result in facilities of lasting use.**

Hopkins' new agency was called the Works Progress Administration (WPA). After a year it employed 3 million people; during its life, 8.5 million. Its employees built half a million miles of highway, nearly a hundred thousand bridges, and eight thousand parks. It was also criticized for creating make-work and for being used by Democratic Party bosses for political patronage. Harold Ickes' Public Works Administration (PWA) also received new funds, and his meticulous administration kept the PWA from much controversy. Though slow to get started, eventually the PWA built such big projects as LaGuardia Airport in New York City, the San Francisco-Oakland Bay Bridge, and the aircraft carriers *Yorktown* and *Enterprise*.

Doubleday Field at the Baseball Hall of Fame in Cooperstown, New York. Harry Hopkins had his fingers in everything.

Ickes did not accept the WPA as he had the CWA in 1934. He was furious at Hopkins for choosing the name WPA, so like that of his own agency, convinced it was a deliberate attempt to confuse the public. The WPA was supposed to engage in smaller projects which employed large numbers of people, while the PWA was devoted to bigger projects requiring long term planning and heavy equipment. In practice, though, the lines dividing these projects were fuzzy, and Ickes accused Hopkins of treading on his territory, as well as his budget. The two men engaged in a public feud so nasty that it made Ickes paranoid and gave Hopkins an ulcer.

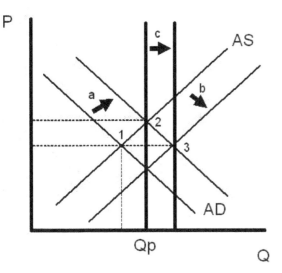

Figure 6-4. Hopkins vs. Ickes. Start with output below potential (1), a depression. Hopkins' rapid spending on small projects increased aggregate demand fast (a). Ickes' projects required more planning, so they affected aggregate demand more slowly. The shift from 1 to 2 would take years. But, after those years, the added infrastructure would reduce resource costs, increasing aggregate supply (b) and potential output (c). Output winds up bigger, and prices lower (3).

- *What was the difference for the economy between the effects of the PWA's big projects and the WPA's small projects?*

Ickes' big projects didn't increase aggregate demand much at first because they took so long to plan. Hopkins' projects increased aggregate demand right away. But in the longer run, Ickes' projects probably affected aggregate *supply* more than Hopkins' projects did. The dams reduced electricity costs; the highways, bridges and airports reduced transportation costs. These lower resource costs meant increases in aggregate supply and potential output. We're still getting good use out of LaGuardia Airport and the San Francisco-Oakland Bay Bridge. In the long run Ickes' projects increased output more. But as Hopkins once said, "people don't eat in the long run, they eat every day."

- *What was the difference for the economy between deficit spending with the private sector buying Treasury bonds, and the Federal Reserve buying Treasury bonds?*

There would have to be big deficits if fiscal policy was to be used to bring the economy out of depression. Unlike Budget Director Douglas, Marriner Eccles, the new head of the Federal Reserve Board, feared that the Federal Reserve would *not* buy the Treasury bonds when the government ran a deficit. The deficits would be big, and if banks had to buy the bonds, they would have little left over for private lending. That would reduce private investment spending even as government spending increased. Eccles didn't use the term, but he was worried about crowding out.

> *Deficit spending requires borrowing, which could increase real interest rates. If the Fed increases the money supply, interest rates won't increase, but inflation might.*

So, Eccles thought, the Fed would have to buy the bonds. But would the Fed act? Open market operations were controlled by a large committee dominated by the regional banks. There was no assurance that the Fed would even consider cooperating with the administration's fiscal policy.

150

When Roosevelt asked Eccles to become the head of the Federal Reserve, Eccles said he'd take the job only if the Federal Reserve's structure was reformed. Roosevelt agreed, and Eccles' ideas became the banking bill of 1935. The bill's most important feature was that it reorganized the Federal Open Market Committee, making the Chairman of the Federal Reserve Board its head, and limiting participation by the regional banks. Power over monetary policy would be concentrated in Washington, D.C.

The bill passed and President Roosevelt signed it on August 24, 1935. The Federal Reserve was reborn, in essentially the form we know today.

The National Recovery Administration
Hoover, Eccles, Douglas, Ickes, and Hopkins disagreed, but they had one thing in common: they were all concerned about demand. Each in his own way wanted to increase the willingness and ability of consumers and businesses to buy the things that industry could produce. Hoover and Douglas wanted to create conditions for businesses to borrow and invest, so they would demand more materials and labor. Eccles, Ickes, and Hopkins each promoted government spending on public works. But this was just one strand of thinking in the Roosevelt administration. The President had pledged to "try something," and with the National Recovery Administration (NRA), he tried something big.

Blue Eagle. The National Recovery Administration's logo, placed in shop windows of businesses that had signed on.

What was the cause of the downward spiral of prices and wages? Some in the administration answered, "cut-throat competition." The problem, said former brigadier general Hugh Johnson, who headed the NRA, was "the murderous doctrine of savage and wolfish competition, looking to dog-eat-dog and devil take the hindmost." A business would cut its prices in its desperation to sell what it could produce. Its competitors would have no choice but to cut their prices, too. Lower prices meant less revenue, so businesses had to lay off employees or cut their wages. Fewer employees with lower wages could not buy what business produced. The (too) simple solution, then, was to stop prices from falling. That's what the NRA was for.

The NRA's idea was to get businesses in each industry to agree with one another not to cut prices. They would do this by establishing industry codes, which would limit the amount each firm would produce. Without "overproduction," prices and wages could be stabilized.

For a year and a half starting in mid-1933 General Hugh Johnson ran a vigorous campaign to encourage businesses to sign on to industry codes and persuade consumers to shop at businesses that adhered to a code—despite their higher prices. A business could display a poster in its window, showing a blue eagle and the slogan "We Do Our Part," to let customers know that they followed an NRA industry code. It was hoped that customers patriotically would shop at stores displaying the blue eagle, even if their prices were higher because of the codes.

- *What was the problem with the NRA's supply-side approach to recovery?*

The Depression problem was that the quantity of goods that consumers demanded was less than the quantity that business could supply. It was "underconsumption" said supporters of deficit spending, who said "let's increase demand." It was "overproduction" said supporters of the NRA, who said "let's decrease supply." The NRA enabled businesses to form government-sponsored cartels, to restrict production and fix prices. Labor was included. To decrease its supply, the NRA's

> **The National Recovery Administration allowed businesses to form cartels. This would raise prices by restricting aggregate supply. It was declared unconstitutional in 1935.**

legislation encouraged businesses to restrict workers to a 40-hour week and to end child labor. To support the price of labor—wages—the NRA encouraged workers to form unions. And it enacted a minimum wage.

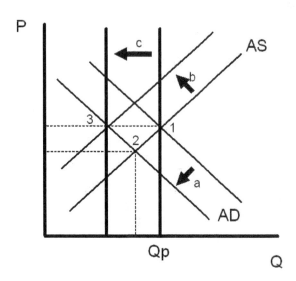

Figure 6-5. NRA. The decline in aggregate demand (a) reduces prices (1 to 2). It's a depression. Eventually second shift #1 would cause wages and resources prices to fall, too, increasing aggregate supply, as in figure 6-1(a). To stop the deflation, the NRA restricted supply by allowing businesses to form cartels and workers to form unions. Aggregate supply decreases (b). Prices are higher, but output is even lower (3). If the NRA supply restrictions become permanent, potential output would decline as well (c).

If it worked, the NRA would stabilize prices and wages, perhaps even reduce unemployment—but at a lower level of national output than could be achieved with competitive production. It didn't work. General Johnson was a flamboyant promoter of the NRA, but he was an erratic administrator, and his ultimate problem (unknown at the time) was that the idea at its core was flawed. Yes, restricting output could raise prices, but wouldn't it be better if price increases were the result of added demand and *increased* output?

Roosevelt became disenchanted with Johnson and fired him in October 1934. In May 1935 the Supreme Court mercifully (and unanimously) declared the whole thing unconstitutional.

People still favored the abolition of child labor and limits on working hours. Some restrictions on aggregate supply are made for social, cultural, or humanitarian reasons—the public is willing to "pay" with lower output to have them. (Abolition of child labor, though, probably increases potential output in the long run. If they're not in the factories, the kids are in school. This results in a more educated labor force that adds to productivity.) Limits on working hours and child labor, the minimum wage and the right to organize unions were re-authorized in later legislation, which the Supreme Court upheld.

The Roosevelt Recession
In 1937 after four years of expansion the real GDP had finally topped its 1929 level. The unemployment rate had dropped, but it was still 9.2%. That was excellent compared to the 1932 rate of 22.9%, but terrible compared to the 1929 rate of 2.9%. In 1938 unemployment rose back to 12.5%, and real GDP dropped by 4.0%. Deflation re-emerged. The interest rate spread increased.

It was a recession in the midst of the Great Depression. Since it took place during the Roosevelt administration—the President had been re-elected in 1936—it's called the *Roosevelt recession*.

Roosevelt Recession

Year	Real GDP Growth	CPI Inflation	Unemploy- ment Rate	Interest Rate Spread	Gov't Budget Balance (% GDP)
1936	14.0%	1.5%	10.0%	1.5%	-5.1%
1937	4.4%	3.6%	9.2%	1.8%	-2.4%
1938	-4.0%	-2.1%	12.5%	2.6%	-0.1%
1939	7.9%	-1.4%	11.3%	2.0%	-3.0%

By now you should recognize what's needed in the goods and money markets to explain the 1937-38 recession. Almost the same diagrams used for the Panic of 1907 (Figure 4-7) and the Great Depression of 1929-33 (Figure 5-2).

Since both output and prices decreased in 1938, aggregate demand must have decreased. The recession was caused by a decrease in spending. Since unemployment was above 5% in 1937 and even higher in 1938, output was less than potential before and after the change in aggregate demand. Real GDP fell in 1938, so income must have decreased. That year's deflation shows that prices decreased. The drop in both income and prices in 1938 means that money demand must have decreased. But the interest rate spread increased, so the money supply must have decreased enough to more than offset the drop in money demand. It's all there in Figure 6-6.

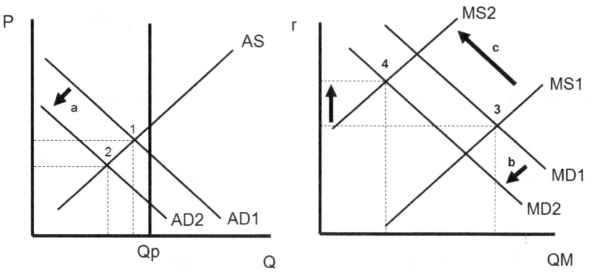

Figure 6-6. Roosevelt Recession. Output is still less than potential in the goods market (1). The Roosevelt administration attempts to balance the government's budget, with tax increases and spending cuts. Aggregate demand falls (a), output decreases and is further from potential, indicating added unemployment (2). Meanwhile, the Federal Reserve increases reserve requirments, which reduces the money multiplier. Money supply decreases (c) and the real interest rate rises (3 to 4). Second shift #2 decreases investment spending, and aggregate demand falls some more.

Here's the story. The recovery had progressed enough that in 1937 President Roosevelt decided to try for a balanced budget. Though he had agreed to all that deficit spending in his first term, he was at heart a balanced budget man. The Federal government made a
large bonus payment to veterans of World War I in 1936. These were transfer payments, adding directly to the incomes of consumers. No such bonus was scheduled in 1937. Spending on transfer payments dropped. In 1937, social security taxes were collected for the first time. Benefits were not scheduled to start for several years, however, so the initial effect of this new program was a large tax increase. Higher taxes subtracted from the incomes of consumers.

The budget balance fell from -2.5% of GDP in 1937, to -0.1% in 1938. That is, there was deficit spending above taxes equal to 2.5% of GDP in 1937, but in 1938 the budget was nearly balanced. (That's fiscal year 1938, July 1 1937 to June 30 1938, which accounts for the timing difference).

Having nearly achieved a balanced budget, Roosevelt didn't want to give it up. He resisted added spending for relief and public works. But in the Spring Harry Hopkins and his staff produced a memo which described what was needed. Gross Domestic Product needed to be $88 billion to achieve full employment, the memo read. It was now $56 billion, $32 billion short. The memo said "if money invested or spent turns over two or three times a year, it would require between 7 and 10 billion dollars per year of additional investment or spending, public or private, to get reasonable full employment."

Hopkins was arguing for the *multiplier effect*. If the Federal government (or a private business) spends a thousand dollars on road construction, say, that thousand dollars became paychecks for workers and equipment suppliers. They would spend their new income on food and clothing and housing and appliances, causing each of these industries to increase production and employment. The incomes of *these* employees would rise, and they would spend more, too.

Roosevelt reluctantly agreed, government spending increased again, and in 1939 the budget deficit was back to 3.2% of GDP. Fiscal policy increased aggregate demand.

The Federal Reserve surveyed the scene in late 1936 and decided (somehow) that the threat of *inflation* was the economy's chief problem. Prices had been rising since 1933. The Fed took the opportunity to use a new policy tool that it had been granted by the 1935 banking bill: setting reserve requirements. Banks keep a fraction of their deposits in reserve so they can meet customer demands for withdrawals. The Fed now had the power to set a minimum percentage of deposits that had to be kept in reserve.

The percentage is called the *required reserve ratio*. If the Fed lowers the required reserve ratio, banks could lend more of their deposits. The money multiplier would increase, so would the money supply, interest rates would fall and investment would increase. If the Fed raises the required reserve ratio, banks must keep higher reserves. They'll have to lend less, the money multiplier would decrease, the money supply would decrease, interest rates would rise and investment would decrease.

The required reserve ratio is a Federal Reserve policy tool that fixes the minimum percentage of deposits that banks must hold in reserve.

Between August 1936 and May 1937, the Fed nearly doubled reserve requirements, from 13% of deposits to 25%. Banks had been holding excess reserves above the minimum required by the Fed. Banks did this probably because it had been only four years since the bank runs had ended, because they still had dim expectations about the ability of borrowers to repay, and because the demand for loans by businesses was still relatively small. The Fed thought that banks would not respond by increasing their reserves very much when the required ratio went up because many already held enough reserves to meet the new required ratio.

The Fed was wrong. Banks increased their reserves so they could continue to have an excess beyond the new higher requirements. They cut back their lending, and business investment fell. Marriner Eccles had gone along with the required reserve increase. But with the recession cutting the gains of the previous four years, he argued for rescinding the ratio increases, or at least using open market operations to buy a large quantity of bonds, to try to increase lending again. George Harrison, still at the New York Bank, argued against this, and he carried the day. Ironic, because the arguments he used were the same as had thwarted his own expansionary ideas back in 1930.

Unemployment Insurance

When Franklin Roosevelt was elected President in 1932, he asked Frances Perkins to head the Department of Labor. Perkins had worked as his industrial commissioner when he was Governor of New York, and she was a long-time activist on labor issues.

She told him she'd take the job if he would support her policy ideas. It was a long list. Prohibit child labor. Enact a minimum wage. Even upgrade the unemployment numbers produced by the Bureau of Labor Statistics. Maybe most important, she'd work for unemployment insurance and old age pensions. Roosevelt agreed with her goals. But he was an agreeable man, so she pressed him. "Are you sure you want these things done? Because you don't want me for Secretary of Labor if you don't," she said. He agreed to back her, and she took the job. She was the first woman cabinet secretary.

In June 1934 Perkins became chair of a group called the Committee on Economic Security. Unemployment was the nation's most immediate problem, so they spent much of their time debating unemployment insurance. The Labor Department's economists told them that, had unemployment insurance existed in 1929, "it would have had a most pronounced stabilizing effect at a very crucial time."

An unemployment insurance program collects taxes from businesses based on their employee payrolls, and pays benefits to people when they become unemployed. When unemployment increases, the unemployed apply for benefits, and transfer payments (R in the consumption function) increase. Business payrolls are smaller, so unemployment insurance taxes (T) decrease. When unemployment decreases, the reverse happens; transfers decline and taxes increase.

> *Unemployment insurance is an automatic fiscal stabilizer. When recessions occur, spending increases and taxes decline without the need for new legislation.*

The whole process works automatically. When a recession starts and unemployment rises, benefit payments go up because the unemployed themselves apply for benefits. Taxes go down because business payrolls are smaller. Unemployment insurance is an *automatic fiscal stabilizer*. It's an automatic form of counter-cyclical fiscal policy, in good times and bad.

It's "automatic" because no new act of Congress is required. No need for Congress to recognize a recession, debate and pass legislation, and only then cut taxes or start spending, perhaps too late. Taxes and benefits vary automatically with the number of employed and unemployed people. It's "fiscal" because it deals with the government's budget, taxing and spending. And it's a "stabilizer" because it adjusts aggregate demand to offset recession and inflation. With an automatic stabilizer such as unemployment insurance, the fluctuations in aggregate demand are smaller. Equilibrium output remains closer to potential. Recessions are milder, and inflation is less severe.

Social Security

Francis Townsend was a doctor who found himself unemployed at age 66 in 1933. On September 30, 1933 his local Long Beach newspaper published a letter he had written describing a plan to pay aged people a generous monthly pension, paid for with a kind of national sales tax. Within a few weeks an entire page of the newspaper every day was devoted to letters debating the *Townsend*

Plan. People would come by his house looking for further details. By the end of November the doctor decided to devote himself full time to his Plan. In just one year, by the fall of 1934, there were 5,000 Townsend clubs nationwide. Townsend coined the slogan "age for leisure, youth for work."

Under the Townsend Plan, people over 60 who agreed not to work would receive $200 a month, which they would be required to spend. That would increase consumption spending, Townshend explained. Benefits would be paid for by a 2% transaction tax, which was a tax on every sale, business to business or business to consumer.

Today we know that the Plan could not have worked. The added transfer payments would have increased consumption, but the added taxes would have discouraged almost as much spending as the pensions created. Aggregate demand would not have increased by much. Further, the pension of $200 per month was astoundingly generous. Prices have risen 17.9 times since 1934, so $200 then could buy what $3,580 bought in 2016. By comparison, the average monthly Social Security payment for a retiree in December 2016 was about $1,320. Townsend's promise (adjusted for inflation) is almost triple what we pay to retirees. Further, with 12 million Americans 60 years old or older in 1934, a monthly income of $200 would have meant annual pension payments of about $29 billion. Gross Domestic Product for the whole United States in 1934 was $66 billion, which meant that 44% of GDP would be funneled through this government program to make payments to 9% of the population. (To be fair, national income figures were not yet widely available. Townsend probably didn't know the size of U.S. GDP.)

The Townsend Plan was introduced in Congress in January 1935. Dr. Townsend himself came to Washington to testify. Both Democrats and Republicans subjected the doctor to relentless questioning until he admitted that he had no idea how much revenue his 2% transactions tax would raise.

Still, millions of people belonged to Townsend Clubs. Frances Perkins would write later that "one hardly realizes nowadays how strong was the sentiment in favor of the Townsend Plan . . . The pressure from its advocates was intense." We have to have old age pensions, Roosevelt told Perkins, "Congress can't stand the pressure of the Townsend Plan unless we have a real old-age insurance system."

President Roosevelt was adamant about one point: there must be a pension fund. People would pay into the fund while they were working, and draw on the fund once they retired. Funding payments to older people out of current revenues was welfare—the dole. "Mustn't have a dole," Roosevelt said, time and again. Perkins and relief administrator Harry Hopkins tried to point out the many problems with a pension fund scheme.

- Millions of retired people were in desperate need now, in 1934. They'd never paid into a fund, because there was no program while they were working.
- Building a reserve fund meant collecting taxes now, but paying benefits later. A tax hike in the midst of the Depression would cut consumer spending and make things worse.
- Then there was a technical problem. How would the reserve fund be invested? The fund would be enormous if everyone contributed. If the money was invested in stocks, like a

private pension, the government would soon own a large share of private industry. Frances Perkins' Department of Labor might own a majority interest in General Motors. A solution was to invest the fund only in the government's Treasury bonds. But there weren't enough Treasury bonds in existence for the fund to buy, once it got big.

Roosevelt would not be persuaded. The pension plan had to be based on worker contributions. "I guess you're right on the economics," he would say later, "but those taxes were never a problem of economics. They are politics all the way through. We put those payroll contributions there so as to give the contributors a legal, moral, and political right to collect their pensions and their unemployment benefits. With those taxes in there, no damn politician can ever scrap my social security program."

The bill was introduced in Congress in January 1935 by Senator Robert Wagner and Representative David Lewis, long-time supporters of social insurance. It included unemployment insurance, social security old-age pensions, and (for good measure) the first major Federal welfare program, known as Aid to Dependent Children. With reason, they called it *The Big Bill*.

The debate was fierce. Unemployment insurance would encourage people to loaf, its opponents said. Old-age pensions would keep them from saving. "Isn't this socialism?" demanded Senator Gore of Oklahoma. "Oh, no," Secretary Perkins replied. "Isn't this a teeny-weeny bit of socialism?" the Senator asked, sarcastically.

But the Big Bill was conservative compared to the Townsend Plan, and the public clearly wanted Congress to do something. It passed, and Roosevelt signed it on August 14, 1935.

Unemployment insurance taxes were first collected in 1936. By July 1937 every state had an unemployment insurance program. During World War II unemployment was very low, so few benefits were paid. Tax payments accumulated in the unemployment insurance funds. With the first post-war recession, in 1948-49, benefit payments surged and tax collections dropped. The program has performed this stabilizing role in every recession since.

> *The "Big Bill" containing unemployment insurance, Federal welfare and Social Security became law in 1935. In a sense, it marks the beginning of the U.S. social safety net, or the U.S. welfare state.*

- *How did Social Security become a "pay-as-you-go" program? Why did no trust fund accumulate for the first 40 years?*

Working people began paying social security taxes on January 1, 1937. Within months the Roosevelt recession began. So, before the first benefit check was cut, Social Security was reformed. The first payments were moved from 1942 to 1940. The first increase in the tax rate was postponed. Scheduled benefit payments were increased. Provision was made for widows and orphans to receive survivor's benefits. The reforms increased benefits and cut taxes to such a degree that the pension's reserve fund would not accumulate *at all*. A small contingency fund would be kept to insure prompt payment of benefits. Social security became a pure pay-as-you-go system after all, with the taxes collected from workers paid out almost immediately to current retirees.

Ida May Fuller from Ludlow, Vermont had worked most of her life as a legal secretary. She turned 65 in October, 1939, and while on an errand in Rutland she dropped by the government office to ask about Social Security benefits. She remembered "It wasn't that I expected anything, mind you, but I knew I'd been paying for something called Social Security and I wanted to ask the people in Rutland about it." She'd been paying into the system, of course, only since 1937. Her payments over those three years *totaled* $24.75.

> *Social Security was purely a "pay-as-you-go" system until the 1980's. Benefits to retirees were paid out of taxes from working people. No trust fund accumulated.*

She retired at the end of 1939, and one day during the first week of February 1940 she received Social Security benefit check 00-000-01, for $22.54. It wasn't a lot—she'd been earning about $75 a month at the law firm. It supplemented income she had from some stocks she owned and on an apartment she rented out (no pension from her employer, though). By the first week of March, 1940, when her second check arrived, Ms. Fuller had received more in benefits than she had paid in payroll taxes. Since she lived to be 100 years old, during her retirement she received many times the value of her tax payments.

This was possible because Social Security had become a *pay-as-you-go program*. Ms. Fuller was not paid out of a reserve fund with her name on it, built from the premiums she paid during her working years. That was impossible, because the program hadn't existed for most of her working years. Instead, her benefits came from the taxes paid by people working in 1940 and after. No reserve fund accumulated.

Social Security and the Baby Boom
The story of the first 40 years of Social Security was one of expansion. Benefits were increased to keep up with inflation. In 1972 Congress created an annual *cost of living adjustment (COLA)*. The automatic adjustments started in 1975, and since then each year benefits have increased automatically by the amount of inflation, as measured by the percentage increase in the Consumer Price Index.

For forty years the revenues collected each year from the payroll tax were enough to pay the benefits owed to retired people, disabled people and surviving families. But cracks in the system began to appear in the mid-1970s. It became evident that revenues would not cover promised benefits forever, and that the small reserve fund might not support benefit payments for much longer.

The problem resulted from the *baby boom*. For all of U.S. history fertility rates had fallen. Each successive generation of families had fewer children, on average. But in 1946 newly-returned soldiers made up for their years away and the number of births increased. This would have been an amusing historical footnote, except that the number of births kept increasing for the next decade, and remained above historic trends into the 1960's.

The explanation had to be more than just returning soldiers. The parents of the boomers were the children of the Depression. Perhaps the economy of the 1950s and 1960s so exceeded their expectations that they felt free to have larger families. Whatever the cause, though, the boom faded after 1964, succeeded by a "baby bust" or "birth dearth."

The baby boom threatens the Social Security program. The boomers began to retire in 2008. Kathleen Casey-Kirschling, known as the first boomer because she was born at one minute after midnight on January 1, 1946, applied for benefits on October 15, 2007.

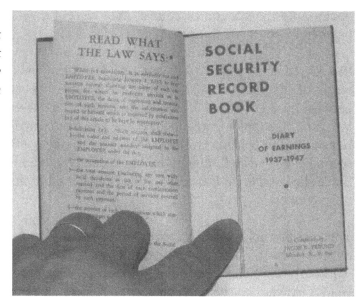

Now the government does it. A notebook printed in 1936 to be used to keep track of earnings for ten years. Social Security benefits were and are based in part on total earnings.

- *Why does the baby boom create problems for the Social Security system?*

By the second decade of the 21st century enormous numbers of new retirees will be owed benefits each year. Under the pay-as-you-go system, these benefits would be paid from the taxes of current workers. But these workers are the product of the birth dearth. There aren't very many of them. In 2016 there were 2.8 workers for every retiree; by the mid-2030's there would be only 2.1. There would not be enough payroll taxes from so few working people, at current tax rates, to pay benefits to all those boomer retirees, at current benefit levels.

The Reagan Administration took a stab at solving the problem in 1983. For the first time there would be a true Social Security pension fund. Tax rates were raised above the amount required to pay current benefits. The reserve fund began to grow in size. As of December 2016, it amounts to about $2.8 *trillion* dollars. That's a lot of money. It's not enough.

- *What is the Social Security trust fund?*

Just what is the *trust fund*? There is a filing cabinet in the Treasury Department's Bureau of the Public Debt in Parkersburg, West Virginia that contains $2.8 trillion in Treasury bonds in which the Social Security trust fund is invested. That's why it is often said that social security taxes are lent right back to the Federal government. The money can only be invested in Treasury bonds, which cover the government's spending beyond its revenues. The reason only Treasury bonds are allowed was understood way back in the 1930's. If $2.8 trillion was invested in stocks, the government would be a major owner of American industry. There's little support for an idea like that.

Payroll taxes fund most social security benefits, but now the tax revenue is falling short. The Social Security administration will cover this deficit and make the full benefit payments by drawing on the trust fund. They will open that filing cabinet in West Virginia and take out Treasury bonds and present them to the Treasury for repayment. The Treasury (and Congress and the President) will meet this obligation by either borrowing from the bond market, cutting other government spending, or raising taxes. Because of the bonds, the Treasury will have a legal and moral obligation to pay.

> *As a result of the baby boom, there will be more retirees than workers can support at current benefit levels and tax rates. The trust fund will cover the difference until 2036. After that, only three-quarters of benefits can be paid, unless a policy solution is found.*

But in 2034 the filing cabinet will be empty. The trust fund will be exhausted. With fewer workers supporting each beneficiary, current payroll taxes will support only three-quarters of promised benefits. Beneficiaries will have no legal claim on Treasury revenues without the Treasury bonds in the trust fund. The Social Security Administration may ask Congress and the President to continue to pay benefits, doing the same things they did when there was a trust fund: borrowing, cutting other spending, or raising taxes. But the "moral authority" of the trust fund bonds will be gone.

The Social Security trust fund, then, is the moral authority that the Social Security Administration has to demand that the shortfall in payroll tax revenues be covered out of the Federal budget.

Fiscal Policy in the Great Recession
The Great Recession began in December 2007. In response, Congress passed and President George W. Bush signed an income tax cut, which took effect in the Spring of 2008. Taxpayers received $600 per adult and $300 per child.

The effects of the tax cut faded in later summer 2008, then the financial crisis made the Great Recession worse in the Fall. In response, in February 2009, Congress passed and President Obama signed a stimulus bill worth $787 billion in added spending and tax cuts. The bill provided tax cuts to families and businesses, aid to state and local governments, and direct spending on "shovel ready" infrastructure projects. Separate bills extended unemployment insurance benefits.

The tax cut in 2008 and the stimulus bill in 2009 were efforts by the President and Congress to increase aggregate demand, and so increase output and employment. It was *discretionary counter-cyclical fiscal policy*. "Discretionary" because it required a special act of Congress. "Counter-cyclical" because it was intended to offset (or "counter") the decreases in spending that were causing the recession and slow recovery. "Fiscal" because that's the word we use to describe policy dealing with taxes and spending, the government's budget.

The intent of the tax cut was to increase consumer spending. Some people did exactly as expected and spent their refunds, which became income of businesses and their employees. The new income was in turn spent, and the effect of the tax cut multiplied through the economy. The income multiplier increased the effect of the tax cut on aggregate demand and output.

The equation for the multiplier is

$$1 / (1 - MPC)$$

where the MPC is the marginal propensity to consume ("b" in the equations above). The multiplier is bigger if the MPC is bigger. But suppose that people save their tax refunds, or use them to pay down debt, which are prudent things to do in a recession. Then the MPC for the added after-tax income will be smaller. That will make the multiplier smaller, and that means the tax cuts have a smaller effect on aggregate demand.

- *Did the tax rebate and the stimulus program help shorten the recession and strengthen the recovery?*

The Congressional Budget Office is the non-partisan research arm of the U.S. Congress. They reviewed the evidence on the effects of the 2008 tax cut in a June 2009 publication. Based on survey data of individual households, they found that consumers spent about 33 percent of their rebates during 2008. That would imply a multiplier of about 1.5
(= 1 / [1 - .33]).

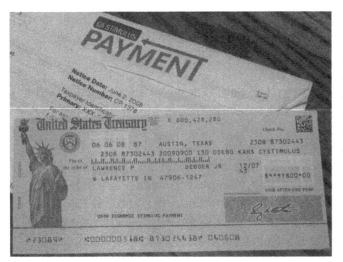

I Knew Those Kids Would Come in Handy. The author's 2008 stimulus payment, otherwise known as the tax rebate. That's $1,800: $600 for the author, $600 for the spouse, and $300 for each of two kids. We spent it more than once, though in the aggregate, the MPC can't be greater than one.

The total 2008 tax rebate was about $95 billion. With a multiplier of 1.5, it would have increased real GDP by $143 billion. That amounts to an additional one percent of GDP for 2008.

The government was trying to use tax cuts to increase spending during a recession. But when unemployment is rising people become cautious in their spending. The marginal propensity to consume shrinks and so does the income multiplier. One solution to this problem could be to give tax cuts to low income people. Households with low income or few assets tended to spend more of their rebates, and save less. Low income people tend to have higher marginal propensities to consume. They use the extra income for necessities.

In May 2011 the Congressional Budget Office estimated the effects of the American Recovery and Reinvestment Act (ARRA), the stimulus bill passed in February 2009. ARRA provided spending increases and tax cuts totaling $830 billion (a re-estimate from the original $787 billion). About 20 percent of the impact occurred in the first 6 months of the program, and another half took place in fiscal 2010 (October 2009 to September 2010). Most of the rest of the impact was effective by June 2011.

Its peak effect was in 2010, when half of the $830 billion in spending and tax cuts took place. That's $415 billion. CBO estimates that GDP was 1.5 percent to 4.2 percent higher as a result. Given the size of GDP, that amounts to $220 to $615 billion, which amounts to a multiplier between 0.5 to 1.5.

A look at the multiplier equation begs the question: how could the multiplier be less than one? If the marginal propensity to consume is zero, the multiplier equation produces one. It may be that government activity replaced some private activity, rather than adding to it. Federal spending on road construction, for example, may have diverted construction equipment from private sector uses. Federal construction may have replaced private construction.

We used this idea before, for potential output. Scarce resources limit the amount that output can increase. Of course, in 2010 equilibrium output was well below potential output, so there must have been unemployed resources that the government could employ. But did the unemployed resources match what the government wanted to buy? Perhaps factory workers were unemployed, while the government was looking for construction workers. Construction workers would then be pulled from private projects, while factory workers remained unemployed.

The CBO found that direct government spending appears to have the biggest bang for the buck. But as Hopkins and Ickes knew, it takes time to start spending on such projects, even if they are "shovel ready." One complaint about the 2009 stimulus bill was how long it took to get spending on roads and buildings started.

Increases in transfer payments—like unemployment insurance—also may provide a big bang. Lower income people spend most of what they receive in transfers. Their marginal propensities to consume are high. Tax cuts for upper income people are less likely to increase spending. Upper income people save more. Their MPC's are lower. Temporary tax cuts are less effective than permanent tax cuts. People are less likely to spend a windfall if they think it won't last.

The effects of ARRA were all but exhausted by mid-2011. CBO's estimated impact on GDP in 2011 is only half what it was in 2010. Output was still less than potential, but Congress and the President had moved on to discussions of cutting the Federal budget deficit. Additional stimulus was not provided.

Terms in this Chapter, in order of appearance
The New Deal
Liquidationists
Fiscal policy
After-tax income
Transfer payments
Government purchases
Treasury bonds
Deficit spending
John Maynard Keynes
The General Theory of Employment, Interest and Money
Consumption function
Disposable income
Marginal propensity to consume (MPC)
Autonomous consumption
Income multiplier
Budget balance
Counter-cyclical fiscal policy
Government budget surplus
Tax Increase of 1932
Pro-cyclical fiscal policy
Roosevelt recession
Multiplier effect
Required reserve ratio
Unemployment insurance
Automatic fiscal stabilizer
The Townsend Plan
Social Security
The Big Bill
Pay-as-you-go program
Cost of living adjustment (COLA)
Baby boom
Trust fund
Discretionary counter-cyclical fiscal policy

Notes
Eccles' memoir is a source for details on his career and his thinking, though supplemental sources like Kettl, Stein and Friedman and Schwartz are needed to temper some of Eccles' special pleading, especially on the recession of 1937-38. The story of the banking bill of 1935 is told by Eccles (pp. 200-229), Kettl (pp. 48-52), and Davis (pp. 537-541).

Lewis Douglas' laid out his ideas in a series of lectures at Harvard University in 1935, published in Douglas. The quote about the end of western civilization is in Kennedy (p. 143). Douglas' relationship with Roosevelt and his effect on policy are taken from Perkins (p. 270), Eccles (pp. 96-97, 133-34), and Schlesinger (pp. 10-11, 290-91).

The New Deal spending programs of Ickes and Hopkins are discussed in Kennedy and Davis. Hopkins' temporary CWA program is described by Davis (pp. 307-314) and Kennedy (175-76). Davis relates the story of signing the bill on Vincent Astor's yacht (p. 467). Information about Ickes' PWA is from Kennedy (p. 152, 178, 252). Hopkins' WPA is discussed in Kennedy (pp. 252-53). The bitter conflict between Ickes and Hopkins is in Davis (pp. 470-71), and it is he who says Ickes became paranoid and Hopkins developed an ulcer.

Kennedy (pp. 177-89, p. 328) tells the story of the NRA.

The story of Keynes' meeting with Roosevelt is told in Moggridge (p. 582), Perkins (pp. 225-226), Davis (pp. 319-21) and Stein (149-51). Perkins has the quotes from Keynes about Roosevelt and from Roosevelt about Keynes. Moggridge has another from Keynes. Keynes' 1933 letter to Roosevelt is in Keynes' *Collected Works*, volume 21, pp. 289-97 (Moggridge, editor). Stein (p. 162) gives the "young was very heaven" quote from Samuelson. It was originally written by the English poet Keats after he read Homer for the first time.

Sometimes old movies from 1933 and 1934 will still include the National Recovery Administration logo at the start or the end. The movie studios had a code too, pledging not to reduce theater ticket prices. Amaze your friends with this information!

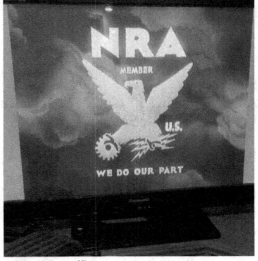

The monetary policies leading up to the recession of 1937-38 are discussed in Friedman and Schwartz (pp. 523-528). The fiscal policies are discussed in Stein (pp. 98-110). Keynes' discussion of the multiplier and the marginal propensity to consume are in the *General Theory*, pp. 113-131. That's a tough read, though.

Roosevelt's speeches and fireside chats are available on a website, the New Deal Network, at newdeal.feri.org (no "www").

The discussion Frances Perkins had with Roosevelt when she was appointed Secretary of Labor is described in her memoir (pp. 150-152) and in Martin (pp. 238-241).

Estimates on the accumulated reserve of an unemployment insurance program in the 1920's are from the Report of the Committee on Economic Security (1935), on the Social Security Administration's website. Perkins' comments on stabilization are from her memoir (p. 285). Davis has a good description of the arguments over unemployment insurance (pp. 450-51). Chimerine et. al. (1999) and U.S. Department of Labor (1986) discuss the history of unemployment insurance legislation and its stabilizing effect.

Perkins (pp. 282-85) and Kennedy (pp. 266-68) describe Hopkins' and Perkins' arguments with FDR over old age pension contributions. Schlesinger (pp. 308-09) is the original source for the "no damn politician" quote.

Holtzman (1963) describes the origins and details of the Townsend plan. Kennedy (pp. 224-25) and Davis (pp. 401-02) describe the Townsend movement. Dewitt (2001) provides a modern economic analysis of the Plan. Perkins' take on Townsend is in her memoir (pp. 278-79 and p. 294).

The debate on social security is described by Perkins (pp.298-299) and Schlesinger (pp. 311-312). Brown (1969) and Altmeyer (pp. 88-98) describe the amendments to Social Security in 1939.

Dewitt (1996) gives details about Ida May Fuller's tax payments and benefits.

The Congressional Budget Office (2001 and 2009) provides summaries of Social Security's features and problems.

The 1977 and 1983 Social Security reforms are detailed in Kollman. The annual Social Security Trustees report gives the accounting view of the problem. It's on the web (www.ssa.gov/OACT/TR/.

Sources
Altmeyer, Arthur J. 1966. *The Formative Years of Social Security.* Madison, Wisconsin: The University of Wisconsin Press.

Bender, Ray. 1955. "Our First Claimant," *Oasis* 7.

Brown, J. Douglas. 1969. "The Genesis of Social Security in America." Princeton, New Jersey: Princeton University Industrial Relations Section. Available on the Social Security Administration website, www.ssa.gov/history/jdb5.html.

Chimerine, Lawrence, Theodore S. Black and Lester Coffey. 1999. "Unemployment Insurance as an Automatic Stabilizer: Evidence of Effectiveness Over Three Decades." Unemployment Insurance Occasional Paper 99-8. Washington, D.C.: US. Department of Labor, Employment and Training Administration.

Congressional Budget Office. 2001. *Social Security: A Primer.* Washington D.C.: U.S. Government Printing Office.

Congressional Budget Office. 2010. *Did the 2008 Tax Rebates Stimulate Short-Term Growth?* Washington D.C.: U.S. Government Printing Office.

Congressional Budget Office. 2011. *Estimated Impact of the American Recovery and Reinvestment Act on Employment and Economic Output from January 2011 Through March 2011.* Washington D.C.: U.S. Government Printing Office.

Congressional Budget Office. 2014. *CBO's 2014 Long-Term Projections for Social Security: Additional Information.* Washington D.C.: U.S. Government Printing Office.

Davis, Kenneth S. 1986. *FDR: The New Deal Years, 1933-37, A History.* New York: Random House.

DeWitt, Larry. 1996. *Details of Ida May Fuller's Payroll Tax Contributions.* Research Note 3, Social Security Administration website, www.ssa.gov/history/idapayroll.html.

Dewitt, Larry. 2001. *The Townsend Plan's Pension Scheme.* Research Note 17, Social Security Administration website, www.ssa.gov/history/townsendproblems.html.

Douglas, Lewis W. 1935. *The Liberal Tradition.* New York: D. Van Norstrand Co., Inc.

Eccles, Marriner S. 1951. *Beckoning Frontiers: Public and Personal Recollections.* New York: Alfred A. Knopf.

Friedman, Milton and Anna Jacobson Schwartz. 1963. *A Monetary History of the United States, 1867-1960.* Princeton, New Jersey: Princeton University Press.

Holtzman, Abraham. 1963. *The Townsend Movement: A Political Study.* New York: Bookman Associates.

Kennedy, David M. 1999. *Freedom From Fear: The American People in Depression and War, 1929-1945.* New York: Oxford University Press.

Kettl, Donald F. 1986. *Leadership at the Fed.* New Haven: Yale University Press.

Keynes, John Maynard. 1936. *The General Theory of Employment, Interest and Money.* New York: Harcourt, Brace, Jovanovich.

Keynes, John Maynard. 1971. *The Collected Writings of John Maynard Keynes. Volume 21, Activities 1931-39.* Donald Moggridge, editor. Cambridge, U.K.: MacMillan and Cambridge University Press.

Kollman, Geoffrey. 1996. "Summary of Major Changes in the Social Security Cash Benefits Program: 1935-1996." CRS Report to Congress 94-35 EPW. Washington, D.C.: Congressional Research Service, The Library of Congress.

Martin, George. 1976. *Madam Secretary: Frances Perkins.* Boston: Houghton Mifflin Company.

Moggridge, Donald E. 1992. *Maynard Keynes, an Economist's Biography.* London: Routledge.

Perkins, Frances. 1946. *The Roosevelt I Knew.* New York: Viking Press.

Schlesinger, Arthur M., Jr. 1958. *The Coming of the New Deal.* Boston: Houghton Mifflin.

Slemrod, Joel and Mathew D. Shapiro. "Did the 2008 Tax Rebates Stimulate Spending?" NBER Working Paper No. 14753, February 2009.

Social Security Administration. *The 2013 Annual Report of the Boar of Trustees of the Federal Old-Age and Survivors Insurance and Federal Disability Insurance Trust Funds.* May 2009. Website: www.ssa.gov/OACT/TR/.

Stein, Herbert. 1996. *The Fiscal Revolution in America (2nd Revised Edition).* Washington, D.C.: The AEI Press.

United States Department of Labor. 1986. "Fifty Years of Unemployment Insurance—A Legislative History: 1935-1985." Unemployment Insurance Occasional Paper 86-5. Washington, D.C.: U.S. Department of Labor, Employment and Training Administration.

News Articles
Goodman, Peter S. "Consumers Lean on Rebate Checks for Bills and Gas," *New York Times,* June 1, 2008.

Kornblut, Anne E. "Bush Renews Focus on His Plan for Revamping Social Security," *New York Times*, April 6, 2005.

Social Security Administration. "Nation's First Baby Boomer Files for
Social Security Retirement Benefits -- Online!" *Social Security News Release*, October 15, 2007.

Chapter 7
War and Inflation

We've seen the Panic of 1907, the recession of 1920-21, the Great Depression and finally the Roosevelt recession within the Great Depression. For forty years the United States grappled with the problem of recession and depression. But with the end of the Great Depression the United States' policy problem changed. While recessions are still a concern, inflation has become an equally important problem in the years since 1940.

Recession and Inflation
How sharp was the change in the policy problem facing the United States starting in the 1940's? The table in Figure 7-1 shows one answer. The table shows the number of recession months and inflation rates by decade, from the 1880's to the 2000's. Recession months are measured by the National Bureau of Economic Research business cycle dates. The months from peak to trough are recessions. There are 120 months in each decade, of course. The inflation rate is the average yearly rate in the all-items consumer price index, or estimates before 1913.

From the 1880's to the 1930's the average decade saw 51 months of recession. There was very little variation in this number. The best decade was the 1900's, with 48 months, and the worst was the 1910's, with 54 months. This disguises the depths of the downturns—the 1890's and 1930's saw the worst depressions—but the economy was in recession more than four years in every ten during these six decades.

Inflation was not often a problem. Inflation averaged 0.7% per year for sixty years. Deflation troubled the economy in the 1880's, 1890's and 1930's. Inflation was mild in the 1900's and prices were stable in the 1920's. Only the 1910's saw inflation, because of the four years of double digit inflation during and after World War I. The consumer price level was only 36% higher in 1939 than it was in 1880, and that was entirely due to World War I. Without those four war inflation years, the average inflation rate rounds to 0.0%. That's price stability. Except for World War I, prices in 1939 were the same as in 1880.

The story changes in 1940 and after. Starting with the 1940's the average decade had only 19 months of recession—about a year and a half out of ten. The 1960's and 1990's had less than a year of recession. The worst decades were 1970's and 2000's with 27 and 26 months of recession, respectively. That was just a bit more than half the average number of recession months before 1940.

But now inflation was a problem. Inflation averaged 4.0% per year from 1940 to 2009. The 1970's saw the most inflation of the whole 130 year period, 7.1%. (And the 1970's had more recession months than any other post-1940 decade. A nasty ten years, they were.) During the 1950's, 1990's and 2000's inflation was not as much of a problem. Those decades still saw higher inflation than any pre-1940 decade, aside from World War I.

Decade	Number of Recession Months	Average CPI Inflation Rate
1880s	51	-0.8%
1890s	51	-1.0%
1900s	48	0.9%
1910s	54	6.9%
1920s	49	0.1%
1930s	52	-1.7%
1940s	19	5.6%
1950s	18	2.1%
1960s	10	2.3%
1970s	27	7.1%
1980s	22	5.6%
1990s	8	3.0%
2000s	26	2.6%
Average Decades		
1880s-1930s	51	0.7%
1940s-2000s	19	4.0%

Figure 7-1. Number of months of recession and average CPI all-items inflation rates, by decade, 1880-2009. The number of recession months are measured by the NBER peak and trough business cycle dates. There are 120 months in each decade, of course. The inflation rates are simple averages of the all-items inflation rates for each year in the decade. Decades are defined by the first three digits of the year, for example, the 1880s are 1880 to 1889.

The consumer price index was 1,433% higher in 2009 than it was in 1940. That's a percentage that needs some explaining. Prices increased about 15-fold. What cost a dollar in 1940 cost $15.33 in 2009. What cost a dollar in 2009 cost about 7 cents in 1940. Pennies meant something back then!

- *Why have recessions been less frequent and inflation higher since 1940?*

We know some answers already. First, until 1933 the United States was on the *gold standard*. Gold limited the amount of money that could be created. Even after the creation of the Federal Reserve in 1913, gold put a ceiling on the amount of Federal Reserve notes. Without too much money chasing too few goods, sustained inflation cannot happen.

Sometimes the gold standard required governments to adopt pro-cyclical policies. When the money supply approached its gold standard ceiling in 1920, the Fed sharply increased interest rates, causing the recession of 1920-21. When Britain left gold in 1931 and the U.S. faced a gold drain, the Fed increased interest rates and held them high for two years, making the Great Depression worse (more on that in Chapter 8).

Without the gold standard, the Federal Reserve has no limit on money creation, and a greater scope for countercyclical policy. The result is more inflation and fewer recessions.

A second change was in fiscal policy, particularly the *automatic fiscal stabilizers*. The Social Security program created a group of income recipients who are immune to the ups and downs of the economy. Recessions come along, and social security recipients keep on spending. The unemployment insurance program automatically cuts taxes and increases benefits when recessions hit. Deposit insurance prevents bank runs, which supports bank lending. All three forms of insurance—old age, unemployment, bank deposits—support aggregate demand during recessions.

But these income supports added to inflation, too. As we'll see, these supports to incomes gave people the ability to resist the wage cuts that usually took place in recessions prior to 1940. Prices were less likely to fall without the drop in business costs.

World War II

It was Columbus Day, 1942. The United States had been officially at war for more than ten months. President Franklin Roosevelt had just completed a tour of the Midwest and West Coast, visiting defense plants and military bases. He reported what he saw to his radio audience in another of his fireside chats.

"The main thing that I observed on this trip is not exactly news," he said. "It is the plain fact that the American people are united as never before in their determination to do a job and to do it well."

The United States had just begun to mobilize, he continued.

> Germany and Japan are already realizing what the inevitable result will be when the total strength of the United Nations [the name used for the U.S. and its allies] hits them. . . . In the last war, I had seen great factories; but until I saw some of the new present-day plants, I had not thoroughly visualized our American war effort.

The war effort was enormous. Fifteen million men and hundreds of thousands of women entered the armed forces, and three-quarters were sent overseas. All of these soldiers had to be paid and equipped. More than that, the United States supplied a large amount of the equipment used by Great Britain and the Soviet Union in their struggle with Germany and Japan. British convoys across the Atlantic used American-made ships. Russian soldiers defended Stalingrad in American-made boots.

Federal government spending increased ten-fold during World War II. The unemployment rate dropped to its lowest level ever, 1.2% in 1944. The Great Depression was over.

Hitler had invaded France in 1940 with an army of 2,500 tanks, supported by 3,000 aircraft. By the end of the war the United States had produced 102,000 tanks and 296,000 aircraft, as well as 88,000 warships and almost 2.5 million trucks.

All of these soldiers and all of this equipment had to be paid for. Federal spending increased from seven billion dollars in 1938 to seventy billion dollars in 1945. During World War II the United States government spent more than it had spent during the entire period from 1789 to 1940.

It was the greatest expansionary spending program in history, and it ended the Great Depression. Unemployed factories reopened to produce for federal contracts. Employers hired unemployed workers to build the weapons of war. The unemployment rate had been 11.3% in 1939. By 1944 it was 1.2%, the lowest rate of the twentieth century.

Here's the data; let's apply the model. The United States declared war on Japan on December 8, 1941, the day after the Pearl Harbor attack. War was declared on Germany on December 11. But the U.S. had been actively aiding Great Britain since 1939. Exports of war material to Great Britain had been growing.

The unemployment rate still well above 5% in 1940, the 11th straight year that output had been less than potential. (Think of all the added goods and services that could have been produced!) Real GDP grew extraordinarily fast during the whole period 1940 to 1944. The unemployment rate fell to the lowest level ever recorded in 1944, so output was well above potential. Inflation topped 10% in 1942, but was lower in 1943 and 1944. This differs from what happened in World War I, when inflation increased and stayed high.

World War II

Year	Real GDP Growth	CPI Inflation	Unemploy-ment Rate	Interest Rate Spread	Gov't Budget Balance (% GDP)
1940	7.7%	0.7%	9.5%	1.9%	-2.8%
1941	18.2%	5.0%	6.0%	1.6%	-3.8%
1942	19.9%	10.9%	3.1%	1.5%	-12.4%
1943	19.8%	6.1%	1.8%	1.2%	-26.9%
1944	8.4%	1.7%	1.2%	0.9%	-21.2%

Still, rising output and rising prices mean that aggregate demand must have increased. Output moved from less than potential to more than potential. The enormous budget deficits in 1942-44 show why. Government purchases increased, but taxes did not rise as much. This added spending increased aggregate demand.

For this war, we've got the data for our BAA-AAA corporate interest rate spread, and it fell steadily during the World War II years. Money demand must have been rising rapidly with income growth and inflation, so money supply must have increased even more to hold interest rates down. The goods and money market diagrams are shown in Figure 7-2.

The model explains the data But there are some questions here. Why did the inflation rate fall in 1943 and 1944? In World War I, the inflation rate stayed well above double-digits during the war. How did the interest rate spread remain so low in the face of rising money demand? If the money supply increased to hold down interest rates, why did it not increase inflation? Output remained above potential for three straight years, 1942-44. Why didn't rising input costs decrease aggregate supply, raising prices and decreasing output?

We'll just have to look to the story to find out.

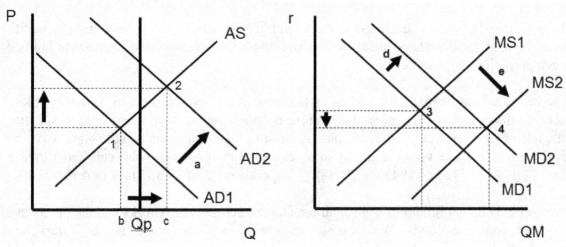

Figure 7-2. World War II. In the goods market, output is less than potential in 1940 (1, b). Government purchases rise, increasing aggregate demand (a). Output grows and prices rise (1 to 2). Unemployment falls below 5%, so output is above potential (c). In the money market, rising incomes and prices must have increased money demand (d). Since the interest rate spread fell from 1940 to 1944, money supply must have increased more (e). The real interest rate fell (3 to 4).

Battling Wartime Inflation

In his fireside chat Roosevelt mentioned "the serious problem of the rising cost of living." Like most wars, World War II threatened to create inflation. It was exactly the opposite problem from Depression. In Depression there was little spending, so factories cut back production, laid off workers, and cut wages and prices. Now, there was a lot of spending. Factories ran round the clock and hired all available workers, and still couldn't produce enough. They bid up wages and invented new benefits, trying to attract workers from other places or industries. They paid for wage increases with higher prices—but prices didn't rise as much as expected.

- *What policies were used to hold down inflation during World War II?*

An expanded labor supply could counter inflation. "I was impressed by the large proportion of women employed," Roosevelt said in his radio chat, "Doing skilled manual labor running machines. As time goes on, and many more of our men enter the armed forces, this proportion of women will increase." Women's labor force participation—the percentage of women old enough to work who were working for pay or looking for paid work—increased from 27% in 1940 to 35% in 1944. Five million women entered the labor force. Partly it was the attraction of a paycheck after a decade of depression. Partly it was a patriotic desire to help with the war effort. Partly it was the encouragement of the War Production Coordinating Committee's "Rosie the Riveter" campaign. Can women do the job? "We Can Do It," said the famous poster.

Defense jobs were opened to African American workers. Under pressure from civil rights leaders (and his wife Eleanor), Roosevelt issued Executive Order 8802 on June 25, 1941, which said

"There shall be no discrimination in the employment of workers in defense industries or government because of race, creed, color or national origin." In his radio chat he said

> In some communities, employers dislike to employ women. In others they are reluctant to hire Negroes. In still others, older men are not wanted. We can no longer afford to indulge such prejudices or practices.

In part the increased employment of women and African Americans countered inflation. More goods were available to buy because so many more people were working to produce them. But mostly the added workers were in defense plants, building planes and tanks and ships. Civilian production did not increase very much. In some cases entire industries were converted to war production. Between 1942 and 1945 the Chrysler Corporation made 25,507 tanks—and no cars.

Higher taxes could counter inflation. Take a larger share of people's paychecks and they will have less to spend on consumer goods. With less spending prices wouldn't rise as much. Taxes were increased. In 1939 a family with a $5,000 income paid $48 in income taxes. In 1944 they paid $755. And the taxes were now withheld from paychecks. Before, taxpayers had to send the government a check at the end of the year. Now, the government withheld the taxes during the year, and sent the taxpayer a check at the end of the year if a refund was due. That encouraged tax compliance a lot. Still, the government did not have the nerve to raise taxes enough to pay for all the added spending. Tax revenue rose seven times, but spending rose ten times. The Federal budget deficit reached 26.9% of Gross Domestic Product in 1944.

War bond drives could counter inflation. Bonds were sold directly to the public, with campaigns that featured Hollywood stars and war heroes. If people lent their money to the government by buying bonds, they would be saving more and spending less. The marginal propensity to consume (MPC) in the consumption function would be smaller. Saving did go up. Americans saved about a quarter of their after-tax incomes during the war. Part of this was due to war bonds, but much was due to the fact that there was very little to buy. There were no cars or refrigerators to be had, so people saved their money. Maybe they could buy when the war was over.

Buy war bonds and stamps for victory. The matchbox could have added: And to hold down inflation.

Price controls place legal ceilings on the prices of products. Higher incomes increased demand, which created shortages. Goods in short supply were rationed.

Finally, the government resorted to price controls. Each controlled product had a ceiling price, and it was illegal to charge more. The Office of Price Administration (OPA) enforced the controls. This kept inflation low, but it created new problems. So many people had so much new income that everything available could be sold at the controlled prices and still people would want to buy more. The result was shortages of price-controlled goods. Gasoline, tires, meat, sugar, butter, cigarettes and many other goods were in short supply.

They weren't going to be available for the duration. Shortages could be more than inconvenient. How could Rosie the Riveter go to work if she had to wait in line at the grocers to get food for her kids? What if doctors couldn't make emergency house calls because they weren't first in line for gasoline?

The answer to shortages was rationing. Every product now had two prices—one in money, and one in ration stamps. Both were needed to buy a rationed product. Money was earned on the job, and there was more than enough money around. Ration stamps were distributed to everyone by the OPA, and they were kept scarce. Auto owners with "A cards" in their windows could buy three gallons of gasoline a week (doctors got more). Controls kept the price of gasoline down. Lots of auto owners had the money to buy as much as they wanted at the controlled price—but three gallons was all they were allowed.

Wartime inflation was countered by employing more labor to increase the supply of goods, by imposing higher taxes, which reduced disposable income available for spending, with war bond drives, which increased saving and decreased spending, and with price controls and rationing.

All these efforts held down inflation, but the price controls were especially effective. From 1942 to 1945 inflation averaged only 3.4% per year. In a sense, though, inflation happened; it just took other forms. Goods were sold on the black market at illegal high prices to people without enough ration stamps. Businesses would make second-rate goods to hold their costs down and earn more profit under the controlled price. And in a sense, a good that is unavailable has an infinite price—it can't be bought for any money. None of this was recorded in price indexes.

So let's modify the goods market analysis in Figure 7-2, to answer the questions at the start of this section. Recall the consumption function,

$$C = A + b (Y - T + R).$$

Mr. Ernsberger's War Ration book. To buy rationed goods, he needed money and ration stamps. By ration book number four, the back of the book had a warning: "Never buy rationed goods without ration stamps. Never pay more than the legal price." Come on people, don't buy on the black market!

Taxes (T) increased, and income tax withholding was introduced. That reduced disposable income. War bond drives and the lack of consumer goods decreased the marginal propensity to consume (b). With less disposable income and less consumption out of income, consumption spending (C) was lower than it would have been. The increase in aggregate demand was reduced.

Wages and benefits were bid up and businesses searched for workers. But women and African Americans were added to the labor force, so more workers were available. This increased potential output and aggregate supply, which held down inflation. Input cost increases were smaller, so aggregate supply did not decrease as much. That explains the absence of second shift #1.

Finally, inflation was illegal. Businesses were not allowed to increase prices on many consumer goods. Figure 7-3 modifies the goods market to take account of the story.

The Fed in the War
What about the Federal Reserve? Inflation can be controlled if the Fed had kept the money supply growing slowly. The big demand for funds by the government would have increased interest rates and cut back business and consumer spending. When inflation is the problem, raising interest rates is the counter-cyclical monetary policy.

- *Why didn't the Federal Reserve use monetary policy to control inflation?*

The Treasury was trying to sell lots of bonds, to borrow lots of money, competing with other borrowers for the money that banks had to lend. Borrowers would bid interest rates higher. The Treasury feared that higher interest rates would raise the cost of borrowing, and so raise the cost

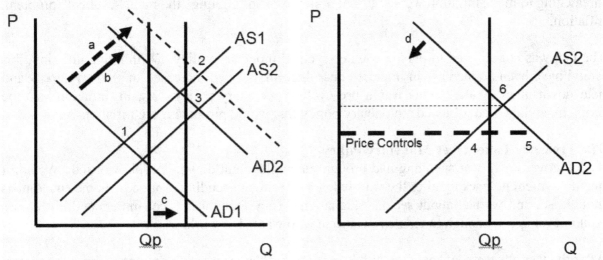

Figure 7-3. World War II inflation. The huge wartime increase in government purchases increases aggregate demand a lot (a), ending the Depression (1, less than Qp), but creating inflation, at (2). Taxes and bond drives reduce disposable income and the MPC, so aggregate demand does not rise as much as it could have (b). Added female labor force participation and less discrimination against African Americans increased aggregate supply (AS2) and potential output (c), which also holds inflation down (3). Equilibrium output is not so far beyond newly higher potential, so second shift #1 is a lesser problem. Price controls complete the wartime anti-inflation drive (shown on the second diagram). At the below-equilibrium price level, output demanded (5) exceeds output supplied (4), a shortage. Rationing is used to divvy up the short supply among consumers. When the controls are dropped at the end of the war, prices jump (6). Pent-up consumer demand keeps aggregate demand from falling (d doesn't happen) with the fall in government purchases.

of the war. They feared that if they offered their Treasury bonds at lower interest rates, they would not sell. Not enough money would be raised for the war effort.

So the Treasury demanded that the Fed hold interest rates down. If interest rates began to rise, the Fed would buy Treasury's bonds. The Fed would create this money, so the money supply would rise. Interest rates would fall back to fixed levels. Often the Fed would buy the bonds directly from the Treasury, in effect financing the war with newly printed dollars. This meant, though, that the Fed was not allowed to raise interest rates to combat inflation. Counter-cyclical monetary policy was set aside for the duration of the war. The money supply increased, even as inflation became a problem (as in Figure 7-2).

- *What were the fiscal and monetary policies used during World War II?*

Output was below potential in 1940, and unemployment was the problem. That means increased government purchases were a counter-cyclical fiscal policy. Spending increased aggregate demand, and equilibrium output reached potential, probably by the end of 1941. After that, added government purchases became a pro-cyclical fiscal policy. Output was above potential and inflation was the problem. Bigger budget deficits added even more to aggregate demand, threatening to make inflation worse. Fiscal policy was "promoting" the main "cyclical" problem, inflation.

The Fed was not allowed to pursue counter-cyclical monetary policy. With rising inflation, this would have been an increase in interest rates. Instead, the Fed increased the money supply and held down interest rates. This was a pro-cyclical monetary policy. Again, inflation was the problem, and the Fed followed a monetary policy that would promote more inflation.

The Treasury Takes Over Monetary Policy

Added government war spending had brought unemployment down. People worried: wouldn't unemployment go back up after the war, when government spending dropped? Some economists thought so, and warned about secular stagnation. They thought that consumers and businesses could never spend enough to employ everyone who wanted to work.

After the war government spending did drop, a lot, but the Depression did not return. Consumers and businesses took up the slack. Many people had been unable to buy consumer goods during the Depression, and consumer goods had been unavailable in the war years. During the war people had saved a big share of their incomes. Economists called it pent-up demand, and now, in 1946, this demand was released. Consumers used their savings to buy the consumer goods they'd been denied so long. Businesses saw their opportunity and converted war plants or invested in new factories to produce these goods.

There was no deep recession with the war's end, as there had been after World War I. Real GDP dropped a lot. The unemployment rate increased, but only to 4.4% in 1947, closer to the 5% rate consistent with potential output. Output dropped back near potential. Inflation increased, averaging more than 10% per year from 1946 to 1948. Congress let the price controls expire all at once in 1945, and prices shot up.

Marriner Eccles was still the chairman of the Federal Reserve. Eccles had signed on with the Roosevelt administration to make sure that monetary policy was consistent with New Deal deficit spending. That meant expanding the money supply so rising interest rates wouldn't choke off recovery.

Now things had changed. Roosevelt was dead, and Eccles had trouble establishing a relationship with the new President, Harry Truman. Perhaps the problem was the unpleasant advice Eccles had to offer. Depression wasn't the problem anymore. Inflation was. Eccles recommended to the President a fiscal policy of higher taxes, less government spending, budget surpluses, and a continuation of price controls. Truman didn't like it.

Eccles also wanted to raise interest rates, but here he had a problem. The new Treasury Secretary, John Snyder, insisted that interest rates remain fixed. The huge budget deficits during the war had been paid for by borrowing. The Treasury borrowed by selling bonds to investors. The sum total of those bonds was the amount the Treasury owed to investors, known as the national debt. The national debt was now enormous, measured at more than 100% of GDP. Some of the bonds were short term, which meant the Treasury had to pay back the bondholders in a few months or a few years. The Treasury did this by borrowing more from other investors, which was called refinancing or rolling over the debt.

So, every year the Treasury had to borrow billions in the bond market to refinance the part of the national debt that came due. Treasury Secretary Snyder demanded that Eccles's Federal Reserve fix interest rates low to keep borrowing costs low. And he demanded that the Fed buy any bonds that the Treasury couldn't sell to private investors at the low interest rates the bonds offered.

Eccles chafed under these demands. The money supply needed to contract and interest rates needed to rise to fight inflation, he thought. The Treasury treated the Fed as if its sole responsibility was to assure a stable market for Treasury bonds, at interest rates of the Treasury's choosing. The Fed's mission was much bigger than that, Eccles thought. It should be using monetary policy to stabilize the economy, fighting recession with low interest rates and fighting inflation with high rates. It should be using counter-cyclical monetary policy.

The Federal Reserve had been created to be an independent agency. The Fed had to match money demand with the money supply that would fix the equilibrium interest rate at the rate chosen by the Treasury. In effect, the Treasury controlled the quantity of money, not the Fed (see Figure 7-4).

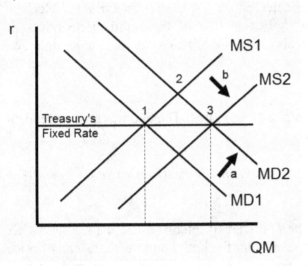

Figure 7-4. The Treasury controls monetary policy. The Treasury sets a fixed real interest rate (1). Inflation increases money demand (a), which would increase the interest rate (2). The Treasury requires the Fed to buy bonds, increasing the money supply (b). The fixed rate is restored (3), but the quantity of money has increased (1 to 3). By setting the fixed rate, the Treasury has required the Fed to set a particular quantity of money. The Treasury effectively controls monetary policy.

At the core of this argument was the question of who should make monetary policy. The Federal Reserve was created as an independent agency so it could make policy decisions free from politics. Eccles accused the Treasury, and the executive branch of government, of having a "chronic bias for cheap money in all seasons." Leave it to the politicians, his thinking went, and low interest rates would create so much spending that inflation would rise and rise. Treasury Secretary Snyder found this offensive. The promotion of economic stability, he said, "cannot be carried out by an agency such as the Federal Reserve, which has no responsibility to the electorate. . . ." The nation's elected leaders should judge what was in the overall interest of the economy.

Supporters of an independent Fed pointed out that elected officials are subject to the voters. Many more voters are borrowers than are lenders. Borrowers prefer lower interest rates, and since they vote in large numbers, elected officials prefer low interest rates, too. Left to elected officials, interest rates would be too low, and that would create inflation. Critics of the Fed responded by pointing out that the Fed is the banker's bank. Banks are lenders, and lenders prefer higher interest rates. They make more profits that way. If Fed policy is "captured" by bankers, the Fed will keep interest rates too high. Elected officials should have a say in the Fed's policies.

President Truman found Marriner Eccles annoying. The man pushed too hard for an anti-inflation

> **During and after World War II, the Treasury set interest rates on Treasury bonds and expected the Federal Reserve to guarantee that the bonds would sell at those rates. In effect, the Treasury controlled monetary policy.**

fiscal policy, Truman thought, and his stand on interest rates threatened the stability of the bond market. So, in January 1948, Truman refused to reappoint Eccles as chairman of the Fed. When Eccles asked why, Truman said the reasons were best known to himself alone. Eccles's term on the Federal Reserve Board would continue for several more years, so Truman offered to appoint him as vice-chairman. Eccles accepted, and then waited for months for Truman to act. The appointment never came. Eccles finally withdrew his name from consideration.

The new chairman was Thomas McCabe, who had been head of the Philadelphia Federal Reserve bank. McCabe was a more conciliatory man than Eccles, so it must have been a trial for McCabe to have Eccles still on the Reserve board. With Eccles free of the political restraints of chairmanship, he became even more outspoken about ending fixed rates and regaining Fed independence.

The Fed vs. the Treasury
There was actually no legal reason for the Fed to maintain fixed rates. The Fed was an independent agency and could have increased rates at any time.

- *Why didn't the Fed make monetary policy independently of the Treasury after World War II?*

First, throughout most of the 1946-1950 period, the Fed wanted interest rates just a little higher than the Treasury's fixed rates. Inflation had moderated after the initial burst with the end of price controls. The Federal budget was in surplus, and Truman had actually asked Congress for new price controls (he was refused). There was no sharp difference of opinion with the Treasury.

Second, in 1949 the economy entered a mild recession. Now the Fed needed to reduce interest rates, and the Treasury thought that was fine. Fixed rates, it turned out, meant a ceiling on rates, not a floor. The Treasury didn't mind if refinancing the national debt cost less.

Third, and perhaps most important, was the power of the President. In Washington one bucks the President at one's peril, as Eccles found out. Eccles told McCabe what would likely happen if the Fed tried to raise interest rates without the Treasury's consent. The Treasury, Eccles said, "would no doubt take the issue directly to the President who, in turn, would take it to the Congress if the Open Market Committee remained adamant. There can hardly be any doubt as to what the result might be." The Fed was a creature of the Congress. The President would try to get Congress to change the rules, to make the Fed toe the line.

Eccles liked to tell a joke: A central banker in another country was asked if his bank had the right to defy the government. He replied "Yes, we value that right very greatly and wouldn't think of exercising it." Eccles said that it was not the Fed's place to "enforce its will." He hoped Congress would lend a hand.

Paul Douglas had been elected Senator from Illinois in 1948. He was an economist from the University Chicago, and his work as an economist is still remembered today (ask any economics graduate student about the "Cobb-Douglas" production function, an equation that describes how businesses combine labor and machinery to produce output). In December 1949 Douglas's subcommittee on monetary policy began hearings into the Federal Reserve-Treasury conflict, and the desirability for an independent monetary policy. Snyder, McCabe, and Eccles were called to testify.

Snyder and McCabe denied that there was any conflict. No one likes to air their dirty laundry in public. But the Senator got an earful from Eccles. The Treasury ignores the Fed's advice, Eccles declared. "Decisions are apparently made by the Treasury largely on the basis of a general desire to get money as cheaply as possible." Fixed rates meant the Fed had no control over the money supply.

Senator Douglas's subcommittee report favored Fed independence. It said, "The freedom of the Federal Reserve to restrict credit and raise interest rates for general stabilization purposes should be restored even if the cost should prove to be a significant increase in service charges on the Federal debt and a greater inconvenience to the Treasury."

Douglas was a junior Senator; he had been in office for only a year. Yet his opinion carried weight. Knowledge is power in any group. Support for the Fed grew in the Congress. Perhaps, Eccles thought, there was enough support in the Congress to overcome the Treasury's demands for fixed rates.

The Accord
President Truman had just arrived at his home in Independence, Missouri, for his first visit since Christmas. June 24, 1950, was hot and humid, as if summer had turned itself on with the calendar. The phone rang at 9:20 p.m.. It was Secretary of State Dean Acheson. "Mr. President, I have very serious news," he said. "The North Koreans have invaded South Korea."

The Cold War was on. Mao Zedong's communists had taken over China. Joseph Stalin's Soviet Union had detonated an atomic bomb, ending the American monopoly on nuclear weapons. North Korea was communist, with a large army equipped by the Soviet Union. South Korea was allied with the U.S., without much of an army at all. Truman flew back to Washington the next day and, stepping into his limousine at National Airport, told his defense secretary "By God, I am going to let them have it."

The Treasury expected budget deficits. The U.S. army had been demobilized after World War II. The army was actually smaller in mid-1950 than it had been on Pearl Harbor day. To fight in Korea, military spending would have to increase. Deficits would be financed by borrowing. Bond issues would now be needed to support national defense, not just for national debt refinancing. The Treasury needed a stable bond market with low interest rates, and it needed the Federal Reserve to buy the bonds that investors would not.

To the Federal Reserve, though, the war meant one thing: inflation. The money supply would expand if the Fed was forced to buy bonds. That would be a pro-cyclical policy, a policy that would make inflation worse. It was exactly the opposite of the stabilization policy required. Now, more than ever, it was time to break with the Treasury and raise interest rates. Now, suddenly, the conflict over fixed rates really mattered.

Events seemed to confirm the Fed's worst fears. People remembered the last war, only five years before. They expected a return to shortages and rationing. Consumers reacted by buying everything in sight. Businesses reacted by ordering as much inventory as they could. Production and employment increased, but so did prices. Inflation jumped from virtually nothing in the year before June 1950, to 9% in the year after.

Eccles said "it was time the System, if it expected to survive as an agency with any independence whatsoever, should exercise some independence." In August, 1950, the Federal Open Market Committee resolved to increase interest rates beyond the fixed ceilings. Treasury Secretary Snyder fought back, issuing bonds with low interest rates. Investors would not buy them if other investments paid more, which they would if the Fed raised rates.

This put the Fed in quite a bind. If they sold bonds, using open market operations to raise interest rates, rates in the market would exceed those on the new bonds the Treasury was offering. Private investors could make more money buying bonds in the market than buying bonds from Treasury. So the Treasury debt issue would "fail," meaning investors would not lend money to the Federal government. If the Treasury couldn't borrow (and refused to budge on the interest they would pay), how could it pay for the war effort? The Fed gave in and bought Treasury bonds in October and November. Emboldened, Secretary Snyder announced a new debt issue for December and January, again at the fixed rates.

Eccles was unhappy with this situation, but so was Treasury Secretary Snyder. Now, he realized, the Treasury was at the mercy of the Fed. Should the Fed decide not to buy its bonds, the Treasury would have no choice but to offer higher interest rates to private investors, and pay the higher borrowing costs. Snyder decided to take the matter to President Truman, and the President sent a letter to McCabe in December, saying that "I hope the Board will realize its responsibilities and not allow the bottom to drop from under our securities. If that happens that is exactly what Mr. Stalin wants." Will the Fed be a tool of the communist dictator? That is political hardball.

The Federal Open Market Committee was scheduled to meet on January 31. On January 30, McCabe received a call from the White House, inviting the whole FOMC to meet with the President at 4:00 p.m. the next day. This was most unusual, McCabe told the President's appointments secretary. The Fed's policy-making body had never met with the President in all its history. But the White House announced the meeting to the newspapers, so McCabe felt he had no choice but to accept.

President Truman started the meeting with a warning. "The present emergency is the greatest this country has ever faced, including the two world wars and all the preceding wars." The Treasury had to borrow at low rates. The Fed shares your concerns, McCabe told Truman. But economic stability was the Fed's main job.

The meeting ended with smiles and handshakes. They agreed to "protect the credit of the United States." To the Treasury, that meant maintaining fixed rates, so it could sell its bonds. To the Fed, that meant raising interest rates, to prevent inflation. Each side knew that the policy of other side had not changed, even as they were shaking hands. It was, wrote economist Herbert Stein, "a masterpiece of deliberate misunderstanding."

The next day Fed chair McCabe received a letter from Harry Truman. "Dear Tom," it said, "I want the members of the Federal Reserve Board and the members of the Federal Open Market Committee to know how deeply I appreciate their expression of full cooperation given to me yesterday in our meeting."

> As I understand it, I have your assurance that the market on government securities will be stabilized and maintained at present levels in order to assure the successful financing requirements and to establish in the minds of the people confidence concerning government credit.

It was outrageous. No one at the Fed had made any such commitment. McCabe decided that his only course was to confront the President in private, and ask him to withdraw the letter. The Federal Reserve Board members agreed that McCabe would meet with the President the next day to request that his letter be withdrawn.

But that night, as Marriner Eccles was about to leave his office, a reporter called him on the phone.

"Listen to this," the reporter said, and read him the text of President's letter.

"Where did you get that?" Eccles demanded. He'd thought the letter was confidential.

"The White House has just released it to the world. What have you got to say to that?"

Eccles told the reporter he'd call him back. Now it was clear that the Treasury and the White House intended to convince the public that the Fed had agreed to hold rates constant. Then any attempt to raise interest rates to fight inflation could be portrayed as a betrayal of the Fed's word, and of the war effort. Eccles figured he had to act fast, before public opinion hardened.

Without telling anyone of his intentions, he got a hold of the Fed's confidential minutes of the meeting with the President. His secretary stayed until eleven o'clock typing copies. Then he called the reporter back. He said, in effect, that the President of the United States had lied.

The front pages of the Sunday papers on February 4 shouted the news. The minutes of the meeting showed that the Fed had not agreed to hold rates constant. The President had not even asked. Senator Douglas issued a statement in support of the Fed. Other Senators followed his lead. Truman and Snyder had little support in Congress.

At a meeting of the Open Market Committee that day, some members criticized Eccles for releasing a confidential document. But Allan Sproul, head of the New York Fed, said he had "temporarily retrieved our place in the financial community and with the public."

They decided to confront the President with their own letter. It amounted to the Fed's declaration of independence. The policy of fixed rates, the letter said, meant

> . . . more and more money and cheaper and cheaper dollars. This means less and less public confidence. Mr. President, you did not ask us in our recent meeting to commit ourselves to continue on this dangerous road. Such a course would seriously weaken the financial stability of the United States. . . .

In the face of a determined Fed, and without support in Congress or the press, the Treasury surrendered. Over the next month the Treasury and the Federal Reserve worked out an agreement, known as *The Accord*. The Fed would allow rates to rise gradually for a time, but after that it would act independently in the interest of economic stabilization. The Treasury would have to sell its bonds by offering market interest rates, even if those rates were higher than they preferred.

> *In 1951 the Fed and the Treasury signed "The Accord", which gave control over monetary policy to the Federal Reserve.*

At the end of February, as negotiations were wrapping up, Truman called Chairman McCabe into his office and told him that his services were no longer satisfactory. The President cannot fire the chairman of the Fed, but in the face of such Presidential disapproval McCabe felt he had to resign. The President appointed a Treasury official, William McChesney Martin, as the new chair.

The Federal Reserve's headquarters in Washington, D.C. Also known as the Marriner S. Eccles Federal Reserve Board Building.

Marriner Eccles resigned on July 14, 1951, after 17 years with the Federal Reserve. His career is defined by its contradictions. He was a banker who came to Washington to support the New Deal. He was the head of the monetary policy agency who thought that fiscal policy should be used to fight the Depression. He spent much of his career subordinating monetary policy to the Treasury's fiscal policy, first to finance the New Deal, then to finance two wars. Yet his first important act was to consolidate Federal Reserve policy-making in Washington, and his last was to strike a blow for the Fed's independence. By the beginning of the 1950's, the Federal Reserve was largely what Marriner Eccles had made of it. The Fed's headquarters in Washington D.C. is named for him.

The Korean War
It's ironic. After all the debate about the Accord, all the concern about how to finance Korean War budget deficits, the Korean War was paid for with taxes. There were no deficits to finance.

Korean War

Year	Real GDP Growth	CPI Inflation	Unemploy- ment Rate	Interest Rate Spread	Gov't Budget Balance (% GDP)
1950	8.7%	1.3%	5.1%	0.6%	-1.0%
1951	9.9%	7.9%	2.7%	0.6%	1.8%
1952	4.3%	1.9%	2.9%	0.6%	-0.4%
1953	3.7%	0.8%	3.6%	0.5%	-1.7%
1954	-0.6%	0.7%	6.8%	0.6%	-0.3%

Here's the data for the Korean War period. The war itself lasted from June 1950 to July 1953. Clearly, its effect on the economy was much smaller than during World War II. Real growth was high for two years, but growth had been double-digits for three years during World War II. Inflation was high for just one year, then very low in 1952 and after. The unemployment rate fell below 5%, but it was below 2% for three years during the earlier war. The interest rate spread was stable during the Korean War. It had fallen during World War II.

It's the government budget balance that shows the reason why. During World War II taxes increased, but not nearly enough to cover the increase in Federal spending. Budget deficits rose to 27% of GDP. That increased aggregate demand, and the price level. The Federal Reserve was required to hold interest rates constant. They would buy the Treasury bonds used to finance the deficit at low, fixed interest rates. When the Fed buys bonds, the money supply increases. The increase in the money supply created inflation. Price controls held inflation rates in check during the war, but inflation spiked upward as soon as the controls were lifted.

During the Korean War the Truman administration increased taxes enough to cover increased spending. Individual and corporate income tax revenues doubled between 1950 and 1953. No extraordinary budget deficits developed—in fact, the budget was in surplus in 1951 and nearly balanced in 1952. In wartime! With no deficit to finance, there was no need to buy Treasury bonds and no need to increase the money supply. Without an increase in the money supply, there was no sustained inflation.

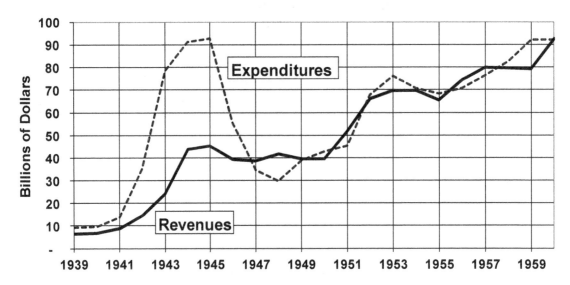

Figure 7-5. Tale of Two Wars. Federal Government Expenditures and Revenues, 1939-1960. Revenues rose during World War II (1941-45), but spending rose a lot more. The Federal Government ran a large deficit, Federal Reserve increased the money supply to help finance it. During the Korean War (1950-53), however, revenue increases matched spending hikes, no large deficit developed, and the Fed did not have to create money.

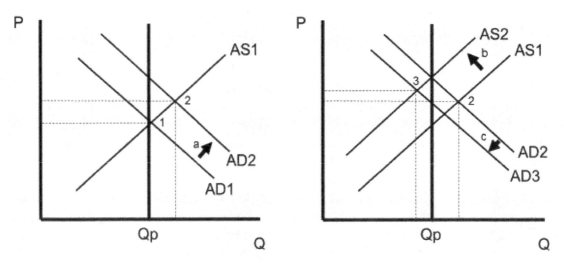

Figure 7-6. During and After the Korean War. Consumer spending increased at first, then small budget deficits added to aggregate demand (a). Output moved beyond potential (1 to 2). There was little inflation after the initial burst in 1951, and the unemployment rate edged upward after 1951. After the war higher costs resulted from output above potential, which caused a small second shift #1 (b). The move towards a balanced budget decreased aggregate demand too (c). The result was a mild recession with low inflation in 1954 (2 to 3).

What about that burst of inflation from 1950 to 1951? Consumers remembered the last war, and now here was war again. They remembered the rationing and the shortages. So this time, when war broke out, they took their savings and bought everything in sight. Stock up now while you can! The marginal propensity to consume increased, and that increased aggregate demand even without a boost in the money supply. The Truman administration instituted a price control program, but it was not as comprehensive as during World War II. It didn't need to be. Consumer purchasing power was being taxed away. The Korean War has a small effect on the economy, and the post-war recession was mild as well (Figure 7-6).

No matter what is happening to the government's budget, if the quantity of money doesn't increase, prices won't either. If the budget deficit is financed by an increase in money, though, inflation results.

Wars create inflation, but only when budget deficits are financed by money creation. That's what happened during World War I, World War II, and (we will see) the Vietnam War. The Korean War is the exception that proves the rule.

The end of the fixed rate policy presented the new Federal Reserve chairman, William McChesney Martin, with a policy problem. When rates had to be held fixed, it was obvious what the Fed should do in any situation. If the market was pushing interest rates up, the Fed bought bonds, increasing the money supply, causing interest rates to fall. If the market was pulling interest rates down, the Fed sold bonds, and interest rates would rise again. Now the Fed needed a new guiding principle.

Martin proposed one at his nomination hearing. "Our purpose is to lean against the winds of deflation or inflation, whichever way they are blowing," he said. If deflation and recession threatened, the Fed would buy bonds, cut the discount rate, reduce reserve requirements. The money supply would expand and interest rates would fall. If inflation was the problem, the Fed would contract the money supply to raise interest rates. It was a declaration that the Fed would follow counter-cyclical monetary policy. *"Leaning against the wind"* became a Fed policy catch-phrase. Of course, problems remained: how to decide what direction the wind was blowing, and how hard to lean.

Who Should Make Monetary Policy?
It's the second decade of the 21st century, and many members of Congress want to limit the powers of the Federal Reserve. One proposal seeks to *"audit the Fed,"* by subjecting monetary policy decisions to review by the Government Accountability Office. Another wants to ban bankers from serving on the Fed's boards. A more stringent proposal seeks to fix a formula for making monetary policy, and require the Fed to justify any deviations from the formula's result.

Supporters of these measures come from both the right and the left of the political spectrum. Traditionally Democrats criticize the Fed for holding interest rates too high, to the benefit of bankers. Democratic Presidential candidate Bernie Sanders, a Senator from Vermont, continued that argument during his campaign, writing that "an institution that was created to serve all Americans has been hijacked by the very bankers it regulates." Sanders would ban bankers from serving on Fed boards and from choosing its staff.

Republicans have criticized the Fed for holding interest rates too low. Republican Representative Scott Garrett from New Jersey told Fed chair Janet Yellen that "The people pushing back on your decisions are those arguing for a tougher monetary policy, not a looser one. This flies in the face of the original stated rationale for political independence in monetary policy." There have been Republican proposals to strengthen the role of the banking industry in the Fed's governance, the opposite of Senator Sanders' position.

Some politicians and economists recommend that the Fed's interest rate decisions be made by formula. One such formula is called the *Taylor Rule*, after economist John Taylor from Stanford University. The rule would require the Fed to raise the federal funds rate when inflation increased or unemployment decreased, and reduce the federal funds rate when the opposite happened.

The Fed has pushed back against audits and rules. In testimony Fed chair Yellen said such a rule would restrict the Fed's ability to respond to a crisis, and "would essentially undermine central bank independence."

We've had this argument before. President Truman's Treasury Secretary declared that monetary policy "cannot be carried out by an agency such as the Federal Reserve, which has no responsibility to the electorate. . . ." The Fed is not accountable to the public. But Marriner Eccles claimed that elected officials have a "chronic bias for cheap money in all seasons." Elected officials want low interest rates, even if rising inflation requires high interest rates.

Before that, when the Federal Reserve was founded, supporters of a central bank wanted a single institution based in New York or Washington, to make policy independent of politics. Those who feared centralized power wanted many banks dispersed across the states, and a political appointee at the head of the board in Washington.

The question of who should control monetary policy is an old, old debate in the United States. Now we're having that debate again.

Different countries have organized their central banks in different ways. Some are more independent, some less. Economists Alesina and Summers used this fact to research the relationship between central bank independence and inflation. The authors rank 16 developed country central banks from less to more independent (see Figure 7-7). Sure enough, countries with less independent central banks—those more subject to pressures from elected officials—generally had higher inflation rates from 1955 to 1988.

Supporters of Fed independence point to the 1978 Humphrey-Hawkins Act, which charged the Fed to minimize inflation and maximize growth and employment. This is known as the Fed's *dual mandate*. Since inflation has been low and unemployment high since the end of the Great Recession, the Fed has held interest rates low.

Legislators like Representative Garrett would like to repeal the high employment part of the mandate, so the Fed would focus only on low inflation. The central banks of Europe and Japan have mandates to address inflation only.

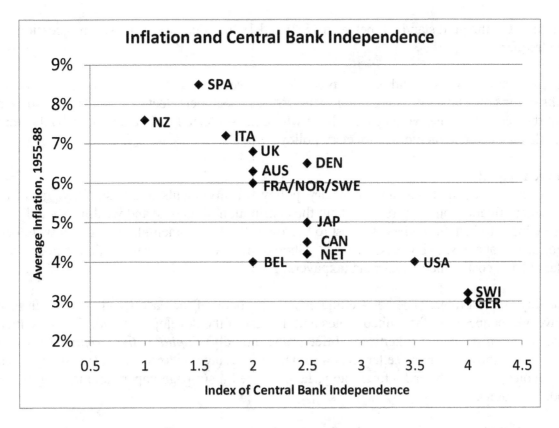

Figure 7-7. Independence and Inflation. Alesina and Summers' (1993) analysis of the relationship between central bank independence and average inflation for 16 developed countries. The index of central bank independence based on legal and administrative characteristics of the banks. More independent banks are less subject to political influence from elected officials. Countries with more independent central banks have generally experienced lower inflation rates.

Some officials want an even more stringent rule to govern monetary policy: a return to the gold standard. During a debate, presidential candidate Ted Cruz, a Republican Senator from Texas, said "Instead of adjusting monetary policy according to whims and getting it wrong over and over again and causing booms and busts, what the Fed should be doing is keeping our money tied to a stable level of gold."

Do we need a central bank? Could we return to the gold standard? There are many technical issues involved. It's unclear whether the gold standard would work if just one country adopted it, for example.

There's an important political issue involved. The voters expect their elected officials to promote growth, employment and stable prices. When the economy is in recession, elected officials lose elections (as Herbert Hoover, Jimmy Carter and George H. W. Bush could attest). With a gold standard and no central bank, the money supply is determined by the stock of gold, which is influenced by mining and trade. The money supply cannot be used to stabilize the economy. On the gold standard, elected officials give up one of the tools that can be used to influence the economy. On the gold standard, between 1880 and 1940, prices were stable but recessions were more frequent.

Perhaps a return to gold would only be possible if the voters were willing to accept the economic results of the gold standard. But as long as the voters expect their elected officials to do something about the economy—and vote against those who don't—elected officials will probably want all the tools they can get, including monetary policy.

Income Inequality

The arguments about fiscal and monetary policy are arguments about stability, growth and government finance, but they're also about the distribution of income and wealth. Should interest rates be high, to benefit lenders at a cost to borrowers? Should unemployment be low, to benefit wage earners at a cost to business owners? Should the government provide aid the poor, the sick or the old at a cost to income-earning taxpayers?

Inequality is a hot topic. The best-selling economics book of the past decade was about income and wealth inequality in the United States and the rest of the developed world. It was written by French economist Thomas Piketty, and titled (rather grandly) *Capital in the Twenty-First Century*. It was briefly the number one seller on Amazon books, even with its 685 pages (including 77 pages of footnotes). A tough read—fortunately, he published a six-page paper summarizing the most important points.

Piketty based his analysis on a massive database that he and his colleagues gathered about income and wealth in the developed world. Data go back two centuries in some cases. The series on wealth in France starts in 1820. Data for the United States dates to the beginning of the Federal income tax in 1913.

There are many ways to measure income distribution, but Piketty chooses something straightforward. If you stack income earners from top to bottom, how much of total income is earned by the top 1% of the population, the top 10%, or the bottom 90%? In other words, how much is earned by each *income percentile*? Figure 7-8 shows the result for years from 1913 to 2015.

From 1913 to 1940 inequality was high. This is shown by the high percentage of income earned by the top 1% of income earners, almost 24% of total income at the peak in 1928. The remaining top 10% earned another 25%, which left the lower 90% of the population with just over half of all the income.

Inequality fell from 1940 to 1980. At the peak in 1970 the lower 90% of the population earned almost 70% of total income. The top 1% earned about 8% of total income, and the remaining top 10% earned 22% of total income.

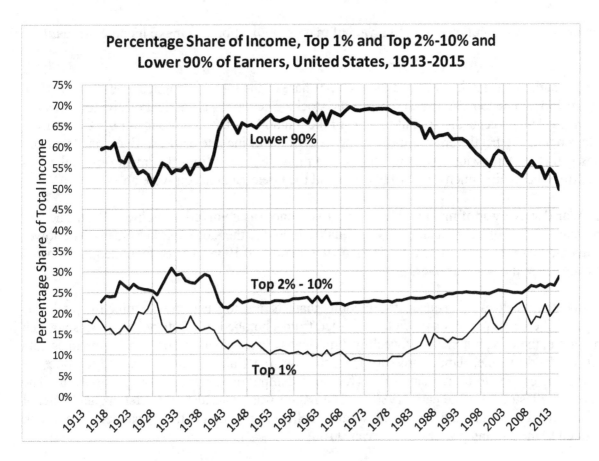

Figure 7-8. Income inequality in the United States, 1913-2015. The lower line labeled "top 1%" shows the percentage of total income earned by the top 1% of income earners. The middle line shows the top 10%, less that top 1%. The higher line shows the percentage earned by everyone else, the lower 90%. The total sums to 100% in any one year.

After 1980 inequality began increasing again, and this has continued to the present day. As of 2015, the top 1% earn 22% of all income, the remaining top 10% earn 28%, and the lower 90% of the population are making do with about half.

Piketty and others try to explain these fluctuations. Why did inequality fall in the 1940-1980 period? Why did it increase again after 1980? What will happen in the future?

Our macroeconomic model does not have much to contribute to the inequality questions. That's because it treats output and income in the aggregate. If output and income rise, there is no way to know who is benefitting and who is being left behind. So we must look to other models and other explanations for the answers. Here are a few.

Crises. Stanford historian Walter Scheidel has investigated the long, long history of income and wealth distribution, and has come to a bleak conclusion. He finds that only four things regularly reduce inequality for any length of time. One is epidemics or pandemics, like the Black Death in Europe in the 14th century. So many workers died that the wages of those who remained went up. The complete collapse of states will do it, such as the fall of the Roman Empire. If everyone loses, the rich lose the most. Revolution can reduce inequality. Think of the nobility in the

French or Russian revolutions. Finally, wars of mass mobilization can make income inequality fall.

The stock market crashed in 1929 and the income share of the top 1% dropped from 24% in 1928 to 15% in 1931. The top 1% owned most of the stock. They lost a great deal of dividend income in the crash. The percentages of total income of the remaining 10% and the lower 90% increased. This does not mean that the crash improved the lives of lower income earners. Everyone lost from the crash and the Depression. The top 1% just lost more. Scheidel finds that most financial crises do not affect inequality much. The 1929 crash and the Great Depression were an exception.

World War II was a war of mass mobilization. Everyone was involved in the war effort. The war had an even bigger effect reducing U.S. inequality than did the stock market crash. The lower 90% saw their earnings share rise from 55% in 1940 to 66% in 1945. The drop in inequality lasted for decades after the war was over.

In Europe the world wars reduced the income share at the top because so much capital was destroyed. There was not much profit to be earned from a bombed-out factory. There was no such destruction in the U.S., but plenty of wealthy Americans owned stock in European companies, and so lost dividend income. Under pressure from the war, the United States increased tax rates on upper-income earners to more than 90%. That put a damper on the pursuit of great wealth. The high tax rates lasted until the early 1980's. The nation was grateful to its veterans, and offered them benefits such as the G.I Bill. Vets went to college, and universities expanded enrollment. This added to the earning power of the lower 90%.

Eventually, though, the effects of the crash, Depression and World War II faded. Inequality began to increase again, and that's normal according to Scheidel.

Growth. Inequality fell between 1940 and 1980. Potential output grew rapidly from 1941 to 1973, by more than 4% per year (see Chapter 3). According to Piketty, this is no coincidence.

Wealth is distributed more unequally than income. Wealth is made up of assets like houses, factories and office buildings, land, savings accounts, stocks, and bonds. In 2014 the top 10% of wealth-holders owned 73% of the wealth, compared to earning 50% of the income. So anything that changes the value of wealth will affect the top earners more. Anything that changes wage growth will affect low earners more.

Piketty compares the growth of output to the rate of return on assets. The wages of the lower earners tend to rise with growth. But a large share of the incomes of the top earners come from interest, rents and profits, which derive from the ownership of assets. If the rate of return on assets is greater than the growth of wages, income inequality will increase. Throughout most of history that was true. Growth was very slow prior to the industrial revolution, and land owners earned between 4% and 5% on the value of their land. As upper income people accumulated more and more assets, their incomes grew faster than those of working people. Inequality increased.

In the middle of the twentieth century this changed. Growth increased, especially due to the increase in productivity. The rate of return on assets dipped with the Depression and the high tax rates of World War II and after. Inequality decreased. Growth slowed after 1973, and especially in the past ten years. The rate of return recovered, and income inequality increased again.

Education. Piketty's comparison of asset returns and growth explains why the owners of capital first lost and then gained income relative to working people. But MIT economist David Autor points out that inequality has increased among working people too. Inequality has increased within the lower 99%. In particular, the incomes of higher-skilled, more-educated people have increased compared to the incomes of less-skilled, less-educated people.

Technological advance increases business demand for college-educated employees. If the supply of college-educated employees does not grow to match this added demand, the wages of college-educated employees rise compared to high school-educated employees. Income inequality among wage-earners will increase. If the supply of college-educated employees rises faster than the demand, college-educated employee wages fall, and so does inequality.

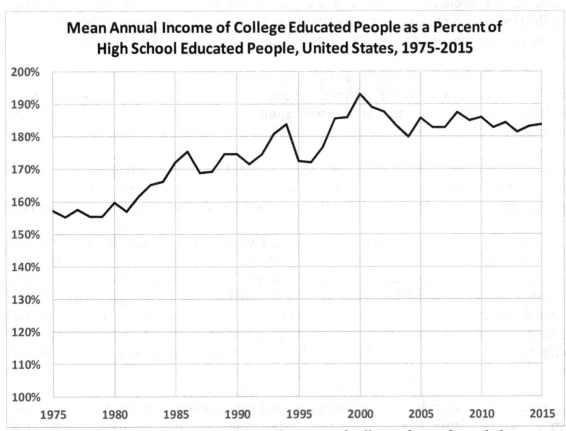

Figure 7-9. The College Income Premium. Incomes of college educated people have risen relative to incomes of high school educated people. In 1975 college incomes were 157% of high school incomes (that is, 57% higher). In 2015 college incomes were 184% higher (84% higher). The period between 1980 and 2000 saw the biggest increase.

Figure 7-9 shows the increase in the college income premium from 1975 to 2015, based on Census data on average annual earnings of workers by education level. The premium was 57% in 1981 (That is, college educated people earned 157% of what high school educated people earned, or

57% more.) The premium began to increase in the early 1980's, peaked in 2000 at 93%, then stabilized around 85% through 2015.

Autor claims that there's been a steady increase in the demand for college-educated employees, and explains the changing college income premium based on variations in the growth of supply. The supply of college graduates grew rapidly in the 1970's, but slowed in the 1980's and 1990's. During the Vietnam War male college students were granted deferments from the military draft. With this incentive the number of young people in college increased. As a result, large numbers of college-educated employees became available in the 1970's. This increase in supply caused the college earnings premium to stagnate under 60%.

College attendance growth slowed when the war and the draft ended in the early-1970's. The stagnation of the income premium also discouraged attendance growth. With slower growth in supply, the pay of college educated employees increased relative to high school educated employees. Inequality increased. Young people have come to recognize the value of college education, which has accelerated attendance and supply since 2000. The slowdown in productivity growth in the past ten years may have reduced demand growth as well. Since 2000 supply and demand have grown at the same pace, and the income premium has stabilized near 85%.

Winners-Take-All. Back in the day, every town had a vaudeville theater. People would pay to see live entertainment, and thousands of acts toured the circuit. George Burns and Gracie Allen were a "Dumb Dora" comedy act—a straight man with a ditzy woman—the best of many such acts. They played the big city palaces and the lesser acts played to audiences in small towns.

Then came radio. Burns and Allen got a radio show and people could hear them in their homes each week. Why go to the theater to see a second rate act, when the best was available at home? Burns and Allen got rich, vaudeville died, and the lesser acts found other occupations at lower pay.

New technologies can magnify the reach of superstars. Two economists named Robert Frank and Philip Cook wrote a book called *The Winner-Take-All Society* explaining how these technologies could concentrate income among the most talented people. Radio allowed Burns and Allen to compete with lesser comedians. Movies did the same for Fred Astaire and Ginger Rogers. Lesser dancers could not compete. There were once many piano manufacturers. Then came rail transportation and the very best pianos could be shipped nation-wide. The best manufacturers could compete for more customers. They expanded and got rich. Lesser producers went out of business.

Local accountants must compete by tax software designed by accounting experts. Local professors must compete with academic superstars offering on-line courses. Brick and mortar stores must compete with the vast selection offered by Amazon. Automobile factories used to employ thousands of people on assembly lines. Now a few hundred skilled technicians run a factory full of robots. The technicians earn a lot, the owners of the robots earn even more, and the factory workers struggle for what they can find.

Apple released its first desk-top computer in 1976. By the early 1980s computers appeared on office desks. The internet linked them together and popular browsers became available in the

1990's. The advances in information technology roughly correspond to the increased inequality that began in 1980. Perhaps the winners are taking all.

The Future of Inequality. Piketty thinks continued slow growth will cause inequality to increase. The wealthy will continue to reap the income from their assets, while working people will see only slow wage growth. Scheidel would agree that increasing inequality is the normal course of events, absent catastrophes. We may have moved beyond plagues, world wars or the collapse of nations. Perhaps catastrophic climate change?

Over the past decade the growing supply of college-educated employees has matched the growing demand. The expansion of on-line higher education may increase supply. Slower productivity growth may keep demand growing slowly. The college income premium may not resume its increase, so that source of wage-earner inequality may not rise. There's talk in 2017 of a retail apocalypse, with the shift to on-line shopping now emptying malls and causing big retailers like Sears and Macy's to close stores. On-line retailing may be the winner that takes all, concentrating income with fewer sellers.

But there's an opposing view to Winners-Take-All, called the *Long Tail*. Information technology reduces the costs of production and distribution. Everyone can offer content on the internet. Produce a video, a song, a novel and who knows? It might go viral, and you could launch a career. Small manufacturers might find on-line niche markets, reaching consumers that they would never find otherwise. Perhaps technology will spread the wealth, not concentrate it.

Though most authors discuss inequality as if it were a bad thing, most also recognize that some inequality is necessary. Output growth probably would stagnate in a society with absolute equality of incomes. Without the possibility of earning more, people would not go to the trouble of acquiring education and skills. Businesses would not invest and expand. Some inequality is necessary to provide incentives and rewards for the activities that create growth.

But growth probably would stagnate in a society with absolute inequality too. If one person or family owned everything and received all the income above subsistence, there would be little opportunity for anyone else to get ahead. A poor person might invent something new, but the added income would be taxed away, if the big guy was the government, or taken in higher prices and rents, if he was a private monopoly, or simply stolen, if he was a crime boss. Again, people would not go to the trouble to acquire education, and businesses would not invest if all the profits go to the Godfather.

If growth is near zero at absolute equality, and near zero at absolute inequality, there must be some optimal level of inequality in between. The question is, how much inequality is enough?

Terms in this Chapter, in order of appearance
Gold standard
Automatic fiscal stabilizers
World War II
Expanded labor supply
Taxes
War bonds
Price controls
Rationing
Black market
Infinite price
Counter-cyclical monetary policy
Counter-cyclical fiscal policy
Pro-cyclical fiscal policy
Pro-cyclical monetary policy
Secular stagnation
Pent-up demand
National debt
Rolling over the debt
Korean War
The Accord
Leaning against the wind
Audit the Fed
Taylor Rule
The Fed's Dual Mandate
Income inequality
Income percentile

Notes
FDR's October 12, 1942 fireside chat is available on the internet, at www.presidency.ucsb.edu/site/docs/pppusyear.php?yearindex=1942.

Manchester (289-327) and Kennedy (746-797) give histories of the home front during World War II. Stein (1994, pp. 65-70) and Friedman and Schwartz (546-591) cover the war's economic policies.

Manchester (1974, p. 296) offers the statistics on wartime equipment production. Kennedy writes of the changes brought about by the war, including women's labor force participation (pp. 776-780), and executive order 8802 (pp. 765-768).

Kettl (1986, 59-62), and Friedman and Schwartz (pp. 561-563) discuss the Fed's deal with the Treasury during the war. Friedman and Schwartz discuss the ways inflation makes itself felt when there are price controls (pp. 557-558). Stein discusses war time tax policy (1994, pp.68-69).

McCullough (pp. 774-776) tells the story of Truman's reaction to the start of the Korean War.

The story of the fixed interest rate policy of World War II, and the struggle between the Treasury and the Fed over the Fed's independence, is told by Kettl (1986, pp. 45-81), Meltzer (2003, pp. 579-712) and Stein (1996, pp. 241-280). All the quotes in the text come from these sources. It's a dramatic story that can be told from different points of view. Kettl, for example, emphasizes the role of Marriner Eccles, while Meltzer focuses on New York Bank head Allan Sproul. I followed Kettl's approach here.

The story of Eccles' release of the confidential minutes of the meeting with President Truman is told by the man himself in Eccles (1951, pp. 486-499).

Both of Stein's books (1994, 1996) focus on the development (and breakdown) of the consensus on stabilization policy. Stein (1996) provides a detailed description of fiscal policy during the Eisenhower administration (pp. 281-371). The Eisenhower quotes come from Stein (1996, p. 367 and p. 368). Stein (1996, pp. 370-71) and Wicker (pp.180-181) tell of Richard Nixon's attempts to get Eisenhower to support a tax cut. Stein speculates that Eisenhower's tight fiscal policy cost Nixon the election in 1960.

Kettl (1986, pp. 88-91), Degen (1987, 119-126) and Friedman and Schwartz (1963, pp. 624-632) touch on monetary policy during the Eisenhower years. Kettl discusses Chairman Martin's relationship with Eisenhower.

The quote from Sen. Sanders if from Sanders (*New York Times*, 2015). The quote from Rep. Garrett is from Appelbaum (*New York Times*, April 7, 2015). The quote from Sen. Cruz is from Appelbaum (*New York Times*, December 1, 2015)

Alesina and Summers (1993) provide research on the relationship between central bank independence and inflation.

It was reported that the five most highlighted text passages by electronic book readers were all in the first 26 pages of Piketty's book. Apparently most readers struggled to get past the introduction. Try that Piketty and Suez's six-page paper before plunking down your $25.

Piketty's income and wealth data are available on the World Wealth and Income Database, at wid.world. The U.S. Bureau of the Census has data on income by educational attainment, at www.census.gov/data/tables/2016/demo/education-attainment/cps-detailed-tables.html

Sources

Alesina, Alberto, and Lawrence H. Summers. 1993. "Central Bank Independence and Macroeconomic Performance: Some Comparative Evidence," *Journal of Money, Credit and Banking* 25 (May): 151-162.

Autor, David H. "Skills, Education and the Rise of Earnings Inequality Among the 'Other 99 Percent,'" *Science* 344 (May 23): 843-851.

Degen, Robert A. 1987. *The American Monetary System.* Lexington, Massachusetts: D.C. Heath and Company, Lexington Books.

Eccles, Marriner S.. 1951. *Beckoning Frontiers.* New York: Alfred A. Knopf.

Frank, Robert H. and Philip J. Cook. *The Winner-Take-All Society: Why the Few at the Top Get So Much More Than the Rest of Us.* New York: The Free Press, 1995.

Friedman, Milton and Anna Jacobson Schwartz. 1963. *A Monetary History of the United States, 1867-1960.* Princeton, New Jersey: Princeton University Press.

Kennedy, David M. 1999. *Freedom From Fear: The American People in Depression and War, 1929-1945.* New York: Oxford University Press.
Kettl, Donald F. 1986. *Leadership at the Fed.* New Haven: Yale University Press.

Keynes, John Maynard. 1936. *The General Theory of Employment, Interest and Money.* New York: Harcourt, Brace, Jovanovich.

Manchester, William. 1973. *The Glory and the Dream.* New York: Bantam Books.

McCullough, David. 1992. *Truman.* New York: Simon and Schuster.

Meltzer, Allan H. 2003. *A History of the Federal Reserve. Volume 1: 1913-1951.* Chicago: University of Chicago Press.

Piketty, Thomas. 2014. *Capital in the Twenty-First Century.* Cambridge, Mass.: Harvard University Press.

Piketty, Thomas and Emmanuel Suez. 2014. "Inequality in the Long Run," *Science* 344 (May 23): 838-843.

Stein, Herbert. 1994. *Presidential Economics (3rd Revised Edition).* Washington, D.C.: The AEI Press.

Stein, Herbert. 1996. *The Fiscal Revolution in America (2nd Revised Edition).* Washington, D.C.: The AEI Press.

News Articles
Appelbaum, Binyamin. "Yellen Says Restraining the Fed's Oversight Would Be a 'Grave Mistake'," *New York Times*, July 16, 2014.

Appelbaum, Binyamin. "In Republican Attacks on the Fed, Experts See a Shift," *New York Times*, April 7, 2015.

Appelbaum, Binyamin. "G.O.P. Candidates Viewing Economy's Past Through Gold-Colored Glasses," *New York Times*, Decenmber 1, 2015.

Cohn, Emily. "Not Many People Got Past Page 26 Of Piketty's Book," *HuffPost*, July 7, 2014.

The Economist. "Apocalypse Then: The Lessons of Violence and Inequality Through the Ages." March 2, 2017.

Frank, Robert H. "Winners Take All, but Can't We Still Dream?" *New York Times*, February 4, 2014.

Sanders, Bernie. "Bernie Sanders: To Rein in Wall Street, Fix the Fed," *New York Times*, December 23, 2015.

Chapter 8
Trade and Exchange Rates

There's a big world out there, and we have to deal with it. So far our macroeconomic model doesn't say much about the rest of the world. We know that exports and imports influence aggregate demand, but that's about it. In this chapter we'll do better. We'll start with another economic indicator, exchange rates, which are determined in a third market, the exchange market. Then we'll apply this model all the way from the 1930's to now.

Exchange Rates

The *exchange rate* of the dollar is the number of foreign currency units that one dollar trades for on international currency markets. The *value of the dollar* is the same thing. We'll call it the exchange value of the dollar, just to be clear. There are more than one hundred international currencies that have exchange rates with the dollar. The value of the dollar against most foreign currencies changes every day, even every hour or every minute, depending on how many dollars people want to buy and sell. Prior to 1973, most exchange rates were fixed and often unchanged for years at a time.

In our models and in this book the U.S. exchange rate will be measured as foreign currency units per dollar. That's how much it costs a foreigner to buy a dollar, measured in another currency. This makes sense of the term "value of the dollar," and it means that when the dollar gets "stronger", or it "appreciates" or is "revalued," the exchange rate goes up. When the dollar gets "weaker," "depreciates" or is "devalued," the exchange rate goes down.

> **The exchange rate of the dollar can be measured as the number of foreign currency units per dollar. This is also known as the "value of the dollar."**

On average in 2016, one dollar exchanged for 0.90 European euros (used in France, Germany, Italy, Spain, Greece and many other European countries). It took 90 "eurocents" to buy a dollar. In 2001, a European would have needed 1.12 euros to buy a dollar. By 2008 the value of the dollar was 0.68 eurocents. It had depreciated in value. Since then the dollar has appreciated again, rising a lot in 2015. The dollar is "weaker" than it was in 2001, but "stronger" than it was in 2008.

Exchange rates can be inverted to measure the number of dollars per foreign currency unit. The exchange rate between the dollar and euro is often presented in dollars per euro, not euros per dollar. On average in 2016 one euro exchanged for $1.11 because 1 / 0.90 = 1.11. In 2008 one euro exchanged for $1.47 (1 / 0.68 = 1.47). When the dollar gets weaker, it costs more dollars to buy a euro. The value of the euro goes up. Since "weaker" sounds more like down than up, we'll measure exchange rates in foreign currency units per dollar.

The value of the dollar is important for imports and exports. When the dollar is stronger, foreign currencies are less expensive. To buy foreign imports, importers must first buy foreign currency, and then use that currency to buy foreign products. If the foreign currency is cheaper, so are the foreign products, as measured in dollars. Likewise, when the dollar is stronger, it costs foreigners more to buy U.S. exports, because the dollars they buy in order to purchase U.S. goods are more expensive. The value of the dollar influences the amount of goods and services that the U.S. imports and exports.

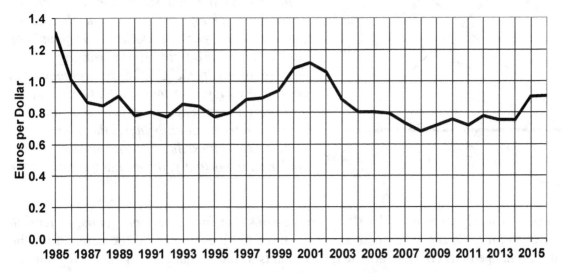

Figure 8-1. Exchange rate, euros per one dollar, 1985-2016 (estimated before 1999). The euro is the European multi-national currency. It replaced the German mark, French franc, Italian lira and several other national currencies in 1999. Prior to 1999 the data here are averages for those currencies. The value of the dollar in euros was high in the mid-1980s. It remained stable around 0.8 euros per dollar from 1990 to 1996. Then the value increased, mostly because there was a world financial crisis. International investors wanted to buy more dollars, in order to invest in nice, safe U.S. Treasury bonds. That pushed the value of the dollar up. Large U.S. trade deficits in the 2000's helped bring the value of the dollar down, but in late 2008 this reversed again as a new financial crisis caused the world to buy dollars. Successive European crises have caused much of the fluctuation in the value of the dollar since then, including a substantial increase in 2015.

The Exchange Market
The exchange rate helps determine exports and imports. The exchange rate itself is set in the exchange market. The price in the exchange market is the exchange rate or the exchange value of the dollar, its price in foreign currency units. The quantity is the number of dollars traded. And, of course, the equilibrium exchange rate is determined by the *exchange demand for the dollar* and the *exchange supply of the dollar*.

The dollar and the world's other currencies are traded in exchange markets around the world. U.S. currency traders who want yen or pounds or euros offer dollars in exchange. They supply dollars in order to demand other currencies. Japanese or British or European currency traders who want dollars supply their currencies in exchange. They supply their currencies in order to demand dollars.

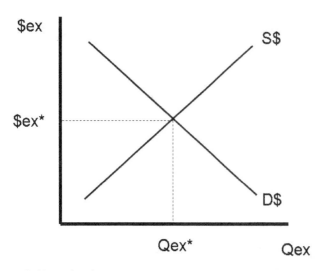

Figure 8-2. The Exchange Market. Quantity (Qex) is the number of dollars traded on foreign exchange markets; price is the exchange value of the dollar or the exchange rate ($ex), measured as the number of foreign currency units that exchange for one dollar (like euros per dollar or yen per dollar). Demand for dollars comes from foreigners wanting to buy, lend or invest in the U.S. Supply comes from Americans supplying their dollars in exchange for foreign currencies, to buy, lend or invest in other countries. Equilibrium is the intersection, which determines the quantity traded (Qex*) and most importantly, the exchange value of the dollar ($ex).*

But why would a foreigner want dollars? Three reasons: to *buy American goods*, to *lend to Americans*, or to *invest in American assets*. These three motives lie behind the demand for the dollar in the exchange market. Here are the determinants of the exchange demand for the dollar.

- If foreigners have more income, they'll want to buy more goods from all over the world, including the United States. They'll demand dollars in order to buy U.S. goods.
- If U.S. goods improve in quality relative to goods from other countries, foreigners will want to buy them. They'll demand dollars in order to buy U.S. goods.
- If U.S. goods are produced more efficiently than goods in the rest of the world, they'll have lower prices. Foreigners will demand dollars to buy lower priced U.S. products.
- If U.S. interest rates are higher than interest rates in the rest of the world, foreigners will want to lend in the U.S. They'll demand dollars in order to lend to American businesses and governments.
- If owning businesses in the U.S. is seen as more profitable or less risky than in the rest of the world, foreigners will want to invest in the U.S. They'll want to buy U.S. businesses or build factories or offices in the U.S. They'll demand dollars in order to make these investments.

So, the demand for the dollar depends on the world's income, U.S. goods quality, U.S. goods prices, U.S. interest rates, and expectations about the U.S. economy. When the world's income rises, when quality or expectations improve, when goods prices fall or when interest rates rise, the demand for the dollar goes up. The opposite changes make the demand for the dollar go down.

In the exchange market, shifts in the demand for and supply of the dollar cause changes in the dollar's exchange rate.

These reasons explain why the supply for the dollar slopes upward. If the exchange value of the dollar rises, the dollar exchanges for more foreign currency. It can buy more foreign goods, buy more foreign assets, and support more foreign lending. So Americans supply more dollars in exchange for foreign currencies. This also explains why the demand for the dollar slopes downward. If the exchange value of the dollar rises, the dollar is more expensive, so foreign currencies buy fewer dollars. That makes American goods, assets and lending more expensive, so foreigners demand fewer dollars.

Exchange demand and supply are mirror images of one another. Unlike the goods or money markets, in the exchange market the same factors determine both demand and supply. Dollars are supplied by Americans who want to trade them for other currencies. Americans will supply dollars in order to buy foreign goods, lend to foreigners, or invest in foreign assets.

If American incomes go up, or if foreign goods improve in quality or price relative to U.S. goods, the demand for foreign goods will increase, and the demand for foreign currencies will increase. Americans must offer dollars in trade for foreign currencies, so the *supply* of dollars will increase. Likewise, if foreign interest rates rise relative to U.S. rates, Americans will want to lend to foreigners, so they will demand foreign currencies, so they will supply more dollars. If owning businesses in foreign countries is seen as more profitable or less risky than in the U.S., Americans will want to buy foreign businesses or build in other countries. They'll demand foreign currencies and supply dollars.

This happened in a big way in 2015. The U.S. economy was growing faster than the European economy. The European central bank was cutting interest rates, while the U.S. Federal Reserve was considering an interest rate hike. Europeans wanted to invest in U.S. businesses, and they wanted to lend at higher U.S. interest rates. So they exchanged their euros for dollars, to do that buying and lending. This increased the demand for the dollar, and the exchange value of the dollar went up.

You can see the increase in the value of the dollar against the euro in 2015 in Figure 8-1. This means, by the way, that the exchange rate between the dollar and the euro is a good indicator of the trends in European economies relative to the U.S. economy. When investors are pessimistic about Europe, the value of the dollar in euros goes up.

Figure 8-3 shows two exchange market diagrams. The diagram on the left shows just the increase in demand. This represents the desire of Europeans to trade their euros for dollars, in order to invest and lend in the U.S. The diagram on the right adds a supply shift. Americans have the same intentions as Europeans, to invest and lend in the U.S. Since Americans start with dollars, that means they'll demand fewer euros, and so supply fewer dollars. The exchange supply of the dollar decreases. Both shifts increase the exchange value of the dollar. Since we don't have data on the quantity of dollars exchanged, we can't determine whether quantity rises or falls, so we can't decide which shift dominates. We're most interested in changes in the exchange rate, so this is not a big concern.

Since the determinants of demand and supply are the same, but in opposite directions, an increase in exchange demand will always correspond to a decrease in exchange supply. Likewise, a decrease in exchange demand will always be accompanied by an increase in exchange supply. We can find the correct direction of change in the exchange rate with either demand, or supply, or both.

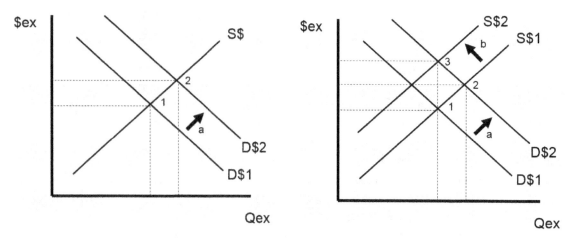

Figure 8-3. Surprise Rise. In the early 2015 international investors sought to invest in U.S. businesses and lend at U.S. interest rates. They demanded dollars in order to make these transactions. On the left, demand for the dollar increased (a), increasing the equilibrium exchange value of the dollar from 1 to 2. Americans invest and lend in the U.S. as well, so they trade fewer dollars for euros. On the right, the supply of the dollar decreases (b). Both shifts increase the exchange value of the dollar (1 to 2 to 3).

Changes like these can be important in the long run, too. From the 1950's to the end of the 1980's Japan's economy developed rapidly. Before World War II it had produced cheap manufactured goods. As late as the mid-1960's, the phrase "made in Japan" could evoke laughter in children. After the war Japan began developing electronic and industrial products among the best in the world. The world beat a path to its door.

To import from Japan the world needed yen, so the demand for the yen grew. Japan ran a trade surplus, so its demand for foreign currencies like the dollar grew less. The exchange value of the yen increased. In 1971 100 yen exchanged for 28 cents. By 1994 100 yen exchanged for one dollar. The yen's exchange value against the dollar increased almost four-fold in 23 years. U.S. products didn't deteriorate during those 23 years; Japan's products simply improved relative to U.S. products.

Long run trends are why economists and currency traders sometimes use the words "stronger" and "weaker" to describe increases or decreases in a currency's value. When a currency's value increases, it *might* be because the nation's economy is stronger, that is, it is producing a larger quantity of higher quality products efficiently, relative to another country. Its currency, like its economy, is getting stronger. When a currency's value decreases, it *might* be because the quality of a nation's products a lagging. Its currency is getting weaker. But don't be fooled. A weak economy's currency sometimes rises in value, and a strong economy's currency sometimes drops.

Second Shift #4: Exchange Market to Goods Market.
We've got a whole new market added to our macroeconomic model. That means we've got the potential for a few more second shifts. We'll focus on two (which brings the total to five).

Exports and imports are part of spending and aggregate demand in the goods market. The rest of the world spends on U.S. exports. Americans buy imports from the rest of the world. Export spending adds to aggregate demand for U.S. output. Import spending subtracts from it, because when people buy imports they are not spending on U.S. output.

The exchange rate helps determine export and import spending. When the value of the dollar rises, it exchanges for more yen or pounds or euros. A dollar buys a lot of goods and services sold by Japanese or British or European firms. So, when the value of the dollar rises, Americans buy more imports.

> **Second Shift #4: In the exchange market, dollar demand or supply shifts and the equilibrium exchange rate changes. This affects exports and imports in the goods market, causing aggregate demand to change.**

A higher value of the dollar implies a lower value of the yen, pound or euro. That makes U.S. exports more expensive for foreigners to buy, so they buy less. U.S. exports fall. A higher value of the dollar increases import spending and decreases export spending. Aggregate demand decreases.

A lower value of the dollar has the opposite effect. Imports are more expensive, so import spending decreases. Exports are less expensive, so export spending increases. Aggregate demand increases.

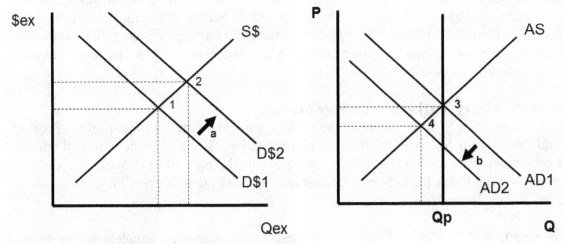

Figure 8-4. Dollar up. The demand for dollars in the exchange market increases (a). The exchange value of the dollar rises (1 to 2). This makes U.S. exports more expensive, so export spending decreases. This also makes U.S. imports less expensive, so import spending increases. Both changes decrease aggregate demand (b). Output falls (3 to 4).

Exports and imports depend on the exchange rate. And the exchange rate is determined in the exchange market. This leads to second shift #4. The demand for the dollar or supply of the dollar changes in the exchange market. The exchange rate adjusts up or down. Export and import spending are affected in the goods market. Such spending is included in aggregate demand, so aggregate demand shifts. And that changes output and the price level.

Suppose Americans decide to lend more money overseas. Perhaps interest rates in Japan, China, Germany, or Mexico are higher than they are in the U.S., so more profits can be earned by lending in those countries. To lend in Germany, Americans must acquire euros. To acquire euros, Americans must trade dollars. The supply of dollars increases.

Traders find that they can offer fewer euros for dollars and still make a deal, since so many dollars are being supplied. Americans become a little desperate to get euros, so they accept fewer euros in exchange for their dollars. The value of the dollar falls.

With a lower exchange value of the dollar, U.S. imports become more expensive, and U.S. exports become less expensive. It takes more dollars to buy the euros needed to import goods from Germany. That makes all German imports more expensive, so people buy fewer. Over in the goods market, import spending declines, and Americans spend more on goods produced in the U.S. It takes fewer euros to trade for the dollars needed to buy goods from the U.S. That makes all U.S. exports cheaper. People around the world buy more. Export spending increases.

Aggregate demand is based on spending, and spending is the sum of consumption, investment, government purchases, and exports less imports. If export spending rises and import spending falls, aggregate demand increases. U.S. output rises, and so does the price level.

Second shift #4 can work in reverse, too. Suppose the demand for the dollar increases, which increases the exchange value of the dollar. This happened in 2015 as international investors saw more opportunity for profits in the U.S. economy. But this increased the cost of U.S. exports around the world and contributed to slower growth in export spending. U.S. aggregate demand increased more slowly as a result.

Second Shift #5: Money Market to Exchange Market.
The demand for and supply of the dollar in the exchange market depends in part on the level of the U.S. real interest rate compared to rates in other countries. The higher the U.S. real interest rate, the more attractive it is to lend in the U.S., and the more dollars will be demanded in order to make such loans. The lower the U.S. real interest rate, the less attractive is U.S. lending, so the fewer are the dollars demanded.

The real interest rate is determined in the money market. When money demand rises or money supply falls, the real interest rate goes up. When money demand falls or money supply rises, the real interest rate goes down. Real interest rate changes affect dollar demand and supply in the exchange market. And that's second shift #5.

Suppose the money supply increases. Perhaps the Federal Reserve is increasing the money supply, trying to encourage borrowing and spending. The real interest rate falls.

The exchange market reacts. Around the world people decide that lending in the U.S. is less profitable than lending in their own countries. They demand fewer dollars in the exchange market. That decreases the exchange value of the dollar.

This is a good reason for taking the words "stronger" and "weaker" with a big grain of salt. Consider Japan. The Japanese economy had grown slowly for almost two decades. In

> **Second Shift #5: In the money market, money demand or supply shifts and the equilibrium real interest rate changes. This affects dollar demand and supply in the exchange market, causing the equilibrium exchange rate to change.**

2013 Japan's central bank tried to stimulate their economy with expansionary monetary policy. The increase in the money supply reduced Japan's real interest rates.

As a result, the value of the yen fell. International investors looked elsewhere for places to lend, and the demand for the yen decreased. Japanese people looked elsewhere for places to lend, too, so the demand for other currencies increased, and so did the supply of the yen. The value of the yen fell from $1.29 per 100 yen in mid-2011 back to one dollar per 100 yen in mid-2013. That's second shift #5. Japan's stock market and businesses were excited. If Japan's exports were cheaper, the world would buy more, and aggregate demand would increase. Output and employment would rise. That's second shift #4. The yen got weaker, but the policy was intended to make the Japanese economy stronger.

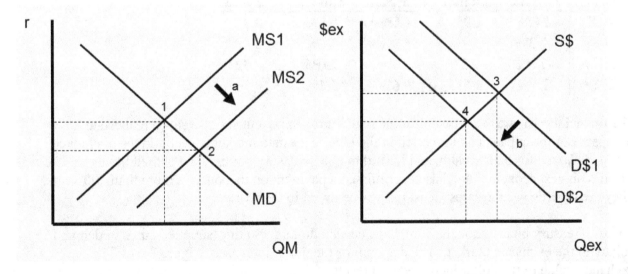

Figure 8-5. Looking elsewhere. The Federal Reserve increases the money supply (a), which decreases the real interest rate (1 to 2). The lower real interest rate makes lending in the U.S. less attractive, so international investors demand fewer dollars (b). The exchange value of the dollar falls (3 to 4).

The combination of second shifts #4 and #5 offers another path for monetary policy to affect output. Increase the money supply and the real interest rate will fall. Second shift #5 will reduce the exchange value of the dollar. Second shift #4 will cause export spending to increase and import spending to decrease, which will increase aggregate demand and increase output.

Of course, the neighbors might object. If the dollar is less valuable, the pound, euro and yen are more valuable, and exports to the U.S. from Great Britain, Europe and Japan will fall. Monetary policy moves by central banks are sometimes criticized by the nation's trading partners for this reason.

Data, Model, Story: The Great Recession *Revisited*

In Chapter 3 we looked at the Great Recession of 2007-09 using the goods and money markets (see Figures 3-13 to 3-15). Now we've got the exchange market. What can we add to our story?

Here are the data. The last column now shows the exchange rate in euros per dollar. The exchange value of the dollar had been falling during the 2000's, but it bottomed out in 2008 and began climbing in 2009 and 2010.

The Great Recession

Year	Real GDP Growth	CPI Inflation	Unemploy-ment Rate	Interest Rate Spread	Exchange Rate Euros/$
2007	1.8%	2.9%	4.6%	0.9%	0.73
2008	-0.3%	3.8%	5.8%	1.8%	0.68
2009	-2.8%	-0.3%	9.3%	2.0%	0.72
2010	2.5%	1.6%	9.6%	1.1%	0.76

The financial crisis was the reason for the rise. European countries also saw a real estate collapse. European banks had invested in the U.S. real estate market as well. Investors looked for a *safe haven* for their wealth, and looked to U.S. Treasury bonds. The United States has the world's biggest economy, and has never missed a payment on its bonds in more than 200 years. They are regarded as the safest, least risky investment in the world.

To buy Treasury bonds, though, Europeans needed dollars. So they supplied euros to demand dollars in the exchange market. The demand for the dollar increased (Figure 8-6). The exchange value of the dollar increased as a result.

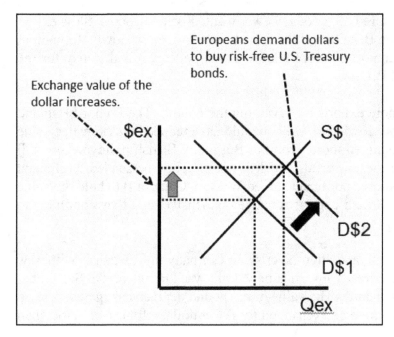

Figure 8-6. Increased demand for the dollar in the exchange market.

We're interested in the exchange market mostly because exports and imports depend on the exchange rate. With a higher exchange value, U.S. exports become more expensive, and U.S. imports become cheaper. Both exports and imports were reduced by the recession. Lower incomes in the U.S. reduced import spending; lower incomes in Europe reduced spending on U.S. exports. But the higher exchange value of the dollar contributed to an added reduction in exports. Aggregate demand fell, reducing output, increasing unemployment and reducing the inflation rate.

The Exchange Market and the Great Depression

The trouble started in May 1931 with a run on the largest bank in Austria, the Credit-Anstalt. International investors looked for an alternate place to keep their wealth. The exchanged their deposits for gold and shipped it out of Austria. With too little gold to support its money supply, Austria left the gold standard.

Gold was flooding out of Germany too. The financial dislocations left over from World War I were still disrupting the German economy. Germany owed enormous war reparations payments to France and Britain; France and Britain owed enormous war debts to the United States. Germany paid in gold, and investors recognized the precarious situation and moved their gold elsewhere. Germany left the gold standard.

With Austria and Germany down, investors wondered about Great Britain. The British economy had been in trouble since the end of World War I. To see why, we need to know something about how the gold standard influenced trade between nations.

The United States Treasury pledged to exchange one ounce of gold for $20.67. Great Britain pledged to exchange one ounce of gold for about four and a quarter pounds. Since the values of the two currencies were both fixed to gold, the exchange rate between the currencies was fixed too. The *fixed exchange rate* between dollars and pounds was $4.86 per pound. This had been the dollar-pound exchange rate for as long as anyone could remember.

But that exchange rate no longer worked for Britain. The U.S. economy had been developing rapidly for decades. U.S. goods were now as desirable as British goods. People around the world, and people in Britain, wanted to buy more U.S. goods. Fewer wanted British goods. Slow export growth held down aggregate demand in Britain, and the British economy grew slowly throughout the 1920's. And, since Britain was importing more than it was exporting, it had to pay for the excess with gold. Gold flowed out of Britain.

The British could have encouraged more exports by devaluing the pound. The Bank of England could have offered more pounds per ounce of gold, which would have reduced the exchange value of the pound. That would have encouraged more exports. But many British policymakers still thought of the pound as a symbol of the powerful British Empire. They persuaded a reluctant Chancellor of the Exchequer (a well-known politician named Winston Churchill) to hold the value of the pound at its traditional value. British exports remained expensive, and they continued to lag. Gold drained from British banks.

International investors saw this weakness, and after the crisis in Germany they began to withdraw gold from Britain. With gold reserves already low, this new drain was too much. On September 19, 1931, Great Britain left the gold standard. The value of the pound depreciated against foreign currencies. This meant that the pound could be exchanged for fewer dollars, francs, or marks than before.

That was just what international investors were afraid of. Investors who held funds in pounds suffered a loss in wealth. They had purchased some stock in a British company, (say) a thousand pounds worth. At $4.86 per pound, that was $4,860 dollars to an American. In September 1931 the exchange rate fell to about $3.50 per pound. Now the thousand pound investment was worth only $3,500. Almost overnight British assets were worth about 25% less to a foreign owner.

Now international investors focused on the United States. Would the U.S. be next? Would wealth kept in dollars lose value if the U.S. left the gold standard? Within days after Britain left gold, investors began withdrawing funds from U.S. banks and from the U.S. itself. The United States lost 11% of its gold supply in a month.

The New York Fed was charged with international policy. George Harrison knew what to do (and Benjamin Strong probably would have agreed). The classic response to a gold drain was to raise interest rates, so that keeping funds in the country was more attractive to investors. Higher interest rates meant a greater return on funds kept in dollars. On October 8 the Fed raised its discount rate a point to 2.5%, and a week later to 3.5%. It was the largest increase over so brief a period in the Fed's history, before or since.

- *Why did the Fed raise the discount rate in response to the gold drain in 1931?*

Figure 8-7 shows the analysis. International investors feared that the U.S. would leave the gold standard, and that the dollar's exchange rate would drop. This would reduce their wealth. So they tried to sell their dollars before the dollar was devalued. The supply of dollars increased. These days such an event would reduce the exchange rate. But in the era of fixed exchange rates, it created a surplus of dollars instead. More dollars were supplied than demanded at the fixed exchange rate.

The U.S. was still on gold, so investors had another option. They traded their dollars for gold at $20.67 an ounce. Gold drained from the Treasury's vaults.

So the Fed raised the discount rate. An increase in the real interest rate makes lending in the U.S. more profitable, and so will increase the demand for the dollar. That's second shift #5. It worked. The demand for the dollar increased enough so that quantity demanded equaled quantity supplied. There was no longer reason to convert dollars to gold. Sure enough, the gold drain stopped. The U.S. gold stock was about the same at the end of 1933 as it was in October 1931.

Figure 5-6 in Chapter 5 shows the increase in the discount rate in 1931. Now you know why the Fed followed this *pro-cyclical monetary policy*. The economy was in depression. Unemployment was rising and prices were falling. Yet the Fed increased interest rates, to support the gold standard's fixed exchange rate. The gold standard turned out to be a mechanism for transmitting crises from one country to another.

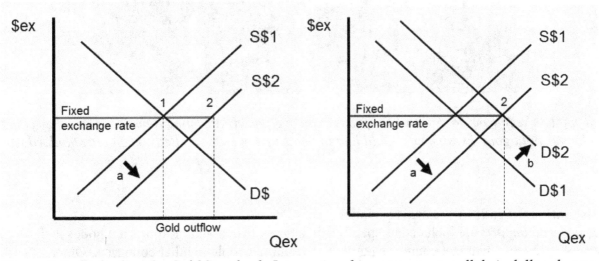

Figure 8-7. Defending the Gold Standard. International investors try to sell their dollars because they fear it will be devalued. The supply of dollars in currency markets increases (a). At the fixed exchange rate, there is a surplus of dollars (1 to 2). There are more dollars supplied than demanded. Unable to trade their dollars for other currencies, investors demand gold in exchange for dollars from the Treasury. Gold drains away. The Fed increases interest rates to make lending in the U.S. more attractive, which increases the demand for dollars (b). That's second shift #5. Equilibrium is restored at the fixed exchange rate (2). The gold drain stops.

Almost as an afterthought, the United States left the *gold standard*, with a whimper, not a bang. There was no single, economy-quaking announcement, as in Great Britain in 1931. Instead, the Roosevelt administration chipped away at the standard with a series of acts. The Federal Reserve was allowed to use both gold and government bonds as a currency reserve, meaning gold hardly limited the money supply at all. It was then made illegal for U.S. citizens to own gold for monetary purposes. Private citizens were required to turn over to the government all gold not used in industry or jewelry (they were allowed to keep their gold dental fillings, too).

In effect, the Treasury no longer pledged to U.S. residents that it would exchange dollars for gold. Finally, in early 1934, the official price of gold was increased from $20.67 to $35 per ounce for international trade purposes, a devaluation of the dollar in foreign exchange. Gold still played a role in international trade, but by the end of 1933, the U.S. money supply was no longer backed by gold, nor was the size of the money supply influenced by gold in any significant sense. From then until now, U.S. money has been *fiat currency*, money by government decree.

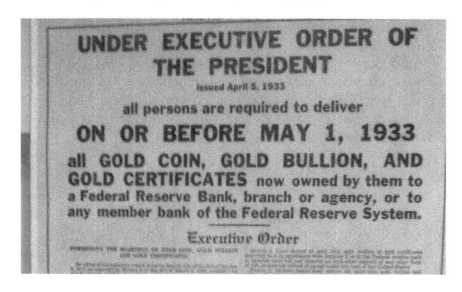

But you can keep your gold teeth. A reproduction of a poster informing Americans that they could no longer hold gold investments. Gold had to be turned over to the Fed. The gold standard was over.

International Trade in the Macro Model

Exports and *imports* are included as spending in aggregate demand. Exports are goods and services produced within a country's borders and sold to people in other countries. Other countries' spending adds to aggregate demand. Imports are goods and services produced in other countries but purchased in the country. Imports subtract from aggregate demand because the spending is diverted from the country's production.

An increase in the volume of *international trade* will increase both exports and imports. It's trade, after all. A country's imports are mostly bought with its exports. If both exports and imports increase by the same amount, aggregate demand will remain unchanged. Trade may have no effect on aggregate demand, output and prices. This is shown in the left diagram in Figure 8-8.

Why all the concern about trade, if it has no effect? Because the benefits of trade mainly show up in aggregate supply.

Comparative Advantage in Trade

"It is sometimes said," wrote economist Paul Douglas in his memoir, "that if all economists were laid end to end, they would not reach a conclusion." But that's not the case with trade, Douglas continued. "Almost unanimously, from Adam Smith on, they have favored *free trade* between localities and nations."

Why are economists so nearly unanimous in supporting international trade? It goes back to a British economist named *David Ricardo*. Ricardo was a successful stockbroker who took up economics after reading Adam Smith's *Wealth of Nations*. In 1817 he published his own book, **On the Principles of Political Economy and Taxation.** There he elaborated his theory of trade.

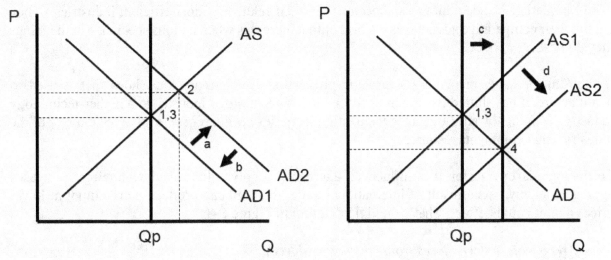

Figure 8-8. Higher Tech Supply. Exports and imports are included in aggregate demand. An increase in spending on a nation's exports increases aggregate demand (a). This would increase output and the price level (2). An equal increase in spending for imports would move aggregate demand back to the original equilibrium (b, 1,3). Specialization in the nation's most efficient industries improves average technology. Both increase potential output and aggregate supply (c, d). Output is higher and prices are lower with increased trade (4).

Trade is obviously beneficial in the case of *absolute advantage*. If one nation can produce coffee at low cost, and another can manufacture airplanes at low cost, it makes sense for the two nations to specialize in their low cost activities and trade. The United States imports coffee from Columbia, where it is easy to grow. It would be very expensive for the United States to try to grow coffee. Without trade, there would not be a Starbucks on every block.

Absolute advantage is the basis for only a small amount of trade, however. Most trade occurs because of a more powerful (and more difficult) idea, *comparative advantage*. What counts, Ricardo and every

Comparative advantage means that a nation can produce a product at lower cost, relative to the other products it produces. World output increases if nations specialize in the products for which they have a comparative advantage.

economist since have said, is the *relative* cost of producing products. Nations that are less efficient at producing everything can still export goods. Nations that are more efficient at producing everything can still import goods.

As an example, consider modern dentistry. A dentist is probably more skilled at cleaning teeth and at oral surgery than is the dental hygienist. Why, then, does the dentist hire the hygienist? Because the dentist is far more skilled at surgery, and only a little more skilled at teeth cleaning. The dentist has the comparative advantage in surgery, but the hygienist has the comparative advantage in cleaning teeth. The dentist's office can serve more patients (and make more money) if the hygienist cleans teeth while the dentist performs surgery.

With international trade nations can *specialize* in their relatively most efficient industries. They exploit their comparative advantages. World output increases when nations specialize in the things they do best.

If the United States increases its airplane production, and imports the shoes that it used to manufacture, it has shifted its resources from a lower-technology industry to a higher-technology industry. Moving towards greater specialization increases the aggregate level of technology of the industries that employ its resources.

Technology is one factor that influences aggregate supply. Improved technology increases aggregate supply. As a result of international trade, the U.S. can produce more output at lower prices than it could before. That's the right diagram in Figure 8-8.

- *Who wins and who loses from international trade?*

If international trade offers us more output for lower prices, why is trade so controversial? Because, while nations as a whole benefit from trade, not everyone in a nation benefits. Increased trade involves a shift in resources towards the industry that produces the exported goods, and away from the industry that competes with the imported goods.

This can be hard. In our example, employment in the airplane industry will increase; employment in the shoe industry will decline. But maybe airplanes are produced in Seattle while shoes were made in Tennessee. Will shoe workers have the skills to work in the airplane factories? Will they have to uproot themselves to move to Seattle? Will the communities in Tennessee that depend on the shoe industry even survive?

This is one inequality issue that our macroeconomic model can analyze. The United States has a comparative advantage in the production of high-technology goods, like airplanes. Mexico and China have comparative advantages in producing low-tech goods, like shoes. Total world output increases if the U.S. makes airplanes and China makes shoes. But that increases the demand for higher-skilled workers in high technology industries in the U.S., and decreases the demand for less-skilled workers in low technology industries in the U.S. Income shifts toward higher-skilled workers. Less skilled workers are left behind. Most of the decline in lower-tech manufacturing jobs and pay in the U.S. is due to automation ("Winners-Take-All" from Chapter 7). But some is due to importing products that the U.S. used to produce itself.

Consumers are better off with trade, because of increased output and lower prices. Businesses and employees in the export industries are better off too. But those in the import-competing industries lose out.

The Smoot-Hawley Tariff

Tariffs are taxes on imported goods, and are they are usually intended to restrict trade. These taxes raise the prices of imports, making them less attractive to consumers. Instead, consumers buy the goods produced by domestic farmers and manufacturers, who employ more workers and make more profits. Tariffs help domestic businesses that compete with imports, and they help their employees. Tariffs hurt consumers and businesses that must buy the higher priced imported goods.

The tariff question had been a hot-button issue throughout the 19th century and into the 20th. Republicans, with their electoral base in the east, supported high tariffs to protect eastern manufacturers from European imports. Democrats, with their electoral base in the south and west, supported moderate tariffs. They recognized the need for tariffs as the main source of revenue for the government, but feared the effect tariffs would have on the prices their constituents had to pay.

> *A tariff is a tax on imported goods, designed to raise its price. Consumers switch their purchases to domestic goods, and imports are reduced. This raises employment and profits for domestic industries.*

Since Republicans held the Presidency for most years from Lincoln to Taft (1861 to 1913), U.S. tariffs were high. When Democrat Woodrow Wilson became President in 1913, tariffs were cut substantially. The tariff reduction was made possible partly because the new income tax became the biggest source of revenue for the government.

When the Republicans regained power with President Harding, however, they passed the Fordney-McCumber tariff in 1922, which sharply increased tariff rates. The average percentage tacked onto the price of imports in 1920 was16%. After the 1922 tariff, the rate was 38%. During the 1920's, falling farm incomes reduced opposition to tariffs in the south and west. Some Democrats joined Republicans in support of higher tariffs.

Herbert Hoover had pledged to help farmers by restricting imports of foreign farm products during the campaign of 1928. Senator Reed Smoot of Utah and Representative Willis Hawley of Oregon sponsored a tariff bill, but they couldn't get it through Congress in 1929.

Then the Great Depression began. One policy that seemed likely to help was to restrict imports, to preserve the dwindling U.S. market for American goods. Senator Watson of Indiana said that if the tariff bill passed, "within a year from this date we shall have regained the peak of prosperity."

Economist Paul Douglas was aghast (yes, he's the future Senator from Chapter 7). Douglas joined with another economist, Clair Wilcox, to draft an appeal to President Hoover to veto the Smoot-Hawley tariff. The letter pointed out that other countries needed to sell their goods to the U.S. in order to earn the dollars to buy U.S. exports. They couldn't earn dollars if the U.S. wouldn't buy their exports. The tariffs also would provoke other countries to retaliate with tariff increases of their own. Raising tariffs to cut imports would surely lead to an offsetting reduction in U.S. exports. The tariff was self-defeating. No fewer than 1,028 economists signed the letter.

President Hoover signed the bill anyway. At the June 17, 1930 signing ceremony he used six gold pens, and handed them to Smoot and Hawley and other supporters as souvenirs.

In our macroeconomic model a tariff seems like a reasonable anti-recession policy. A tariff is a tax on imported goods, intended to reduce imports. Imports are subtracted from the spending that makes up aggregate demand—recall C+I+G+X-M. If imports are reduced, consumers will spend more on domestic output, from the import-competing domestic businesses. Aggregate demand will increase. An increase in aggregate demand will increase output. Jobs are brought home from overseas.

That's just one of the effects of a tariff, however. To buy American goods, other nations need to earn dollars, and they can only do that by exporting goods to the U.S. The less they export to the U.S., the less than can afford to import from the U.S. Furthermore, other nations may respond to a tariff with trade restrictions of their own. Other nations did increase their tariffs on American goods, after the Smoot-Hawley tariff was passed. These tariffs reduced U.S. exports. A reduction in exports *reduces* aggregate demand.

Trade restrictions reduce imports, which increases aggregate demand. They reduce exports, which decreases aggregate demand. They raise input costs and reduce the level of technology employed, which reduces aggregate supply. Overall, output is lower and the price level is higher when trade is restricted.

Tariffs interfere with the most important benefit of free trade, which is the more efficient allocation of production among nations. The principle of comparative advantage means that each nation has something to contribute to world output. With trade, a nation specializes in the industries in which it is most efficient, relative to its other industries. It produces more from its resources. Trading this output in the world's markets earns it more income than it could have had without trade.

When the U.S. imported less, it switched resources to industries in which it was relatively less efficient. That means that U.S. output was produced with lower average efficiency. The same resources were used in less efficient ways, so they produced less total output. That's like a reduction in technology, and that reduces aggregate supply.

Imposing a tariff also means that imported equipment and materials are more expensive. A tariff on steel, for example, increases the cost of steel to auto and appliance manufacturers. And a tariff means that resources are used less efficiently. Aggregate supply is reduced, and, if the tariff is permanent, potential output is reduced too. Tariffs reverse the increases in aggregate supply and potential output in Figure 8-8.

Netting it all out, the Smoot-Hawley tariff increased domestic demand for the output of import-competing industries (increasing aggregate demand), decreased the foreign demand for the output of exporting industries (decreasing aggregate demand), and raised resource costs and reduced average technology (decreasing aggregate supply and potential output). In the end, the tariff reduced output and raised prices.

U.S. imports fell, by 36% in real terms from 1929 to 1933. That's what the higher tariffs were meant to achieve. But real exports fell 45%. The U.S. trade position actually got worse in the first years after Smoot-Hawley. Both exports and imports had been around 5.5% of Gross Domestic Product in 1929. In 1933 both were near 3.5%. GDP had fallen, but trade had fallen faster. The volume of trade fell around the world, partly because of rising tariffs, partly because of falling incomes.

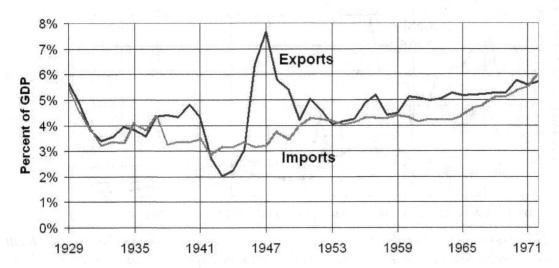

Figure 8-9. U.S. Exports and Imports as Percent of GDP, 1929-1972. Both exports and imports dropped radically from 1929 to 1932, because of the world depression and the Smoot Hawley tariff. Trade as a share of GDP was cut nearly in half. Demand for U.S. exports was huge after World War II, while other nations had little capacity to export. The U.S. had an enormous trade surplus. The surplus got smaller and smaller during the 1950's and 1960's as the rest of the world recovered. By 1972 U.S. had a trade deficit, imports exceeded exports. But only then did the share of trade in GDP permanently reach its 1929 level.

There is little doubt that the drop in trade contributed to the Depression. Still, trade was a small part of American economy. The effect of falling consumption and investment was much bigger. The Smoot-Hawley tariff didn't cause the Great Depression. But it probably made the Depression worse.

From GATT to the WTO
The Democrats gained control of the Presidency and Congress in 1933. Historically, when that happened they would pass a reduction in U.S. import tariffs, as they had during the Woodrow Wilson administration. Democrats had opposed the Smoot-Hawley tariff.

But the Great Depression presented special problems. Most other countries had raised their tariffs too, in response to Smoot-Hawley and their own economic depressions. A U.S. tariff cut might not be followed by tariff reductions in other countries, and that would put U.S. businesses at a disadvantage.

217

The U.S. decided to push for *bilateral trade agreements*. It would negotiate tariff reductions with other countries, one country at a time. Congress approved the *Reciprocal Trade Agreement Act (RTAA)* in 1934. It authorized the President to negotiate bilateral agreements. Congress gave prior approval to whatever agreements the President might negotiate. The tariff reductions would not have to be ratified by Congress. It was the first time Congress had ever delegated such powers to the President. The RTAA was good for three years, after which it could be reauthorized.

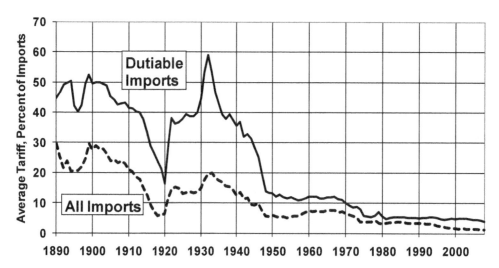

Figure 8-10. Average U.S. Tariff Rates, 1890-2008. The black line shows the average tariff collected as a percent of all imports subject to tariffs ("dutiable imports"). The dashed line shows the average tariff as a percent of all imports, including those not subject to tariffs. The two lines tell the same story. Tariffs were high at the start of the 20th century. They fell during the Wilson administration (1913-1921). The Fordney-McCumber tariff increased the rate in the 1920's, and then Smoot-Hawley raised tariffs again in 1930-31. The rate on dutiable imports reached almost 60%, the highest in U.S. history. Reciprocal agreements began to reduce tariffs during the 1930's. Then the negotiation of GATT in 1947 cut tariffs in half. Reductions from the 1960's to the 1980's came from successive rounds of GATT negotiations. In the new century tariffs are at their lowest levels in U.S. history.

By the end of the decade the U.S. had negotiated 21 bilateral agreements with its trading partners. Tariffs were reduced, but they remained as high as they had been before Smoot Hawley. Little was changed during World War II. Then, starting in April 1947, representatives of 23 nations met in Geneva, Switzerland to discuss new trade rules. The result was the *General Agreement on Tariffs and Trade*, known as *GATT*. The average U.S. tariff was cut in half.

Attempts to found an International Trade Organization to enforce the GATT failed, but eventually a GATT Secretariat was headquartered in Geneva to administer the rules. Nations gathered every few years to negotiate further tariff reductions and other trade rules. These gatherings were known as "*rounds*," usually named after the place where they first met. Sometimes the rounds succeeded, sometimes they did not. But tariff rates trended ever lower, and world trade increased.

The United States also undertook trade negotiations apart from the GATT framework. The *North American Free Trade Agreement (NAFTA),* for example, did away with most trade restrictions between Canada, Mexico and the United States. It passed Congress in 1993.

The last round of GATT negotiations started in Uruguay in 1986. It became known as the Uruguay Round. Trade negotiations had become more complex over the decades. In the 1940's most of the world's trade was in tangible goods like cars, machinery, or wheat. Now new products were being traded. New communications technology allowed trade in services, such as telephone answering or computer programming. Rules were needed to cover trade in services. Sometimes ideas and technologies were bought and sold over international boundaries, so rules were needed defining intellectual property rights.

In the 1940's most of the barriers to trade were tariffs, which were easily measured taxes on imports. As tariffs were reduced, however, nations found other ways to protect their industries from foreign competition. Nations could require importers to obtain licenses, and then make the licensing procedures difficult. Nations could apply more stringent environmental regulations to imported goods than domestically produced goods. They could design their health and safety rules to discriminate against particular nations' products. Of course, some of these rules and restrictions were legitimate, designed to protect national security, the environment or consumer health. Negotiating the line between a nation's attempts to protect its security, environment or health, and its attempts to protect its domestic industries from trade, was much tougher than simply cutting a tariff rate in half.

> *Trade negotiations have reduced tariffs, but now must contend with new issues such as trade in services and intellectual property, and environmental and labor regulations.*

Rules could be written and agreed to, but they were open to interpretation. How to resolve disputes between nations over trade? The Uruguay round created a new organization, the *World Trade Organization (WTO)* to resolve trade disputes. The agreement was signed in April 1994. By the end of the year the U.S. Congress had agreed. In January 1995 the new trade rules came into effect, and the WTO began operation. The WTO has been the focus of trade negotiations—and controversy—ever since.

Brexit

Brexit means Great Britain's exit from the *European Union.* The European Union is partial economic and political union of 28 countries in Europe. In particular, it tries to maintain a single market for all its territory, so people and goods can move easily among the member countries. There are no tariffs or other trade barriers, and no limits to immigration. In 1999 the European Union create a standard currency for its member countries, called the *euro.* Most of the EU countries adopted the euro—the Germans abandoned the mark, the French abandoned the franc, the Italians left the the lira—but Great Britain kept the British pound. (Chapter 11 discusses the consequences of adopting the euro for Greece.)

In a referendum on June 23, 2016, 52% of the British electorate voted to leave the European Union. On March 29, 2017, the British government invoked Article 50 of the European Union treaty, which started the process of negotiating the country's withdrawal from the EU.

Leaving the EU means Britain will be able to set its own immigration policy, but it also means that it will no longer be part of the EU's single market. There will be tariffs and trade barriers on British exports to Europe.

Some economists expected an immediate recession after the referendum. The pro-Brexit vote was a shock to many, and their warnings about the costs of trade restrictions in the long run influenced their thinking about the immediate future. There was no recession. British real GDP grew 2.3% in the second half of 2016, about the same as the previous four years.

The first effect of Brexit was a drop in the exchange value of the pound. That did happen right away. The exchange rate in dollars per pound dropped from $1.48 per pound on June 23, 2016, the day of the referendum, to $1.36 on June 24, when the voting results were announced. That's an 8% change in one day. Currency traders knew that tariffs would likely reduce the amount of trade between Britain and the world. With less trade, there would be less need for British pounds. The demand for the pound fell, and so did its exchange value.

The drop in the pound's value decreased the cost of Great Britain's exports to the rest of the world, and increased the cost of imports from the rest of the world. Lower export costs should increase British exports, eventually. But remember, elasticities are smaller in the short run and bigger in the long run (see Chapter 2). At first, a change in the exchange rate may not affect the quantity of exports very much. If British exports are cheaper other countries may want to buy from Britain, but they'll have to make contacts, negotiate contracts, obtain financing. This takes time. Eventually exports respond to a change in a currency's exchange value, but not right away.

Likewise, when the exchange value of a currency falls, imports may continue unchanged for a time. Contracts have been written, deals have been made, trades go through no matter what happens to the exchange rate. If imports are no longer profitable, though, imports eventually will decline. It usually takes more than a year for exchange rate changes to affect exports and imports significantly.

What did happen, though, is the price of those imports went up. Importers passed their higher costs to consumers in higher prices. The British annual inflation rate increased from 0.4% in June 2016 to 2.6% in April 2017.

Then first quarter real GDP growth came in at 0.8%, a significant slowdown from 2016. It's just one quarter, but the British magazine *The Economist* reported that "the Brexit slowdown is under way." If that's true, Britain is experiencing a fall in real GDP growth and a rise in inflation. If that real GDP growth turns negative, we would show it as a decrease in aggregate supply in the goods market. Higher costs for imported inputs reduce the profitability of production, so British firms cut output. The exchange market has given Great Britain a preview of the effect of Brexit on its economy.

Eventually British exports will benefit from the lower exchange value of the pound. But by that time Brexit will raise the trade barriers to British goods in Europe. The result should look like the effect of the Smoot-Hawley tariff on the U.S. economy way back in 1930, a reversal of Figure 8-8. There's no net effect on aggregate demand, a decrease in aggregate supply, and (if the new trade barriers are permanent) a decrease in potential output.

How to Equilibrate the Exchange Market?

The exchange market must be equilibrated. The quantity of a currency demanded must equal the quantity of currency supplied. Some mechanism must bring that result about.

In most markets flexible prices equilibrate quantity demanded and supplied. That happens in the exchange market if exchange rates are allowed to fluctuate. If dollars demanded exceed dollars supplied, desperate traders will begin to offer more euros (or yen or pounds) for those dollars. The exchange value of the dollar will rise. This will encourage some traders to offer more dollars (I can get more euros for my dollars!), and it will discourage some traders from trying to buy dollars (I don't want them at that price!). We've equilibrated the exchange market by changing the exchange rate.

We accept this, but in the 19th and early 20th centuries the world was used to the fixed exchange rates that existed under the gold standard. Fixed exchange rates do have advantages. Business decisions are more predictable. The profits or interest an American earns in European euros or Japanese yen will not be eroded by a drop in the value of the dollar. With less uncertainty, a business will more likely to make an investment or a loan. International trade may grow faster if exchange rates are fixed from year to year.

But suppose the quantity of dollars demanded and supplied are not equal at that fixed exchange rate? That's the situation shown in the top left diagram in Figure 8-11. The equilibrium exchange rate is less than the fixed exchange rate, so there is a dollar surplus. More dollars are supplied than demanded. Some trades will not go through—there just won't be anyone wanting to buy those dollars at that exchange rate price. Desperate traders will offer more dollars per foreign currency unit, and the value of the dollar will fall, unless something is done.

Suppose, though, that the nation has committed to *support the fixed exchange rate*. One thing that could be done is to raise interest rates. With higher interest rates, more people would want to lend in the United States, and for that they need dollars. More dollars would be demanded. Interest rates could be raised until demand increased enough to match supply at the fixed exchange rate.

Or, taxes could be increased. Then people would have less after-tax income to buy imports. They would need fewer foreign currency units, so they would supply fewer dollars to get them. Dollar supply would decrease until demand and supply were consistent with the fixed exchange rate. This is shown in the top right diagram in Figure 8-11.

But what if the economy was in recession? Then interest rate hikes and tax increases would make the

> *Three desirable features of an international payments system are fixed exchange rates, independent stabilization policy, and free flow of capital. One of these must be given up to equilibrate the exchange market.*

recession worse. Those are pro-cyclical monetary and fiscal policies in recession. Policy would create more economic hardship, just to support the fixed exchange rate. We've equilibrated the exchange market, but we've given up independent stabilization policy—the ability to set monetary and fiscal policy to our economy's needs.

Or, perhaps dollar supply could be restricted directly. Make importers acquire a license to import foreign goods, make foreign investments or lend in other countries, and deny licenses when the supply of dollars is too great. That would limit the supply, so the fixed exchange rate would be consistent with exchange market equilibrium. That's shown in the lower left in Figure 8-11.

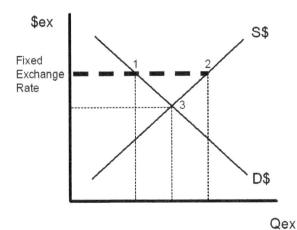

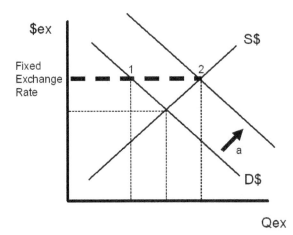

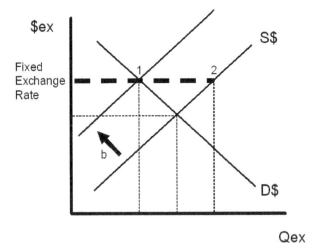

Figure 8-11. Two out of three. Here the fixed exchange rate of the dollar is above the equilibrium value. At the fixed rate, the number of dollars demanded (1) is less than the number supplied (2). There are three ways to solve this problem and equilibrate the exchange market. The U.S. could allow the dollar's value to fluctuate. It would drop to equilibrium (3), and the number of dollars demanded and supplied would be equal. But the fixed exchange rate has been sacrificed. It could raise interest rates and raise taxes. Higher returns on lending would make the dollar more attractive to foreign investors (second shift #5). The demand for dollars would rise (a). But independent stabilization policy has been sacrificed. It could restrict imports and foreign transactions. If Americans don't import foreign goods or invest or lend in foreign countries, they will not supply dollars in exchange for foreign currencies. The supply of dollars will decrease (b). But free trade and the free flow of capital have been sacrificed, and the world won't produce as much as it could.

But wait—the exchange system is supposed to *encourage* trade! Restricting the ability to trade currencies across borders discourages trade. I have willing customers for imported German cuckoo clocks, and clock craftsmen in Germany ready to produce them. But I can't get a license to exchange dollars for euros. Transactions that will make buyers and sellers better off don't take place. We've given up the free flow of capital and currency across international boundaries.

There are three features the world would like to have in an exchange market: *fixed exchange rates, independent stabilization policy*, and the *free flow of capital* across national boundaries. Fixed exchange rates make business decisions more predictable. Discretionary stabilization policy lets governments respond to recessions and inflation with counter-cyclical policy. The free flow of capital increases the world's wealth by allowing trade to allocate resources to their most productive uses.

> *The choice between independent stabilization policy, the free flow of capital, or fixed exchange rates, is sometimes called the "impossible trinity." Economist Robert Mundell thought it up.*

But the world can only have two out of three. One of these three goals must be sacrificed to equilibrate the exchange market.

A Canadian economist named *Robert Mundell* had given this problem a lot of thought. And why not? It was the central economic problem Canada faced in the 1950's and 1960's. Canada was closely linked to the United States. Currency, trade and investment flowed freely across its long U.S. border. But this meant, Mundell pointed out, that Canada had to choose between a fixed exchange rate and independent stabilization policy. Unlike other developed nations, Canada chose to let its exchange rate fluctuate. It kept its independent stabilization policy. The choice of which of the three desirable features to sacrifice came to be called *Mundell's "impossible trinity."*

- *How has the world solved the exchange market equilibrium problem?*

The gold standard had fixed exchange rates and the free flow of capital, but sacrificed independent stabilization policy. Since each nation tied its currency to gold at a fixed price ($20.67 per ounce in the U.S.), each currency exchanged for a fixed amount of every other currency. Gold was accepted in payment everywhere, though, so money could flow freely across boundaries. There was free flow of capital.

But a nation tried to import more goods and it exported, it would have to pay for the difference in gold. Gold would flow out of the country. The nation's money supply would decrease, interest rates would rise, and aggregate demand would decrease. This would happen even if the economy were in recession. Stabilization policy was not independent—it was not set by each country based on that country's needs.

The gold standard broke down during the Great Depression, and something new was needed. In 1944 the U.S. and Great Britain called for an international conference to thrash out a new system. The U.S. representative was a prominent Treasury official, Harry Dexter White. Great Britain sent the world's most famous economist, John Maynard Keynes.

Where would the conference be held? World War II still raged; Britain was under the threat of German rocket attacks. In the U.S., then. But a conference in July in hot, humid Washington, Keynes wrote White, would be "an unfriendly act." They picked the Mount Washington luxury hotel in the mountains of New Hampshire for its cool climate. The hotel had been closed for two years due to wartime travel restrictions,

> *An international conference in 1944 established the Bretton Woods system of fixed exchange rates, and created the International Monetary Fund.*

but the management scrambled to get it ready. The hotel's train station gave the conference its name: *Bretton Woods.* Forty-four countries sent delegations. Seven hundred delegates filled the hotel to overflowing. But Harry Dexter White and John Maynard Keynes ran the show.

Wish you were here! The Mount Washington Hotel, Bretton Woods, New Hampshire, in a 1920's postcard.

They came up with a mixed system. Exchange rates would be fixed, most of the time. Stabilization policy would be independent, most of the time. That left the problem of equilibrating trade and currency flows. This would be accomplished at first by restricting the supply of each nation's currency in exchange markets. International lending and investing would be restrained. These restrictions were lifted by the end of the 1950's.

Each nation was expected to set fixed exchange rates against other currencies. The U.S. dollar would be the main international currency. Nations would fix their exchange rates relative to the dollar, and hold dollars in reserve, to support their fixed exchange rates. That gave the U.S. an advantage, because it could print all the dollar reserves it wanted. So, for international trade purposes, the U.S. fixed the dollar relative to gold, at $35 on ounce. That would restrict the amount of dollars that could be released into the world's trading system. Other countries had the right to exchange their dollars for gold, which meant the U.S. would have to be careful about the supply of dollars.

Countries were expected to "defend" their fixed exchange rates. For example, if traders wanted to buy more French francs than others wanted to sell, the value of the franc would rise. Under the rules France would sell francs at the fixed exchange rate until buyers were satisfied. If traders tried to sell more francs than others wanted to buy, the value of the franc would tend to fall. France then was expected to buy francs at the fixed rate, using their reserves of dollars or gold.

If a country's dollar or gold reserves ran short, they could borrow reserves from a new institution, the *International Monetary Fund (IMF)*. This would allow a country to maintain fixed rates if the imbalance in buying and selling was temporary. As a condition of the loan, however, the IMF might recommend higher interest rates to increase the demand for its currency, and higher taxes and less government spending, to reduce the country's imports. Stabilization policy was to be independent, unless the IMF said otherwise.

If the imbalance was longer term—a "fundamental disequilibrium"—then the country could apply to the IMF to adjust their exchange rates. Again the IMF might enforce contractionary monetary and fiscal policies. If these were tried and the imbalance persisted, a cut in the exchange rates would be permitted. Exchange rates were fixed, unless the IMF said otherwise.

The Bretton Woods system faced problems in the 1960's, and broke down in the early 1970's. The United States dollar was the anchor of the system. All currency values were fixed to the dollar, but now the dollar itself was over-valued. The cold war with the Soviet Union caused the U.S. to spend a lot on foreign military aid. It fought a war in Vietnam. And it kept interest rates low, which encouraged inflation and discouraged dollar demand. The quantity of dollars supplied exceeded the quantity demanded in international exchange markets.

The dollar was the only currency tied to gold, at $35 an ounce. This was supposed to keep the U.S. from allowing dollar supplies to increase too much. It hadn't worked. By the end of the 1960's, there were more dollars in foreign hands than there was gold in Fort Knox.

In 1971 Great Britain tried to exchange dollars for gold. President Richard Nixon met with his advisors at the *Camp David* retreat in the hills of Maryland. On Sunday night, August 15, 1971, President Nixon spoke to the nation about the state of the economy. When he got to gold, he said

> I have directed Secretary Connally to suspend temporarily the convertibility of the dollar into gold or other reserve assets, except in amounts and conditions determined to be in the interest of monetary stability and in the best interests of the United States.

The United States had closed the gold window. It would not back the dollar with gold, as the Bretton Woods system required. The Bretton Woods system was dead.

Since 1971, the world has solved the Exchange Market problem with flexible exchange rates. Capital flows are enormous, and stabilization policies are independent. But some countries still face Mundell's impossible trinity—when their governments attempt to set the exchange values of their currencies.

China, the Yuan and the Dollar

China began to abandon communism as a way to organize its economy in 1978, and turned increasingly to market organization. Chinese real gross domestic product began to grow fast, averaging 10% per year from 1980 to 2010 (the U.S. economy grew 2.7% per year during this time.). Growth fell below 8% only twice during these three decades, in 1989 and 1990. Those were the years of unrest surrounding the massacre at Tiananmen Square. The lesson was not lost on the Communist Party leaders. Keep the economy growing, or the party's hold on power could slip.

Lets look at the exchange market from China's point of view, so we'll measure the value of the Chinese currency, called the yuan or renminbi, in dollars per yuan. In 1994 China devalued the yuan from 17 U.S. cents per yuan to 12 cents per yuan, then fixed it at that rate for ten years. A devaluation of 5 cents may not seem like much, but it's the percentage change that matters. The devaluation made Chinese exports cheaper by 33%. Exports grew rapidly (that's second shift #4). A cheap yuan made imports expensive, however, which discourage Chinese people from buying. The end of the communist economy also meant the end of the "iron rice bowl." No more free medical care, support for the elderly in retirement, or subsidized housing. The Chinese people responded by spending less and saving more.

With exports cheap and little spending on imports, China exported much more than it imported. China ran enormous trade surpluses, especially with the United States. Ordinarily such a surplus would result in a rise in the value of the yuan and a fall in the value of the dollar. Americans would supply dollars into foreign exchange markets, trying to buy yuan in order to buy Chinese products. The Chinese would not demand so many dollars, since they weren't buying many American products. With dollar supply rising faster than dollar demand, the value of the dollar should have increased.

> *To keep the value of the Chinese yuan from rising, China created yuan and bought dollars. It invested these dollars in U.S. Treasury bonds, which helped keep U.S. interest rates low.*

Let's say the same thing from China's point of view. China was not importing much from the U.S., so few yuan were supplied, but the U.S. was buying a lot from China, so many yuan were demanded. That should have increased the exchange value of the yuan.

A rising yuan would have made Chinese exports more expensive, threatening the economic growth upon which China's growing economy depended. So the Chinese central bank began *buying dollars* to prevent the dollar from falling and the yuan from rising. That's a form of government exchange market intervention. The added supply of yuan kept its exchange value low. The added demand for dollars kept its exchange value high (again, that's the same thing).

What did China do with all those dollars they had purchased? China lent them back to the United States, buying U.S. Treasury bonds and other U.S. assets. By 2014 China owned more than a foreign exchange reserves of $4 trillion dollars, much of it in American bonds. In effect, China acted as a kind of central bank, buying Treasury bonds for money. The money supply increased. U.S. banks and other lenders had more dollars to lend, which kept U.S. interest rates low. For a time in the 2000's the Fed was trying to restrain U.S. growth by selling bonds and raising interest rates, but China was offsetting this policy with their bond purchases. All that money flowing into the U.S. helped keep interest rates low.

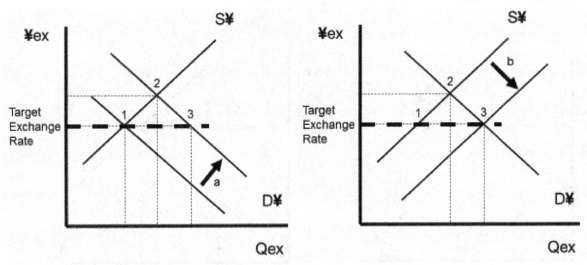

Figure 8-12. Buying dollars for fun and profit. International businesses demand even more yuan to buy China's increasing exports (a). This increases the equilibrium exchange value of the yuan (2) above the lower target rate (1). To hold the yuan's value low, China prints new yuan and supplies them in the exchange market (b), trading them for dollars and other foreign currencies. The yuan's value is held down (3). China invests the dollars it buys in U.S. Treasury bonds, which holds down U.S. interest rates.

China's exchange rate policy may have helped keep U.S. interest rates low, adding to investment spending. But Americans accused China of *currency manipulation*, for holding the exchange value of the yuan low.   This increased China's exports to the U.S. (which are U.S. imports) and decreased U.S. exports to China.   China's manufacturing employment grew, but U.S. manufacturing employment never recovered from the 2001 recession. Much of the reason was technological advance and automation, but Chinese exchange rate policy gets some of the blame.

Under pressure from the U.S. Congress and its own central bank, China allowed the yen to rise in value, slowly, starting in mid-2005. But the central bank still had to buy billions of dollars to keep the yuan from rising too fast. By 2016 China owned xxx in American bonds.

China's real GDP growth averaged 10% per year from 1980 to 2010. Over 30 years that's a 17-fold increase in output—an astounding rate of development for 1.3 billion people. But growth dropped below 8% in 2012, and below 7% in 2015. There's no doubt that China's output growth is slowing down. Why?

China's based its growth strategy exports and investment. Keep the value of the yuan low and the world will buy China's exports. Manufacturing employment will increase. Increase government spending on infrastructure. Build lots of highways and power plants. Adopt proven technologies from around the world, to increase productivity.

But now the world's growth has slowed, and so have its purchases of China's exports. Rates of return on investment have fallen. Eventually the *Law of Diminishing Returns* kicks in (from Chapter 2!). The country can use only so many miles of highway and gigawatts of power. More won't add as much to output growth. And China's technology reached the cutting edge. New technologies must be developed if productivity is to increase.

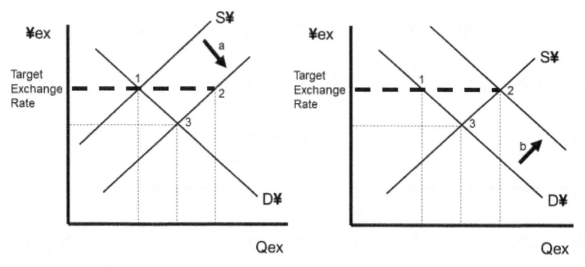

Figure 8-13. China's Trilemma. China keeps its interest rates low to encourage output growth, but this causes Chinese people to supply yuan in exchange for other currencies looking for better returns in other countries. Yuan supply increases (a). The equilibrium exchange rate (3) falls below China's target rate (1). There is an excess supply of yuan in the exchange market (2 is more than 1). China could raise interest rates to encourage international lending in China (b), or restrict the ability of Chinese people to supply yuan (reverse a). All three results are unwanted (falling exchange rate, higher interest rates, restricted currency flows). So China uses its vast foreign currency reserves to buy excess yuan (b), supporting the value of the yuan at the target exchange rate.

For years Chinese leaders have discussed a new development strategy based on the development of services and added consumer demand. This means closing factories and laying off construction workers, however, in hopes that they'll move to consumer services. The leadership sees the possibilities for unrest.

The transition would be easier if growth wasn't so slow, so the Peoples Bank of China (China's central bank) has kept interest rates low. Low interest rates in China, though, have caused Chinese people to want to lend in other countries were rates of return are higher. They are supplying yuan in exchange for dollars, yen and euros. This is putting downward pressure on the exchange value of the yuan.

That could help China's exports, but Chinese leaders see a different problem. International investors won't want to lend in China if they think the yuan will fall in value. Think of the British pound or U.S. dollar in 1931. A withdrawal of international investment might hurt more than an increase in exports would help. China wants to support the exchange value of the yuan, to keep it from falling too fast.

China faces the consequences Mundell's impossible trinity. It's been called a "trilemma." They want a higher exchange value of the yuan. They want low interest rates. They want to open up their economy to international capital flows. In the long run, they can only have two out of three (see Figure 8-13).

As a temporary stopgap, China is using its enormous reserves of foreign currencies to support the value of the yuan. It sells some of those Treasury bonds for dollars, and then uses the dollars to buy yuan in the exchange market. This adds to the demand for the yuan, and keeps the exchange value of the yuan from falling too much. This policy works as long as China has foreign currency reserves to spend. By 2016 reserves were down by a trillion dollars. At that rate reserves will last for just a few years.

China was accused of being a currency manipulator during the American Presidential campaign in 2016. It was, and it still is. Now though, China is not holding down the value of the yuan to support its exports, it's trying to keep the yuan from falling, to sustain investor confidence.

Terms in this Chapter, in order of appearance
Exchange rate
Value of the dollar
Exchange demand for the dollar
Exchange supply of the dollar
Buy American goods
Lend to Americans
Invest in American assets
Second shift #4: exchange market to goods market
Second shift #5: money market to exchange market
Safe haven
Fixed exchange rates
Pro-cyclical monetary policy
Gold standard
Fiat currency
Exports
Imports
International trade
Free trade

David Ricardo
Tariffs
Absolute advantage
Comparative advantage
Specialize
Smoot-Hawley tariff
Tariff
Bilateral trade agreements
Reciprocal Trade Agreement Act (RTAA)
General Agreement on Tariffs and Trade (GATT)
Trade negotiation "rounds"
North American Free Trade Agreement (NAFTA)
World Trade Organization (WTO)
Fixed exchange rates
Brexit
European Union
Support a fixed exchange rate
Independent stabilization policy
Free flow of capital
Robert Mundell
Impossible trinity
International Monetary Fund
Bretton Woods System
Camp David meeting
The gold window
Winners and losers from trade
Flexible exchange rates
Currency manipulation
Law of Diminishing Returns

Notes
Paul Douglas tells the story of the Douglas-Wilcox tariff appeal in his memoir (p. 71). In a 600+ page book, he devotes one paragraph to it. The man led an eventful life (we've seen him before, as a U.S. Senator in chapter 7). He tells the old "end-to-end" joke on page 475.

Eichengreen (1986) and Irwin (1997) analyze the causes and effects of the Smoot Hawley tariff. The quote by Watson is from Schlesinger (1956, p. 164).

Ahamed (2009, pp.224-240) tells the story of the British gold standard debate.

Eichengreen (1996) describes the operation of the gold standard and the instability between the wars.

Eichengreen (1996) and Solomon (1982) provide excellent histories of the rise and fall of Bretton Woods. Volcker and Gyohten (1992) give a first-hand account of the struggles to preserve the system during the 1960's and 1970's. Hallwood and MacDonald (2000) provide a textbook treatment.

The description of the Bretton Woods conference comes mostly from Van Dormael (1978, pp. 168-223), Moggridge (1992, pp. 721-755) and Rees (1973, pp. 221-235).

Irwin (1997), Eichengreen (1996, pp. 100-102) and Crowley (2003) describe the Reciprocal Trade Adjustment Act, the General Agreement and Tariffs and Trade and the failure to ratify the International Trade Organization.

Frieden (2006, pp. 460-61) describes how Canada's exchange rate problem influenced Robert Mundell's work on the "impossible trinity." Mundell was awarded a Nobel Prize in Economics for his work in 1999. Later, in 2002, he appeared on *The Late Show with David Letterman*, reading the "Top Ten Ways My Life Has Changed Since Winning The Nobel Prize." Number 10: "Can end almost any argument by asking, 'And did you ever win a Nobel Prize?'" Number 4: "When I call K-Rock to request Aerosmith, they play Aerosmith." Number 3: "Any meaningless crap I say, the next day it's in the *Wall Street Journal*." That last one might well be true. Mundell's delivery was so good that Letterman had him back several times.

Wicker's biography of Richard Nixon (pp. 542-568) and Wells' biography of Arthur Burns (1994, pp. 74-77) describe Nixon's Camp David meeting. So do Volcker and Gyohten (pp. 76-80), Stein (1994, pp. 176-180) and Safire (1978, pp. 659-686). Volcker, Stein and Safire write first-hand: they were there.

Hicks and Devaraj (2017) attribute 88% of manufacturing job loss in recent years to productivity improvements, and the remainder to trade. U.S. manufacturing output continues to increase.

Sources

Bernanke, Ben S. 2016. "China's Trilemma—and a Possible Solution," *Brookings Institution* (March 9).

Boughton, James M. 2000. "From Suez To Tequlla: The IMF As Crisis Manager." *Economic Journal.* 110 (January): 273-291.

Crowley, Meredith A. 2003. "An Introduction to the WTO and GATT." *Economic Perspectives* 27 (Fourth Quarter) 42-57.

DeLong, J. Bradford and Barry Eichengreen. 2002. "Between Meltdown and Moral Hazard." Pages 191-254 in Jeffrey A. Frankel and Peter R. Orszag (eds.), *Economic Policy in the 1990's.* Cambridge, Massachusetts: MIT Press.

Douglas, Paul. 1972. *In The Fullness of Time.* New York: Harcourt, Brace Jovanovich.

Eichengreen, Barry. 1996. *Globalizing Capital.* Princeton, New Jersey: Princeton University Press.

Frieden, Jeffry A. 2006. *Global Capitalism: Its Fall and Rise in the Twentieth Century*. New York: W.W. Norton.

Hallwood, C. Paul and Ronald MacDonald. 2000. *International Money and Finance*. (3rd edition.) Malden, Massachusetts: Blackwell.

Hicks, Michael J. and Srikant Devaraj. 2017. *The Myth and the Reality of Manufacturing in America*. Muncie, Indiana: Ball State University Center for Business and Economic Research.

Irwin, Douglas A. 1997. "From Smoot Hawley to Reciprocal Trade Agreements: Changing the Course of U.S. Trade Policy in the 1930's." National Bureau of Economic Research Working Paper 5895 (January). Cambridge, Massachusetts: NBER.

Ketchum, Richard M. 1989. *The Borrowed Years, 1938-1941*. New York: Random House.

Lawrence, Robert Z. 2002. "Trade Policy." Pages 277-327 in Jeffrey A. Frankel and Peter R. Orszag (eds.), *Economic Policy in the 1990's*. Cambridge, Massachusetts: MIT Press.

Moggridge, D. E. 1992. *Maynard Keynes: An Economist's Biography*. London: Routledge.

Rees, David. 1973. *Harry Dexter White*. New York: Coward, McCann and Geoghegan.

Safire, William. 1975. *Before the Fall*. New York: Ballantine Books.

Schlesinger, Arthur M., Jr. 1956. *The Crisis of the Old Order*. Boston: Houghton Mifflin Company.

Solomon, Robert. 1982. *The International Monetary System, 1945-1981*. New York: Harper and Row.

Stein, Herbert. 1994. *Presidential Economics*. (3rd edition.) Washington, D.C.: American Enterprise Institute.

United States International Trade Commission. 2004. "Value of U.S. Imports for Consumption, Duties Collected, and Ratios of Duties to Values, 1891-2004," USITC (May).

Van Dormael, Armand. 1978. *Bretton Woods: Birth of a Monetary System*. New York: Holmes and Meier.

Volcker, Paul and Toyoo Gyohten. 1992. *Changing Fortunes*. New York: Times Books.

Wells, Wyatt C. 1994. *Economist in an Uncertain World*. New York: Columbia University Press.

Wicker, Tom. 1991. *One of Us: Richard Nixon and the American Dream*. New York: Random House.

News Articles

Andrews, Edmund L. "Greenspan Suggests Rates May Increase Without Pause," *New York Times*, February 17, 2005.

Bradsher, Keith. "How China Lost $1 Trillion," *New York Times*, February 7, 2017.

Gough, Neil. "As China's Economy Slows, a Look at What Could Happen," *New York Times*, October 18, 2016.

Landler, Mark. "Chinese Savings Helped Inflate American Bubble," *New York Times*, December 26, 2008.

"The Brexit Slowdown is Under Way," *The Economist*, May 31, 2017.

Chapter 9
The Great Inflation

The United States had seen a surge of inflation after World War II, and then a telling lack of deflation after the 1957-58 recession. Still, it may not have been clear at the beginning of the 1960's that inflation was about to become a policy problem fully equal to that of recession.

But that's what happened. Everyone knows that the worst economic decade of the 20th Century was the 1930's, the time of the Great Depression. Less well known is that the second worst economic decade of the 20th Century was the 1970's: the time of the *Great Inflation*.

The End of Deflation
Recessions had always been accompanied by *deflation*. When the demand for their products fell, businesses would cut prices. When unemployment increased, workers would accept lower wages. Prices had fallen during the Depression, of course, but also in the recessions of 1937-38, 1948-49 and in 1955, after the recession of 1953-54. But the recession of 1957-58 did not bring deflation. The inflation rate fell, but it never became negative.

All the peacetime recessions and depressions up to 1955 were accompanied by deflation. At some point during or just after the recession, the price level fell. But there was no deflation in any recession for the next fifty years.

- *Why was there no deflation associated with any recession from 1956 to 2008?*

In the goods market, when output is less than potential, we expect deflation to result from an increase in aggregate supply. Unemployment causes workers and suppliers to accept lower wages and prices, and the decline in input costs causes firms to employ and produce more output. That's second shift #1. Perhaps, since 1955, second shift #1 has been slow off the mark. Something is slowing the downward adjustment of input costs.

It's the "pain" of unemployment that convinces people to accept lower pay rather than remain unemployed. What is this pain? Watching your savings melt away. Worrying about how your mortgage will be paid. Postponing your bill payments and facing down creditors. Denying your family the luxuries and then the necessities of life. In the face of these anxieties, workers might accept a job even if the wage is low.

But as of the 1950's there was unemployment insurance, Social Security and welfare. All the programs passed by the Big Bill in 1935 were operating and well-known to the public. Now the pain of unemployment could be held off for a time. Workers could wait longer for recall to their old job, or search longer for a job at a higher wage. Input costs were less likely to fall right away. Aggregate supply would increase more slowly.

The *Employment Act of 1946* had encouraged the government to "promote maximum employment, production and purchasing power." During recessions countercyclical fiscal and monetary policies would be used to increase aggregate demand. Aggregate demand would recover more quickly than it did before.

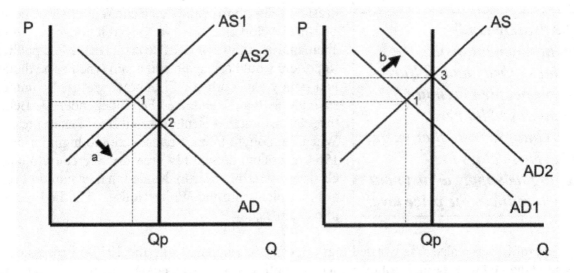

Figure 9-1. Legacy of the Big Bill? The economy starts in recession, with output less than potential (1). Second shift #1 should increase aggregate supply (a), because input costs decrease with unemployment and unused capacity. The price level falls (1 to 2). The big bill of 1935 established a safety net which may delay the pain of unemployment, and so delay the aggregate supply shift (a). Meanwhile, the government more readily uses countercyclical fiscal and monetary policy to increase aggregate demand (b). The price level rises (1 to 3). If shift (a) is slow and shift (b) is quick, the price level may never decline.

So, while aggregate supply was responding more slowly to recessions, aggregate demand was responding more quickly. The sluggish increase in aggregate supply, which would reduce the price level, is overwhelmed by the quicker increase in aggregate demand, which increases the price level. The recession never sees deflation. Perhaps the absence of deflation from 1955 to 2008 was partly the result of the more generous "*safety net*" which protects people from some of the misfortunes of recession, and the countercyclical efforts of government to end recessions as quickly as possible.

Dwight Eisenhower was President of the United States from 1953 to 1960, and he was determined to halt this continuing inflation. He later wrote in his memoirs,

> Critics overlooked the inflationary psychology which prevailed during the mid-fifties and which I thought it necessary to defeat. . . . The administration believed that if wages and prices could increase during a recession, we could get into real inflationary trouble in time of prosperity.

As soon as the 1957-58 recession was over the President began a drive to turn the Federal government's recessionary deficit into a big budget surplus. He reduced Federal spending and resisted all calls for tax cuts.

The "safety net," unemployment insurance, social security and welfare, allows people to remain unemployed longer, searching for a higher wage job. This delays the aggregate supply adjustment which reduces the price level.

President Eisenhower and Fed chair William McChesney Martin developed a new working relationship. Unlike Truman, Eisenhower refused to criticize the Fed publicly. Reporters would ask again and again whether he thought Fed policy was correct. Eisenhower refused comment, saying only that he endorsed Fed independence. Behind the scenes, though, Eisenhower felt free to exert pressure. When he thought interest rates were too high during the 1954 recession, he sent his Treasury Secretary to talk to Chairman Martin. Martin decided that he couldn't resist a direct plea from the White House. The Fed reduced interest rates.

The Federal Reserve also was worried that prices hadn't fallen during the 1957-58 recession. It presented the Fed with a tough policy choice. Its policy was to "lean against the wind." But which wind? If the economy could suffer from inflation and unemployment at the same time, it wasn't clear which way to lean. The Fed chose to fight inflation. Chairman Martin thought they had allowed interest rates to stay too low for two long in the 1953-54 recession. So, as soon as signs of recovery became clear, the Fed began raising interest rates. By mid-1960 the discount rate was at four percent, the highest rate in thirty years.

With Eisenhower's restrictive fiscal policy, and Martin's restrictive monetary policy, it is no surprise that the recovery from the 1957-58 recession was sluggish and short. Inflation was just 1.6% percent in 1960, but the unemployment rate averaged 5.5% and GDP was growing by just 2.3% per year. For the time, those were disappointing numbers.

Vice President Richard Nixon was particularly concerned about the economy's mediocre performance, since he was the Republican presidential nominee in 1960. Nixon knew that an election year recession could ruin his hopes for the Presidency. He pleaded with the President for a tax cut, to stimulate consumer and business spending. Eisenhower was focused on inflation. The unemployment rate was 4.8% in February 1960. By election day in November it was up to 6.1%. Richard Nixon lost the election by 119,000 votes, two-tenths of one percent. The new President would be a Democrat, John F. Kennedy.

Kennedy's Economists

John F. Kennedy entered the Presidency with few fixed economic ideas. He had criticized the Eisenhower economic performance—three recessions in eight years—and had promised to "get this country moving again." He had little idea of how to accomplish this goal, however, and now, in January 1961, a lingering recession was his problem.

He sought advice from some of the best economists of his generation. He assigned Paul Samuelson to write a report on the economy during the November to January transition of administrations. In

1970 Samuelson became the first American winner of the Nobel Prize in Economics. On the Council of Economic Advisors was James Tobin (Nobel Prize 1981). On the Council's staff were Kenneth Arrow (Nobel Prize 1972) and Robert Solow (Nobel Prize 1987). These were Ivy League professors—Kennedy was a Harvard man. But to head up his Council of Economic Advisors, he went to the Big Ten. He appointed Walter Heller, an economist from the University of Minnesota.

Heller and the Council decided to give the President an education in economics. Heller had a knack for clear, colorful writing, and began sending Kennedy memos on economic topics. He sent about 300 in three years, and Kennedy read them.

The press called it the "New Economics," but it was nothing new to Kennedy's economists. It was just *Keynesian economics*, with enough added features that they took to calling it "neo-Keynesian," or even "the Keynesian-classical synthesis." What was new was that, for the first time, a President would propose a Keynesian fiscal policy for Keynesian reasons, using Keynesian language.

Kennedy's economists diagnosed the economy's troubles this way. The Federal budget had some *automatic stabilizers*. Income taxes automatically fell with incomes during recessions, and unemployment insurance spending automatically increased. This helped keep recessions mild. When the economy boomed, the stabilizers helped restrain inflation. It was during recoveries that the economists saw a problem. Taxes started rising and spending started dropping just as soon as the economy turned around. This slowed recovery and could even prevent the economy from reaching potential output before the next recession hit.

The problem seemed to be getting worse. The 1949-53 expansion lasted 45 months, the 1954-57 expansion 39 months, the 1958-60 expansion just 24. During this first expansion the unemployment rate had dipped to 2.5%, during the second, 3.7%. In the last expansion the rate had fallen to only 4.8%, in February 1960, before turning up again. Now, at the start of the Kennedy administration in January 1961, the rate was 6.6%.

The Kennedy administration decided that expansionary policy was needed. But what kind? John Kenneth Galbraith advocated increased public spending. Galbraith was an economist and a long-time Kennedy advisor who had written a book called *The Affluent Society* in 1958. We've got lots of consumer goods, he wrote, but not enough "public goods." We drive our huge cars with their big tail fins past crumbling schools and polluted rivers. Raise Federal spending to shift the mix from private to public consumption, Galbraith said, and reduce unemployment as a side benefit. The administration tried, early on, to increase spending. Congress wouldn't have it.

James Tobin wanted a policy to promote long run growth. He was not satisfied to simply get *to* potential output, he wanted potential output to grow faster. Increase the number of buildings, factories and machines that the economy uses to produce output. Get the Federal Reserve to cut interest rates to encourage extra business investment in plant and equipment. Run a budget surplus and retire part of the national debt. With fewer Treasury bonds available, investors have to put their money in stocks and corporate bonds. That's money for business expansion.

This idea ran smack into the exchange market problem, however. High interest rates encouraged the demand for the dollar. Reduce them, and the United States would have trouble supporting the fixed exchange value of the dollar, which was required by the Bretton Woods system. This was one of the reasons that the Fed held interest rates high. Mundell's "impossible trinity" restricted discretionary monetary policy, for the sake of fixed exchange rates.

That left Walter Heller's idea, a big, permanent tax cut. Heller argued that the tax structure had been developed during World War II, when the problem was to hold down spending to restrain inflation. But now it created *fiscal drag*, restraining recovery.

> *"Okun's Law" said that each one percent drop in the unemployment rate produced a 3% increase in real GDP. The Kennedy economists used this relationship to calculate the size of the tax cut needed to return to the economy to potential output.*

Heller and his staff figured it this way. The unemployment rate in mid-1961 was about 6.5%. They estimated that it could get down to about 4% without triggering inflation. That was full employment (they thought). Arthur Okun, a staff economist on the Council, calculated that each one percent drop in the unemployment rate produced about 3% in extra output. With tongue in cheek, they dubbed that ratio *Okun's Law*. A 2.5% drop in unemployment, to get to 4%, meant a 7.5% increase in GDP. That was potential output, what the economy could produce without inflation, if everyone and everything was employed as usual. In 1961 7.5% of GDP was about $35 billion.

- What did the size of the GDP gap imply for the size of the tax cut?

The economists turned to the *income multiplier*, the same idea that Keynes had described to Francis Perkins almost thirty years before. If consumers spent more, businesses would produce more, they would pay more wages to more workers, and their workers would spend more, too. That would cause businesses to produce even more output. They thought the multiplier was about three: for every one dollar reduction in taxes, output would increase by three dollars. So, to close a GDP gap of $35 billion, the tax cut needed to be one-third that amount, somewhere around $10 to $12 billion dollars.

Kennedy didn't buy it. His economists were disappointed when the President-elect told them he would not increase the deficit to deal with the recession. Kennedy's margin of victory had been razor thin. He did not want business people and the Congress to label him as an irresponsible spender.

Kennedy Proposes a Tax Cut
Heller started sending his memos, but Kennedy resisted. Then, early in 1962 the recovery faltered. Real GDP was growing more slowly than projected, and a "Kennedy recession" seemed possible. That did it. Kennedy committed to the tax cut that summer, as an anti-recession policy. If it passed the Congress the tax cut would take effect in 1963.

In December 1962 Kennedy spoke to the Economic Club of New York about his tax cut.

The President was "an apt pupil," Heller thought, and now it showed. "This economy is capable of producing without strain $30 to $40 billion more than we are producing today," he told his audience. That was the GDP gap, the difference between actual output and potential output. The way to close this gap was

> to reduce the burden on private income and the deterrents to private initiative which are imposed by our present tax system; and this administration pledged itself last summer to an across-the-board, top-to-bottom cut in personal and corporate income taxes to be enacted and become effective in 1963.

Then the President said that his tax cut would not be inflationary.

> If the economy today were operating close to capacity levels with little unemployment, or if a sudden change in our military requirements should cause a scramble for men and resources, then I would oppose tax reductions as irresponsible and inflationary; and I would not hesitate to recommend a tax increase, if that were necessary.

With output less than potential—the GDP gap—added spending would create greater output, not higher prices. Of course, if a big increase in military spending pushed output beyond capacity, a tax *increase* might be needed. Apparently, Vice President Lyndon Johnson wasn't listening.

The administration's people began lobbying Congress for the tax bill. They met much resistance. The "traditional budget balancers" had accepted the need for deficits in a recession. But this was different. It was a tax cut during a recovery, with a budget already in deficit.

Walter Heller testified before the Ways and Means Committee. "How is it that you're trying to give people a tax cut, and they don't seem to want it?" asked a sympathetic Congresswoman. Heller replied off-the-cuff, "Maybe it's the Puritan ethic." "Heller denigrates the Puritan Ethic!" said the headlines the next day. And on the floor of Congress, a Congressman declared "I'd rather be a Puritan than a Heller." The tax cut was not passed in 1963, but Kennedy sensed that he was making progress, and held out hopes for 1964.

The Great Society
President Lyndon Johnson met with Kennedy's shocked and somber advisors on the night of John Kennedy's funeral, November 25, 1963. The business of government goes on, and Heller anticipated a long effort to persuade the new President to support the tax cut. He was surprised to find Johnson already convinced that the tax cut was needed.

Johnson had decided that the painful transition to his administration would be eased if he took responsibility for Kennedy's legacy. Two days later, in a speech before a joint session of Congress, he urged them to pass the civil rights bill which Kennedy had championed. And, he said, "no act of ours could more fittingly continue the work of President Kennedy than the early passage of the tax bill for which he fought all this long year."

Johnson thought that a tax cut would be the best thing for the economy. But he had other incentives. There would be a Presidential election in less than a year. A tax cut would please the voters. Just as important, pushing a tax cut through Congress—where Kennedy's team had failed—would demonstrate that Johnson was in charge.

Johnson had been the majority leader of the Senate before becoming Vice President. He was known as a master deal-maker. Kennedy tried to get things done through education and persuasion. Johnson knew how to make deals. The tax cut passed, and Johnson signed it on February 26, 1964.

It was a big tax cut, amounting to $11.5 billion dollars, compared to a total budget of just under $100 billion. The tax rate on the lowest income individuals fell from 20% to 16%, and on the highest income individuals from 91% to 70%. The corporate profits tax rate was cut from 52% to 48%.

When the tax cut took effect in July 1964, the unemployment rate was 5.2%, and the inflation rate over the previous year had been 1.3%. By the end of 1965, the unemployment rate was 4.0%. and the 12-month inflation rate was 1.9%. The tax cut seemed to have done just what Heller and company had expected: brought the economy up to capacity, with unemployment at the estimated full employment level of 4.0%. But the inflation rate had risen to 1.9%. Not a big increase, but (as it turned out) it was the beginning of a trend. Still, with the economy booming and unemployment falling, Johnson was elected in a landslide in November 1964.

Lyndon Johnson was now the elected President of the United States, and he was determined to build a legacy of his own. He had first come to Washington in the 1930s, during the late stages of the New Deal. Franklin Roosevelt was his hero. With his electoral landslide and a Congress stocked with members of his Democratic party, now was the time, he thought, to extend the New Deal. He called it the *Great Society.*

He had coined the term in a speech in the Spring of 1964, and now he used it again and again. The Great Society would channel the nation's extraordinary prosperity to its public needs. He listed his proposals in his January 1965 State of the Union speech: Job training, extension of the minimum wage and unemployment compensation, high-speed railroads, a stepped up war on poverty, voting rights enforcement, immigration reform, preschool education, college scholarships, hospital care for the elderly, regional medical centers, medical research and education, services for mentally retarded, urban planning, housing programs in a new Department of Housing and Urban Development, training and equipment for police officers, new national parks and seashores, highway beautification, programs for clean air and water, pollution control research, research on distilling fresh water from the sea, establishment of a National Foundation on the Arts, and reforms of the electoral college.

With his deal-making skills, and big Democratic majorities in Congress, Johnson managed to get most of his agenda passed. His chief aide calculated that in 1965 and 1966 they had proposed 200 major pieces of legislation, and passed 181. Johnson was intensely proud of this achievement. The Great Society programs were "his babies."

The Vietnam War

North Vietnam was Communist, allied with mainland China. South Vietnam was anti-Communist, allied with the United States. The two Vietnams were at war. The United States had several thousand military advisors in the south at the beginning of 1964. Lyndon Johnson was ambivalent. "I don't think it's worth fighting for and I don't think we can get out," he told an advisor, "Of course, if you start running from the Communists, they may just chase you right into your own kitchen." Most of his advisors, many left over from the Kennedy administration, urged him to commit U.S. forces to defend the South. Senator Barry Goldwater of Arizona, his opponent in the November election, advocated commitment as well. Johnson felt that he had to appear strong in the face of Communist aggression, as strong as Kennedy had been in the Cuban Missile Crisis.

Johnson hesitated for almost a year. But by July 1965 it appeared to the President and his advisors that the United States had to commit to a larger war, or get out. Weakness in the face of Communist aggression was not possible, they decided. The escalation began. By the end of 1965 the number of troops in South Vietnam approached 200,000.

The Great Society programs were expensive. The President had convinced Congress that a small deficit in the near term would eventually be balanced by revenues from rapid economic growth. Escalation in Vietnam made these calculations obsolete. Johnson feared that if the Congress knew how expensive the war would be, they would gut his Great Society programs. And, he feared, higher spending would give the Fed an excuse to raise interest rates. So for months the administration hid the projected spending numbers. They cancelled a meeting that was usually held to inform the Federal Reserve about the coming year's budget proposal.

William McChesney Martin had been chair of the Fed for 14 years, and he had his own information sources in the Pentagon. War spending was going to increase a lot. "These things are going to go way beyond what the administration has admitted,'" he told his colleagues. At an October meeting with the President, Martin asked how much the budget would need to rise to pay for the war. "[Defense Secretary] McNamara says it very likely will be less than $5 billion for the rest of 1966," the President said. Martin had heard much higher numbers from his sources. Increased defense spending with the economy near capacity meant that business and consumer spending would have to be restrained. Interest rates would have to rise.

President Johnson's "guns and butter" policy increased Great Society social spending and escalated the Vietnam War. The increase in aggregate demand threatened to increase inflation. His economists advocated a tax increase. He refused. In 1965 the Fed increased interest rates instead.

War spending also disturbed the new head of the Council of Economic Advisors, Gardner Ackley. Ackley figured that rising revenues from the growing economy could pay for the new Great Society programs, or escalation of the war. But if the President insisted on both the war and the social programs—*guns and butter* the reporters called it—then a tax increase was needed. If taxes didn't rise, consumer, business and government spending together would outstrip the economy's ability to produce, and inflation could result. He remembered later, "we had all the evidence we needed to conclude without any question, certainly by November or early December, that a tax increase was absolutely necessary if we were going to avoid substantial inflation in 1966."

Ackley also warned the President that "monetary policy stands at the crossroads." Martin was sure to restrain spending with higher interest rates if taxes weren't raised to do the job. Sure enough, on Friday, December 3, 1965, the Fed raised the discount rate half a point.

President Johnson was furious. "It made him ill to think about those bankers collecting 12 percent interest," Ackley said. He released a mild statement to the press: "I regret, as do most Americans, any action that raises the cost of credit, particularly for homes, schools, hospitals, and factories." But he had his allies in Congress step up the pressure. Senator Proxmire demanded hearings "to determine what action must be taken to prevent this creature of Congress from endangering the nation's prosperity and from doing so in defiance of the President of the United States."

Martin could not be persuaded. At a meeting in December Johnson, Martin, Ackley and others talked about what kind of tax increase would be needed. Ackley was convinced that Johnson would ask for a tax hike in his upcoming State of the Union speech.

Johnson knew that leaders in Congress were unwilling to consider higher taxes. Instead, in the January 1966 speech, Johnson asked for more Great Society programs: ending discrimination in jury selection and housing, development aid for rural areas, urban renewal, improved unemployment insurance, a higher minimum wage, a teacher corps, assistance for renters, pollution control, highway safety, consumer protection, research on a super-sonic passenger jet, and campaign finance reform.

He declared, "This nation is mighty enough, its society is healthy enough, its people are strong enough, to pursue our goals in the rest of the world while still building a Great Society here at home." He would pursue the Vietnam War and the Great Society at the same time. Guns and butter spending would continue. But he would not raise taxes.

Congress passed most of the President's social programs. The Vietnam escalation continued. By the end of 1966, there were almost 400,000 American soldiers in Vietnam. The inflation rate in 1965 had been 1.9%. By April 1966 it was 2.9%. By August, 3.5%. It had not been so high since 1958. Martin's Fed continued to tighten monetary policy, selling bonds to slow growth of the money supply and raise the federal funds rate, from 4.4% in January to 5.8% in November.

The Income Tax Surcharge
Ackley told the President that the Fed was hinting that "if we do move on taxes, the Fed is ready to move on money." Raise taxes, and Martin could allow interest rates to fall. But throughout 1966 Johnson did not think the Congress or the country was ready for a tax hike. Opposition to the war was mounting. Now a push for a tax hike would not only threaten social spending, it could threaten the country's luke-warm support for the war.

Late in 1966 Johnson finally came around, persuaded by rising inflation and higher interest rates. With Martin's implied offer before him, he said in his January 1967 State of the Union address, "I recommend to the Congress a surcharge of 6 percent on both corporate and individual income taxes--to last for two years or for so long as the unusual expenditures associated with our efforts in Vietnam continue." A *tax surcharge* was a tax on a tax. Taxpayers would calculate how much income tax they owed, and then tack on an extra six percent.

Towards the end of 1966 tight money started to affect the economy. Housing construction fell. In the first half of 1967 output growth slowed to a crawl. The unemployment rate edged upward from 3.6% to 4.0%. Inflation stopped rising. Johnson's advisors were now concerned that an immediate tax hike would push the economy into recession. They decided to wait until mid-year to send the tax hike proposal to Congress. The President finally submitted the tax hike proposal—now revised to a ten percent surcharge—on August 3, 1967.

> *The 1968 income tax surcharge was a fiscal policy designed to decrease aggregate demand and reduce inflation. It didn't work.*

The climb of inflation had stopped, and the President had come through with a tax hike recommendation. Martin kept his promise. The Fed reversed its interest rate policy in February 1967, now buying bonds to reduce the federal funds rate. In April it cut the discount rate back to four percent. Now interest rates were back to where they were in early 1965. The tax proposal got nowhere in Congress. Leaders demanded big cuts in social spending as the price for considering a tax hike. Johnson agonized, "You can't ask me to slaughter my own babies."

Meanwhile, the economy had turned again. In the second half of 1967 output growth resumed. In the first half of 1968 it boomed. Inflation resumed its rise, up to 4.0% by February 1968. Martin allowed the federal funds rate to creep upward again, but did not feel he could take decisive action. He had promised Johnson not to raise rates if there was a tax hike proposal. And, he thought that tighter monetary policy would take the pressure off Congress to pass the tax hike. Raise interest rates, and Congress would think that monetary policy had done the job. Martin kept money looser than he would have in other circumstances.

Finally in 1968 the President agreed to some cuts in his Great Society programs, and the tax surcharge passed, at a rate of ten percent. As of July 1968 people saw their take-home pay reduced as the surcharge increased income tax withholding.

That's the story. Let's check the data and the model.

Here are the data for the five years 1964 to 1968. An exchange rate isn't included—it was fixed by the Bretton Woods system, so exchange rates were constant—but the budget balance and the real federal funds rate are included, as measures of fiscal and monetary policy, respectively.

The goods and money market diagrams are shown in Figure 9-2. We start with equilibrium output at potential output. The unemployment rate in 1964 was near the 5% level that we use as an indicator of output at potential. Of course, the Kennedy-Johnson economists thought full employment was 4%. Looking back, we know they were wrong.

Output grew rapidly in most of these years, and the inflation rate increased too. So aggregate demand must have increased, and pushed output above potential after 1964. The unemployment rate dropped below 5%.

The Great Society and Vietnam

Year	Real GDP Growth	CPI Inflation	Unemploy-ment Rate	Interest Rate Spread	Budget Balance (% GDP)	Real Federal Funds Rate
1964	5.8%	1.3%	5.2%	0.4%	-0.9%	2.2%
1965	6.5%	1.6%	4.5%	0.4%	-0.2%	2.5%
1966	6.6%	2.9%	3.8%	0.5%	-0.5%	2.3%
1967	2.7%	3.1%	3.8%	0.7%	-1.1%	1.1%
1968	4.9%	4.2%	3.6%	0.8%	-2.9%	1.5%

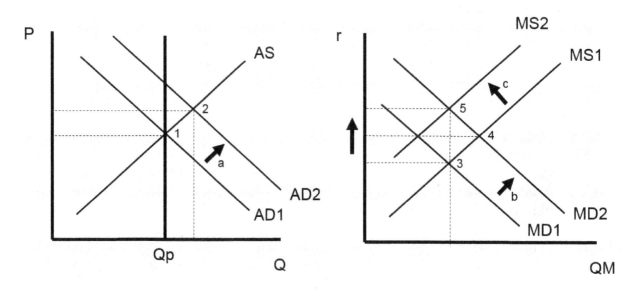

Figure 9-2. Let's Make a Deal. Output was near potential in 1964 (1). Aggregate demand increased (a) due to the Kennedy tax cut, added government transfers (the Great Society) and added government purchases (for the Vietnam War). The budget balance became more negative (a rising deficit). Output moved above potential and inflation increased (2). Rising incomes and prices increased money demand (b), which increased the real interest rate (3 to 4). For a time in 1966 the Fed increased the federal funds rate, which decreased the money supply (c) and increased the real interest rate more (4 to 5). Output growth slowed in 1967. Then the Fed reversed course in 1967 so both fiscal and monetary policy were expansionary.

In the money market, rising incomes and prices must have increased money demand, which increased the real interest rate. That would be enough to explain the rise in the BAA-AAA corporate interest rate spread. As people demanded more money for transactions, banks had less to lend, especially to more-risky businesses. But at the end of 1965 the Fed increased its interest rates, which must have raised the spread more. This slowed output growth in 1967, stopped the fall in the unemployment rate, and slowed the increase in inflation. That was *counter-cyclical monetary policy* at a time of rising inflation.

But the Fed and the President made an implicit deal. The President pledged to raise taxes, and the Fed would cut interest rates. The President made the pledge, the Fed delivered the rate cut—but taxes didn't increase for another year and a half. Both fiscal and monetary policies were expansionary at a time of low unemployment and high inflation. Those are *pro-cylclical fiscal and monetary* policies. The Great Inflation had begun.

The Phillips Curve
With the tax surcharge in place, the administration's economists expected unemployment to rise and inflation to fall. Arthur Okun remembered thinking

> You could go down that curve just as you went up that curve. Why can't we get back to where we were in 1965, the good old days? That's exactly what we thought would happen. That's exactly what didn't happen.

The "curve" he was talking about was the *Phillips Curve*. It had been first drawn by A.W. Phillips, a New Zealand econometrician (that is, an economist who uses statistical techniques with economic data), in 1958. The curve showed the relationship between the unemployment rate and a measure of inflation. It showed a tradeoff. When unemployment was high, inflation was low; when unemployment was high, inflation was low.

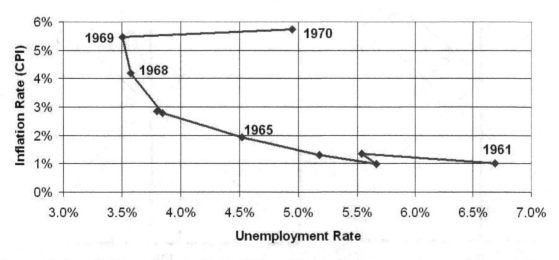

Figure 9-3. Phillips Curve, 1961-1970. The inflation rate is on the vertical axis, the unemployment rate on the horizontal axis. In 1961 unemployment was high and inflation was low. From 1961 to 1969 the economy traced a perfect Phillips Curve, with falling unemployment and rising inflation. In 1968 Johnson's economists thought the surtax would cause the economy to retrace its steps, back to the "good old days" of 1965. Instead, unemployment fell and inflation rose again in 1969, then the economy jumped off the Phillips Curve in 1970, with higher inflation and higher unemployment. Unemployment was about where it had been in 1964, but inflation was almost 5 percentage points higher.

The 1960's had traced a perfect Phillips Curve (Figure 9-3), which helped convince many economists that Phillips had discovered an essential economic tradeoff. By 1969 inflation was too high and unemployment was too low, but no matter. The tax surcharge would take care of that. The economy would just trace its path back down the curve, to the "good old days" of 1965.

Imagine their shock, then, when in 1970 unemployment went up—but so did inflation! We know what happened. Here's the data we need for the goods market. Figure 9-4 shows the goods market diagram. The low unemployment rate shows that output was above potential. Inflation was increasing, and so were input costs. The competition by businesses for scarce resources increased wages and the prices of other resources. In the goods market that is shown as a decrease in aggregate supply (second shift #1).

The First Stagflation

Year	Real GDP Growth	CPI Inflation	Unemploy-ment Rate
1969	3.1%	5.5%	3.5%
1970	0.2%	5.7%	5.0%
1971	3.3%	4.4%	6.0%
1972	5.3%	3.2%	5.6%

Real GDP did decrease for a while in 1970—there was a recession that year—but growth in the rest of the year put the overall growth rate just above zero. Still, for a time output was decreasing while inflation was rising. The unemployment rate went up to 5.7%. We saw in Chapter 3 why the unemployment rate is often a lagging indicator, meaning it continues to rise after real GDP begins to grow. This is a picture of stagflation, simultaneous increases in unemployment and inflation. It was the first stagflation of the 1970's. It was not the last.

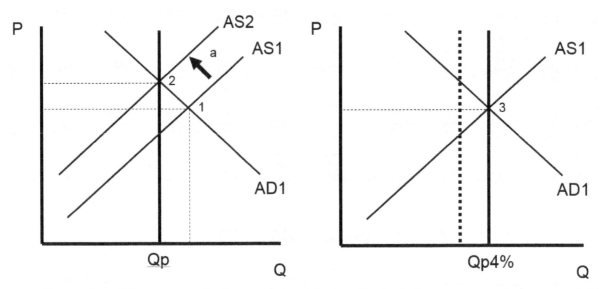

Figure 9-4. What was, and what might have been. On the left, output was above potential in 1969, with the unemployment rate at 3.5% (1). Input costs rise and aggregate supply decreases (a), due to second shift #1. Inflation increases but output falls back towards potential (2). The unemployment rate rises. On the right, what if the unemployment rate had been 4% at potential output, as the Kennedy economists thought. Then output would have been near potential in 1969 (3), and second shift #1 would not have happened.

The Phillips Curve in Figure 9-3 shows stagflation too. The economy jumped off that perfect curve of the 1960's, with both unemployment and inflation rising from 1969 to 1970. That jump is the same event as the decrease in aggregate supply shown by (a) in Figure 9-4.

Many economists were shocked by the stagflation. Not Milton Friedman, an economist from the University of Chicago. *Inflationary expectations* explained why the economy had jumped off the Phillips Curve in 1970. In fact, Friedman said, the whole Phillips Curve had shifted upward and outward, because people had come to expect inflation. Amazingly, he explained this in a speech to the American Economic Association in December 1967, two years *before* the event.

The Phillips Curve wasn't stable. Friedman said

> Implicitly, Phillips wrote his article for a world in which everyone anticipated that nominal prices would be stable and in which that anticipation remained unshaken and immutable whatever happened to actual prices and wages.

Most of Phillips' data came from the world of 1880 through 1940, when the price level was stable over the long term. Inflationary expectations would not develop in a stable price environment.

The Phillips Curve shows the relationship between the inflation rate and the unemployment rate. It's another way to express aggregate demand and supply changes.

But now inflation would create the expectation of more inflation. Businesses would expect their costs to rise, so they would raise prices. Workers would expect prices to rise, so they would demand wage hikes. The economy could slow and unemployment increase, but people would, for a time, continue to expect inflation. The same unemployment rate could correspond to lots of different inflation rates, depending on inflationary expectations. Since inflationary expectations were higher in 1970 than they had been in 1965 (after five years of inflationary experience), the economy could not slide back down the Phillips Curve. In 1970, 5% unemployment would correspond not to 2% inflation, as in 1965, but to 6% inflation. The Phillips Curve had shifted.

There was a further implication, Friedman said. "There is always a temporary trade-off between inflation and unemployment; there is no permanent trade-off." If was not possible for policymakers to set the unemployment rate permanently below the *natural rate of unemployment*, which was the rate that existed when the economy was at full capacity. If policymakers tried to hold the unemployment rate below the natural rate (as they did in 1966-69), eventually market forces would push the economy back to the natural rate, but with a higher inflation rate.

What Friedman had found was an aggregate supply curve that shifted when costs began to respond to inflationary expectations. He discovered what we call second shift #1. John Maynard Keynes had explained aggregate demand in our macroeconomic model. Milton Friedman explained aggregate supply. We could call it the *Keynes-Friedman macroeconomic model*.

Friedman's analysis had one more unfortunate, and ominous, implication. Once inflation got going, it was not possible to slow the economy a little to bring it back down, as the stable Phillips Curve implied. If expectations of inflation were high enough, only a long, deep recession would work. Policymakers spent much of the 1970's looking for an alternative to that recession. They didn't find one.

Price Controls

In the summer of 1971 both the unemployment and inflation rates remained unacceptably high. Yet, what could be done? Fiscal and monetary policy could attack inflation, or unemployment, but not both. Adopt policies to bring down inflation, and unemployment would rise. Bring down unemployment, and inflation would go up. Democrats in Congress demanded a different policy solution, price controls, and surprisingly many business people agreed. They wanted help in resisting union wage demands.

As a young man President Richard Nixon had worked as a low-level official for the Office of Price Administration, the agency in charge of price controls and rationing during World War II. He came away from that experience disillusioned with government's attempt to micro-manage the economy. But facing the difficult economy (and with an election looming in 1972), he decided to go for a dramatic policy change, a "long bomb." He called his advisors to a meeting at Camp David on August 13, 1971.

Looking back after more than forty years, the most important decision made at that Camp David meeting was to close the gold window. This ended the fixed exchange rate system that had existed since the Bretton Woods conference in 1944. Most of the developed world has been using flexible exchange rates since. At the time, though, it was wage and price controls that created the sensation.

In his speech on Sunday night, August 15, 1971, President Nixon said

> The time has come for decisive action—action that will break the vicious circle of spiraling prices and costs. I am today ordering a freeze on all prices and wages throughout the United States for a period of 90 days.

Prices would be frozen for ninety days. It was hoped that three months of zero inflation would reduce inflationary expectations. Then controls would gradually be lifted in a second phase. If expectations stayed low, inflation would be lower without higher unemployment.

The President set up a policy-making body, the Cost of Living Council, headed by Donald Rumsfeld and his deputy, Dick Cheney (the future Defense Secretary and Vice President during the second Bush administration). Day to day decisions were made by a Price Commission, which eventually employed 700 people. This was much, much smaller than World War II's OPA, but perhaps bigger than the President envisioned.

Inflation was low during the freeze, about 1%. It had been 6% in the three months before August. In November the Price Commission began to administer Phase II, which was a program of gradual decontrol. Phase II may have had some success: in the year before the freeze, inflation had been 4.6%; in the first year of Phase II, it was 3.7%. Some success, but not much.

Price controls are a form of *incomes policy*. Inflationary expectations cause a wage-price spiral. Workers expect price increases. They demand wage increases to maintain the purchasing power of their incomes. Businesses expect wage increases. They raise their prices to maintain the purchasing power of their profits. In a sense, an incomes policy tries to mediate between these groups. If workers and businesses could just agree on who should get what, inflation could be stopped without a recession. It's hard to get agreements like that, though.

> *"Incomes Policies"* are attempts to restrain wage and price increases through persuasion or legal controls. Price controls are a kind of incomes policy.

- What kinds of market difficulties did price controls create?

A trucker had concluded a contract for higher wages with his drivers before the freeze. He had not yet re-negotiated his price with his only customer, a grocery chain, when the freeze was imposed. He asked for an exception to the freeze, claiming he'd go broke paying high wages while charging low prices. The Internal Revenue Service investigated his case and agreed that he probably would go broke. It was early in the freeze, though, and the Cost of Living Council wanted to appear tough. They ruled against the trucker.

> *The 1971 price controls may have held inflation down for a brief time, but they created shortages. Eventually their effectiveness wore off.*

The hay crop was big one year during the price controls. Farmers needed more steel wire to tie up the hay bales. Ordinarily, the price of wire would have risen, signaling steel companies to shift production from other products to wire. But the price could not rise under the controls, and a wire *shortage* developed. A large part of the hay harvest was left in the fields. That, in turn, meant a smaller supply of animal feed, and of beef, than the nation could have had.

After a while, labor union leaders refused to cooperate with the Price Commission. If it was clear to the union members that their wage increases were set in Washington, they reasoned, what was the justification for having a union, and paying union dues?

After a while, it became clear that a much larger bureaucracy would be needed to enforce the controls. Most businesses cooperated with the 90-day freeze, but as Phase II wore on business lawyers began to search for and find loopholes to evade the controls. The Price Commission would need to match these lawyers with their own if the controls were to continue.

Perhaps most important, the Nixon administration fell into a trap that they'd sworn to avoid. The danger was that with price controls in place, policymakers would feel free to attack unemployment with expansionary fiscal and monetary policies. This added demand would put pressure on the controls system—more employed people working at higher incomes would demand more goods, but with fixed prices businesses would have less incentive to produce more. *Shortages* would result. This had been the result of many price control episodes around the world, as Nixon's economists knew well.

The Federal Reserve had increased interest rates through most of 1971. Now the Fed began a rapid increase of the money supply. Interest rates fell in the first part of 1972. The economy began to grow faster. GDP increased 4.6%, and the unemployment rate fell to 4.9% by January 1973. Burns was accused of trying to aid in the re-election of the President, a charge that he and the Nixon administration denied.

Still, politically motivated or not, in fact monetary policy was expansionary in 1972. The resulting rapid increase in spending torpedoed the strategy behind the wage and price controls. The controls were supposed to reduce inflationary expectations. But as prices pushed against their controlled ceilings, people began to expect that inflation would explode once the controls were eliminated. As 1972 turned into 1973, it was clear that the price control program was in trouble.

OPEC and Oil Prices

In 1960 the oil producing counties of the Middle East along with Venezuela combined to form *OPEC*, the *Organization of Petroleum Exporting Countries*. OPEC's main goal, at the start, was to negotiate better terms with the big oil companies. The oil companies had the upper hand because their contracts had been signed during the time when the Middle Eastern countries were colonies of Britain and France. Middle Eastern nationalism was on the rise, especially after the 1967 war between Arab countries and Israel.

> *The Organization of Petroleum Exporting Countries (OPEC) is a cartel which restricts the supply of oil in order to raise its price.*

The demand for oil was also rising. When the 1967 Six-Day war cut exports for a time, it began to dawn on OPEC that they controlled a substantial part of the world's limited supply of oil. The developed world's ever-increasing thirst for oil might be used to OPEC's advantage. Then, in 1973, Israel again fought a war with Arab countries. The United States and other western nations supported Israel. OPEC responded by imposing an oil embargo on the United States, cutting off oil exports to the U.S. in October 1973. The price of crude oil nearly tripled; the average price of a gallon of gasoline increased from 36 cents in 1972 to 57 cents by 1975, coincidently a 57% hike.

OPEC was now a *cartel*. A cartel is an organization of countries or businesses in a particular industry, which tries to manipulate supply to influence the good's market price. If enough of an industry's output is controlled by the cartel, it can reduce the supply of the good, driving the price up. A cartel can analyze its industry's costs and the demand for its product to adjust supply to make its profits as high as possible. Each member is assigned a share of the restricted output to produce, and thus a share of overall revenue. A cartel's problem is to keep its members in line. It is always profitable for any one member to exceed its output quota—to sell more at the higher price created by the restricted supply. If a large number of cartel members exceed their quotas, though, the overall supply rises enough to reduce the price, and the cartel fails to keep profits high. But OPEC wasn't failing now, and Americans were shocked.

- *What was the effect of the sudden oil price increase on the economy?*

Here are the data for the goods market. Output was at potential in 1973, with the unemployment rate very near 5%. Then came the *supply shock*. The price of oil and gasoline shot upward. Oil is an input to motor fuel, industrial chemicals, fertilizer, plastics. Increases in oil prices made production of these products more expensive. And, since practically everything must be transported to market, fuel costs had an even wider effect on business. Aggregate supply was suddenly reduced. The result was a simultaneous decrease in output and increase in inflation. Real GDP fell in 1974 and 1975, and inflation rose to double-digits in 1974, nearly that high in 1975. The unemployment rate rose to the highest level since 1940.

Oil Shock

Year	Real GDP Growth	CPI Inflation	Unemploy- ment Rate
1973	5.6%	6.2%	4.9%
1974	-0.5%	11.0%	5.6%
1975	-0.2%	9.1%	8.5%

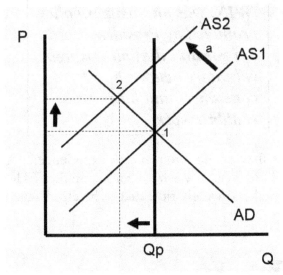

Figure 9-5. Worst of both worlds. A sharp increase in the price of oil increases resource costs. This is a supply shock. Aggregate supply decreases (a). Stagflation results, a rise in the price level (inflation) and a fall in output (recession) (1 to 2).

The price of gasoline had been stable for many years, near 35 cents a gallon. Now the price was climbing to unimagined heights. Just as bad, there were gasoline shortages. Drivers couldn't be sure that their gas station would have gasoline when they needed it. So, when the station had gasoline to sell, cars lined up for blocks to buy it. The expectation of shortages aggravated the shortages.

Oil supplies had been interrupted before, during the Suez crisis in the 1950's and the Six-Day War in the 1960's, without gasoline shortages. This time, though, there were price controls. The rise in the price of gasoline was restricted by President Nixon's controls. Prices went up, but not enough to reduce gasoline purchases down to the lower quantity supplied.

Richard Nixon resigned on August 9, 1974, and Gerald Ford became President. That month the unemployment rate was 5.5%, the inflation rate was 11%. The new President called an Inflation Summit in September, and heard testimony from business people, labor leaders, economists and many others. Then, on October 8, he addressed a joint session of Congress.

251

The new President had decided to adopt policies that people called "the old time religion." Ford asked Congress to limit the coming year's spending, and to enact a five percent tax surcharge on businesses and upper-income taxpayers. These moves would reduce the spending of government, businesses and consumers. He asked consumers to conserve gasoline and food, the goods that had seen the biggest price hikes.

What is most remembered from this speech, however, is his proposal for a big public effort to fight inflation. President Ford reached into his pocket for a red button, and hooked it to his jacket. The button, he said

> bears the single word WIN. I think that tells it all. I will call upon every American to join in this massive mobilization and stick with it until we do win as a nation and as a people.

"WIN" stood for "whip inflation now." A few weeks later, he and Mrs. Ford signed a pledge at a White House ceremony. It read, "I pledge to my fellow citizens that I will buy, when possible, only those products and services priced at or below present levels. I also promise to conserve energy and I urge others to sign this pledge."

In his speech Ford had rejected what he called a "politically tempting" return to mandatory price controls. He said that Americans knew the problems they create "from recent experience." A purely voluntary program would not create such problems. But it wasn't a solution either. The WIN buttons and consumer pledges were mostly ignored and widely ridiculed. The effort faded by the end of the year.

> *"Whip Inflation Now" (WIN) was an incomes policy promoted by President Ford to restrain inflation through voluntary actions by consumers and businesses. It didn't work.*

Whip Inflation Now. Was it nonsense? Or a worthwhile ingenious nostrum.

So did the "old time religion." The unemployment rate had been edging upward in 1974, but in 1975 it soared. In May 1975 it hit 9%, the highest rate since the Great Depression. The target of policy switched from inflation to unemployment. At the Fed, Arthur Burns had been raising interest rates through most of 1974. Now in 1975 the discount rate was cut almost three points. President Ford reversed course and asked Congress for a tax cut.

Double-Digit Inflation
The legacy of the Watergate scandal and stagflation worked against President Ford in the 1976 election. He lost to the former governor of Georgia, Jimmy Carter. Carter remembered later that inflation barely had been mentioned during the campaign. Inflation, Carter said "was not a burning issue. The only thing was, what are we going to do about jobs." The inflation rate had fallen after the 1973-75 recession, from 13% in October 1974 to 5% in January 1977. Unemployment, on the other hand, was still 7.5%. The Carter administration increased spending on employment programs. But the inflation rate began to creep upward.

In March 1978 President Carter appointed a new Fed chair, G. William Miller. Miller was a businessman, the chairman of the board of the Textron Corporation. Before the year was out, however, confidence in Miller's management of Fed policy had faded. Yes, the Fed had increased the discount rate six times in 1978, normally a sign that the Fed was trying to restrain spending. But inflation was rising even faster. By October the influential business magazine *Fortune* ran an article titled "Why the Fed is a Flop at Managing Money." It pointed out that "what actually affects the behavior of business and consumers is the *real rate of interest*—the nominal rate minus the expected rate of inflation." In 1974, for example, the Fed jacked up interest rates to 12 percent. But lenders anticipated an inflation rate of more than 10 percent, so "business had every incentive to keep borrowing at what, in many cases, amounted to a zero real rate of interest."

> *In the second half of the 1970's the Federal Reserve increased interest rates, but inflation rose just as much. Real interest rates were negative. The Fed's inflation-fighting policy was "behind the curve."*

For five years, from mid-1974 to mid-1979, the federal funds rate was less than the inflation rate most of the time. The real federal funds rate was negative more often than not. Inflation raced higher, and the Fed followed meekly with interest rate hikes that didn't quite keep up. The Fed, it was said, was always *behind the curve*.

Fortune called Miller "a fainthearted inflation fighter," and this view seemed to be borne out when in November the Open Market Committee voted to increase the discount rate. Miller voted against the increase. No one at the Fed could remember a chairman being outvoted on the committee. When inflation topped double-digits early in 1979, Carter's economic team started to worry about the Fed's ineffective policy. The Secretary of the Treasury, Michael Blumenthal, and the head of the Council of Economic Advisors, Charles Schultz, began to campaign for tighter money. They made speeches and they leaked complaints to the press. Again, no one could remember a time when the President's people wanted the Fed to *raise* interest rates, while the Fed resisted. The *Wall Street Journal* called it a "world turned upside down."

The price of oil had faded as an issue by the end of 1978. The price of gasoline remained around 60 cents a gallon from 1975 to 1978. This was much higher than it had been before 1973, but people had adjusted. Conservation measures were taken. Highway speed limits were set at 55 miles per hour. Sales of fuel efficient cars from Japan began to grow.

A 1972 Honda Civic. Honda first exported cars to the U.S. in 1969, and introduced the Civic in 1972. When gasoline prices nearly doubled in 1973, and doubled again in 1979, Americans looked for fuel efficient small cars. Nearly a million Civics were sold from 1973 to 1979.

Then in 1979 Iranian fundamentalists overthrew the Shah of Iran. Iran's oil exports fell during the chaos. In 1980, Iraq invaded Iran, beginning a war that was to last for eight years. Now neither Iraq nor Iran was exporting crude oil. With two of its members at war, OPEC decision-making was paralyzed. The cartel could not agree to increase production to hold oil supplies steady.

The price of crude oil jumped from $15 a barrel in January 1979 to almost $40 in April 1980. The price of gasoline rose from 60 cents a gallon in 1978 to $1.35 a gallon in 1981. The oil and gasoline price controls were still in effect—no one had had the nerve to rescind them in the midst of rising inflation—so again there were shortages and gas lines.

Paul Volcker at the Fed
In the summer of 1979 President Carter retreated to Camp David to consult with experts about the economy. The President came down from the mountain and on July 15 gave his famous "malaise" speech. "The erosion of our confidence in the future is threatening to destroy the social and the political fabric of America," he said. Then he fired his Treasury Secretary, and replaced him with Fed chair William Miller. That left a hole at the Fed. The new chair had to be someone willing to fight inflation, to somehow push the Fed ahead of the curve. The very mention of his name should restore respect for the Fed.

One name kept surfacing: Paul Volcker, then head of the New York Federal Reserve Bank. He was a balding cigar-smoking six-foot-eight graduate of Princeton (yes, he was on the basketball team). He had been a figure in the world of monetary policy and international finance for two decades. He had been at Treasury in the sixties, trying to defend the Bretton Woods fixed exchange rate system. He had been at Richard Nixon's 1971 Camp David meeting, when the system came crashing down. He was now the head of the New York Federal Reserve Bank, in the heart of the nation's financial district. He was known to be an inflation "hawk."

- *What are the Fed's policy choices when faced with stagflation?*

Volcker was surprised to get the call, and he went down to Washington without expectations. He walked into the Oval Office and sprawled on a couch. He puffed on his cigar and started talking. "Mr. President," he said, "You must understand my concern about the importance of an independent central bank and the need for tighter money—tighter than Bill Miller wants."

Paul Volcker recognized the difficult trade-off that the oil shocks, inflationary expectations and stagflation presented the Federal Reserve. With both inflation and unemployment high, the Fed had to choose. It could increase the money supply and decrease interest rates, to bring down unemployment. But that would aggravate inflation. It could decrease the money supply and increase interest rates, to bring down inflation. But that would aggravate unemployment. William Miller leaned towards attacking unemployment, and so voted against further interest rate increases. But Volcker was an inflation hawk. He wanted interest rates higher, to bring down inflation, even at the cost of higher unemployment.

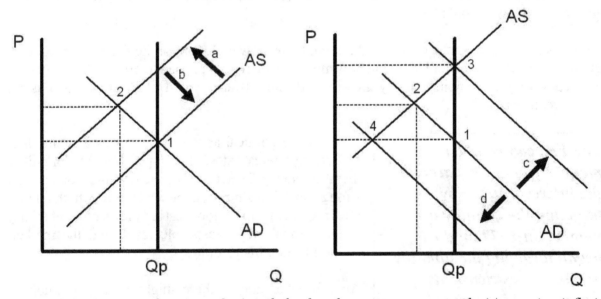

Figure 9-6. Accommodate or not? An oil shock reduces aggregate supply (a), causing inflation and recession (1 to 2). The Federal Reserve has a choice. It can fight recession by increasing the money supply. Interest rates fall and investment increases, increasing aggregate demand (c). The recession ends quickly, but there is even more inflation (2 to 3). It can fight inflation by decreasing the money supply. Interest rates rise and investment decreases, reducing aggregate demand (d). Inflation is brought under control, at the cost of a deeper recession (2 to 4). A third choice is to make no policy change. Left alone, with output less than potential, workers and suppliers will eventually be forced to accept lower wages and prices (or smaller wage and price increases). Second shift #1 means aggregate supply will increase (b). The price level falls back to (1), with oil prices up and other prices down. This requires a lengthy period of unemployment, however.

Jimmy Carter appointed Paul Volcker chair of the Federal Reserve, and Volcker took office in August 1979. Within a week he persuaded the Open Market Committee to raise interest rates. The vote in the committee was 4 to 3 in favor of the rate hike. Volcker knew he had the votes to raise rates some more, but the markets saw the close vote as a sign that the Fed would not be tightening again. Perversely, the rate hike probably increased inflationary expectations. It was time, Volcker thought, to find a new policy to "shake up" inflationary psychology.

In making monetary policy, the Fed could target either the money supply or the interest rate. To target the interest rate, the Fed adjusted the supply of money to meet the amount of money demanded. To target the money supply, the interest rate would rise or fall to equate the supply to the amount demanded. The Fed had always targeted interest rates in the past. It made policy by setting the federal funds rate.

The Fed was "behind the curve." Volcker wrote that it had been "reacting too slowly and too mildly only after the evidence was abundantly clear, which by definition was too late." *Targeting the money supply*, on the other hand, offered the Fed several advantages.

There was an academic advantage. The University of Chicago's Milton Friedman had advocated that the Fed to follow a policy of stable money supply growth. Pick a growth rate near the average rate of growth in GDP, and stick to it through good times and bad. There then would be no sustained inflation, and at least the Fed would not contribute to recessions. The policy was called *monetarism*. Now it would be tried.

There was a tactical advantage. The Fed did not know how high to raise the federal funds rate to fight inflation. It had a better idea about how much the money supply had to grow to keep inflation low. They would set money supply growth, and interest rates would rise just as much as the markets required.

The Fed can conduct monetary policy by targeting the interest rate, or by targeting the quantity of money. In 1979 the Fed began targeting the quantity of money, restricting its growth, and interest rates soared.

There was a political advantage. "It was a camouflage for raising interest rates," said Open Market Committee member Nancy Teeters. The Fed would come under strong attack if it simply announced the very high interest rates required to do the job. Instead they would set money supply growth at a reasonable level, and the markets would increase interest rates.

And, Volcker hoped, there might be a psychological advantage. "People don't need an advanced course in economics to understand that inflation has something to do with too much money," Volcker thought. Announce a money growth target loud and clear—so loud and clear that the Fed could not back off—and the Fed's credibility might be restored. People would understand what the Fed was doing and why, and they would believe the Fed would follow through. Their expectations of future inflation would drop. "We would have a chance of affecting ordinary people's behavior," Volcker thought.

Chairman Volcker called a secret meeting of the Open Market Committee on Saturday, October 6, 1979. Volcker described his idea, and warned committee members that interest rates would be more volatile, and would likely rise a lot. The Committee supported him. Some of the members were eager to go ahead.

That Saturday night Volcker announced their decisions. He announced changes in all three of the Fed's tools, all at once. The *discount rate* would rise by another point. There would be new higher *reserve requirements* on commercial bank deposits. And, most important, the monetarist approach to *open market operations* would be adopted. The money supply would be targeted, and interest rates would rise as they would.

And they did. When the markets opened on Monday, October 8, the federal funds rate was 11.6%. By the end of the day the rate was 13.9%. In two weeks it was 17.6%. But it wasn't a steady rise. The next day the rate dropped to 15.7%, it was 10.9% on November 7, 14.2% on December 10. The federal funds rate was higher and more volatile, just as Volcker had warned. Other interest rates followed suit. The home mortgage rate averaged 11.3% in September. By April it was 16.3%. The monthly payments on a new 30-year mortgage rose by 40%.

Interest rates rose higher than Volcker had thought they would, yet the inflation rate did not come down. It was 12.2% in September 1979, 14.8% in April 1980. This was partly the result of rising oil prices, but the hoped-for psychological impact on inflationary expectations never appeared. "We soon learned that any dreams we might have had of changing public expectations by the force of our own convictions were just that—dreams," Volcker said.

The Great Recession of 1981-82

There was a short, sharp recession in 1980. It was enough to defeat President Carter and elect Ronald Reagan, but not enough to bring down inflation. "It was in a way a mostly wasted year restoring credibility in the attack on inflation," Volcker recalled later. But now he and the Fed resolved to renew the attack. The federal funds rate was 12.8% in October, with a real rate near zero. By January, as President Reagan gave his inaugural address, the federal funds rate was 18.9%, and the real rate was about 7%. The federal funds rate would remain above ten percent for the next year and a half.

The recovery ended after only one year. This new recession would be sharp, but not short. It is marked from July 1981 to November 1982. At 16 months it was the longest recession since the Great Depression (to that time). It was a "double-dip," a second recession almost on top of a first. The economy was in recession for 22 of 34 months from 1980 through 1982.

> *The Great Recession of 1981-82 was the result of the Federal Reserve's efforts to bring down inflation. It worked, but at great cost in high unemployment and lost output.*

The unemployment rate remained above 10% for ten straight months in 1982 and 1983, topping out at 10.8% in December 1982. It was and is the highest unemployment rate since the Depression. Unemployment in the Midwestern "rust belt" soared. The unemployment rate topped 10% for 27 straight months in Indiana, peaking at 12.4%.

The home mortgage interest rate hit 18.5% in October 1981. People built and bought many fewer houses. "For a while my office was deluged with sawed-off wooden two-by-fours in a campaign organized by homebuilders to lower interest rates and stimulate their business," Volcker remembered. Farmers blockaded Fed headquarters with their tractors for a day to protest high interest rates.

Great Recession 1981-82

Year	Real GDP Growth	CPI Inflation	Unemploy- ment Rate	Interest Rate Spread	Real Federal Funds Rate
1979	3.2%	11.3%	5.8%	1.1%	-0.1%
1980	-0.3%	13.5%	7.2%	1.7%	-0.1%
1981	2.5%	10.3%	7.6%	1.9%	6.1%
1982	-1.8%	6.2%	9.7%	2.3%	6.1%
1983	4.6%	3.2%	9.6%	1.5%	5.9%

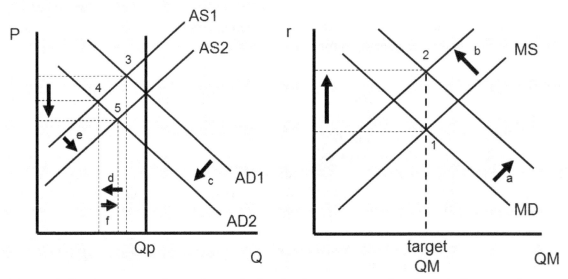

Figure 9-7. Not as complicated as it looks. In the money market, high inflation is increasing money demand (a). The Fed decreases money supply (b) to hit the target quantity of money. The real interest rate increases a lot (1 to 2). In the goods market, output is less than potential (3). This high interest rate reduces investment, and aggregate demand declines (c). Output falls (d). Output remains less than potential until businesses and workers are convinced to accept lower prices and wages. Aggregate supply increases (e), and output begins to recover (f). The inflation rate falls.

Some members of the Reagan administration began to speak against the Fed's policy. Two things saved it. President Ronald Reagan never wavered in his support for the Fed's independence. And, most important, Volcker's strategy was working. Inflation remained above 10% through the end of 1981. Then it started to drop. In January 1982 it was 8.4%. By July, 6.4%. And in December, 3.8%. The inflation rate had not been so low since January 1973.

The unemployment rate in 1979 was already above 5%. It increased to 7.2% with the short 1980 recession. Output starts less than potential in Figure 9-7. Fed chair Paul Volcker adopted money supply targeting, which is modeled in the money market diagram to the right of Figure 9-7. The target is a quantity of money—in real life, a money growth rate—and money supply is adjusted to hit that target. High inflation meant money demand was increasing, so money targeting produced a big rise in the real interest rate. The real federal funds rate increased from near zero to 6.1% in 1981, a huge one-year increase, and the interest rate spread increased too. The Fed was now ahead of the curve.

The high real interest rate caused a big decline in investment spending, and aggregate demand fell. Real GDP decreased. With output well below potential, and unemployment high, inflationary expectations began to fall. Businesses realized that they could not raise prices with sales so low. Workers realized that they had to take lower paying jobs with job opportunities so limited. In 1983 real GDP increased and the inflation rate fell. An increase in aggregate supply is the only shift that can produce that result. Unemployment remained high, however, so output is still below potential. It stayed there through most of the 1980's.

Hyperinflation
The United States in the 1970's and early 1980's saw the Great Inflation, the worst peacetime inflation of the 20th century. Double-digit inflation was a huge problem, but it wasn't nearly enough to call it *hyperinflation*. Inflation has to get much worse to call it that.
Sometimes it does. Sometimes the inflation rate rises to hundreds, thousands or even millions of percent per year. We know what causes hyperinflation: way too much money chasing too few goods. Only governments print money, so only governments can cause hyperinflation. But why would a government do such a thing?

One reason is lack of tax revenue. If a government must provide services, but cannot raise taxes, it might print money to fund the budget deficit. The United States effectively did that in World Wars I and II. If taxes are really low, and spending is really high, there may be so much money created that hyperinflation results

> *Hyperinflation can occur only if the government prints vast amounts of money.*

A second reason for hyperinflation is that governments sometimes have policy objectives which are more important than economic stability. Hyperinflations are often associated with wars. A government might risk printing too much money if there's a war to be won.

Probably the most famous hyperinflation was in Germany after World War I. The inflation rate hit almost 30,000 percent *per month*. It wiped out middle class savings and helped pave the way for Adolph Hitler. There were several big hyperinflations after World War II, including the worst hyperinflation every recorded, in Hungary in 1946. More recently, there was hyperinflation in Bolivia in 1984-85, in Argentina, Brazil and Peru in 1989-90, in Ukraine in 1991-94, and Yugoslavia in 1992-94.

Zimbabwe saw hyperinflation in 2006-08. It began with a botched land reform that devastated agriculture. The government of President Robert Mugabe began seizing thousands of big white-owned commercial farms in 2000. Unfortunately, many of the farms' new owners knew little about farming. By 2008 the big farms produced less than a tenth of the corn that they did in the 1990s.

In the chaos foreign investors fled, manufacturing ground to a halt, goods and foreign currency needed to buy imports fell into short supply, and prices shot up. With manufacturing and farming less productive, government tax revenues fell. Prices were rising, though, so government employees demanded higher pay. President Mugabe's government began printing more Zimbabwean dollars to keep ministries functioning and to protect the salaries of supporters against further price increases.

I'm a hundred-trillionaire (Zimbabwean). Towards the end of the hyperinflation in Zimbabwe the central bank printed $100 trillion bills. They exchanged for less than one U.S. dollar.

This presents a third reason for hyperinflation: a government that lacks legitimacy. President Mugabe hadn't been elected in a free and fair election. He could not impose taxes and expect them to be paid. So the government printed money to pay government employees, the police and the army, to keep the President in power.

Inflation reached an annual rate of 1,281 percent by mid-2006. It hit 410,000 percent by mid-2007. Inflation was officially 231 million percent in July 2008. John Robertson, an independent economist in Zimbabwe, estimated that it actually had reached eight quintillion percent — that's an eight followed by 18 zeros—by the end of the year.

These inflation rates are hard to believe. A glance at the picture of the one-hundred-trillion Zimbabwean dollar bill confirms them. It exchanged for 33 cents, American, but the end of the hyperinflation.

The hyperinflation caused great hardship for the people of Zimbabwe. Most of the nation's schools ceased to function. Teachers quit showing up because their salaries no longer covered the cost of the bus fare to work. Hospital workers faced the same situation, and many hospitals shut down. Cities couldn't buy the chemicals to treat the water supply, and taps ran dry. Late in 2008 a cholera epidemic began. With no sanitation and no hospital care, people died by the thousands.

Hyperinflations usually end with currency reform, and Zimbabwe saw two such reforms in 2008 and 2009. The first reform simply lopped ten digits off prices and currency denominations. That made it easier to make change, but since the government kept printing money, it did not stop inflation.

The second reform killed the Zimbabwean currency. The government quit printing it. U.S. dollars or South African rand circulated instead. Since the government cannot print these currencies, the increase in the money supply stopped, and eventually so did inflation.
Add Zimbabwe to the list of the great hyperinflations in history.

Terms in this Chapter, in order of appearance
The Great Inflation
Deflation
Employment Act of 1946
Safety net
Keynesian economics
Automatic stabilizers
Fiscal drag
Okun's Law
Income multiplier
Kennedy tax cut
The Great Society
The Vietnam War
Guns and butter
Tax surcharge
Counter-cyclical monetary policy
Pro-cyclical fiscal policy
Pro-cyclical monetary policy
Phillips Curve
Inflationary expectations
Natural rate of unemployment
Keynes-Friedman macroeconomic model
Incomes policy
Price controls
Shortages
Organization of Petroleum Exporting Countries (OPEC)
Cartel
Supply shock

Stagflation
Whip Inflation Now (WIN)
Double-digit inflation
Real interest rate
Behind the curve
Paul Volcker
Money supply targeting
Monetarism
Discount rate
Reserve requirements
Open market operations
The Great Recession, 1981-82
Hyperinflation

Notes
Both of Stein's books (1994, 1996) focus on the development (and breakdown) of the consensus on stabilization policy. Stein (1996) provides a detailed description of fiscal policy during the Eisenhower administration (pp. 281-371). The Eisenhower quotes come from Stein (1996, p. 367 and p. 368). Stein (1996, pp. 370-71) and Wicker (pp.180-181) tell of Richard Nixon's attempts to get Eisenhower to support a tax cut. Stein speculates that Eisenhower's tight fiscal policy cost Nixon the election in 1960.

The story of Martin, Johnson and the December 1965 discount rate hike is told in Hargrove and Morley (1984, pp. 248-249), Kettl (1986, p.104) and Califano (2000, pp. 106-109).

Two of Kennedy's economists, Solow and Tobin (1988, p.6), say that Kennedy had no fixed economic ideas when he took office. Heller describes the economic education of President Kennedy in Hargrove and Morley (p.175). Stein (1996, pp. 379-384), Heller's piece in Hargrove and Morley (p. 196) and Solow and Tobin (pp. 10-11) catalogue Galbraith, Tobin and Heller's views on expansionary policy.

The GDP gap, Okun's Law, multiplier calculation is based on a 1961 essay by the Council of Economic Advisors, published in Tobin and Weidenbaum (1988, pp. 29, 58-59). Prior to about 1990, policy debates like this used Gross National Product (GNP), not Gross Domestic Product (GDP). I've used GDP throughout this book, for consistency.

Kennedy's speech to the Economic Club of New York is available on the internet at www.presidency.ucsb.edu/site/docs/pppusyear.php?yearindex=1962. Heller tells the story of lobbying for the Kennedy tax cut, describes Kennedy's strategy of persuasion in Hargrove and Morley (pp. 205-209).

Heller (Hargrove and Morley, pp.209-211) talked about the transition to the Johnson administration. Heller also describes Johnson's skills at making deals (p. 181). President Johnson's speeches are available online at www.presidency.ucsb.edu/site/docs/index_pppus.php.

Joseph Califano's memoir of his years on Johnson's staff is an excellent source of policy details. He calculates that the administration passed 181 of 200 bills in 1965 and 1966 (Califano 2000, p. 149). Gardner Ackley notes that the Great Society programs were Johnson's babies (Hargrove and Morley, p. 247)

Ackley in Hargrove and Morley (pp. 247-249), Okun in Hargrove and Morley (pp. 293-95), Kettl (pp. 103-105) and Califano (pp. 106-109) tell the story of Fed chair Martin's response to the added spending required by Vietnam in 1965. Ackley describes Johnson's reaction to the Fed's tight monetary policy (pp. 232-238). Kettl describes the dance between Johnson and Martin over the tax surcharge and looser monetary policy (pp.107-109). Arthur Okun in Hargrove and Morley (pp. 305-306) and Califano (pp. 284-288) discuss the legislative battle to pass the tax surcharge.

Okun in Hargrove and Morley (pp. 306-308) talks about the failure of the tax surcharge to restrain growth or inflation. Solow and Tobin (p.15) report that the Kennedy-Johnson economists were using the Phillips Curve. Milton Friedman's speech to the AEA convention is in Friedman (1968).

The story of Volcker's appointment and his new policies is told by the man himself in Volcker's memoir with Toyoo Gyohten (1992, pp. 163-170), in Mussa (1994, pp. 95-97) and in Biven (2002, 237-244).

McCracken in Hargrove and Morley (p. 345) mentions Nixon's interest in a dramatic "long bomb" policy change.

Wicker (1991, pp. 552-560), Stein (1994, pp. 166-168, 176-187), McCracken in Hargrove and Morley (pp. 344-57), Stein in Hargove and Morley (pp. 390-401), and Safire (1975, pp. 659-686) tell the story of the wage and price controls and its problems. The story of the baling wire is from Sterba (1973).

Sources for Burns' alleged support of Nixon's reelection through loose monetary policy in 1972 are the original Rose article (1974), Wicker (pp. 563-564), and Kettl (p. 116).

Skeet (1988) provides a history of OPEC. The formation of OPEC is covered on pages 15-34, the first oil crisis on pages 99-123, and the second oil crisis on pages 157-177. Stein (pp. 190-193) and Stein in Hargrove and Morley (pp. 403-405) describe the interaction of the oil embargo and the price controls.

Stein (pp. 213-216) describes Ford's economic policies, including the WIN buttons. Greenspan in Hargrove and Morley (pp. 440-458) discusses his time at Ford's economic advisor. Ford's speeches are available online at www.presidency.ucsb.edu/site/docs/index_pppus.php.

Biven (2002) provides a study of Jimmy Carter's economic policies. He mentions Carter's recollection that inflation had not been a 1976 campaign issue (p.85). Biven (pp. 69-83) and Hargrove and Morley (pp. 476-481) discuss the Carter stimulus package of 1977.

Kettl covers the Miller Fed and mentions Miller's egg timer (p. 169). The phrase "behind the curve" to describe Fed policy in the late 1970s appears in many sources, such as Mussa (p. 92) and Volcker and Gyohten (pp. 165-166). Kettl (pp. 169-170) and Hargrove and Morley (p. 485-486) tell the story of the administration's campaign for higher rates.

Kettl sketches Volcker's biography (pp. 172-73). Volcker's quotes are from Volcker and Gyohten (p.166). Mussa (pp. 96-97) catalogues the tactical, political and psychological advantages of targeting money growth. The Teeters quote is in Kettl (p.177). Volcker's "dreams" quote is from Volcker and Gyohten (p. 170).

Volcker called 1980 a wasted year in the inflation fight in Volcker (1994, p. 148). He remembers the two-by-fours in Volcker and Gyohten (p. 176). Kettl mentions both the homebuilder and farmer protests (p. 187). The criticisms of the Fed from the Reagan administration and Congress are from Kettl (pp. 180-181). Kettl describes the decision to back away from money targeting (pp.183-184).

Sources

Biven, W. Carl. 2002. *Jimmy Carter's Economy: Policy in an Age of Limits.* Chapel Hill, N.C.: University of North Carolina Press.

Califano, Joseph A., Jr. 2000. *The Triumph and Tragedy of Lyndon Johnson.* College Station, Texas: Texas A&M University Press.
Dallek, Robert. 1998. *Flawed Giant: Lyndon Johnson and his Times, 1961-1973.* New York: Oxford University Press.

Friedman, Milton. 1968. "The Role of Monetary Policy" *American Economic Review* 58 (March): 1-17.

Hargrove, Erwin C. and Samuel A. Morley (eds.). 1984. *The President and the Council of Economic Advisors: Interviews with CEA Chairmen.* Boulder, Colorado: Westview Press.

Kettl, Donald F. 1986. *Leadership at the Fed.* New Haven: Yale University Press.

Mussa, Michael. 1994. "Monetary Policy," Pages 81-145 in Martin Feldstein, *American Economic Policy in the 1980s.* Chicago: University of Chicago Press.

Rose, Sanford. 1974. "The Agony of the Federal Reserve," *Fortune* 90 (July): 91-93.

Rose, Sanford. 1978. "Why the Fed is a Flop at Managing Money." *Fortune* 98 (October): 53-68.

Schlesinger, Arthur M. 1965. *A Thousand Days.* Boston: Little, Brown and Co.

Skeet, Ian. 1988. *OPEC: Twenty-Five Years of Prices and Politics.* Cambridge, U.K.: Cambridge University Press.

Solow, Robert M. and James Tobin. 1988. "Introduction: The Kennedy Economic Reports." Pages 3-16 in James Tobin and Murray Weidenbaum, *Two Revolutions in Economic Policy*. Cambridge, Massachusetts: The MIT Press.

Stein, Herbert. 1994. *Presidential Economics (3rd Revised Edition)*. Washington, D.C.: The AEI Press.

Stein, Herbert. 1996. *The Fiscal Revolution in America (2nd Revised Edition)*. Washington, D.C.: The AEI Press.

Volcker, Paul A. 1994. "Monetary Policy." Pages 145-151 in Martin Feldstein, *American Economic Policy in the 1980s*. Chicago: University of Chicago Press.

Volcker, Paul A. and Toyoo Gyohten. 1992. *Changing Fortunes*. New York: Times Books.

Wells, Wyatt C. 1994. *An Economist in an Uncertain World: Arthur F. Burns and the Federal Reserve, 1970-1978*. New York: Columbia University Press.

Wicker, Tom. 1991. *One of Us: Richard Nixon and the American Dream*. New York: Random House.

News Articles

Dugger, Celia. "Cholera Epidemic Sweeping Across Crumbling Zimbabwe," *New York Times*, December 12, 2008.

Dugger, Celia. "Fragile Signs of Hope Emerging in the Gloom of Mugabe's Rule," *New York Times*, March 20, 2009.

Dugger, Celia. "Life in Zimbabwe: Wait for Useless Money," *New York Times*, October 2, 2008.

Wines, Michael. "As Inflation Soars, Zimbabwe Economy Plunges," *New York Times*, February 7, 2007.

Wines, Michael. "Caps on Prices Only Deepen Zimbabweans' Misery," New York Times, August 2, 2007.

Wines, Michael. "Freeze on Wages Is Latest Step to Stanch Inflation in Zimbabwe," New York Times, September 1, 2007.

Wines, Michael. "Zimbabwe's Prices Rise 900%, Turning Staples Into Luxuries," *New York Times*, May 2, 2006.

Chapter 10
Deficits and Goldilocks

How frustrating, that policymakers had to choose between inflation and recession. How devastating, that apparently the only way to beat double-digit inflation was with a Great Recession. So it's perhaps no surprise that, in the midst of simultaneous recession and inflation—stagflation—ideas would bubble up to offer another choice.

It's December 4, 1974, at the Two Continents restaurant in Washington, D.C.

The Laffer Curve

According to legend, it began on a napkin. Economist Arthur Laffer had dinner with two companions, Jude Wanniski, an editor at the *Wall Street Journal*, and Dick Cheney, a member of the Ford administration. Talk turned to the budget problems faced by the new administration. The budget was in deficit, and Wanniski and Cheney supposed that a tax increase would be needed.

A tax increase can *reduce* tax revenue, Laffer told them. Cheney and Wanniski were mystified. Laffer grabbed a cocktail napkin and sketched a diagram. He drew a vertical axis and labeled it "Income tax revenue." He drew an axis and labeled it "income tax rate," and he drew a half-moon shaped curve.

How much revenue would the government raise if the tax rate was zero? he asked. Nothing, of course, was the answer. How much revenue would be raised if the tax rate was 100%? After a pause, Laffer told them, also nothing. If government took all the earnings from working or saving or investment, then no one would have any reason to work or save or invest. The *tax base* would be zero. As the tax rate rises from zero, at first revenue increases. But after a while, people stop working as much, and higher tax rates will bring in less revenue.

> *The Laffer curve shows the relationship between tax rates and tax revenues. Revenue is zero when the tax rate is zero, and when it is 100%. This means that, when tax rates are very high, a decrease in the tax rate could increase revenues.*

It was a revelation to Jude Wanniski. If taxes were lower workers would supply more hours of work. Businesses would supply more goods and services. Taxes affected the behavior of businesses and employees. As he stared at this *Laffer curve*, Wanniski realized something else: if taxes were high, a tax *cut* could stimulate so much new output, income and wealth that tax revenue could *increase*.

Taxes didn't just affect spending, the demand for goods. They affected the supply of work and savings too. It looked like a new kind of economics: *supply-side economics*.

Back in New York Wanniski persuaded the *Wall Street Journal* editors to adopt the supply-side idea in their editorials about tax policy. He wrote a book extolling the Laffer curve. He and Laffer explained the idea to the new Congressman from Buffalo, a former NFL quarterback named Jack

Kemp. Kemp was so impressed that he and Delaware Senator William Roth proposed a bill to reduce tax rates by 10% a year three years in a row, a 30% cut altogether. By 1978 Kemp-Roth tax cut was part of the Republican platform in the Congressional elections.

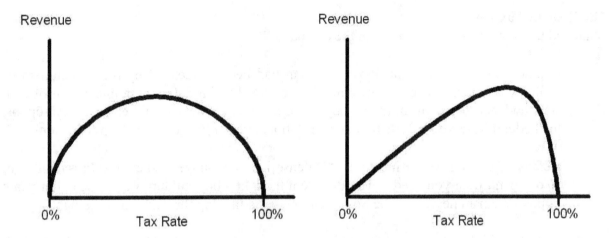

Figure 10-1. Two Laffer Curves. Revenue is on the vertical axis, the income tax rate is on the horizontal axis. The Laffer curve was often pictured as at left, with the peak near the 50% tax rate. There is a large section of the curve to the right of the peak where reductions in the tax rate will increase revenue. However, for most taxes and most taxpayers, the response of hours worked to the income tax rate was relatively small. The Laffer Curve actually looked as it does at right, with a peak nearer to 100%, and little room for tax cuts to increase revenue.

Ronald Reagan had been a well-known actor, and was the former Governor of California. He had been a New Deal Democrat until the end of the 1940's (he'd voted for Truman in 1948), but his concern about the threat of communism made him turn to the right. He entered politics as a Republican. Reagan made his first political splash in a speech endorsing conservative Republican Barry Goldwater for the 1964 presidential nomination. He ran for the Republican nomination himself in 1968, and again in 1976, nearly taking the nomination from President Gerald Ford.

Now, in 1980, he was running for the nomination again. He was 69 years old, so this was his last chance. His chief opponent, George H. W. Bush, unexpectedly won the Iowa caucus in January. The New Hampshire primary was next. It would make or break Reagan's candidacy.

Reagan's campaign managers set up a seminar on national issues for their candidate, to prepare him for the crucial primary. Among the instructors were Arthur Laffer, Jude Wanniski and Congressman Jack Kemp. They told him about the Laffer curve. He understood instantly.

"I came into the big money making pictures during World War II," he told them. The tax rate in the top bracket was raised to 90% during the war. Those with the highest incomes kept only a dime of every extra dollar they earned. "You could only make four pictures and then you were in the top bracket," Reagan said, "so we all quit working after four pictures and went off to the country." Had the tax rate been lower, he would have made more movies. Lower tax rates meant more work, higher incomes, and, plausibly, more tax payments and revenue. Reagan had lived on the right side of the Laffer curve.

The Reagan campaign emphasized tax cuts as the centerpiece of their policy proposals. George Bush called it "voo-doo economics." But it persuaded the voters. Reagan won in New Hampshire, and in November he won the Presidency.

The Reagan Tax Cut

What had the new President promised in the campaign?

- Inflation would be brought down. Reagan had been influenced by the monetarism of Milton Friedman. The economy could be stabilized and inflation kept under control with slow and steady growth in the money supply. The President would consistently support the Federal Reserve's efforts to reduce inflation, even at the cost of a deep recession.

- Defense spending would increase. "Defense is not a budget issue," the President said, "You spend what you need." The President thought a big buildup was needed after years of post-Vietnam neglect. The Soviet Union was still a big threat, Reagan thought.

- Taxes would be cut. Reagan favored two existing tax proposals. One was the Kemp-Roth tax cut bill, which would reduce income taxes on individuals by 30% over three years. The other was a bill to allow businesses to depreciate their facilities and equipment more rapidly for tax purposes. This would reduce taxes on businesses, and make it cheaper to invest in plant and equipment.

- The budget would be balanced. As a candidate Reagan had repeatedly criticized Carter administration budget deficits. And Republicans had always been for balanced budgets.

More generally, the President thought that *free markets* could promote the efficient use of resources and technical innovation. "Free" meant free of government regulation or interference. In this the Reagan administration was part of a world-wide trend toward greater reliance on markets. The Carter administration had deregulated trucking and air travel. Margaret Thatcher's new government in Great Britain was moving in this direction. Amazingly, so was China's communist government under its new premier, Deng Xiaoping.

On February 18, President Reagan announced his economic program in a speech to a joint session of Congress. He proposed a litany of spending to be cut: federal aid to education, subsidies to arts and humanities, the synthetic fuels program, funds for local economic development, trade adjustment assistance, grants to states and local governments, postal subsidies, NASA space programs. Eligibility rules would be tightened for Medicaid, food stamps, welfare, and the school lunch program.

He cited the Soviet military threat to justify a defense buildup. Then came the tax proposal. What was needed, he said, was

> a tax program which provides incentive to increase productivity for both workers and industry. Our proposal is for a 10-percent across-the-board cut every year for 3 years in the tax rates for all individual income taxpayers, making a total cut in the tax rates of 30 percent.

The tax debate lasted through the Spring and Summer. Republicans controlled the Senate, but Democrats had the majority in the House, so some compromise was needed. But President Reagan was known as the "Great Communicator" for his ability to persuade the public to support his policies. Public support for the new President was strong.

The Democrats would propose an additional cut, such as a tax cut for savers. The Republicans would adopt it too, and add another, like a tax cut for small businesses, which the Democrats would then try to top. The bidding war was on. "I don't like this poker game of calling and raising," said Jim Wright, a leading House Democrat. But he added, "frankly, we'll put anything in the bill if it will buy votes."

This put the House Democrats in a political bind. Republicans and their conservative Democratic allies appeared to have the votes to pass the tax bill. The Democrats needed a tax cut bill of their own, to compete with the President's proposal. And so began what has been called a "one-time, sixty-day breakdown in the normal partisan checks and balances of the fiscal process," or more simply, a "feeding frenzy" and a "bidding war."

Then, in late July, came one addition that had profound long-term effects. When there was inflation, the Federal income tax was subject to a phenomenon called *bracket creep*.
The Federal income tax is progressive, which means that people with higher incomes pay a higher percentage of their incomes in taxes. This is accomplished by having income tax brackets. People with incomes in the $14,000 and $16,000 bracket paid 37% of each extra dollar in taxes; people with incomes in the $16,000 to $18,000 bracket paid 43%, and so forth. As inflation increased prices it also increased pay. People were pushed into higher and higher income tax brackets. The percentage of their income paid in taxes increased, even though their pay had not increased, in real terms. Tax bills went up in real terms even though tax rates hadn't changed. Real after-tax incomes were reduced. The Federal government collected more revenue.

> *Bracket creep is the increase in tax revenues that occurs because inflation pushes incomes into ever higher tax brackets. Income tax indexing increases the brackets with inflation, which prevents bracket creep, but also slows revenue growth.*

Republican Senator Bill Armstrong of Colorado proposed *income tax indexing*. Indexing would increase the brackets each year by the amount of inflation. With indexing inflation would not push taxpayers into higher tax rate brackets. The brackets would increase too, so the taxpayers' rates would stay the same. But this meant that inflation would no longer accelerate tax revenues. Without indexing, the tax rate cuts would eventually be erased by inflation and bracket creep. Revenues would recover. With indexing, the rate cuts in Kemp-Roth would be permanent.

President Reagan supported the idea. The main difference between his proposal and the Democrats', he said, was that the Democrat tax cut was temporary, while the Republican cut was permanent, because of indexing. After one last round of additions (a subsidy for peanut growers to win over Georgia Democrats), Kemp-Roth passed on July 29, 1981.

On August 3 budget director David Stockman ruined a victory luncheon with the bad news. "The scent of victory is still in the air," he declared, "but I'm not going to mince words. We're heading for a crash landing on the budget. . . . It's going to be harder than hell to get to a balanced budget even by 1986."

Stockman had asked for added budget cuts, but they had never been found. One attempt to cut Social Security benefits had been defeated in the Republican-controlled Senate by a vote of 96 to nothing. Stockman's balanced budget had been zapped by the third rail of American politics, Social Security.

The tax cut had been bigger than planned. The spending cuts had been smaller than planned. Then the Great Recession of 1981-82 reduced revenue even more. Revised projections had deficits growing through the middle of the decade.

"What about the revenue feedback from the tax bill?" asked one of the President's political advisors. The big tax cut, after all, was supposed to generate so much added economic activity— more work, more saving, more investment—that the lower tax rates would produce higher revenue. It was the Laffer curve argument, the idea that had started it all.

- *Why didn't the Reagan tax cuts produce enough added revenue to balance the Federal budget?*

It was not that the Laffer curve didn't exist. Of course lower taxes increased the amount of economic activity. The question was *how much* added activity tax cuts would produce, and how high taxes were in the first place. What was the *elasticity of supply* of labor, or investment? How much would it respond to an increase in after-tax wages or returns? If the added take-home pay from a tax cut encouraged people to work a lot more, or encouraged many more people to enter the labor force, then the added earnings might be enough to offset the cut in tax rates. If the added pay encouraged people to work just a little more, or encouraged only a few more people to enter the labor force, then the tax cut would reduce revenue.

As Reagan administration Treasury official (and economist) Donald Fullerton wrote, the economic response to tax rates, and the tax rates themselves, "are both low enough to suggest that broad-based cuts in labor tax rates would not increase revenues." Or, as administration economist Martin Feldstein put it, "for most taxpayers a cut in the tax on wages and

> **The elasticity of supply of labor shows the response of the income tax base to a tax cut. It's too small for a tax cut to increase revenues.**

salaries would increase tax revenue only if the resulting increase in labor supply was much greater than either logic or previous experience suggested was at all likely."

Let's see why. Consider a (relatively) simple example. Suppose the income tax takes 30% of a worker's earnings. She works 2,000 hours during the year earning $20 an hour, for $40,000 in total, and pays 30% in taxes, which is $12,000. Her after-tax take-home pay is $28,000, or $14 an hour. Then the tax rate is cut to 20%. Now, if she works 2,000 hours, her tax bill is $8,000 and her after tax pay is $32,000, $16 an hour. That's more income for the worker, but a revenue loss for the government.

But maybe our worker is inspired by the higher after-tax pay to work more. After-tax pay went up from $14 to $16 an hour, a 14.3% increase. How much more would she have to work to pay the same $12,000 in taxes that she paid at the higher tax rate? The answer is 3,000 hours, 50% more. A 14% rise in pay would have to cause a 50% rise in working hours. That's a *labor supply elasticity* of 3.5 (50% divided by 14.3%). Labor supply elasticities aren't that big. They're usually measured as very inelastic, around 0.1 to 0.4. A 14.3% rise in pay would cause a 6% rise in work (0.4 x 14.3%). But that means the government will lose revenue from an income tax cut. We're almost always on the left side of the Laffer Curve.

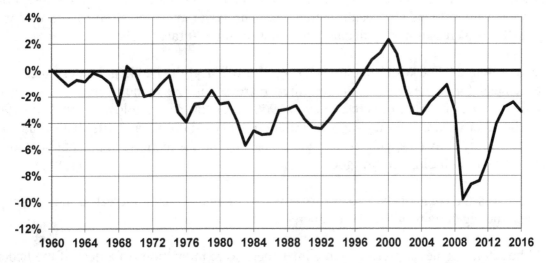

Figure 10-2. Federal budget balance as percentage of GDP, 1960-2016. The budget moves towards bigger deficits during and just after recessions, as in 1970-71, 1974-76, 1979-83, 1989-91, 2000-2003 and 2007-09. The budget moves towards surplus or to bigger surpluses during expansions, as in 1962-65, 1971-74, 1976-79, 1986-89, 1992-2000, 2003-06, 2010-15. In three instances, though, the budget deficit has become bigger or stayed big during expansions: during the Johnson Vietnam War-Great Society spending increase in 1965-1968, and during the Reagan tax cut-defense buildup in 1983-1986. Entitlement payments to baby boomer retirees explain the added deficit in 2016.

The Federal budget deficit had been $74 billion in 1980, the last full year of the Carter administration. In 1982, the deficit grew to $128 billion. Both 1980 and 1982 were recession years, so deficits were to be expected. But 1986 was the fourth year of an expansion, and by then the deficit was $221 billion. At 5% of GDP, it was the largest deficit since World War II up to that time.

The tax cut had passed at the end of July. By September it was clear that deficits would grow huge, and there was talk of new taxes. Over the next five years Congress passed a series of tax increases. President Reagan would not support an income tax rate increase, but did support elimination of many of the feeding-frenzy additions to the tax code.

Deficits and Monetary Policy

Ronald Reagan supported these tax increases because he really did support a balanced budget. At the August 3 victory luncheon he had told Stockman "we can't give up on the balanced budget. Deficit spending is how we got into this mess." Yet the President was not willing to give up any of his other promises to balance the budget. Defense spending would be increased. Tax rates would be cut. Inflation would be brought down. Balancing the budget was apparently the last of these four in importance. So the *budget deficit* increased.

What "mess" did the budget deficit create? In the past big deficits during expansions or wars had increased inflation. But the experience in the 1980s showed that inflation was not a necessary result of deficits. Whether deficits produced inflation depended on the actions of the Federal Reserve. Lower taxes increase consumer and business spending. A bigger defense budget increases spending directly. Incomes rise, and consumers need more money for transactions. Businesses want more loans to expand operations. The government must borrow more for its spending. All this increases money demand, and pushes interest rates higher.

The deficits present the Fed with a choice. During World War II the Fed kept interest rates fixed. With the demand for money rising, this required increases in the money supply. During the Vietnam War the Fed increased interest rates in 1966, but kept them too low in 1967 and 1968. To do this they increased the money supply. Inflation increased during and after both wars. The added money supply allowed aggregate demand to rise beyond the increase in potential output. It was too much money chasing too few goods.

Paul Volcker was the chair of the Federal Reserve, and he could have increased money supply growth when the big deficits of the 1980s emerged. He wrote later

> Although it was never pressed, sometimes there were intimations of a deal; if the Federal Reserve would commit itself to reducing interest rates, that would provide political lubrication for some combination of spending cuts and a tax increase to cut the deficit. History taught me to be cautious about that. Once before, in the late 1960s during the debate over an income tax increase to pay for Vietnam War costs, the Fed eased in anticipation of fiscal tightening. I don't know how much the decision to ease was meant as a political gesture as well as being economically appropriate. But it had become part of Fed lore that it was all a big mistake; the tax increase never had the restraining effect anticipated, the Federal Reserve was for months politically locked into inappropriate policy, and the momentum of inflation speeded up.

Volcker would make no deal. The Fed maintained a strong anti-inflation policy. That meant no added increases in the money supply to bring down interest rates. The hard-won victory over inflation would not be given up.

Crowding Out and the Twin Deficits

Here's our chance to apply the data, model and story like never before. To analyze the mid-1980's we need our five macro indicators, measures of fiscal and monetary policy, all three market diagrams and all five second shifts. This is the moment we've been preparing for!

The data and diagrams take up the following page, in Figure 10-3. The unemployment rate was 9.6% in 1983. It fell a lot in 1984, but remained well above 5%, so output started and finished below potential. Real GDP increased, very rapidly in 1984. But nothing much happened to inflation; there was no big up or down trend.

How to produce a rise in output, towards potential from below, with no change in inflation in the goods market model? It must have been a simultaneous increase in aggregate demand and aggregate supply, with equilibrium output always below potential.

This makes sense. With output less than potential second shift #1 increased aggregate supply. High unemployment was slowing wage and resource cost increases. Meanwhile, tax cuts were increasing consumption spending, and added defense spending was increasing government purchases. The government budget balance was negative and large. Aggregate demand increased.

Aggregate demand was increasing, but not enough to bring output up to potential. In fact, the unemployment rate remained above 5% throughout the 1980's. By the end of this period economists and policymakers were convinced that the *natural rate of unemployment* was closer to 6% than to 5%. That's the unemployment rate at potential output. One reason was entry of the (then) young inexperienced baby boomers into the labor force. Young people change jobs more frequently, so *frictional unemployment* would be higher. Even so, with the unemployment rate above 6% until 1988, output was less than potential through most of the 1980's expansion. Aggregate demand increased slowly.

Why did aggregate demand grow slowly, even with very *counter-cyclical fiscal policy*? That high real federal funds rate tells the story. The Federal Reserve was restraining growth in the money supply, to make sure that inflation did not re-emerge. Money demand must have been increasing, with growing incomes and moderate inflation (that's second shift #3). The interest rate spread was almost unchanged, however, so money supply must have been *increasing*. This is inconsistent with our view of the Fed's policy.

But remember the banking system, and the money multiplier. The Great Recession of 1981-82 was over, and lenders were recovering their optimism. Usually the interest rate spread would have fallen during the early years of an expansion. The rising money multiplier would have increased the money supply more. But from 1983 to 1985 the spread did not decrease. The Fed prevented that from happening. The spread, and real interest rates, were higher than they would have been, without Fed restraint. Figure 10-4 shows one real interest rate that hit record levels in 1983-84, and remained high through 1986.

High real interest rates, especially for more-risky businesses, would have slowed the increase in investment spending, and slowed the increase in aggregate demand. That's second shift #2. In fact, Figure 10-5 shows that the 1980's are the only expansion in the past 57 years when investment as a percentage of GDP declined.

The government spent more on defense. Consumers spent more because taxes were lower. Overall spending was restrained (and inflation held in check) because higher interest rates kept investment spending from growing. As Paul Volcker put it, "the environment for domestic investment was

Crowding Out

Year	Real GDP Growth	CPI Inflation	Unemploy-ment Rate	Interest Rate Spread	Exchange Rate, Euros/$ (est.)	Real Federal Funds Rate	Gov't Budget Balance (% GDP)
1983	4.6%	3.2%	9.6%	1.5%	1.12	5.9%	-5.9%
1984	7.3%	4.3%	7.5%	1.5%	1.27	5.9%	-4.7%
1985	4.2%	3.6%	7.2%	1.4%	1.31	4.5%	-5.0%

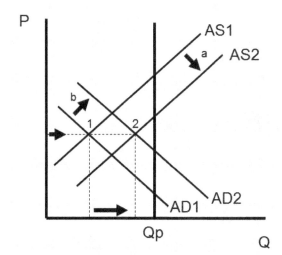

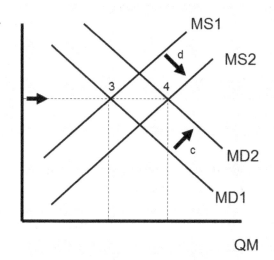

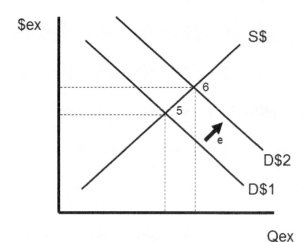

Figure 10-3. Three markets, five second shifts. In the goods market, unemployment is high, so output is much less than potential (1). This holds down input costs, increasing aggregate supply (a). That's second shift #1. Tax cuts cause big government deficits, which increases aggregate demand (b). Inflation is unchanged, output rises but remains below potential (1 to 2). In the money market, rising incomes and inflation increase money demand (c). That's second shift #3. The interest rate spread is unchanged, so money supply must be increasing (d). However, the high real federal funds rate implies that the Fed is holding back money supply growth. The real interest rate and the interest rate spread remain high. This limits investment spending growth, slowing the growth in aggregate demand and output, which is second shift #2. In the money market, the high real interest rates cause international investors to demand dollars, in order to lend in the U.S. Dollar demand increases (e). That's second shift #5. The exchange value of the dollar rises (5 to 6). This reduces exports and increases imports—second shift #4—which also limits the increase in aggregate demand.

not as good as it should have been. We had the longest peacetime expansion in history, but it was not exceptional for either its increases in productivity or for new investment in plant and equipment."

This is a phenomenon known as *crowding out*. Government activity crowds out private activity, because government borrowing crowds out private borrowing.

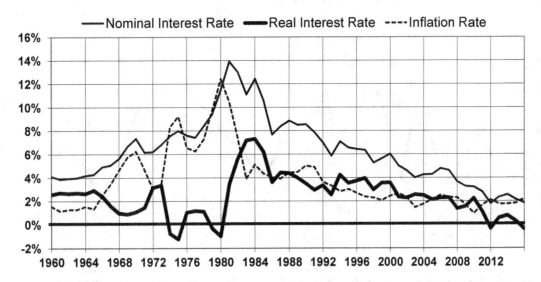

Figure 10-4. Real Interest Rate, 1960-2016. Treasury 10-year bond rate minus Consumer Price Index inflation, core rate. The real interest rate was near 3% through the mid-1960's, but dipped lower in the second half of that decade. During the second half of the 1970's it was lower, even negative, reflecting the Fed's accommodation of inflation. The real interest rate shot upward after 1980, because of the Fed's tight monetary policy. It remained especially high through 1986, and higher than usual into the 1990s because of the combination of big Federal budget deficits and tight money. The real rate has fallen steadily since then. It's been very low since 2010, reflecting the Fed's low interest rate policy.

> **Budget deficits and contractionary monetary policy in the 1980's raised real interest rates. Investment spending declined as a share of GDP. This was "crowding out."**

Martin Feldstein became head of the Council of Economic Advisors in 1982. He began speaking about the crowding out problem. "During the Fall of 1982," he wrote later, "I spent considerable time explaining publicly as well as inside the administration that the recent deficit surge was cyclical but that, as the economy recovered, we would still face a substantial structural deficit." During the recession year of 1982, a deficit was to be expected. This was not a problem—in fact, the lower taxes and added spending would help with recovery. But the deficits would remain as the economy expanded. This was a problem. With the economy at capacity, a big deficit would keep interest rates high.

"I explained also that a persistent structural deficit would inevitably lead to reduced investment in plant and equipment and therefore to lower levels of future real income," Feldstein wrote. That was the main problem with crowding out. Today's investment is tomorrow's capital stock. Less investment today means a smaller stock of machinery and equipment tomorrow. With fewer tools to work with, employees are less productive, and, over the years, potential output grows more slowly. Feldstein advocated bigger tax increases and bigger spending cuts to reduce the budget deficits, to the dismay of the President's political advisors.

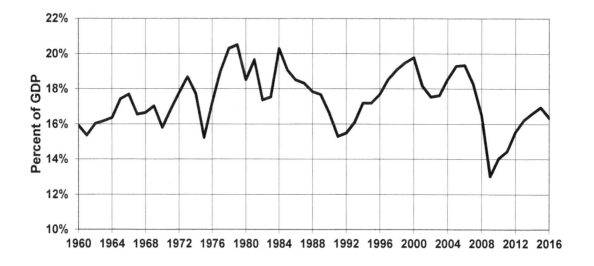

Figure 10-5. Investment as a Percentage of GDP, 1960-2016. Investment is more variable than GDP, so it usually falls more in recessions and grows more in expansions. That means it usually falls as a share of GDP during recessions (as in 1973-75, 1979-82, 2001 and 2007-09) and rises during expansions (the 1990s, 2009-14). During the 1980's, however, investment fell as a percentage of GDP. The slow growth of investment may be evidence of crowding out.

The Exchange Value of the Dollar
That's the interaction between the goods and money markets, for 1983-85. But Figure 10-3 shows the exchange market too. The table shows the exchange value of the dollar against the euro. Of course, the euro didn't exist in 1983-85; it became Europe's currency in 1999. But a value for the euro can be calculated from the values of the currencies that the euro replaced. This calculation makes the euro a sort of price index of the values of the German mark, French franc, Italian lira and other European currencies of the time.

The exchange value of the dollar was increasing. On the exchange market diagram the equilibrium exchange rate rises on the vertical axis. In Figure 10-3 the reason is an increase in the demand for the dollar. Again, the high real interest rates explain the rising demand for the dollar. Interest rates were higher in the United States than they were in the rest of the world. International investors saw this as an opportunity to earn a higher return on their wealth. They exchanged their own currencies for dollars, in order to lend them. This increased the demand for the dollar in the exchange market. The value of the dollar increased. That's second shift #5. The exchange market diagram could also show a decrease in the supply of the dollar. Americans with dollars decided to lend in the U.S., to take advantage of higher interest rates. So they cut their lending elsewhere, and supplied fewer dollars in exchange for marks, francs or lira. An increase in the demand for the dollar and a decrease in its supply would have the same cause, and the same result: a rise in the exchange value of the dollar.

To some extent foreign lending reduced the crowding out effect of high real interest rates. The U.S. was not limited to its own savings for investment in plant and equipment since it could borrow funds from abroad. Fed chair Paul Volcker wrote, "the shortage of domestic savings was compensated in substantial part by an enormous inflow of mainly borrowed capital from abroad." The amount that could be borrowed, he remembered, "turned out to be far larger than I had thought possible."

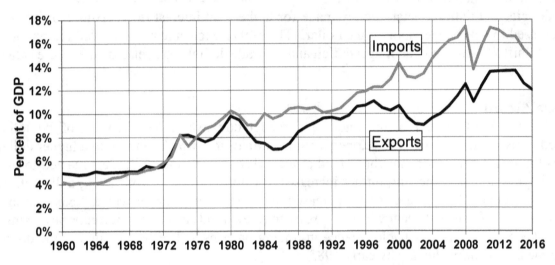

Figure 10-6. Total exports and imports as a percentage of GDP, 1960-2016. The rising percentage of exports and imports in GDP shows the growing importance of trade during most of this period. The gaps between exports and imports are the trade balance. It's been negative—a trade deficit— since 1977. Crowding out explains the big gap in the mid-1980s. The gap almost closed in 1991- 92, after the Plaza Accord and the fall in the dollar's exchange value. The Asian crisis started the increase in the trade deficit after 1997. The growth in the U.S. economy relative to Europe and Japan, and the too-high value of the dollar relative to the Chinese yuan and the Japanese yen, explained the biggest-ever trade deficit in the mid-2000's. The falling value of the dollar against most currencies during the 2000's finally began to close the deficit later in the decade. In 2009 trade volumes dropped because of the world recession. Since imports fell more than exports, the trade deficit got smaller. Both exports and imports have dropped as a share of GDP since 2014.

But with the dollar's value higher, U.S. exports became more expensive, and U.S. imports became cheaper. So (after about a year) U.S. exports began to shrink, and U.S. imports began to expand. The *trade deficit* grew. Look at the gap between exports and imports in Figure 10-6.

U.S. exporters found their sales declining. For example, the American earth-moving equipment manufacturer, Caterpillar, was engaged in intense competition with its Japanese rival Komatsu in the early 1980s. The company found it impossible to reduce its costs enough to maintain its competitiveness with international buyers, in the face of the rising value of the dollar. Komatsu's equipment became cheaper, Caterpillar's more expensive to international buyers. Increasingly, Komatsu made sales and Caterpillar was shut out.

In a sense, it was another form of crowding out.

> *Federal budget deficits and tight monetary policy increased real interest rates during the 1980's. Higher interest rates increased the demand for the dollar, which increased its exchange value. This made U.S. exports more expensive, and led to a trade deficit. The budget and trade deficits were called the "twin deficits."*

Budget deficits and tight monetary policy made for higher real interest rates. High real interest rates increased the exchange value of the dollar. The higher exchange rate crowded out exports. It's second shift #4. The Federal budget deficit and the trade deficit were related: they were called the *twin deficits*.

The Plaza Accord

In the middle of 1984 the real interest rate began to edge downward. Yet the value of the dollar continued to rise. The dollar had developed a momentum of its own. The trend to a higher dollar began as the world's investors sought to lend at high U.S. interest rates. Traders reacted to this trend by buying dollars, expecting further increases in value. But the act of buying dollars itself increased the demand for dollars, and so increased its value. Paul Volcker wrote, "expectational and 'bandwagon' effects that occur when traders try to ride a trend can create wide currency swings far out of keeping with a reasonable balance in trading patterns." The rising value of the dollar had become a *speculative bubble* by early 1985.

During the first Reagan term, the administration did not try to influence the value of the dollar. But by 1984 manufacturers like Caterpillar, farm groups and labor unions were pressuring the administration to do something. Congress considered bills to force the Treasury to intervene in exchange markets. After his 1984 reelection, Ronald Reagan appointed a new Treasury Secretary, James Baker. When asked about exchange rate policy at his confirmation hearing, Baker said it was "obviously something that should be looked at." Perhaps this pricked the speculative bubble, because in February 1985 the value of the dollar began to fall.

But the fall in the exchange value of the dollar after 1985 was also the result of *intervention*. The Treasury and the Federal Reserve hold reserves of foreign currencies. Intervention means that they buy or sell dollars or foreign currencies in an attempt to influence exchange rates. The Treasury takes the lead in setting policy, and the New York Federal Reserve Bank acts as the Treasury's agent, doing the actual buying and selling.

If the dollar's value is thought to be too low, or if it is falling, the Treasury could buy dollars. Reserves of foreign currencies would be traded for dollars. This adds to the demand for dollars, which should raise the dollar's value, or stop it from falling. If the dollar is thought to be too high, or is rising in value, the Treasury could sell dollars. The added supply should depress the dollar's value, or stop it from rising.

The trouble was, by the 1980's, hundreds of billions of dollars were traded in exchange markets every day. The Treasury would have to buy or sell enormous amounts of currency to affect exchange rates. Intervention is more likely to work if many countries act together. This is called *concerted intervention*. The problem with that, of course, is getting all sides to agree on a particular policy.

- *Why did other countries join the United States in concerted intervention to bring down the exchange value of the dollar in 1985?*

> *Governments intervene in exchange markets when they buy or sell foreign currencies to influence exchange rates.*

In 1985 the new Secretary of the Treasury, James Baker, sensed that the time was right for concerted intervention. The Europeans had been complaining about the high value of the dollar for several years. While the high value made it easier for Europe to export to the U.S., it increased the prices of U.S. imports in Europe, adding to European inflation. There were rising protectionist pressures in the U.S. Congress. The high value of the dollar was increasing the volume of imports, and many in Congress were pushing for trade restrictions to protect American companies and jobs. The Reagan administration opposed trade restrictions. Its free market beliefs did not stop at the border. The Japanese also feared U.S. protectionism, and were willing to let the yen rise in value relative to the dollar to head it off.

The Plaza Hotel. Here it is in 2007. Twenty-two years before, it was the site of the G-5 meeting that signed the Plaza Accord. In 2007 it was partially converted to condominiums (starting at $1.5 million each).

Baker planned to call a meeting of the finance ministers (secretaries of the treasury) and central bank chairs of five countries: the United States, Great Britain, France, Germany and Japan. These countries were known as the group of five or G-5. They met at the Plaza Hotel on Sunday,

September 22, 1985. Paul Volcker had offered the New York Fed's headquarters building on Wall Street as a place to meet. But Baker didn't want a discreet meeting in the Fed's fortress. He wanted a flashy meeting in a posh hotel, with reporters and television cameras, so the world would take notice. Most of the groundwork had been done already, and the G-5 were in agreement. That afternoon they issued a communiqué:

> The Ministers and Governors agreed that exchange rates should play a role in adjusting external imbalances. In order to do this, exchange rates should better reflect fundamental economic conditions than has been the case. They believe that agreed policy actions must be implemented and reinforced to improve the fundamentals. Some further orderly appreciation of the main non-dollar currencies against the dollar is desirable. They stand ready to cooperate more closely to encourage this when to do so would be helpful.

This sounds obscure to you and me, but it spoke volumes to trades in exchange markets. The main external imbalance was the U.S. trade deficit. The trade deficit and falling U.S. interest rates were fundamental conditions that meant the dollar's value ought to fall. Policy actions meant selling dollars, and they all agreed to cooperate. And, as Volcker said, "the words 'when to do so would be helpful' were quite rightly read to mean *tomorrow*." The mild-sounding statement screamed at currency traders: big increase in the supply of dollars tomorrow! The next day the dollar's value dropped 4%.

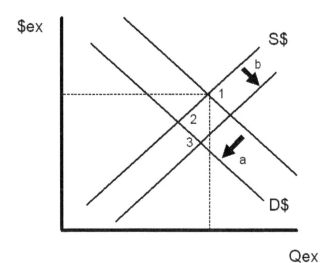

Figure 10-7. Falling value of the dollar. The speculative increases in the demand for the dollar are reversed, and the demand for the dollar falls (a). The value of the dollar falls (1 to 2). Countries try "concerted intervention", supplying dollars into currency markets. The supply of the dollar increases (b) and its value drops some more (2 to 3).

At first no intervention was needed. Market expectations drove the dollar down. Later the United States and other countries sold dollars to sustain the downward trend. The dollar dropped steadily for the next two-plus years, until by the end of 1987 its value against the German mark was down 42% from its September 1985 level and 51% from its February 1985 peak.

After a year U.S. exports began to grow, for the first time since 1980. (There's second shift #4 again.) Exports doubled during the next eight years, 1985-1993. The trade deficit nearly disappeared in the early 1990's.

The *Plaza Accord* marked the first time that major nations had cooperated on exchange rate policy since the end of the Bretton Woods era. The intervention was seen as a success. It seemed that the agreement had caused the dollar's value to fall. But there is some question. The dollar's value had already been falling for seven months at the time of the Plaza meeting. It decreased just a little more rapidly over the next seven months. Real interest rates had fallen since mid-1984. It may be that the markets responded more to changing economic fundamentals than to threats of government intervention.

> *The Plaza Accord in 1985 was an agreement among the major economic powers to sell dollars in exchange markets, to bring down the value of the dollar.*

Counter-cyclical Policy at the Fed

Ronald Reagan had been supportive during Paul Volcker's first term as chair of the Federal Reserve, and had reappointed him to a second term. Now, however, in mid-1987, Reagan's Presidency had only a year and a half to run. There was an election coming up, and it would be very convenient for the probable Republican candidate, Vice President George Bush, if interest rates stayed low and the economy kept growing.

That made Paul Volcker a problem. As Treasury Secretary James Baker said, Volcker was "a known Democrat." More than that, Baker found Volcker aloof and disagreeable. For his part, Volcker resented Baker's attempts to stack the Federal Open Market Committee with new appointees who (Volcker feared) would be administration puppets.

Baker had a Republican candidate in mind: Alan Greenspan. Greenspan was a 61-year old economic consultant, an expert on economic data. He had headed President Ford's Council of Economic Advisors, and had worked with the Reagan administration on Social Security issues in 1982-83. He was well-known for an economist—he had been on the cover of *Newsweek* during the Ford administration. He looked the part of an economic policy maker, sort of like Woody Allen with math skills, according to one observer. President Reagan named Alan Greenspan chair of the Federal Reserve. He took office on August 11, 1987.

Two months later the stock market crashed.

The market had been riding high. The Dow-Jones Industrial Average had passed the 2,000 mark for the first time in January 1987, and stood at a record 2,747 on August 25. But by 1987 the economic expansion was five years old, and problems seemed to be mounting. The trade deficit was huge. So was the budget deficit. Interest rates were rising again, partly because Greenspan's Fed had just increased the discount rate half a point, to prevent inflation from rising.

Again, why the market crashes on a particular day is usually a mystery. But crash it did, on October 19, 1987. The Dow-Jones average fell 22.7% in one day. On the worst day in 1929, it had fallen 11.7%. Five-hundred billion dollars in wealth had disappeared, about the size of the GDP of France. It was (and still is) the biggest single-day drop in stock market history.

But the crash did not lead to a recession. The morning after the crash, Greenspan's Federal Reserve issued a press release.

The Federal Reserve, consistent with its responsibilities as the nation's central bank, affirmed today its readiness to serve as a source of liquidity to support the economic and financial system.

The Fed was willing to act as a lender of last resort. It would lend, freely, to any bank that needed money. Fed officials spent the next weeks putting out financial fires, but within a month it was over. The markets settled down, though it took 15 months for stock values to recover what had been lost on October 19. The overall economy didn't miss a beat. The unemployment rate fell six-tenths of a point in the six months after the crash. Real GDP grew 4.5% in the fourth quarter. It was a lesson on how to handle financial market crises: flood the markets with money. There would be several opportunities to apply that lesson in the coming decades.

The Greenspan Fed probably used counter-cyclical monetary policy more consistently than ever before. Figure 10-8 shows the change in the real federal funds rate, our best indicator of Fed policy. There were two recessions during the Greenspan's tenure from 1987 to 2006. The Fed began cutting the federal funds rate *before* each recession began. Low interest rates probably made each recession shorter and milder. Those years saw one full expansion and parts of two others. In each, the Fed held interest rates low while output recovered towards potential, then increased as the expansion gained momentum, to prevent inflation from rising.

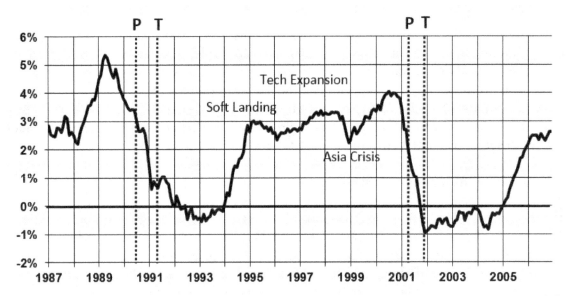

Figure 10-8. The real federal funds interest rate, monthly, 1987-2006. Increases and decreases in the Federal Reserve's main policy interest rate during the Greenspan years. P and T represent the peak and trough dates of the 1990-91 and 2001 recessions.

Perhaps the most famous increase in the federal funds rate was during 1994-95. The Fed changes interest rates to try to influence investment spending. A rule of thumb from Milton Friedman's work on monetary policy is that it takes nine months to a year for interest rate changes to have an effect. That meant that if the Fed was to head off inflation—stop it before it started—it had to anticipate conditions a year in the future. If it could do so, there was a chance for a *soft landing*.

Spending growth would slow enough to stop inflation but not enough to create recession. In our model of the goods market, aggregate demand grows until output equals potential, and stops right there.

If inflation never got started, a future recession would not be required to bring it down. Early in 1994 Greenspan decided to launch a "preemptive strike" on inflation, raising interest rates now to prevent it from ever getting started. Between February 1994 and February 1995 the Fed increased the federal funds rate by three percentage points, in seven separate moves. To make sure everyone knew what they were doing, for the first time the Fed began announcing their federal funds rate decisions on the day they were made. Up until 1994 only the discount rate changes had been announced. The market had had to guess about federal funds rate changes, by watching the direction of interest rates day to day.

> *The Fed probably achieved a "soft landing" with interest rate increases in 1994-95, stopping inflation before it started, without causing a recession.*

Real GDP growth slowed in 1995, and the unemployment rate stopped falling. Over the same period, inflation remained in the 2.5% to 3% range. It was a slowdown, but it was no recession. In 1996 real GDP growth picked up, and remained over 4% in most quarters through the year 2000. The unemployment rate began falling, dropping below 5% in 1997. Inflation did not increase. In fact, it fell, in 1997 and 1998, and remained below 3% until the year 2000.

It appeared that Greenspan had pulled it off: a soft landing. Inflation was held in check without a recession. Criticism of the Chairman all but disappeared in 1996. It was the *Goldilocks economy*. Not too hot, not too cold: just right.

The 1990's: What Good News Looks Like

We've moved from crisis to crisis in our policy history, from panic to war to depression, to war to inflation to recession to panic again. What does the economy look like when there is no panic, no depression, no inflation? What does good news look like? The 1990's provide an example.

Look at these beautiful numbers. Steady real GDP growth averaging more than 4% per year. Unemployment below 5% in 1997 and after. Yet, somehow, despite growth and low unemployment, inflation was falling through 1998, and by 2000 it was just a bit higher than in 1996. A low and stable interest rate spread—financial markets were confident. A stable then rising exchange value of the dollar. A mostly stable federal funds rate, indicating no need for stimulus or restraint. And—miraculously—by 1998 a Federal government budget *surplus*.

The economy hadn't looked this good since the 1920's.

The Goldilocks Economy

Year	Real GDP Growth	CPI Inflation	Unemploy- ment Rate	Interest Rate Spread	Exchange Rate, Euros/$ (est.)	Federal Funds Rate	Budget Balance (% GDP)
1996	3.8%	3.0%	5.4%	0.7%	0.80	5.3%	-1.3%
1997	4.5%	2.3%	4.9%	0.6%	0.88	5.5%	-0.3%
1998	4.5%	1.6%	4.5%	0.7%	0.89	5.4%	0.8%
1999	4.8%	2.2%	4.2%	0.8%	0.94	5.0%	1.3%
2000	4.1%	3.4%	4.0%	0.7%	1.08	6.2%	2.3%

Rising output implies a move to the right along the goods market horizontal axis. An unemployment rate dropping under 5% means output rising above potential. Yet the inflation rate first fell then rose only a little, despite the very low unemployment rate. Figure 10-9 shows what must have happened. Both aggregate demand and supply increased, which held the inflation rate stable. Unemployment fell, but second shift #1 did not restrict aggregate supply growth. Input costs did not rise enough to decrease aggregate supply. That mean potential output must have increased, so equilibrium output equaled potential even at the low unemployment rate.

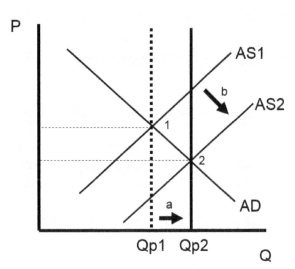

Figure 10-9. New and improved. Equilibrium output equals the original potential output level (1). Technological advance increases productivity, and potential output increases (a). Now output is less than potential. Inputs are more productive, so they are less expensive to employ. Aggregate supply increases (b). Output grows, the inflation rate falls, and the unemployment rate at potential decreases (1 to 2).

Over the years we build new buildings and acquire more equipment. We think up new technologies and apply them to increase productivity. Employees become ever more educated and skilled. We discover new natural resources or learn to exploit existing resources more efficiently. All of these improve *productivity,* the amount of output produced per unit of the economy's labor, capital and other inputs. When labor productivity improves, for example, each worker produces more product. Then businesses could pay higher wages, *but they would not have to raise prices.* With each worker using new technology to produce more product, higher wages could be paid out of higher sales receipts. Wages would rise, profits would rise, but prices would not. Employment could increase without price increases.

> *Productivity is the amount of output produced per unit of input, like output per worker. Productivity growth was slowed from 1973 to 1995, but picked up in the second half of the 1990's.*

All of these increase potential output. Figure 10-9 shows what happens in the goods market when potential output increases. Only an increase in aggregate supply could increase output with falling inflation. Only a matching increase in potential output could keep rising input costs from decreasing aggregate supply again, and increasing inflation.

Between 1941 and 1973, labor productivity—output per worker—increased by 3.0% per year. Then, starting in 1974, this rate of increase dropped. From 1973 to 1996, output per worker rose only 1.2% per year. We looked at the reasons in Chapter 3.

By the mid-1990's the nation was in the midst of a technological revolution. Starting in the early 1980s, personal computers appeared on millions of employee desks, then on top of employee laps. Cell phones had been the richest of luxuries in the 1980s, but were now common. Fax machines came and went, email arrived, and then, in the 1990s, the internet began to grow by leaps and bounds.

Pessimists thought the *information technology* (IT) revolution never would enhance productivity. IT's contribution to productivity just wasn't substantial compared to past innovations. When air travel had replaced rail, for example, a trip from New York to California had shrunk from three days to four hours—*that* was a productivity improvement. The ability to send email instead of making a phone call wasn't comparable.

Optimists pointed out that past innovations had not improved productivity right away. It had taken decades for the introduction of electricity in the 19th century to improve business operations enough to show up in productivity data. Businesses had to experiment with the new technology to discover new and better ways of producing. Now businesses were discovering how to use IT.

In the second half of the 1990's, productivity took off. In the decade after 1995 real GDP per employed worker increased by 2.0% per year. Not quite what it was in the 1950's and 1960's, but nearly a percentage point higher than 1973-96. Information technology fulfilled its promise.

At the Fed, Alan Greenspan was among the first to recognize what was happening. If productivity improved, potential output would grow faster. Equilibrium output could grow and unemployment could fall without increasing inflation. After the experience of the 1980's, it was thought that the unemployment rate at potential output was 6%. But as of 1995 the unemployment rate was less than that. Should interest rates be increased to slow the economy, before inflation started rising?

Greenspan persuaded Fed policymakers to leave the federal funds rate essentially unchanged through 1996, 1997 and into the Fall of 1998. During this time the unemployment rate fell further below 6%, then below 5%. Real GDP kept growing. But not only did inflation not increase, it continued to fall. The 12-month rate dropped under two percent in 1998.

Financial markets loved it. The BAA-AAA corporate interest rate spread remained low, and the stock market boomed. Investment as a percentage of GDP regained what it had lost in the 1980's (Figure 10-5).

Budget Surpluses in the 1990's, Deficits in the 2000's
After the experience of the 1980's, for a time Congress and the Presidents began to take the problem of *structural deficits* more seriously. A structural deficit is one that continues even when equilibrium output is at potential. Structural deficits contrast with cyclical deficits, which occur during recessions when output is less than potential. If the deficit is cyclical, when a recession is over revenues rise and the budget returns to balance. If it's structural, there's a deficit even at potential output.

During President Reagan's second term Congress passed the *Gramm-Rudman-Hollings Act* (usually known only as Gramm-Rudman, one assumes to dismay of Senator Hollings). This set future deficit reduction targets, to be achieved mostly by spending cuts or slower spending growth.

Cyclical budget deficits are caused by the declines in revenues that result from recession. If a deficit remains after the economy recovers, it's a structural budget deficit.

the

But often when the targets threatened to prevent spending that Congress wanted to pass, the deficit targets were changed, or accounting gimmicks were invented to meet the targets in law but evade them in fact. Gramm-Rudman probably restrained spending to a degree, however, because evading the targets required public debate, an added political cost to increased spending. But the continuing expansion may have reduced the deficit more. By the beginning of the Bush administration in 1989, the deficit was down to $153 billion, 2.7% of GDP, from its peak in 1986 of $221 billion and 4.8% of GDP.

The 1980's expansion ended in the 1990-91 recession. With the slowing economy, the deficit began to increase again. This is the counter-cyclical, automatic stabilizing function of the budget, but in the context of the times many in Congress and the administration found it alarming. In the spring and summer of 1990 Congress and the President negotiated a deficit reduction bill. President George H.W. Bush reached an agreement with the Congress to cut spending, and to raise the top income tax rate from 28% to 31%. (This move angered many of the President's supporters. They remembered his 1988 campaign pledge, "no new taxes.")

In the 1990's, the administration of President Bill Clinton also restrained spending and increased taxes. With the Bush and Clinton tax and spending changes, and a recovery from recession, Federal budget deficits began to shrink. By 1996 the deficit dropped below 2% of GDP for the first time since 1979. In 1998 the budget deficit turned to a *budget surplus*. For the first time in 30 years, the Federal government took in more revenue than it spent. The surpluses lasted for four years, peaking in 2000 at $236 billion, 2.3% of GDP.

- *Why did the Federal budget deficits of the 1980's and 1990's turn to budget surpluses at the end of the 1990's?*

This astonishing development had three main causes. First, the 1990s expansion was the longest on record, lasting exactly ten years. Expansion almost always reduces the budget deficit. Income tax revenues rise, automatic stabilizer spending falls. The 1990's expansion lasted so long that it turned the deficits into surpluses.

> *Federal deficits turned to surpluses by the end of the 1990's. The reasons were the long expansion, political stalemate and a stock market boom.*

Second, a Democrat was President, but Republicans won both the House and Senate in the elections of 1994. For the rest of the decade, the Republicans controlled the Congress, the Democrats controlled the Presidency. The result was stalemate. Republicans checked the President's efforts to raise spending; the President blocked the Republican's attempts to cut taxes. Without discretionary spending hikes or new tax cuts, the budget moved towards balance. (Consider that the next time the Republicans controlled the Presidency and the Congress, during the second Bush administration, they passed big tax cuts. And the next time the Democrats controlled both, during the early Obama administration, they passed the Affordable Care Act.)

Third, there was a stock market boom in the second half of the decade. The Federal income tax applies to "capital gains," which is income that comes from the sale of stocks and other assets that increase in value. With the big rise in stock values, capital gains income increased a lot, and so did income tax revenue.

The Asian Crisis

In the 1980s and 1990s Thailand was one of the "Asian Tigers," along with South Korea, Taiwan, Hong Kong, Indonesia, Malaysia, and the Philippines. Thailand's real GDP was growing rapidly, almost ten percent per year from 1986 to 1996. One reason was the fixed value of the Thai currency, the baht. While most of the developed world allowed the values of their currencies to fluctuate, many developing countries tried to keep their exchange rates fixed, relative to the dollar. There were a couple of reasons to do this. Thailand's growth advanced in part due to investment by Japanese automobile and electronics companies. These companies liked the fixed baht, because it eliminated their worries about unpredictable changes in the value of their investments in Thailand.

The fixed value of the baht also promoted prudent monetary policy. Again, because of the impossible trinity (see Chapter 8), to keep a currency's value fixed with an unrestricted flow of capital, a nation must give up an independent stabilization policy. As long as the baht was fixed in value, investors didn't have to worry that the Thai government would adopt inflationary policies which would erode the values of their loans and other assets. Developing countries used the impossible trinity to convince investors that they'd follow prudent fiscal and monetary policies.

The Thai central bank was responsible for keeping the value of the baht fixed. The central bank kept a reserve of foreign currencies—dollars, yen, pounds, marks—for this purpose. If the rising demand for the baht threatened to increase its value, the central bank would sell baht to the market, and build its reserves of foreign currencies. If the rising supply of baht threatened to decrease its value, the central bank would buy baht, using its reserves of foreign currencies.

This worked fine as long as the demand for and supply of foreign currencies were roughly equal. However, in 1996 the central bank found that its foreign currency reserves were shrinking. More people wanted to trade baht for dollars than the reverse. The supply of baht exceeded the demand in the exchange market.

One cause of the baht surplus was *crony capitalism*. Thai businesses borrowed from foreign lenders, but invested in pet projects of influential politicians, their families and their supporters. Loans would go not to projects likely to produce quality goods that could be exported to the world. If the rest of the world didn't want Thai exports, they wouldn't demand Thai baht, either.

An excess supply of baht would make its value fall, unless the central bank acted to purchase the excess baht, adding to baht demand and holding its value up. To buy baht the bank used its foreign currency reserves, earned from past exports. Now those reserves began to run short. Reserves were a state secret, but the markets figure them out. With devaluation looming, they tried to sell even more baht. This drained central bank reserves even faster.

Baht-ulism. A Thai 50 baht note issued in 1997. It was worth $2 on July 1, 1997. It was worth $1.65 on July 2.

Finally, on July 2 1997, reserves were almost gone, and the central bank quit defending the baht. The value of the baht fell instantly, from $4 per 100 baht to $3.30 per 100 baht, an 18% fall in a single day. That was just the start. By January 1998 the exchange rate dipped below $2 per 100 baht. Anyone caught with Thai assets lost half their wealth in six months.

No one would lend in Thailand, for fear of losses due to the falling baht. Construction projects ground to a halt; businesses liquidated their inventories. The effects multiplied through the economy, causing layoffs and bankruptcies. Real GDP fell 11% in 1998, investment spending dropped 44%.

Thailand was one of the Asian Tigers. If one could fail, international investors thought, others can too. Withdrawals from other Asian countries began within the week. On July 11 both Indonesia and the Philippines stopped defending their fixed exchange rates. Malaysia quit defending the ringgit on July 14. By the end of July, it wasn't a Thai crisis, it was an *Asian crisis*. The panic spread from country to country like a plague, which is why economists call it *contagion*.

A currency crisis in Thailand in 1997 caused currency crises in many other developing countries in Asia. This is an example of "contagion."

 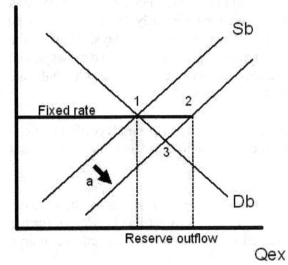

Figure 8-14. Anatomy of a Currency Crisis. Foreign investors increase the supply of baht (labeled Sb) on exchange markets (a), trying to sell their baht assets before devaluation. The Thai central bank uses its foreign currency reserves to buy the excess baht (1 to 2), to prevent a fall in the exchange rate below the fixed rate. Eventually the reserves run out, and the bank has no choice but to let the baht fall in value (3).

Now the problems spread beyond the Asian Tigers. The 1990's was the first decade after the fall of communism, and the Russia was having trouble adjusting to the market economy. Its government ran big budget deficits, mostly because its tax collection bureaucracy was inadequate. It sold state-owned enterprises at bargain prices to political favorites. Uncompetitive businesses were subsidized. Its government and economy survived mainly on its earnings from selling oil.

Now, with most of the Asian Tigers in recession in 1998, the demand for oil declined. The price of crude oil fell by half. That was fine for the United States, which saw gasoline prices drop to 96 cents a gallon by early 1999. It was not so fine for Russia.

International investors tried to sell Russian assets. The supply of rubles outstripped the demand at the going exchange rate. The Russian central bank used its reserves to support the ruble, but reserves ran short. It couldn't earn enough foreign currency to pay interest to its foreign creditors. Finally, on August 17, 1998, Russia defaulted on its government bonds. Russia then restructured its debt, without the consent of its creditors, paying much lower interest over a much longer period of time.

Many of these Russian bonds had been bought on credit. Now the bonds were worth much less than the amount that had been borrowed to buy them. When a large "hedge fund" called Long Term Capital Management collapsed, the bond market froze. Lots of investors wanted to sell bonds; few wanted to buy. Brokers wouldn't buy bonds from their customers for fear that they couldn't be sold again. Business firms hoping to sell bonds in order to raise funds for new investments found no buyers.

Money from all over the world was running the U.S. Treasury bonds, the *safe haven* for wealth in a crisis. Money parked in Treasury bonds is not available for private investment. The demand for the dollar increased, raising the exchange value of the dollar. U.S. exports became more expensive. With investment and exports down, the U.S. economy was on the brink of recession.

The Federal Open Market Committee held its regular meeting on September 29, 1998, and Alan Greenspan proposed a quarter point rate cut. The FOMC agreed unanimously, but the results were disappointing. The stock market dropped 450 points (6%) over the next two days. Usually the market rose with a rate cut. Greenspan had tried to use the quarter point cut to send a message that the Fed was alert to the problem. But the message the markets received from such a small rate change was that the Fed didn't understand just how big the danger was.

The next FOMC meeting wasn't scheduled for a month, but Greenspan set up a conference call with its members on October 15. At 3:30 in the afternoon the Fed announced another quarter point rate cut. The press release said

> Growing caution by lenders and unsettled conditions in financial markets more generally are likely to be restraining aggregate demand in the future. Against this backdrop, further easing of the stance of monetary policy was judged to be warranted to sustain economic growth in the context of contained inflation.

It was a surprise to investors. The Fed hadn't changed rates between meetings in years. The stock market jumped more than 300 points, and continued to gain for the next week. Within three weeks the market had regained everything it had lost since the Russian default. The bond market thawed.

The Fed responded to the 1998 Asian crisis with cuts in interest rates. This reassured investors and helped prevent panic.

What had happened? Fed Governor Lawrence Meyer thought the surprise rate cut sent the message that the earlier cut had not. The Fed understood the problem and was ready to do what was needed. It provided a boost in confidence to investors. Markets began functioning again. The U.S. economy continued to expand, and by 1999 most of the developing countries were growing as well. In a sense it was another application of the lesson from 1987. In a financial panic, flood the markets with money.

Thailand suffered a sharp recession, but it was made shorter by the devaluation of the baht that occurred in July 1997. By 2007 the exchange rate had recovered to 3 dollars per 100 baht, not as high as the old fixed rate of 4 or as low as the panic rate of 2. With the baht cheaper exports began to grow again. Thailand's real GDP dropped almost 11% in 1998, but it grew 4.4% in 1999 and averaged 5% per year in the five years after that. Respectable growth, though nothing like the pace prior to the crisis.

The End of the Longest Expansion
The stock market had been rising since the 1990-91 recession, and by the mid-1990's it was rising a lot. The Dow Jones Industrial Average had dipped below 2,600 during the 1990-91 recession. By October 1996 it topped 6,000, more than doubling in six years. Investors were excited about technological advance (values on the *NASDAQ*, a stock exchange for high tech companies, were rising even faster). They were excited about the new investment opportunities presented by globalization and the collapse of communism. But how much excitement was too much? If values moved upward beyond what firm profits and prospects justified, they could crash. The effects of the crash of 1987 had been contained. The effects of the 1929 crash had not.

Alan Greenspan was concerned, and in a speech in December 1996 he asked, "How do we know when *irrational exuberance* has unduly escalated asset values?" Herbert Stein, a member of the audience and former head of the Council of Economic Advisors, said to himself, "good thing the markets are closed." But when the markets opened the next day, the Dow Jones Industrial Average fell only 55 points, less than one percent. It more than recovered the loss on the next trading day. "Irrational exuberance" may be the most famous two words Alan Greenspan ever said, but they had little effect on the stock market.

Stock values continued to rise rapidly, 26% in 1996, 23% in 1997, 16% in 1998, 25% in 1999. The Dow Jones Industrials topped 10,000 in March 1999, a four-fold increase in less than a decade. People began saying extraordinary things to explain why the stock market boom was not a bubble that would end in a crash. Two respected economists wrote an article and a book called *Dow 36,000*. "Stock prices could double, triple, or even quadruple tomorrow and still not be too high," they said. The headline in *The Wall Street Journal's* special millennium edition on January 1, 2000 read "So Long, Supply and Demand." "There's a new economy out there," the article began, "and it looks nothing like the old one." Of course, people had said the same kinds of things about the market in 1928 and 1929 (and would say them again about the housing boom in the 2000's).

Two weeks later, on January 14, 2000, the Dow Jones Industrial Average closed at 11,723. It wasn't that high again for more than six years. Unlike 1929 or 1987, there is no single day that can be labeled "Black Monday" or "Black Thursday." Traders gradually began to recognize that they'd been irrationally exuberant, and began to sell more than they bought. The Dow fell 6% in 2000, and 7% in 2001. On the *NASDAQ*, the stock market home to the high tech stocks, values fell farther and faster. The NASDAQ index peaked at 5,048 on March 10, 2000. By May 10 it was down 33% to 3,384. It bottomed out on October 9, 2002, at 1,114, a 78% loss from its peak. That compares to the 87% fall of the Dow from high point to low point over 1929-32.

Suddenly it was hard to raise funds for new investment on the stock market. Investment spending began to fall. Suddenly consumers found their portfolios shrinking in value. Some hadn't realized that declines could happen. The wealth effect began working in reverse and consumer spending began to grow more slowly.

There was more.

- The same exuberance that affected the stock market had also affected investment spending, especially in high tech equipment. Businesses spent freely, but by 2000 they were finding that they had the capacity to produce more product than consumers would buy. They cut back on investment spending.
- In 1999 Greenspan and the Federal Reserve finally decided that demand had outpaced productivity growth, and that inflation was a threat. Interest rates were increased. Businesses had yet another reason to cut their investment spending.
- The Asian crisis of 1997-98 had cut demand for oil, driving down its price. In response, the Organization of Petroleum Exporting Countries had cut back on oil supplies. The average price of a gallon of gasoline had been $1.06 in 1998; by 2000 it was $1.51. Consumers had less left over to spend. Business costs increased.
- The Asian crisis had reduced U.S. export growth, and had increased the value of the dollar, making imports cheaper. Lower exports and higher imports reduced spending some more.

Then came the attacks of September 11, 2001. The attacks closed U.S. financial markets for several days. They destroyed the communications equipment used by some banks to make payments. They cut airline travel and tourism. The Federal Reserve responded by flooding the markets with money (again!). Consumer and business spending dropped a lot for a couple of weeks, then resumed in October.

The 9-11 attacks were not a *cause* of the 2001 recession, for the obvious reason that the recession began in March, while the attacks were in September. Can an event in September "cause" another event the previous March? Perhaps in one sense it can. The National Bureau of Economic Research announced in November 2011 their decision to date the start of the recession in March. But they also said "the attacks clearly deepened the contraction and may have been an important factor in turning the episode into a recession." Had the 9-11 attacks not occurred, the 2001 slowdown might not have been severe enough to be labeled as a recession. A later event can change the *perception* of an earlier event.

The Laffer Curve Redux
It's the theory that will not die. In 2017 the Trump Administration supported a large tax cut for individuals and especially for businesses. How would it be paid for? The Secretary of the Treasury, Steven Mnuchin, said

> This will pay for itself with growth and with reduction of different deductions and closing loopholes. The economic plan under Trump will grow the economy and will create massive amounts of revenues, trillions of dollars in additional revenues.

A tax cut that pays for itself. This is, once again, the Laffer Curve idea. Tax cuts will so stimulate the tax base that revenue will increase.

Economists and think tanks were skeptical. The Tax Foundation is a Washington think tank that is generally sympathetic to tax cuts. Their analysis goes like this. The Federal government uses ten-year forecasts of revenues to measure the effects of tax changes. Over ten years the proposed corporate tax cut would reduce Federal revenues by about 5%, which would be $2 trillion. To make up this revenue loss, the economy would have be about 5% larger on average over the ten years. That would require added growth of about one percent per year.

That may not sound like much, but the Congressional Budget Office's projection of growth for the next ten years is 1.9% per year. Growth would have to be 2.9% per year to break even on the tax cut. That's a big increase.

The U.S. economy is at potential output as of 2017. Added growth can come only from labor force increases or rising productivity. The Tax Foundation explains,

> Imagine businesses, spurred by their lower tax rate, start ordering new expensive buildings with new expensive equipment in them. These would generate higher revenues on a per-worker basis, increasing incomes across the board. This is an ordinary concept called "productivity growth," and it certainly could be the result of well-crafted policy.

> Unfortunately, productivity growth has relatively low variance, historically. It usually grows between 1 and 2 percent per year. Policy can probably help us stay towards the higher end of that range, but a single policy is unlikely to move productivity growth for the whole economy by a whole percentage point.

The Tax Foundation's model shows that about the best a tax cut could do would be to increase growth by 0.4 percentage points—2.3% instead of 1.9%.

Except when tax rates are extraordinarily high, they cannot cause an increase in the tax base large enough to increase revenue. Yes, the tax base will increase—a tax cut will increase investment and work—but only enough to reduce the amount of revenue lost.

Why then do policymakers still assert that a tax cut will move revenue up the right side of the Laffer Curve, increasing revenue? Probably because it solves so many problems. If revenue falls with a tax cut, the budget deficit and national debt increase, or government programs must be cut, or some other tax has to be raised. All of these possibilities are unpopular, and make passing the tax cut through Congress more difficult. But if the tax cut does not reduce revenue, or even increases revenue, all of these problems disappear.

It doesn't happen. But wouldn't it be great if it did?

Terms in this Chapter, in order of appearance
Laffer curve
Supply-side economics
Free markets
Reagan tax cut
Bracket creep
Income tax indexing
Elasticity of supply
Budget deficit
Natural rate of unemployment
Frictional unemployment
Counter-cyclical fiscal policy
Crowding out
Trade deficit
Twin deficits
Speculative bubble
Intervention
Concerted intervention
Plaza Accord
Soft landing
Alan Greenspan
Federal budget surplus
Soft landing
Goldilocks economy
Productivity
Information technology (IT)
Structural deficit
Cyclical deficit
Gramm-Rudman-Hollings Act
Budget surplus
Asian crisis
Impossible trinity
Crony capitalism
Contagion
NASDAQ
Irrational exuberance

Notes
Fullerton (1994) tells the Laffer napkin story. The napkin itself is in the Museum of American History in Washington. Here's a link to a picture:
http://americanhistory.si.edu/collections/search/object/nmah_1439217

Feldstein discusses bracket creep (pp. 4-6). Data on tax brackets are available in Edwards (1994, p. 100). Stein (1994) describes Ronald Reagan's career (pp. 257-59). Stockman (1986, p. 10) quotes Reagan on tax rates in the top income bracket. Feldstein also mentions Reagan's unhappiness with high taxes during his movie career (p. 21).

Ronald Reagan's beliefs and policies are described in Regan (157-59), Feldstein (p. 3, pp. 20-22), and Stein (264-67). Stockman tells the stories of efforts to pass the budget cuts in the Senate and House (pp. 159-177), and the battle over the Social Security cuts (pp. 181-193).

Fullerton briefly (pp. 179-182) and Stockman extensively (237-268) describe the tax bidding war of June-July 1981. Stockman (p.270) calls the tax cuts of June-July 1981 a breakdown in partisan checks and balances; Fullerton (p. 181) calls it a feeding frenzy and a bidding war. Stockman (p. 239) quotes Reagan drawing the line at 25%, and Wright on calling and raising (pp. 255-56). Stockman (pp. 269-275) describes the August 3 victory luncheon.

Fullerton (p. 175) quotes himself on the Laffer Curve. Feldstein (p.24) criticizes the extreme supply side claims. McClelland and Mok (2012) review the recent research on labor supply elasticities.

Ronald Reagan may have been on the right side of the Laffer Curve in the 1940's, because the tax rate was so high for the highest brackets. Suppose he earns $1,000 an hour (as a movie star) and works 1,000 hours, so that his before-tax pay is one million dollars. If that's the 90% tax bracket, he takes home $100,000, $100 an hour. He pays $900,000 in taxes. Now the top bracket tax rate drops to 70% (as it did with the Kennedy tax cut). His take home pay goes up to $300 an hour, a 200% increase. At a labor supply elasticity of 0.4—quite inelastic—he works 80% more hours (200% x 0.4), which is 1,800. Now his before-tax income is $1.8 million, and at the new 70% tax rate he pays $1,260,000 in taxes. If the tax rate starts out really high, a tax cut can increase government revenue. At high tax rates we can be on the right side of the Laffer Curve.

Volcker and Gyohten (p. 178) describe the relatively low domestic investment during the 1980s, and (pp. 181-182) describe the fiscal-monetary policy deal that he refused to make. Feldstein (p. 53) recalls what he told his Reagan administration colleagues about crowding out, and discusses the campaign against him (p. 57). Volcker records his surprise at the amount that could be borrowed from abroad (p. 179). He describes the effects of trends on currency trading (pp. 230-31).

Gramm-Rudman is described in Feldstein (1994, pp. 61-62). The Bush and Clinton administration's budget policies are detailed in Elmendorf et. al. (2002, pp. 60-70).

Frankel (p. 321) uses Caterpillar's example of the problems of the high valued dollar for American exporters. Frankel (p. 302) quotes Baker's confirmation hearing comment. Volcker (pp. 232-235) describes the roles of the Treasury and Fed in exchange intervention. Volcker describes his discussion with Baker about the Plaza meeting in Volcker and Gyohten (p. 243).

Woodward's (2000) history of the Greenspan Fed, *Maestro*, is the source of many of the stories told here.

Woodward (2000, p. 16) has Baker's quote about Volcker as a known Democrat. Martin (2000, p. 127) compares Greenspan to Woody Allen. Martin (pp. 153-155) and Woodward (2000, pp. 15-25) cover Greenspan's appointment.

The story of the 1987 stock market crash is pieced together from Woodward (2000, pp. 35-47), Martin (pp. 171-183) and Litan (1994, pp. 536-538).

Woodward (2000, pp. 61-63, 81-83, 88-94) and Martin (196-198) report the Bush administration's efforts to influence Greenspan's policies. Woodward (2000, pp. 69-71) and Elmendorf (pp. 70-71) discuss the monetary policy response. Martin (p. 198) gives Bush's "disappointed" quote.

Mankiw offers a review of monetary policy in the 1990's (2002, pp. 19-43). Greenspan's pre-emptive strike on inflation, aiming for a soft landing, is discussed in Woodward (2000, pp. 115-124) and Martin (pp. 204-209). Blustein (2003, p. 329) is one among many who define the "Goldilocks economy."

Baily (1986) reviews the possible explanations for the productivity slowdown. Greenspan's interpretation of productivity growth are in Woodward (2000, pp. 166-168, 171-174).

Blustein has a chapter on the Russian default (pp. 235-277). The story of Long Term Capital Management is told by Blustein (pp. 305-325) and Woodward (2000, pp. 199-208). Woodward reports on the Fed's interest rate decisions in Fall 1998 (2000, pp.203-212), and so does Blustein (pp.325-331, 349-355).

Martin (pp. 214-217) describes the "irrational exuberance" speech. "Dow 36,000" is from Glassman and Hassett (1999); "So Long, Supply and Demand" is from Petzinger (2000).

The National Bureau of Economic Research puts its press releases on its website, at www.nber.org.

Alan Cole offers the Tax Foundation's analysis of why the Trump Administration's tax cut can't pay for itself.

Sources
Baily, Martin Neil. 1986. "What Has Happened to Productivity Growth?" *Science* 234 (October 24): 443-451.

Bhagwati, Jagdish. 2002. "Trade Policy: Comments." Pages 333-340 in Jeffrey A. Frankel and Peter R. Orszag (eds.), *Economic Policy in the 1990's.* Cambridge, Massachusetts: MIT Press.

Blustein, Paul. 2003. *The Chastening (revised edition).* New York: PublicAffairs.

Cole, Alan. 2017. "Could Trump's Corporate Rate Cut to 15 Percent by Self-Financing?" *Tax Foundation* (April 25).

Elmendorf, Douglas W., Jeffrey B. Liebman and David W. Wilcox. 2002. "Fiscal Policy and Social Security Policy During the 1990's." Pages 61-119 in Jeffrey A. Frankel and Peter R. Orszag (eds.), *Economic Policy in the 1990's.* Cambridge, Massachusetts: MIT Press.

Feldstein, Martin. 1994. "American Economic Policy in the 1980's: A Personal View." Pages 1-79 in Martin Feldstein (ed.), *American Economic Policy in the 1980's*. Chicago: University of Chicago Press.

Frankel, Jeffrey A. 1994. "The Making of Exchange Rate Policy in the 1980's." Pages 293-341 in Martin Feldstein (ed.), *American Economic Policy in the 1980's*. Chicago: University of Chicago Press.

Fullerton, Don. 1994. "Tax Policy." Pages 165-208. in Martin Feldstein (ed.), *American Economic Policy in the 1980's*. Chicago: University of Chicago Press.

Glassman, James K. and Kevin A. Hassett. 1999. "Dow 36,000" *The Atlantic Monthly* (September): 37-58.

Litan, Robert E. 1994. "Financial Regulation" Pages 519-57 in Martin Feldstein (ed.), *American Economic Policy in the 1980's*. Chicago: University of Chicago Press.

Mankiw, N. Gregory. 2002. "Monetary Policy." Pages 19-43 in Jeffrey A. Frankel and Peter R. Orszag (eds.), *Economic Policy in the 1990's*. Cambridge, Massachusetts: MIT Press.

Martin, Justin. 2000. *Greenspan: The Man Behind Money*. Cambridge, Massachusetts: Perseus Publishing.

McClelland, Robert and Shannon Mok. 2012. "A Review of Recent Research on Labor Supply Elasticities," Congressional Budget Office Working Paper 2012-12 (October).

Petzinger, Thomas, Jr. 2000. "So Long, Supply and Demand." *Wall Street Journal* (January 1): R31.

Regan, Donald T. 1988. *For The Record*. New York: Harcourt Brace Jovanovich.

Stein, Herbert. 1994. *Presidential Economics (3rd Revised Edition)*. Washington, D.C.: The AEI Press.

Stockman, David. 1986. *The Triumph of Politics*. New York: Harper and Row.

Volcker, Paul and Toyoo Gyohten. 1992. *Changing Fortunes*. New York: Times Books.

Woodward, Bob. 2000. *Maestro: Greenspan's Fed and the American Boom*. New York: Simon and Schuster.

News Reports
Hirschfeld Davis, Julie and Alan Rappeport, "White House Proposes Slashing Tax Rates, Significantly Aiding Wealthy." *New York Times*, April 26, 2017.

Chapter 11
Modern Times

Economists call it the *Great Moderation*, and it lasted from the mid-1980's until 2007. There were just two short recessions, and two of the longest expansions in United States history. After the 1981-82 recession faded, the unemployment rate topped 7% in only one year, and actually dropped to 4% in 2000. Inflation topped 5% in only one year, and the rate was often less than 3%. Interest rates trended downward throughout the period.

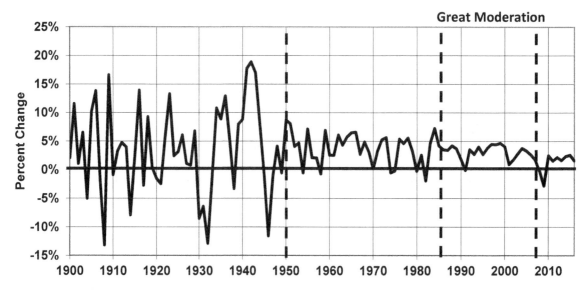

Figure 11-1. Real GDP growth rates, 1900-2012. Prior to 1950 the variation from year to year was enormous. Between 1950 and 1984, much less. Between 1984 and 2007, less still. That was the Great Moderation. Then came the worst recession since the Great Depression: oops. If anything, though, growth has been even more stable since 2010.

The Great Moderation can be seen in a simple graph of real GDP growth since 1900. It's in Figure 11-1. Prior to 1950 the ups and downs in growth were huge. You can spot declines of more than 10% per year in the Panic of of 1907-08, the Great Depression downturn 1929-33, and the World War II demobilization in 1946. But also see the recoveries with growth rates above 10% per year after 1908 and 1933, and the war years 1917-18 and 1941-45. There are no rates of growth or decline that big after 1950.

From 1950 to 1984 there were several years of growth above 5%, and six years where real GDP declined. From 1985 to 2007, though, growth was never above 5%, and there was just one year where real GDP declined. Real GDP growth was more stable during this period. It's evidence of the Great Moderation.

We can measure the variation in a series of numbers by using the *standard deviation*. This statistic is essentially the average difference between each value in a number series and its average. The higher the standard deviation, the more variable is the series. Let's divide our economic indicators into three major periods: 1900 to 1949, 1950 to 1984, and 1985 to 2007. Let's add 2008 to 2016 for good measure. The results are in Figure 11-2. The top section shows the averages, the bottom section shows the standard deviations.

		Real GDP Growth	CPI Inflation	Unemploy-ment Rate	Interest Rate Spread*
Average	1900-1949	3.6%	2.3%	6.8%	1.7%
	1950-1984	3.8%	4.4%	5.6%	0.9%
	1985-2007	2.6%	3.1%	5.6%	0.9%
	2008-2016	1.3%	1.6%	7.3%	1.2%
Standard	1900-1949	7.9%	6.2%	4.8%	0.8%
Deviation	1950-1984	2.8%	3.5%	1.7%	0.5%
	1985-2007	1.6%	0.9%	1.0%	0.2%
	2008-2016	1.8%	1.3%	1.8%	0.4%

* Data from 1919 to 2007

Figure 11-2. Averages and standard deviations for four indicators over three periods, 1900-2007.

These four indicators all show evidence of the Great Moderation. Real GDP growth, inflation, the unemployment rate and the corporate interest rate spread all show smaller standard deviations in 1985-2007 than in the earlier periods. There was less variation in these indicators after 1984 than there was before. (The exchange rate was fixed for most of the first two-thirds of the century. Flexible exchange rates produce larger standard deviations.)

The first half of the century saw much, much wider swings in real GDP growth, inflation and unemployment than the second half of the century. It seems likely that the long-term reforms adopted during the 1930's, plus the sheer growth in the size of government, played a role in that moderation.

- *What caused the Great Moderation?*

Here are some possibilities. Wars cause huge disruptions in the economy, and there were two big ones before 1950. World War I helped destroy the gold standard, and its collapse contributed to the Great Depression. The Vietnam War helped caused the problems of the 1970's as well. Thankfully, there has been nothing comparable since then. With no big wars, the economy has been more stable.

Business management has improved. Businesses kept better track of their sales and inventories starting in the 1980's. Before, a business might continue to produce products for months before realizing that sales were down. Inventories would pile up. Production would be cut, and workers laid off. Inventory control improved with information technology and price scan data. If inventories don't accumulate, production and employment will grow more smoothly.

> *The Great Moderation lasted from the mid-1980's to 2007. There were three long expansions, two mild recessions, low inflation and falling interest rates. Lack of big wars, better business inventory management, and better economic policy were the reasons.*

Economic policy management improved too. The Federal Reserve made huge mistakes during the Great Depression and Great Inflation. Monetary policy has been strictly counter-cyclical since the 1980's. The Fed's responses to financial crises have also improved—consider the stock market crash of 1987 and the response to the Panic of 2008.

Social Security and unemployment insurance created a group of beneficiaries whose incomes are protected during recessions. Automatic stabilizers mean that when recessions come along, some consumer spending continues. Deposit insurance prevents bank runs by the public, which supports bank lending. And (sometimes) the President and Congress have adopted appropriate discretionary counter-cyclical fiscal policies. That was not true in the 1930's.

We've had a decade since the end of the Great Moderation. The standard deviations for 2008-2016 include the Great Recession, but the measures for real GDP growth and CPI inflation are close to those for the Great Moderation. Over the 2010-16 period, not counting the recession, the standard deviation of real GDP growth was 0.4%, the most stable six years since 1900. Average growth was much slower, though.

The Great Depression ended with the increased spending of World War II. The Great Inflation ended with the interest rate increases that caused the recession of 1981-82. The Great Moderation ended too, with the Great Recession of 2007-09, and the Panic of 2008.

Throughout this text we've referred to the Panic of 2008, to turmoil in financial markets. Now it's time to look at this turmoil in detail. What was the Panic of 2008? What caused it?

It began with housing.

The Housing Bubble, 1998-2006
For more than fifty years after World War II, home prices rose at about the same rate as consumer prices. Once in a while house prices would increase faster, but always these booms would fade, home value price increases would slow, and the prices of goods and services would catch up.

Starting in 1998, however, house prices began to rise much more rapidly than consumer prices. By 2001 real home prices had topped any previous boom. By 2006 the real price of houses was nearly double its long run average.

The house price boom was a regional event. In some places house prices rose a lot. In others, not so much. From January 1998 to July 2006, house prices in Los Angeles rose 241%, in San Diego, 218%, in Miami 207%. Population and incomes grew faster in these places, which increased demand. These cities had seen decades of development, so land for new houses was scarce. This restricted supply. Rising demand and restricted supply made for rapid price increases. In Cleveland, though, prices rose only 36%, and in Detroit, 45%. Population grew slowly in those cities, so demand grew more slowly. In Charlotte, North Carolina house prices rose 39% from 1998 to 2006. Population grew faster there, but there was a lot of land available for development.

When income and population increase, and land is scarce, house prices rise. Sometimes this causes people to anticipate even higher prices. The expectation of higher future prices causes demand to rise now. Consumers behave this way (buy before the price goes up). Investors behave this way too (buy low, sell high). The investment demand may cause people to buy houses that cost more than they can afford, because they expect to sell later at a profit. Optimistic expectations cause demand to rise. The demand increase causes the price to rise, and rising prices confirm peoples' optimistic expectation. For a time, optimistic expectations are a self-fulfilling prophesy.

- *Why did house prices collapse?*

Demand rises, but at first nothing much happens to supply. Housing supply is inelastic over shorter periods of time. The added demand raises the price of the existing housing stock. Prices rise a lot. But supply is more elastic over time. Over a longer time period builders had more time to respond to rising prices. Local home builders, home builders in other communities, even business people in other industries see that extraordinary profits can be made in housing. They begin to plan construction. It takes time to acquire land, get zoning and building permits, install utilities and roads, and then build the houses. But eventually supply increases, and this slows the increase in housing prices. If supply increases enough, prices may start to fall.

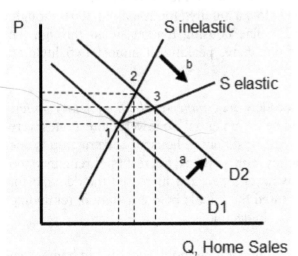

Figure 11-3. More elastic over time. The increase in demand (a) has increased the home price from 1 to 2. In the short run supply is inelastic, but over time it becomes more elastic (b). Price begins to fall (2 to 3). Soon the expectation of falling prices will increase supply more, as speculators try to sell the houses they've been holding. But demand will fall, as buyers wait for lower prices. Higher supply and lower demand will make prices fall fast.

Households notice that prices are not rising. The expectation of future price increases fades, and may change to an expectation of falling prices. Home buyers hold off their purchases, waiting to see how low prices will fall. That causes demand to decrease. People who bought houses as investments, because they thought prices would rise, now try to sell their houses before prices fall more. The supply of existing homes for sale increases, which causes prices to fall some more. Now pessimistic expectations are a self-fulfilling prophesy. For a while, new home supply keeps increasing, because construction plans can't be cancelled right away. Falling demand and rising supply causes prices to fall a lot.

- *Why was the speculative housing bubble so big?*

Demand and supply may explain why and where the *housing bubble* happened, but they don't yet explain why the 1998-2006 bubble was so large. Something must have increased demand more, and for a lot longer, than any previous housing boom. Here are a few possibilities.

Capital Gains Tax Cut. The Democratic President and Republican Congress occasionally agreed on policy. One instance was to eliminate the capital gains tax on most houses. As a result, the tax code treated houses more favorably than other investments. Put your money in stocks, and any gains in value would be taxed when the stock was sold. Put your money in a house, and most of the gains would be tax free. This may have diverted investment funds from other assets, like stocks and bonds, into houses.

Monetary Policy. We described the 2001 recession, which ended the long expansion of the 1990's, in Chapter 10. Alan Greenspan's Federal Reserve cut the federal funds rate twelve times during 2001, from 6% to 1.25%. The rate remained under 2% through the end of 2004. Mortgage rates fell too, after a while, from 7% at the end of 2001 to a low of 5.2% in mid-2003.

In most recessions housing construction drops a lot. Construction can be measured by "housing starts," the number of new homes that builders start each month. In the recessions in 1991, 1982, 1980, 1975 and 1970 monthly housing starts dropped below a hundred thousand. In 2001, though, housing starts remained around 140,000 per month. The housing market sailed through the recession with hardly a pause. Starts increased from there, peaking at almost two hundred thousand per month in mid-2006.

The low interest rates in the first half of the 2000's decade were *counter-cyclical monetary policy*. The economy fell into recession, and output remained below potential, so lower interest rates were appropriate to support aggregate demand. Stimulating investment in housing construction is one of the desired results of counter-cyclical monetary policy. But, perhaps, interest rates remained too low for too long. Low mortgage rates made borrowing cheaper, and increased the demand for housing. A housing slump in 2001 might have punctured the bubble before it started, reminding homebuyers and mortgage lenders that house prices could decline.

Homeownership and Mortgage Innovation. The percentage of households who live in homes that they own—the homeownership rate—varied up and down between 64% and 66% from 1969 to 1995. Then the rate began to grow, peaking at 69% in 2005. It has since fallen back to 64%. If more households own homes, and fewer rent, the demand for houses will rise, and house prices will rise.

The main explanation for the rise in homeownership is greater access to credit. Traditional mortgages require a down payment, have a fixed interest rate, a fixed payment month to month, and payments over a period of thirty years. Mortgage lenders began to invent new mortgage alternatives, and it became easier to get a mortgage starting in the middle-1990s. *Subprime mortgages* also gave more people access to credit. A subprime mortgage is one made to a borrower with no credit history, or who had failed to repay loans in the past, or who had low income relative to the size of the proposed mortgage payment. Traditionally such borrowers would have been denied mortgage loans, because lenders thought that there was too great a risk that the mortgage would not be repaid, and the borrower would default.

Mortgage lenders began to make more subprime mortgages in the 1990's. Because the risk of default was higher, subprime borrowers were charged higher interest rates. This was called "risk-based pricing", and it was an innovation in itself. Prior to the 1990's, riskier borrowers weren't offered mortgages with higher rates. They were denied mortgages all together.

> *An important reason for the housing bubble was the increased availability of mortgage loans to buyers who would have been considered unqualified in earlier times.*

Government policies played a role in encouraging subprime lending. The Community Reinvestment Act was passed in 1977 to encourage lenders to provide loans to borrowers in lower income areas. Since many people in these areas would be regarded as poor credit risks, they would be offered subprime mortgages.

Some analysts worried that home buyers were being lured into risky mortgages against their best interests. Federal Reserve Board member Edward Gramlich was particularly vocal. As early as December 2000 he advocated tighter regulation on subprime mortgage lenders. In 2002 he accused many lenders of charging excessive fees, and promoting mortgage refinancing in order to generate more fees. The Greenspan Fed was relying on industry self-regulation, and Gramlich's warnings went unheeded.

The Secondary Mortgage Market
These factors help explain why the demand for housing rose more during 1998-2006 than it had in the past. But, as usual, the answer to one question generates another question.

- *Where did lenders get the money to make all these additional mortgage loans?*

For decades mortgage lending was done by savings and loan institutions and commercial banks. The main source of the money for making these loans was from the deposits of households in the community. Households deposited their savings in banks and received interest; banks lent this money to mortgage borrowers who paid interest. The mortgage rate was a little higher than the deposit rate, and the difference was bank profits.

A savings and loan crisis at the end of the 1980's changed these practices. Savings and Loans had done much of the lending for houses, using 30-year fixed-rate mortgages. When inflation increased in the 1970's, the real interest rates on these mortgages issued in the 1950's and '60's went negative. Within a decade a large number of the financial institutions that had made mortgages were out of business. Lenders learned that it was risky to make a loan for thirty years at a fixed interest rate, when inflation and interest rates paid on deposits could vary up and down by a lot. What if inflation increased and the interest rate required to attract deposits rose higher than the interest rate being paid on all those old mortgage loans? That's what had caused the savings and loan crisis in the first place.

These problems led to an enormous expansion of the *secondary mortgage market*. Lenders would originate a loan—find the borrower, negotiate the terms, complete the paperwork and lend the money—that was the primary market. Then they would then sell the loan, or the rights to the mortgage payment, to an investor in the secondary market. The lender would receive a money payment from the investor, which could then be used to make another loan, and the investor would receive the mortgage payments, and bear the risk of default. The original lender would make its profits on the mortgage fees, not the mortgage payments.

The secondary mortgage market was a government invention. The Great Depression had increased foreclosures and depressed home construction. In 1938 the Federal government created the Federal National Mortgage Association (FNMA), which became known as *Fannie Mae.* It was Fannie Mae's job to borrow money from investors, buy mortgages from local lenders, and repay investors from the mortgage payments. Local lenders would gain more funds for loans, and get rid of the risk of default. This helped stimulate mortgage lending. Fannie Mae was originally a government agency, but in 1970 it became a private firm, though with a few special privileges. In 1970 a second similar company was created, the Federal Home Loan Mortgage Corporation (FHLMC), known as *Freddie Mac*.

> *In the secondary mortgage market, the rights to receive mortgage payments are bundled and sold as securities to investors. The payments that lenders receive allow them to lend more for mortgages.*

Fannie Mae and Freddie Mac had a peculiar place in financial markets. They were private institutions, not government agencies. Yet when they borrowed money from investors, they were treated as if they were government agencies. The interest rates that they had to pay to borrow money were almost as low as those that the Treasury paid on its bonds. Investors must have expected that, even though they were private firms, should there be trouble the Federal government would come to Fannie's and Freddie's rescue (turns out they were right). The two were labeled "Government Sponsored Enterprises."

Fannie Mae and Freddie Mac wouldn't buy just any loan. They would only buy loans that met certain standards that made the risk of default low. In fact, it was these standards that divided prime and subprime mortgages. A prime mortgage was one that Fannie Mae or Freddie Mac would buy. A subprime mortgage was one they would not buy. Since the number of subprime mortgages increased during the 1990's and 2000's, Fannie and Freddie's share of loans in the secondary mortgage market decreased. In 1989 over 90% of all mortgage loans sold in the secondary market were Fannie and Freddie's. By 2007 their share was less than half.

By 2007 private firms made up the majority of the secondary market. Some of the larger participants in the secondary market were Countrywide Financial, Lehman Brothers and Wells-Fargo. These firms would buy up mortgages and package them together in *mortgage-backed securities* or *mortgage derivatives*, a process known as *securitization*. These new securities would be sold to investors. The mortgage payments would flow from the mortgage borrower through the financial firm to the investors.

The volume of subprime mortgages increased in the early 2000's. By 2006 71% of mortgage-backed securities issued by private financial firms were based on subprime mortgages. In that year financial writer Roger Lowenstein had the rare privilege of watching the staff at Moody's Investors Service analyze a mortgage security. Moody's is a *credit rating service*, meaning it analyzes securities to tell investors how risky they are. (Moody's is the company that rates corporate bonds AAA and BAA, for our interest rate spread data.)

Lowenstein's experience can provide us with an example of how mortgage-backed securities worked. The financial firm wanting to issue the security was unnamed to Lowenstein, and the security was masked with the name "Subprime XYZ." It was a pool of 2,393 mortgages with a total value of $430 million. All the mortgages in the pool were subprime. The borrowers were thought to have a higher-than-usual risk of default. The original lender had provided information on the borrowers and their homes. Three-quarters of the borrowers had adjustable-rate mortgages, which had low initial interest rates which could climb fast. Almost half of the borrowers did not provide verification of their incomes. Twelve percent were for properties in Southern California, which was a risky degree of concentration in a single market (if something went wrong in that one market, potentially up to 12% of the borrowers would default, and the income flow from the security would drop a lot).

The financial firm wished to sell the rights to the pooled mortgage payments to investors. These rights were divided into twelve parts, known as tranches, which Moody's would rate from least risky to most risky. The subprime mortgages themselves were obviously risky. How could they support securities rated at low risk? Because the highest-rated tranche would have first call on the mortgage payments, then the next tranche, then the next. The tranche at the bottom got the highest interest rate. It was the most risky, because it would absorb the first losses if any homeowners defaulted.

Remember, the purpose of the secondary mortgage market was to make more money available for mortgage loans, to more people, at lower interest rates. Mortgage-backed securities were sold in world bond markets, purchased by people and institutions all over the world. This made it possible for anyone in the world with money to invest to lend in a local mortgage market. More money became available for mortgage lending, and that helped keep mortgage interest rates low.

The World's Money
Again, this presents another question.

- *Why would investors in the rest of the world want to lend for U.S. mortgages?*

The first answer is simple: because they could get a higher return on their investments. Perhaps interest rates paid on mortgages or other assets in their own countries were low, compared to the interest rates on U.S. mortgages. In effect, mortgage-backed securities worked because interest rates differed around the world. Investors in countries with low interest rates would lend to borrowers in the U.S., where interest rates were higher. Since the mortgage-backed security interest rate would be higher than the rate in the investor's country, the investor would be satisfied. Since the mortgage-backed security interest rate would be lower than the rate in the borrower's country, the borrower would be satisfied. Both the investor and borrower were better off.

In Chapter 8 we saw how China traded yuan for dollars to hold down the exchange value of the yuan, then lent their dollars in the U.S. A lot of this lending went to the secondary mortgage market, particularly to Fannie Mae and Freddie Mac. China's reserves of dollars supported mortgage lending in the U.S.

Lending came from Japan too. By the end of the 1980's Japan was at the peak of its economic power. The familiar Japanese corporations—Sony, Toyota, Mitsubishi—where producing innovative products that the world wanted to buy. Japan ran big trade surpluses. The value of the Japanese yen had been rising since the end of fixed exchange rates, because of the increased demand for Japan's exports.

This concerned the Bank of Japan, which is Japan's central bank. If the yen became too strong, Japanese exports would become expensive. A decline in exports would slow Japanese growth. So the Bank of Japan cut interest rates. Lower interest rates would make lending in Japan less profitable. The demand for the yen would drop (that's second shift #5), and the rise in the yen's value would slow down.

Interest rates were very low in Japan during the 2000's, so Japanese investors lent money for U.S. mortgages through the secondary mortgage market.

The combination of strong economic growth and low interest rates fueled a spectacular real estate boom. For a while, it was said, the land surrounding the Imperial Palace in Tokyo was worth more than all the real estate in California. Then, of course, the bubble burst. Japanese investors lost trillions of yen as real estate values and stock values fell. Japan's economy suffered two decades of below-average growth and even a period of deflation. Its economy still has not fully recovered, twenty-five years later. The Bank of Japan was slow to respond, but by the end of the 1990's it had reduced its interest rate to near zero, trying to stimulate consumer and business spending.

Japanese families had children to educate and elderly parents to care for. Their savings were earning next to nothing at the near-zero interest rates. So, they looked around for an alternative. In the early 2000's, aided by the newly available internet, they found international stocks, bonds and currencies. An astonishing amount of money flowed out of Japan looking for higher rates of return in the rest of the world. International investors would ask the question: "what are the housewives investing in these days?"

It was called the *yen carry trade*. Housewives, and professional investors and traders, would borrow at near-zero interest rates in Japan, and invest abroad. Some of the money went to nice safe U.S. Treasury bonds. But much of it sought out higher returns, in investments like mortgage-backed securities. Savings from Japan supported mortgage lending in the U.S.

Leverage
A household buys a house for $200,000 cash in California. In three years it doubles in value to $400,000. The homeowner sells, and makes $200,000, a 100% return on the original $200,000 investment.

A more ambitious household buys ten houses for $2,000,000 in California, with a $200,000 cash down payment and a mortgages totaling of $1,800,000. In three years the houses double in value to $4,000,000. The homeowner sells, repays the mortgages plus interest (say $2,100,000), and has $1,900,000 left over. That's an 850% return on the original $200,000 investment.

A mortgage with a down payment is an example of *leverage*. When asset values are rising, borrowing money to invest in assets can multiply profits many times. Investors in many asset markets had to make choices like this, between earning $200,000 in three years, and earning $1.9 million in three years. A lot of investors chose the larger amount.

The leverage ratio in this example is nine to one. The household borrowed $9 for each one dollar in equity, which is the cash down payment. In financial markets during the 2000's, leverage ratios were much bigger. The Bear Stearns investment bank was leveraged at 33 to one (before it failed).

Leverage ratios for homeowners and investment banks are regulated. Homeowners were traditionally required to put 20% down on a standard thirty-year mortgage: a $200,000 house would require a $40,000 down payment. During the housing boom, these terms were relaxed. Some homeowners were allowed to purchase homes with a down payment of 5%, or 3%, or no down payment at all.

The *Securities and Exchange Commission (SEC)* is the agency charged with enforcing leverage ratios on investment banks. It was established during the New Deal to regulate the financial markets, after the stock market crash in 1929. By the early 2000's, many of these regulations were thought to be obsolete. The SEC relaxed its leverage requirements for investment banks in 2004. This allowed the banks to borrow billions of dollars for added investments in mortgage backed securities and other assets.

Credit Default Swaps

A home buyer with a small down payment will often be required to buy mortgage insurance. For a monthly payment from the home buyer, the insurance company will guarantee the bank that the mortgage will be repaid. If the home buyer fails to repay, the insurance company will repay the bank, out of its reserves.

This insurance idea, magnified billions of times, is the idea behind *credit default swaps*. An insurance company accepts a fee from an asset buyer, and in exchange guarantees the asset's value. If the value of the asset falls, the insurer must pay. The insurer has taken on the risk, but receives the fee.

> *Credit Default Swaps are a kind of insurance on the value of assets. The insurance company guarantees the value of an asset in exchange for a monthly fee. If the value of the asset falls, the insurance company pays.*

Credit default swaps are a recent invention. Back in 1998, specialists at the J.P. Morgan investment bank came up with the idea, and approached the American International Group (A.I.G.), a huge insurance company. J.P. Morgan proposed that A.I.G. agree to provide insurance to investors who held mortgage-backed securities and other assets, in case they defaulted. A.I.G. was happy to make the deal. Most of the assets they would insure seemed safe, which meant A.I.G. would collect fees without having to pay much in claims. Activity in the credit default swap market exploded in the 2000's. Starting from nothing in 1998, by 2001 the market was worth one trillion dollars. By 2007, it was worth $45 trillion.

Insurance is a regulated industry, and one thing the regulations address is the ability of the insurance company to pay claims. When a company agrees to insure some risk (be it the possibility that you'll wreck your car, or require hospitalization, or default on your mortgage), it is required to place money in reserve. It can draw on these reserves if claims must be paid. The credit default swaps were so new, however, that they were unregulated. No government agency attempted to guarantee that the insurers had the resources to pay claims, if there were any.

What Went Wrong

This was the situation in the mid-2000's. The economy had seen more than twenty years of the Great Moderation. Home prices were rising rapidly, especially in big cities and on the coasts. Private investors, and the government sponsored enterprises Fannie Mae and Freddie Mac were buying subprime mortgages and selling them in the secondary mortgage market. Mortgage-backed securities based on subprime mortgage payments were in heavy demand. Money flowed into the markets from international investors, especially form Japan and China. Investment banks became highly leveraged in order to multiply their investment returns. Insurance companies offered trillions in credit default swaps, insuring mortgage-backed securities against loss.

What could possibly go wrong?

Home Prices Fall. This whole complex structure rested on rising home prices in the U.S. real estate market. If subprime borrowers were unable to meet their mortgage payments, they could sell at ever-higher prices, repay, and even make capital gains. The potential for default by subprime borrowers was masked by rising home prices.

Home construction started catching up with rising demand, which put downward pressure on prices. Expectations turned by the end of 2006. Now people expected prices to fall, not rise. People holding houses as investments tried to sell before prices dropped further. That increased the supply of houses on the market, and prices dropped some more.

Now many homeowners found themselves *underwater* or "upside-down" on their mortgages. They owed more on the mortgage than their house was worth. That means that, if they couldn't make their payments, they could not sell and pay off the loan. When home prices were rising, default was less likely because the house could be sold to pay off the mortgage. That wasn't possible if the mortgage was underwater. Default and foreclosure were the results.

Subprime mortgages were most likely to wind up in foreclosure. With small (or no) down payments, these homeowners borrowed near the full value of the home. As soon as the price dropped the mortgage was underwater. With mortgage terms that included rising interest and principal payments after a few years, many homeowners found their payments impossible to make. Many had counted on refinancing or selling at higher prices. Now, owing more than their house was worth, they could only default.

> *Rising house prices had masked problems of default. As house prices fell, defaults rose, and mortgage backed securities fell in value.*

The lenders that made these loans, and didn't sell them in the secondary mortgage market, were the first to feel the effects. Big mortgage lenders like Countrywide Financial and Washington Mutual saw rising delinquency rates on the loans that they hadn't yet bundled and sold. Losses mounted and bankruptcy threatened. Countrywide was sold to Bank of America, Washington Mutual to JP Morgan Chase, at steep discounts, in 2008.

Fannie and Freddie are seized. Fannie Mae had been losing its share of the secondary mortgage market, because it would not buy subprime loans. Lenders were threatening to bypass Fannie and sell directly to investors, unless Fannie agreed to buy riskier loans. And, Congress was pressuring Fannie to make more loans available to low-income buyers. Home prices were rising much faster than incomes, legislators pointed out. It was Fannie's responsibility to keep homeownership within reach.

So Fannie and Freddie began buying riskier loans. Between 2005 and 2007, Fannie tripled its purchases of mortgages with down payments of less than 10 percent. This may have encouraged further expansion of subprime lending. When a government sponsored enterprise bought a mortgage, it seemed to have a stamp of approval.

Sometimes warning bells would sound in Congress. Should Fannie be restricted in the kinds of loans it was buying? When that happened, Fannie and Freddie would lobby hard to keep Congress at bay. At one point they made millions of automated phone calls to voters, saying "Your congressman is trying to make mortgages more expensive. Ask him why he opposes the American dream of home ownership." Congress never acted.

As home prices began to fall and default rates rise, Fannie and Freddie found that many of the mortgages they held were not worth what they had paid for them. And, both companies had guaranteed the values of the mortgages that they sold to investors. If those mortgages defaulted and the values of the mortgage-backed securities fell, Fannie and Freddie would have to make up the difference. It would cost billions, money that Fannie and Freddie didn't have.

It was feared that the failure of these two firms would paralyze the mortgage markets. After all, they still bought half the mortgages issued in the U.S. Without them, where would lenders get the money to make mortgage loans? The housing market would be paralyzed. So on September 8, 2008, the U.S. government seized Fannie Mae and Freddie Mac, funneling several hundred billion dollars to the companies to make good on their commitments. Some hoped that the nationalization of Fannie and Freddie would calm financial markets. It may have had the opposite effect. If Fannie Mae and Freddie Mac, the biggest mortgage buyers on Earth, could not survive this crisis, who could?

Mortgage Defaults and Bank Failures. Something odd was happening to the mortgages that provided the income for Subprime XYZ, that mortgage backed security that Moody's Investor Services had rated. Some homeowners fell behind on their mortgage payments within the first 90 days. Six percent of the mortgages were delinquent after six months. These were much higher delinquency rates than analysts had expected.

Government-sponsored mortgage buyers Fannie Mae and Freddie Mac, and investment banks Bear Stearns and Lehman Brothers, had purchased too many mortgage-backed securities. When these securities fell in value, these institutions failed.

Moody's looked into the problem and was dismayed to find that some homes didn't have lawns or landscaping, or that the owner had never moved in. People had bought homes as speculative investments. When housing prices began to fall, they walked away from their mortgages. By the spring of 2007, 13 percent of Subprime XYZ mortgages were delinquent. By early 2008, it was 27 percent, an enormous percentage. It was happening to a lot of the mortgages issued in 2006. The 2007 mortgages did even worse.

The bonds in the lowest tranche of Subprime XYZ became worthless. They didn't earn any income. But with so many defaults, even the middle tranche bonds lost income, and the owners of the highest tranche bonds felt threatened. Now was the time for investors to sell these assets, before their values fell. But, if everyone tries to sell, prices fall.

Lehman Brothers was a 158-year-old investment bank. It too was a big lender for and investor in mortgage-backed securities. Now it was in trouble. Lehman's managers searched in vain for a stronger bank that could buy them out. They pleaded with the government for a bailout. None was forthcoming. On September 15, 2008, Lehman Brothers filed for bankruptcy.

Months before that the government had subsidized the sale of another troubled investment bank, *Bear Stearns*. Why did the Fed and the Treasury assist Bear Stearns, and not Lehman Brothers? Treasury Secretary Henry Paulson claimed, "We didn't have the powers." He said that the law allowed the Federal Reserve to lend to a bank only if it had enough good assets to serve as collateral. Lehman Brothers didn't.

Others dispute this reason. Two possible buyers for Lehman Brothers walked out of meetings when the government wouldn't offer the same loans and guarantees that it had offered for Bear Stearns. Perhaps the Treasury and the Fed were reluctant because they knew that bailouts of elite financial institutions would be unpopular with voters and taxpayers. Perhaps they feared *moral hazard*, that protecting one bank from the consequences of its risky mistakes would encourage others to make more risky mistakes. Perhaps they gambled that Lehman could fail without serious consequences for the rest of the financial system.

If so, they were wrong. The very next day, the government did bail out the biggest insurance company in the U.S., *American International Group, A.I.G.*

Suddenly, A.I.G. was responsible for claims on all those credit default swaps they had issued. These were insurance policies that guaranteed asset values against default. Now mortgage-backed securities were suffering losses from defaults, and any asset tied to Lehman Brothers was worth a lot less than it had been just days before. A.I.G. had not reserved nearly enough to meet all those claims. They would be far more than A.I.G. could pay.

The day after Lehman's collapse, A.I.G. begged for help from the government. The government reversed course and came to the rescue. A.I.G. could not be allowed to fail. Had it collapsed, every asset that it insured would instantly have been worth less, because without the insurance the assets would be riskier. Since A.I.G. insured such a large amount of assets, investors, banks and businesses worldwide would have suffered losses. They may not have been able to repay their own debts, or meet the demands of their depositors. "The spillover effects would have been incredible," said Princeton economist Uwe Reinhardt.

> *The A.I.G. insurance company had made most of the credit default swap guarantees. When asset values fell, A.I.G. couldn't pay, and the government stepped in.*

The government effectively nationalized A.I.G., using government money to buy up its stock. On September 16 the government paid $85 billion; by March 2009 the figure had climbed to $180 billion. The U.S. government owned 80% of A.I.G.'s stock.

But the Lehman Brother's bankruptcy and the A.I.G. failure sparked a world financial panic. Willem Sels, a German banker, said that "when Lehman defaulted, that is the date your money markets freaked out."

Lenders tried to play it safe. Instead of lending to risky businesses, they lent to the U.S. Treasury. This is called a *flight to safety*. The interest rates that Treasury bonds paid wasn't very high, but the money would be repaid. The Treasury has never defaulted, never even missed an interest payment. Now businesses had to pay more to borrow, and the Treasury could pay less.

So much less, incredibly, that during three days in December the interest rate on three-month Treasury securities dropped to zero. So many people wanted to lend to the government that the Treasury didn't have to pay *any* interest. The U.S. Treasury became like a very large mattress. People put the money there for safekeeping, expecting no return at all.

The Great Recession Complete

We first looked at the data from the Great Recession of 2007-09 in Chapter 1. The goods and money market models were applied to the recession in Chapter 3. It was compared to the Panic of 1907 in Chapter 4. The response of monetary was compared to the Great Depression in Chapter 5, and Great Recession fiscal policy was examined in Chapter 6. The exchange market model was added in Chapter 8.

Now we can pull it all together. Figure 11-4 on the following page shows the three market macroeconomic model and the data for the five macro indicators and two policy indicators. Let's roll out a whole bunch of our ideas, and see what we can do with the data and model.

Let's start in the money market. Money demand must have been decreasing in 2009, with the drop in income (real GDP) and the drop to deflation (second shift #3). Since the interest rate spread went up, the money supply must have been decreasing more than money demand. The *shock* to the money market was the main cause of the recession. Banks increased *reserves* and reduced lending, and the *money multiplier* decreased.

> *The shock to the money market increased real interest rates, decreasing investment spending. The wealth effect reduced consumption spending. Rising demand for the dollar raised the exchange rate, which decreased exports. The Great Recession was the result.*

Now check the goods market. Equilibrium output was just above potential in 2007, as shown by the unemployment rate just below 5%. Output dropped a little in 2008 and then a lot in 2009. Inflation increased in 2008—there was an oil price increase—and then in 2009 came the first year of deflation since 1955. The goods market in 2009 can produce these results with a decline in aggregate demand, with equilibrium output falling below potential. Spending must have decreased.

The increase in real interest rates in the money market, especially to risky businesses, reduced investment spending and aggregate demand (second shift #2). The decline in home values and in stock market values created a negative *wealth effect* for consumers. *Autonomous spending* in the *consumption function* declined. The *marginal propensity to consume* decreased too, since people tend to save more when they're concerned for their jobs. Consumer spending fell. As consumers spent less, goods and services that would have been purchased were not produced, employees of those firms were laid off, and they spent less too. The *income multiplier* caused bigger declines in spending, aggregate demand and output.

The Great Recession Complete

Year	Real GDP Growth	CPI Inflation	Unemploy-ment Rate	Interest Rate Spread	Exchange Rate, Euros/$	Federal Funds Rate	Budget Balance (% GDP)
2007	1.8%	2.9%	4.6%	0.9%	0.73	5.0%	-1.1%
2008	-0.3%	3.8%	5.8%	1.8%	0.68	1.9%	-3.1%
2009	-2.8%	-0.3%	9.3%	2.0%	0.72	0.2%	-9.8%

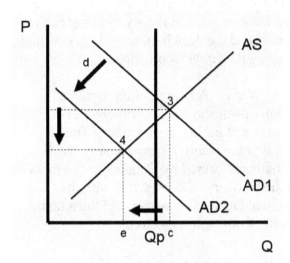

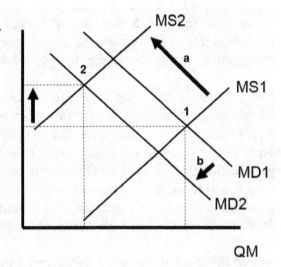

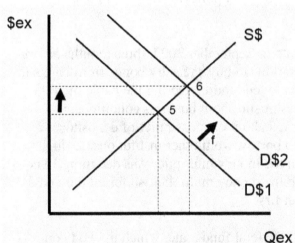

Figure 11-4. All together now. The collapse of financial markets causes lenders to build reserves and restrict lending. The money multiplier falls, which reduces the money supply (a). Money demand decreases with the drop in income and inflation (b, second shift #3). The real interest rate increases (1 to 2). Output is above potential before the recession (c). Aggregate demand declines (d). This happens because collapsing home and stock values reduce household wealth, causing consumption to decline, and the higher real interest rate reduces investment spending (second shift #2). Output and prices fall (3 to 4), and output ends of less than potential (e). Meanwhile, international investors flee risk worldwide and buy U.S. Treasury securities, which increases the demand for the dollar (f). The exchange value of the dollar rises (5 to 6). The higher exchange value of the dollar reduces exports (second shift #4), adding to the effect of the worldwide recession. This reduces aggregate demand, output and inflation even more. The Great Recession is the result.*

Don't forget the exchange market. The exchange value of the dollar increased in 2009. The rising real interest rate may have contributed to an increase in the exchange demand for the dollar (second shift #5). But, in times of crisis international investors look for a *safe haven* for their wealth. They bought U.S. Treasury bonds, and to do that they had to have dollars. The demand for the dollar in the exchange market increased. Recession in the rest of the world was the main reason for the drop in export spending, but the higher value of the dollar made the drop worse (second shift #4). This added to the decline in aggregate demand in the goods market.

The Federal Reserve cut the federal funds rate to near zero, which is *counter-cyclical monetary policy* in a recession. They used *open market operations* to increase the *monetary base*, hoping that second shift #2 would encourage lending and spending. The fact that the interest rate spread went up anyway indicates how pessimistic lenders must have been. The money multiplier fell a lot. But without the Fed's efforts the money market panic, and the drop in money supply, would have been much worse. Remember the Fed's failure during the Great Depression.

The budget balance shows the largest deficit since World War II. A rising deficit during a recession is *counter-cyclical fiscal policy*. Part of the deficit was the result of *automatic stabilizers*. Income tax revenues fell due to unemployment and falling stock values. Transfer payments like unemployment insurance increased. Part was the result of *discretionary fiscal policy*—the Bush tax cut and the Obama stimulus bill that were passed by Congress. The extra spending added to aggregate demand, which hastened the recovery. Contrast this with the Hoover administration's tax increase, which made the Great Depression worse, and the attempt to balance the budget in 1937-38, which contributed to the Roosevelt recession.

We've told the story of the panic. Now here's the story of what policymakers did in response.

Monetary Policy

The Federal Reserve began cutting its federal funds rate in September 2007, three months *before* the recession started. The Fed used open market operations to buy Treasury bonds from banks in exchange for money. Usually, this would cause banks to lend more. During the panic of 2008, banks reserved the money instead. They were too pessimistic about business conditions, too scared about the value of their own assets, too concerned about the possibility of depositor withdrawals, too worried that they wouldn't be able to borrow from other institutions, to do much lending. Higher reserves and less lending mean the money multiplier was declining. The money supply is the product of the monetary base and the money multiplier, so for all the Fed's efforts, the money supply didn't increase very much at first.

Figure 11-4 shows the Fed's difficulty. Ordinarily the federal funds rate, which the Fed controls with open market operations, is nearly the same as the 3-month commercial interest rate, which banks charge for short-term business loans. In March 2008 the two rates differed by less than one tenth of one percent. In most of the next seven months, the Fed cut the federal funds rate, but the commercial rate *went up*. By October the commercial rate was more than two percentage points higher than the federal funds rate. The Fed was buying bonds from banks, but the banks weren't lending. They were reserving the money instead. Loans became scarce, and the interest rate required to get a loan increased.

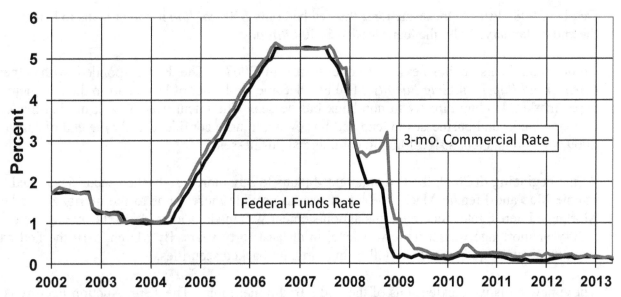

Figure 11-4. The federal funds interest rate and the 3-month commercial interest rate, monthly, 2002-2014. Usually these two interest rates move up and down together. The Fed can reduce the cost of business borrowing for inventories and payroll by reducing the federal funds rate. In mid-2008, though, the Fed cut the federal funds rate from 2.75% to 1%, and the commercial rate went up. Monetary policy wasn't working.

Eventually the commercial rate began to fall, and it converged with the federal funds rate again in 2010. By that time the Fed had stopped reducing the federal funds rate—but not because more rate cuts weren't needed. They were. But on December 16, 2008, the federal funds rate effectively hit zero. It can't go lower.

Federal Reserve Chair Benjamin Bernanke had anticipated this problem. As early as 2004 he was asking the question, what should the Fed do if the federal funds rate was zero? In a speech to the American Economic Association, Bernanke pointed out "that the public might interpret a zero instrument rate as evidence that the central bank has 'run out of ammunition.'" Bernanke invented new policy tools for the Fed, looking for more ammunition.

> *The Federal Reserve cut its federal funds interest rate to near zero, and invented new ways to flood the markets with money.*

The Fed created a new way to lend directly to banks. The Fed's oldest function is as a *lender of last resort*. Banks have been able to borrow directly from the Fed since its founding. But by 2008, few banks took the opportunity. If a bank borrowed from the "lender of last resort," it meant that everyone else thought they were a bad risk. That might signal a bank's weakness to the markets, who might never lend to them again.

William Gavin, a vice president of the St. Louis Fed, wrote that the Fed's new lending program included a "very public campaign to eliminate the 'stigma' associated with borrowing at the discount window. . . ." They called it the *Term Auction Facility*, and it was an auction of money. Banks that wanted to borrow from the Fed would bid an interest rate, with the highest bidder allowed to borrow the money. The auctions began at the end of 2007 and were stepped up in

October 2008. Prior to these auctions, the Fed had only $300 *million* in direct loans to banks. By the end of January, 2009, the loans totaled $630 *billion*.

Commercial loans to businesses became scarce in 2008. The Fed responded with a new *Commercial Paper Funding Facility*. The Fed became the lender of last resort in the commercial paper market, lending directly to non-bank businesses. The intent was to back up that market, allowing banks and businesses to lend and borrow with more confidence. By the end of January 2009, the Fed had lent $316 billion to commercial businesses.

At the beginning of 2009, the Fed announced plans to buy mortgage-backed securities issued by Fannie Mae and Freddie Mac. The intent was to provide more funds to the mortgage market. Mortgage interest rates fell when this announcement was made, and by April the average rate on a 30-year mortgage was at its lowest level in at least forty years. By March 2010 the Fed had bought one and a quarter *trillion* dollars in mortgage-backed securities.

These new tools were extensions of the Fed's traditional tools. The Term Auction Facility is a new way to lend directly to banks. The Commercial Paper Funding Facility extends the Fed's direct lending to other kinds of businesses. Both of these are extensions of the Fed's traditional lending at the discount rate. The Fed's plan to buy mortgage-backed securities is an extension of its open market operations, buying bonds beyond the traditional Treasury securities.

These are a few of the Fed's new policy tools. For decades, we have spoken of the Fed's three policy tools. By May 2009 their website listed eleven.

Bailouts

It was the week of the Lehman Brothers bankruptcy, and the A.I.G. bailout. Investors were pulling money out of even the biggest, most profitable banks. Credit markets had frozen. Fed chair Bernanke and Treasury Secretary Paulson decided that it was time to act. Some aides suggested a "bank holiday", a nationwide closing of banks, as in 1933, but Bernanke and Paulson thought that would just scare people more. So, instead, they "broke the glass" on their most drastic rescue plans.

They met with Congressional leaders in a hastily called meeting to present the outline of a $700 billion plan to rescue the financial system. Bernanke told them, "If we don't do this, we may not have an economy on Monday." When the House of Representatives rejected the first version of the plan, the stock market had its worst day since the crash of 1987. Finally, on October 2, 2009, Congress passed the $700 billion *Troubled Asset Relief Program* (TARP). The money would be distributed in two $350 billion packages.

The original idea was to buy "toxic assets" from banks. Many of these were mortgage-backed securities in the lower tranches, which were taking most of the losses from mortgage defaults. Banks and other institutions that owned these assets were in financial trouble, and this was causing them to increase reserves and reduce lending. If the Treasury bought them for cash, they'd be removed from the banks' portfolios, and the banks would have the added cash to lend.

The plan didn't work. It wasn't clear how much to pay for the toxic assets. Private markets wouldn't buy them, so their prices were effectively zero. But the Treasury couldn't pay a zero price—that wouldn't give added cash for banks to lend.

Instead, in November, the Treasury reversed course and decided to purchase shares in banks, another way to give them cash to lend. Nine of the largest banks in the U.S. were given $25 billion apiece, and a great many smaller banks were offered money as well. This had the side effect of making the U.S. Treasury a part owner of major U.S. banks, an astonishing move, especially for a Republican administration. The Treasury also lent the TARP money more broadly, using the last of the original $350 billion for loans to U.S. auto makers General Motors and Chrysler.

Unfortunately, by the end of 2008 most banks had not lent the TARP money, but had added it to their reserves. They were still too pessimistic and uncertain about their finances and about the prospects of borrowers, to release the money into the economy.

The second $350 billion would be distributed under the new Obama administration in 2009. The Treasury would subsidize private investors to help them buy toxic assets. Banks would undergo "stress tests" to determine their financial health, and those that failed would have to find new investors, or come to the Treasury for more TARP funding, in exchange for a share of ownership.

Later that spring there were some optimistic signs. The interest rate spreads had dropped back towards normal, and some banks were reporting profits. The panic was over, at least partly because of the strenuous efforts by the Fed and the Treasury to stabilize financial markets.

Fiscal Policy
In February 2009 the Obama administration's stimulus package passed the Congress. The *American Recovery and Reinvestment Act (ARRA)* as it was passed contained $787 billion in added spending and tax cuts, about two-thirds added spending, one-third tax cuts. Most of the spending would take place from the second half of 2009 to the first half of 2011.

The tax cuts would not come in the form of rebate checks, as the Bush administration tax cuts had done in 2008. Then, households saved much of their rebate checks, or paid down debt. This time, income tax withholding rates would be reduced. Workers would see a little bit extra in their take-home pay each week or each month. These weekly amounts were small, and this part of the stimulus package was criticized as insignificant.

Another feature was called "fiscal stabilization." State and local governments must balance their budgets. They cannot run deficits like the Federal government can. This is because they cannot borrow as easily from financial markets, and because they cannot print money. When tax revenues fall in recession, state and local governments are forced to cut spending or increase tax rates. Both of these are pro-cyclical policies. If fifty states all act this way, much of the effect of the Federal government's stimulus could be erased. So, a substantial share of the stimulus bill was aid to state and local governments, to try to keep them from cutting spending or raising tax rates as much.

Putting America to Work. A highway sign in 2010 telling us that the funding for a road construction project came from the stimulus bill, known as the American Recovery and Reinvestment Act.

In May 2011 the Congressional Budget Office (CBO) estimated that, at its peak in 2010, the ARRA had increased real GDP by 1.5% to 4.2%, and had reduced the unemployment rate by 0.7 to 1.8 percentage points. This implies that, without the stimulus, the unemployment rate in 2010 would have averaged not 9.6%, but 10.3% to 11.4%. That meant 1.1 to 2.8 million additional people would have been unemployed.

The Not-So-Great Recovery
Wouldn't it be nice if a "Great Recession" were followed by a "Great Recovery"? As of 2017 the economy has recovered, with the unemployment rate near 5% and output close to potential. But it took an exceptionally long time. Once more, here are the data and the market models, in Figure 11-5.

The unemployment rate was high in 2010—it had peaked at 10% in October 2009. Output was well under potential. Real GDP grew steadily, but slowly. Growth has not exceeded 3% since 2005, the longest period of growth that slow in more than a century. Inflation has remained low and fallen a bit. It is under the Federal Reserve's 2% inflation target. The drop in oil prices in 2015 depressed inflation that year and in 2016.

While input costs were held down, second shift #1 increased aggregate supply. Aggregate demand rose more slowly, as indicated by the fall in the inflation rate. It was 3.1% in 2011, and 1.2% in 2016. The slow rise in aggregate demand has several causes. High unemployment, slow wage growth and a slow recovery in home values kept consumer spending growth low. Households were paying down debt rather than taking on more. They increased their savings too.

The Long Slow Recovery

Year	Real GDP Growth	CPI Inflation	Unemploy- ment Rate	Interest Rate Spread	Exchange Rate, Euros/$	Federal Funds Rate	Gov't Budget Balance (% GDP)
2010	2.5%	1.6%	9.6%	1.1%	0.76	0.2%	-8.6%
2011	1.6%	3.1%	8.9%	1.0%	0.72	0.1%	-8.4%
2012	2.2%	2.1%	8.1%	1.3%	0.78	0.1%	-6.7%
2013	1.7%	1.5%	7.4%	0.9%	0.75	0.1%	-4.1%
2014	2.4%	1.6%	6.2%	0.7%	0.75	0.1%	-2.8%
2015	2.6%	0.1%	5.3%	1.1%	0.90	0.1%	-2.4%
2016	1.6%	1.2%	4.9%	1.0%	0.90	0.4%	-3.2%

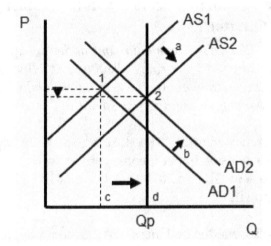

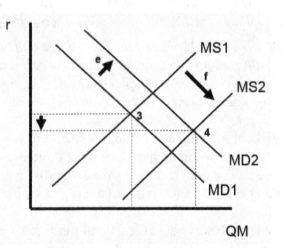

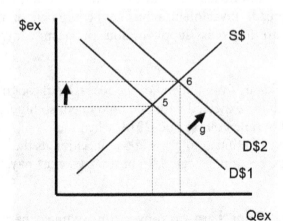

Figure 11-5. A long slow recovery. Output starts well under potential (1, c). Unemployment holds down input costs, so aggregate supply increases (a, second shift #1). Consumers are reluctant to spend and government deficits are reduced. This inhibits aggregate demand growth (b). The inflation rate declines and output grows slowly (1 to 2), but finally reaches potential (d). Money demand rises slowly with low income growth and low inflation (e). The Fed holds the federal funds rate very low to expand the money supply (f). The interest rate spread falls for a time (3 to 4), but lenders remain skittish so investment growth is modest (second shift #2). Sporadic crises in Europe keep the demand for the dollar growing (g), which holds the exchange value of the dollar high (5 to 6). This (and slow growth in the rest of the world) reduces exports (second shift #4), which also holds down aggregate demand growth.

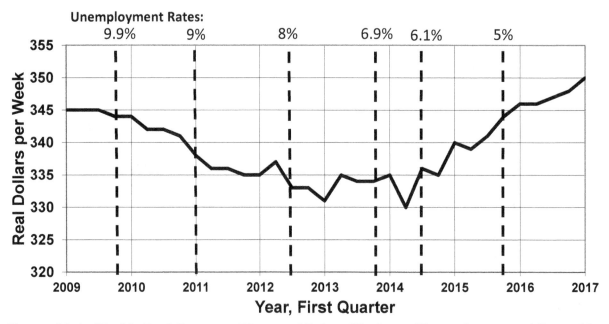

Figure 11-6. Weekly Real Earnings, Wage and Salary Workers. The median or middle weekly wage, adjusted for inflation, and some corresponding unemployment rates. Real wages fell until the unemployment rate dropped below 8%, then remained steady between 8% and 6%. Only when the unemployment rate dropped below 6% did real wages begin to rise steadily.

The Federal government's stimulus spending was not renewed after 2011. Instead, spending was "sequestered," meaning increases were limited, and tax rates on upper income earners were increased. The budget deficit shrank rapidly, from 8.6% of GDP in 2010 to 2.4% in 2015. The shrinking budget deficit reduced aggregate demand growth.

The Federal Reserve held the federal funds rate near zero, and the Fed increased the money supply as never before. Real interest rates were low. But confidence by lenders came and went, as indicated by the downs and ups in the interest rate spread. Investment in business equipment and buildings grew in fits and starts. It took years to sell off the excess supply of houses. Despite low mortgage rates, housing investment lagged.

Policy makers were concerned about slow growth in wages from the end of the recession through 2014. Wages were slow to rise in this recovery, but that's expected with unemployment so high. Figure 11-6 shows that wages adjusted for inflation bottomed out in mid-2014, when the unemployment rate was approaching 6%. Wages have continued to grow above inflation as the unemployment rate has fallen below 5%. Workers are becoming scarce, so businesses must pay more.

Europe suffered several crises, Japan grew slowly, and China's growth slowed from extraordinary to merely rapid. Europe and Japan saw brief recessions after 2010. This in itself reduced export growth. It also held dollar demand and the exchange value of the dollar high, because the world's investors sought the safe haven of U.S. Treasury bonds. In 2015 the European central bank began cutting interest rates, just as the Federal Reserve begin increasing. Lenders demanded dollars to lend in the U.S. (that's second shift #5).

Consumer spending growth was slow. Business investment in equipment, business buildings and houses grow sporadically. Taxes increased and government spending growth slowed. Exports grew slowly with slow growth in the rest of the world, and the rising value of the dollar. It's no wonder aggregate demand grew slowly, and so did real GDP.

Why Has the Unemployment Rate Fallen so Fast?

The unemployment rate came down from 10% to under 5% in a period of six years. A rule-of-thumb (derived from Okun's Law) says that real GDP has to grow about 3% per year just to hold the unemployment rate steady. Less than that, and it will rise. Yet growth has not exceeded 3% in even one year since 2010, and the unemployment rate has fallen almost a point a year.

The reason that real GDP must grow in order to hold the unemployment rate steady is that the labor force keeps growing. Young people turn 16, 18 or 22 and look for jobs. The economy must grow to create more jobs, or the number of unemployed job-searchers will increase.

But labor force growth has slowed. We saw this in Chapter 3. Between 1962 and 1980 the labor force grew an average of 2.2% per year. From 1981 to 2009 the average was 1.3% per year. But since 2010 the labor force has grown only 0.5% per year. During the Great Recession, the labor force actually decreased. It hadn't done that since 1951.

Those years are chosen for a reason: *the baby boom*. The baby boom started in 1946. Those first boomers became eligible to work then they turned 16, in 1962. The end of the baby boom usually is marked in 1964. Those babies turned 16 in 1980. From 1962 to 1980, then, the boomers were entering the labor force. They were all in from 1981 to 2009. In 2009, the first boomers turned 63, and were eligible for early retirement with Social Security. Now the boomers are leaving the labor force, and the labor force is growing more slowly. That slow growth is likely to continue until the last of the boomers retires, when they turn 67 (the new retirement age under Social Security) in 2031.

If there are fewer new job-seekers entering the labor force each year, it takes fewer new jobs to employ them. An early guess is that now real GDP must grow by 1.5% to hold the unemployment rate steady. If real GDP grows faster than that, the unemployment rate will fall, as it has since 2010. That 1.5% figure is important for another reason. If the economy is at potential output, and real GDP grows faster than 1.5%, the unemployment rate will fall below 5%. Second shift #1 will kick in, aggregate supply will decrease, and output will revert to potential. That makes 1.5% the limit for growth once potential is reached.

The Economy at the Lower Bound

After its initial effort in 2008 and 2009, the Fed continued *quantitative easing*. This simply means further increases in the monetary base and quantity of money ("easing" is the opposite of tightening, an increase rather than a decrease). A month-by-month accounting of these policies shows, though, that the Fed acted in fits and starts. There were three episodes of quantitative easing, known as QE-I, QE-II and QE-III. QE-I was the initial response to the recession, and it ended in December 2009. When the economy faltered in later 2010, the Fed began QE-II in

January 2011. These increases continued through July, then stopped. When the economy faltered again, the Fed started QE-III.

From the beginning of the recession in December 2007, to the end of QE-III in August 2014 the quantity of money (measured by M1) doubled from $1.4 trillion to $2.8 trillion. That's an annual average increase of 11.3% per year. Real GDP grew no more than 2.5% in any year during that time, when it was growing at all.

What happened to "too much money chasing too few goods?" This vast increase in the money supply should have created a lot of inflation. But it didn't. Figure 11-2 shows inflation since 2008 to be the lowest since 1900. It peaked at 3.1% in 2011 and fell after that.

The Federal government's budget deficit grew during the Great Recession. Unemployment and falling incomes reduced revenues. The Bush and Obama administrations cut tax rates. Transfer payment spending increased. The Obama administration's stimulus bill increased spending. Congress extended unemployment insurance. The deficit was 9.8% of GDP in 2009, the biggest deficit since World War II. The deficit remained historically high through 2012. The government borrowed trillions of dollars. The sum-total of Treasury bonds in the hands of the public grew from $5 trillion in 2007 to $14 trillion in 2016. That's known as the *national debt*.

What happened to "crowding out?" Surely government deficits that big must increase money demand, and force up interest rates. Put another way, surely the demand for loans by the government must have increased interest rates and reduced borrowing by private businesses. But it didn't. The 10-year Treasury bond interest rate actually fell, 4.1% in December 2007 to 1.7% in December 2012.

What was going on? Had these two rules of economics been repealed? The answer: the rules change when interest rates get really, really low. To see why, we'll have to draw some very strange money market diagrams. They're in Figure 11-7.

Suppose there's a deep recession. In the diagram at left, money demand has decreased a lot. The Federal Reserve increases the money supply a lot. The real interest rate drops to zero. That's the *lower bound* for the interest rate. Now suppose the Fed increases the money supply some more. The equilibrium interest rate is negative, which can't happen. Instead, there is an excess supply of money at the lower bound interest rate, shown by points 3 and 2.

An increase in the money supply has had no effect on the real interest rate, so second shift #2 does not happen, so there is no increase in aggregate demand, no increase in output and no increase in inflation. Too much money does not cause inflation.

What does an excess supply of money mean? Consumers hang on to the money in their checking accounts, too worried about their jobs to spend. Businesses borrow money at low interest rates but don't increase investment spending, because they don't see profitable opportunities during the recession. They hold on to the money instead. Banks keep excess reserves, not sure which borrowers can repay loans. The risk of lending is greater than the interest that can be earned.

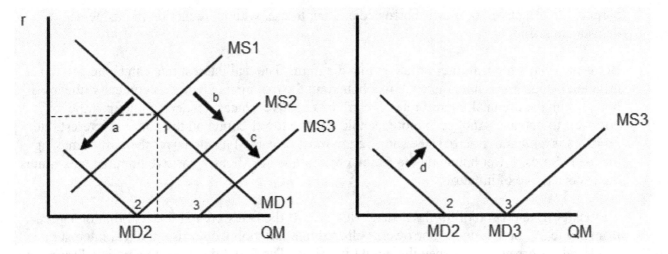

Figure 11-7. Liquidity Trap. The recession reduces prices and incomes, which reduces money demand (a). That's second shift #3. The Federal Reserve responds to the recession with huge increases in the money supply (b, MS1 to MS2), until the real interest rate hits zero. That's the lower bound for the real interest rate. Further increases in the money supply have no effect on the interest rate. An increase from MS2 to MS3 (c) would leave the interest rate at zero (3). There is an excess supply of money at the zero interest rate (2 to 3). It sits idle in bank reserves or savings accounts. Since the interest rate cannot fall further, second shift #2 cannot occur, so changes in the money supply cannot affect aggregate demand. Monetary policy is ineffective, and increases in the money supply cannot cause inflation. Expansionary fiscal policy could increase aggregate demand. Second shift #3 would increase money demand (d, MD2 to MD3) the interest rate will remain at zero. Second shift #3 has no impact on the interest rate, so there will be no crowding out.

Too much money chasing too few goods? There may be too much money. There may be too few goods. But the money isn't *chasing*. Banks, consumers and businesses aren't lending and spending, so there's no added demand for goods, and no inflation.

Now consider the diagram to the right in Figure 11-7. The recession continues. The Federal government increases spending and cuts taxes, leading to the big budget deficit. In the goods market, output begins to increase, prices begin to rise. In the money market money demand increases, shown by the "d" arrow (second shift #3). The equilibrium interest rate is zero, and remains zero as money demand increases. The excess supply of money merely decreases (2 to 3).

With no increase in the interest rate, there is no second shift #2, no decrease in investment, and so no crowding out. Again, what is really happening? There is excess money supply—money that banks aren't lending and businesses aren't borrowing. With a budget deficit, the government borrows and spends the money, which adds to aggregate demand. It creates no reduction in business investment, because that investment was not going to take place.

At the lower bound, expansionary monetary policy is ineffective. The Fed has run out of ammunition if the interest rate can't be reduced further. But expansionary fiscal policy can be particularly effective. Money is borrowed and put to use, with no reduction in business investment spending.

But wait—that's the real interest rate in that diagram. The real interest rate can be negative if inflation is high enough. Is there a lower bound on the real interest rate? Technically, the lower bound is on the nominal interest rate. It can't be negative, since a lender will not pay the borrower to borrow. And, even more technically, the lower bound on the nominal interest rate probably is a bit above zero, since some return must be earned just to cover the cost of making the loan. So the lower bound on the real interest rate is this slightly positive nominal rate, minus the expected rate of inflation.

This suggests another tool for the Federal Reserve. If the Fed were to raise its inflation target, from 2% to 3% or 4%, and if borrowers believed that inflation would rise, the real interest rate would fall. Borrowing and spending might increase. The Fed did not use this policy during the lower bound years. Now that the economy is back to potential, interest rates have risen above the lower bound again.

Fiscal Policy at Potential Output
The Congress did not approve another big stimulus bill after the ARRA, but some smaller stimulus efforts were made. A tax cut and stimulus bill was passed in December 2010. Tax cuts made during the Bush administration in 2001 and 2003 had been due to expire at the end of 2010. The 2012 bill extended these tax cuts for two years, extended unemployment insurance coverage for another 13 months, and cut the Social Security payroll tax from 6.2% to 4.2% for 2011. Later, this cut was extended through 2012. This was the first time a payroll tax cut had been used for countercyclical fiscal policy.

With a Democratic President and a Republican Congress, fiscal policy was in stalemate for much of the 2011-2016 period. The Federal fiscal year begins in October, but in 2013 the Congress failed to pass a budget on time. A budget authorizes spending, so with no spending authorized the government shut down non-essential services. 800,000 Federal employees were sent home. (The websites that provide GDP and unemployment data were offline!).

More serious was the possibility that the Treasury would default on its bonds in mid-October 2013. Congress imposes a *debt ceiling* on the amount of Treasury bonds that the government can issue. This is passed apart from the budget, even though the tax and spending decisions in the budget set the amount of debt required.

The shutdown was a serious threat to financial markets. What if the government could not meet the interest payments on its bonds? Treasury bonds are international investors' safe haven in times of trouble. The foundations of international financial markets would shake if this safe haven turned out not to be safe. Fortunately, last minute agreement raised the debt ceiling just in time.

The Deficit and the Debt
The budget deficit began trending towards zero after 2011 (Figure 11-5). So, when will the budget be balanced?

It won't.

In 2016, as the economy reached potential, the budget deficit *increased*. The budget balance became more negative, dropping from -2.4% to -3.2%. The Congressional Budget Office sees the deficit topping 4% of GDP in 2022, hitting 5% in 2027, and rising from there.

Deficits are projected to rise because of several factors. The baby boomers are retiring. That makes tens of millions of people newly eligible for Social Security and Medicare benefits. Medical costs have been rising faster than general inflation for many years. If that continues, the Medicare and Medicaid programs will become ever more expensive. And, the Affordable Care Act (Obamacare) expands the scope of health care coverage, offering subsidies to help low income people buy health insurance. These transfer payments or *entitlement payments* will increase as a share of GDP. And, adding insult to injury, deficits add to debt, and more debt means more interest to pay.

Tax revenue will increase over the next decade. As incomes rise taxpayers move into higher tax brackets. But the taxes at scheduled rates will not generate enough revenue to cover the promised entitlement benefits.

Continuous deficits add to the *national debt*. The debt is the sum total of the amount the government owes. It's the sum of all past deficits less past surpluses. The debt is usually measured as the *debt held by public*, which subtracts the debt owned by the Federal government to itself. This is mainly money that the government owes to the Social Security trust fund (see Chapter 6).

Figure 11-6 shows the Federal debt as a percentage of GDP starting in 1940, as well as the CBO's projection through 2027. The Great Recession caused enormous increases in Federal budget deficits and Federal borrowing, and so it caused enormous increases in the Federal debt. The national debt was less than 40% of GDP as recently as 2007. As of 2016 it was 77% of GDP. It has not been that high since 1950. By 2027 the CBO expects debt to be 89% of GDP.

The debt is usually measured as a percentage of GDP because the size of the national income shows how much debt the nation can support. Homeowners can pay interest and principle on a bigger mortgage if their incomes are higher. Likewise, the Federal government can pay interest and principle on a larger national debt if its national income is higher. A higher GDP generates more tax revenue, which means more spending of all kinds can be supported, including interest payments.

There are several problems associated with continuous government deficits and rising national debt. Since interest on the debt must be paid, spending on other government services must be reduced. Congress will have less flexibility to respond to national needs. Eventually, investors may hold so many Treasury bonds that they refuse to purchase more. Either the government would not be able to borrow, or would have to pay very high interest rates to attract lenders.

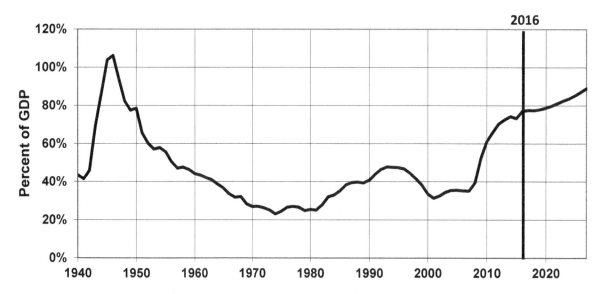

Figure 11-6. Federal debt as a percent of GDP, 1940-2016, and Congressional Budget Office projections, 2017-2027.

Deficits can cause *crowding out*. If the economy is at potential, deficits are *pro-cyclical fiscal policy*. Added government borrowing will increase money demand, raise interest rates, and reduce investment spending. Today's investment is tomorrow's buildings, machinery and technology. With fewer resources and slower growing technology, potential output will grow more slowly, and the nation will be poorer than it could have been. This happened in the 1980's. Deficits can cause inflation, if the Federal Reserve responds with money supply increases to keep interest rates low. This happened in the 1940's and the 1960's.

For these reasons, continuously increasing budget deficits are said to be *unsustainable*.

- *How will the United States ever pay back all that debt?*

After World War II the national debt exceeded GDP. The debt percentage was more than 100%. By 1974 the percentage was down to 23% of GDP. Perhaps we can predict how the U.S. will handle this new debt, by looking at how it handled the huge debt from World War II.

In 1946 and after, the Federal government ran surpluses in just 8 of 29 years. In the rest there were deficits, when the government spent more than revenues, and borrowed the difference. The dollar amount of debt increased by more than $100 billion. The debt from World War II was never paid back.

This does not mean that the U.S. defaulted on its debt. Instead, the debt was "rolled over." The government sold new Treasury bonds to borrow new money when payments came due on old Treasury bonds.

The debt as a percentage of GDP declined even though the government did not run surpluses. The reason is that GDP increased. The debt increased, but GDP increased more, so the debt as a percent of GDP went down. If the annual Federal deficit as a percentage of GDP is less than the amount that GDP grows, then the debt as a percent of GDP will fall. The key to reducing the debt percentage, then, is to reduce the size of the Federal budget deficit to less than the growth in nominal GDP. The CBO thinks that real GDP growth plus inflation is likely to average around 4% over the coming decade.

How will we pay back the national debt? Most likely, we won't. If we can hold the deficit to less than 4% of GDP, though, the national debt as a percentage of GDP will decline. We'll grow the economy enough to handle our debt payments. Unfortunately, the CBO projects the deficit to top 4% of GDP by 2022 and stay higher than 4% after that. At that rate the debt will rise continuously as a share of GDP, with all the implications for interest rates, crowding out, slower growth and currency crises. Those things won't happen this year, or next, but there's no doubt it's a big problem in the long run.

Crisis in Europe: The Greek Tragedy
In 1999 many European countries abandoned their traditional currencies and adopted the euro. France would no longer use the franc, Germany quit on the mark, and the Italian lira was no more. Their economies were tied together in a *currency union*.

Greece joined the *Eurozone* in 2000. The Greeks eliminated their traditional currency, the drachma, and adopted the euro, at a rate of 341 drachma per euro. Effectively, Greece had a fixed exchange rate with their trading partners in the rest of Europe.

The Greek government greatly expanded social programs beginning in the 1980's. By the 2000's the government employed one-third of the labor force, jobs were for life, and retirement before age 60 was common. Tax evasion was a problem, so the government supported its spending by borrowing, mostly from European banks. The banks were willing to lend partly because a country in the eurozone was assumed to be wealthy and well-governed.

In October 2009, however, Greece shocked international lenders by revealing that its deficit was actually more than triple what had been reported. The government had managed to disguise the extent of its borrowing, with the help of some of the larger banks. THe worldwide recession had reduced what tax revenues there were, so lenders feared that Greece could not meet the interest and principle payments on their loans. They were correct. Greece admitted that its debt could not be repaid.

The rest of the *European Union* was concerned. The Greeks had borrowed a lot of money. That meant that European banks held a lot of Greek bonds. Default on these bonds would reduce their value, or make them worthless. Banks that owned such bonds may have defaulted themselves on what they owed other lenders, and on what they owed their depositors. Greek default could have created a crisis for the entire European banking system.

So the European Union and the International Monetary Fund offered loans to Greece. This money allowed Greece to meet its debt payments. Greece and its lenders negotiated a "haircut," which means lenders agreed to take less than the full repayment of their loans. In return, Greece pledged to raise taxes and cut government spending.

European investors looked for a safe place to park their wealth. They found what they always find, U.S. Treasury bonds, the least-risky assets on the planet. To buy bonds they needed dollars, so they supplied euros in the exchange market, and demanded dollars. The exchange value of the dollar rose from 67 eurocents per dollar in November 2009 to 82 eurocents in June 2010, a 22% rise. Now U.S. exports to Europe were more expensive, and that made U.S. recovery from the Great Recession all the more difficult.

The rest of the world had a Great Recession. Greece had a Great Depression. Few banks would lend in Greece. Greek interest rates skyrocketed, and investment spending fell by two-thirds from 2007 to 2013. Real GDP fell every year from 2008 to 2013, by a total of 23%. The Greek unemployment rate hit 27.9% in July 2013, and stood at 23.5% as of January 2017.

What counter-cyclical policies could Greece use to fight this depression? Not monetary policy. There was no drachma. The Greek Central Bank gave up its monetary policy powers to the European Central Bank (ECB) when the euro was adopted. The ECB sets policy for the entire Eurozone, which is dominated by Germany and France. It will not cut interest rates just to help Greece.

How about fiscal policy? Not likely. Greece pledged to try to balance its budget, so taxes can't be cut nor spending increased. Further, if Greece tried deficit spending, it would need to issue Greek Treasury bonds, and who would buy them? Few banks would risk lending to Greece, since it can't make full payments on the debt it already has. The Greeks themselves are in no position to buy debt either.

In a sense, it's Robert Mundell's *impossible trinity*, again. The euro replaced the drachma, so the exchange rate between Greece and the rest of Europe is effectively fixed. Euros move freely among eurozone nations—that's one of the advantages of adopting the euro. It means that capital flows can't be restricted. So, stabilization policy must give way. Greece had to adopt pro-cyclical fiscal policy during its depression.

Devaluation of the currency hastened recover in Thailand and the other Asian countries after the Asian crisis (see Chapter 10). The lower exchange value of the baht encouraged exports. With the euro, this is not an option for Greece. Greece had to encourage exports by promoting "internal devaluation." The cost of its exports is the product of the exchange value of their currency, and the prices of Greek products. Since the exchange value of the euro is fixed, Greek exports can be made cheaper only with a drop in Greek prices. That's deflation. The only way to get sustained deflation is with sustained high unemployment, a long recession. That's what has happened. The Greek consumer price index fell every month from March 2013 to December 2016. Unfortunately, Greek exports have not increased, though they have stabilized. Meanwhile, the depression has reduced Greek spending on imports by 37%.

This could be a very long term problem. Greece's industry is simply not as efficient as Germany's. The world beats a path to Germany's door, demanding euros to buy German products. This supports the value of the euro. But that makes Greece's higher cost, lower quality products more expensive for the world to buy, because the euro's value is high.

It makes tourism to Greece more expensive too. If Greece still used the drachma, and the drachma's exchange value fell by 50% like Thailand's baht did, the cost of tourism in Greece would be cut in half. Tourism would boom. That can't happen with the euro.

> *Greece cannot help solve its currency crisis with exchange rate devaluation, as Thailand did, because it has adopted the euro.*

Perhaps it was a mistake for Greece to adopt the euro. The euro's value will reflect the economies of Germany and France, not the needs of little Greece. As long as people want to buy products from the big European nations, exports from Greece will be expensive too.

Greece considered abandoning the euro, a possibility called *Grexit* (which came before Brexit). Grexit would be difficult. If Greece returned to its old currency, deposits in Greek banks would be automatically converted to drachmas, and this new currency would then depreciate relative to the euro. So, depositors would shift their money out of Greek banks, to avoid this potential devaluation. The resulting bank runs would threaten the Greek banking system, and would decrease the Greek money supply too, making Greek interest rates even higher. The devaluation of the drachma would promote Greek exports and tourism, and allow counter-cyclical stabilization policy. But first there would be a banking crisis, and a lot of inflation, and perhaps a renewed recession. In the end, Greece decided to stick with the euro, at least for now.

What Comes Next

The United States economy is at potential output as of Spring 2017, with the unemployment rate at 4.3%. Counter-cyclical stabilization policy would involve efforts to remain at potential output with low inflation. Federal government budget deficits will grow with the retirement of the baby boomers, which means that fiscal policy will put upward pressure on aggregate demand. That would push equilibrium output beyond potential, unless the Federal Reserve gradually raises interest rates. That's probably what they'll do.

Sudden policy shifts could disrupt this state of affairs. A big tax cut unmatched by spending reductions, or a big infrastructure spending program financed by borrowing would increase aggregate demand more, and so require more rapid increases in interest rates. Crowding out would result.

A recession would change this outlook. The expansion since the end of the Great Recession is eight years old as of June 2017. That's the third longest expansion in U.S. history (after the 1990's and 1960's). Recessions don't die of old age, though, they die of shocks. Think the savings and loan crisis plus the Gulf War in 1990, the tech stock collapse, oil price rise and 9-11 attacks in 2001, and the housing crisis and financial panic in 2008.

Are there any shocks on the horizon that could end our expansion? What a silly question! Shocks are called shocks because they are shocking—unexpected disruptions to the economy. They can't be anticipated. Still, are there any candidates? Let's try a few.

- *Trouble in the European Union.* What if Brexit encourages Grexit, then Frexit (France) and Italexit (Italy)? Renegotiating trade relationships among all those countries, and re-establishing national currencies would disrupt financial markets. Europe might see recession, which would reduce U.S. exports, and contagion might affect U.S. lenders.
- *A Bubble Bursts in China.* What if China has a financial crisis? Some Chinese cities appear to have speculative real estate bubbles like those in the U.S. in the 2000's and Japan in the 1980's. China has tried to sustain growth by borrowing for new construction, but they now have so much debt that the Moody's bond rating agency cut their bond rating. That means they see a higher risk of default on all that debt. If China has a recession, or defaults on its debt, U.S. financial markets could see trouble.
- *U.S. Policy Mistakes.* What if the Fed raises interest rates too much too fast? If inflation bursts above the 2% target, or the unemployment rate drops below 4%, the Fed might decide to raise the federal funds rate more. If the "interest rate elasticity of business investment" is more negative than the Fed expects, an interest rate hike could reduce investment spending enough to create a recession.

What else? A war that creates uncertainty without a big increase in government purchases? A wave of consumer pessimism that reduces consumption? A big hike in oil prices that is not immediately offset by added U.S. production? Renegotiation of trade agreements that disrupts supply chains? Any of these could shock the economy into recession.

What if there is no recession, or only a series of mild recessions? What's the long-run outlook then?

In Chapter 3 we looked at the prospects for long term growth. With the economy at potential, real GDP growth is determined by how fast potential output can grow. And that depends on labor force growth and productivity.

The labor force will grow more slowly for at least a generation (assuming no big increase in immigration). The boomers will retire, and we know how many children will grow up over the next twenty years. The Bureau of Labor Statistics projects the labor force to grow only 0.7% per year through 2050, less than half what it averaged over the previous 40 years.

Productivity has grown slowly in the past decade, just 0.8% per year. If that continues, and we add that to slow labor force growth, we get potential output growth of just 1.5% per year in coming decades, about half what it has averaged since 1960. Why such slow growth?

Maybe slow growth comes from the supply side. Economist Robert J. Gordon argues that the 1928-72 period was exceptional, full of technological advances that added to productivity. Air travel and interstate highways, the power and efficiency of electric machinery, the development of plastics, and the huge investments in the quantity of buildings and equipment that began with World War II all added to productivity. The drop in productivity growth since then is a return to the pre-1928 historic norm. Gordon says that there are no similar productivity-enhancing advances on the horizon.

Maybe slow growth comes from the demand side. Economist Lawrence Summers thinks we're in the grips of *secular stagnation*. Here, "secular" means "trend," as opposed to changes resulting from the ups and downs of expansion and recession. Suppose that people save more. Life spans are longer and retirement benefits are uncertain so they must save more for retirement. The distribution of income is less equal (see Chapter 7). A greater share of income goes to wealthy people, who save a bigger share of their incomes. If saving increases, consumption falls, aggregate demand falls, and so does money demand.

That should reduce real interest rates, which should inspire greater investment, which should take up the slack in aggregate demand. But what if expected returns to investment are lower too? That would offset the lower interest rates. Remember that investment depends on the real interest rate and expected returns. Population is growing more slowly, so there are fewer new consumers to buy increased production. New technologies make investments in "brick and mortar" less profitable. Internet retailers like Amazon mean the construction of new malls is less profitable. Home sharing websites like Airbnb means hotels aren't as lucrative as before. The growing virtual economy simply uses less capital stock. All this means that equilibrium output growth will lag behind growth in potential output.

Maybe there are new technologies on the horizon that will require big new investments. Consider self-driving trucks, for example. If these become feasible the costs of shipment of most products will decline, which will increase the profitability of investment. Lower costs may encourage people to spend more, which could increase consumption. Output will increase and fewer workers will be needed, so productivity will increase.

But what will the truck drivers do? This was discussed in Chapter 7 too. The "superstar" engineer who runs a firm's entire driverless trucking fleet from the home office may be very well paid. The former truckers are out of luck. Savings may increase and consumption spending decrease if new technologies further concentrate income at the top.

And then there's the elephant in the room: climate change. The earth has a limited capacity to absorb the waste products of industrial civilization. We appear to be pushing those limits now. Potential output depends on natural conditions. If natural conditions deteriorate, aggregate supply would be reduced and potential output growth would slow. Inflation would increase too. Can we find policies that reduce industrial wastes without harming the employment, income and profit opportunities of households and businesses? Will we have to divert investment and know-how to defend Miami, New Orleans and New York from rising sea levels, instead of adding to potential output? How would the loss of output and income be distributed among the world's population?

These policy problems will likely outlive the author of this textbook. I hope that this course has helped you develop the skills to analyze, understand and influence macroeconomic policy, as voters or even as policymakers. Pay attention to the data. Analyze and understand by applying the model.

The story of the future is up to you.

Terms in this Chapter, in order of appearance
The Great Moderation
Standard deviation
Panic of 2008
Housing bubble
Capital gains tax cut
Counter-cyclical monetary policy
Mortgage innovation
Subprime mortgages
Secondary mortgage market
Fannie Mae
Freddie Mac
Mortgage-backed securities
Mortgage derivatives
Securitization
Credit rating service
Yen carry trade
China buying dollars
Leverage
Securities and Exchange Commission
Credit default swaps
Underwater mortgages
Lehman Brothers
Bear Stearns
Moral hazard
American International Group (A.I.G.)
Flight to safety
Wealth effect
Autonomous spending
Consumption function
Marginal propensity to consume
Shock
Reserves
Money multiplier
Safe haven
Counter-cyclical monetary policy
Open market operations
Monetary base
Counter-cyclical fiscal policy
Automatic stabilizers
Discretionary fiscal policy
Lender of last resort
Term Auction Facility
Commercial Paper Funding Facility
Bailouts
Troubled Asset Relief Program (TARP)

Quantitative Easing
Accommodative monetary policy
Lower bound
American Recovery and Reinvestment Act (ARRA)
Baby boom
Fiscal cliff
Sequester
Debt ceiling
Entitlement payments
National debt
Debt held by public
Crowding out
Pro-cyclical fiscal policy
Currency union
Eurozone
European Union
Impossible trinity
Grexit
Secular stagnation

Notes

For the history of the "Panic of 2008" I like Alan Blinder's *After the Music Stopped*, despite its tortured references to song lyrics. Eichengreen's *Hall of Mirrors* is fun for its comparison of the Great Recession to the Great Depression. I also used Charles Morris, *The Two Trillion Dollar Meltdown*, which is good for details about mortgage-backed securities and other financial maneuvers, and Paul Krugman, *The Return of Depression Economics and the Crisis of 2008*, which has a nice overview of the causes of the panic. Much of the rest of the information in this chapter comes from news reports, in particular the *New York Times'* series of articles under the title "The Reckoning." Alan Greenspan's 2008 testimony before the Government Oversight and Reform committee is also useful.

The Federal Reserve sponsored a series of papers called *Synopses of Selected Research on Housing, Mortgages, and Foreclosures,* which I relied on for the description of the housing bubble's rise and fall. It's online at www.newyorkfed.org/regional/Synopses.pdf.

Robert J. Shiller's data series on house prices goes back to 1890. It's available in spreadsheet form on his website, at www.econ.yale.edu/~shiller/data.htm.

Information on the impact of ARRA and the long-term budget projections comes from Congressional Budget Office publications, 2010-2011.

Data on Federal deficits and the national debt come from the Congressional Budget Office. The projections for the Federal deficit and national debt come from the CBO's latest review of the budget and the economy.

References

Bernanke, Benjamin and Vincent R. Reinhart. 2004. "Conducting Monetary Policy at Very Low Short-Term Interest Rates," Presented at the Meetings of the American Economic Association, San Diego, California (January 3).

Blinder, Alan. 2013. *After the Music Stopped: The Financial Crisis, the Response, and the Work Ahead.* New York: Penguin Press.

Congressional Budget Office. 2011. *Estimated Impact of the American Recovery and Reinvestment Act on Employment and Economic Output from January 2011 Through March 2011.* Washington D.C.: U.S. Government Printing Office.

Congressional Budget Office. 2017. The *Budget and Economic Outlook, Fiscal Years 2017 to 2027.* Washington, D.C.: Congressional Budget Office (January).

Eichengreen, Barry. 2015. *Hall of Mirrors: The Great Depression, the Great Recession, and the Uses—and Misuses—of History.* New York: Oxford University Press.

Gavin, William T. 2009. "More Money: Understanding Recent Changes in the Monetary Base," *Federal Reserve Bank of St. Louis Review* 91 (March/April).

Gordon, Robert J. 2016. *The Rise and Fall of American Growth.* Princeton, New Jersey: Princeton University Press.

Greenspan, Alan. 2008. "Testimony Before the Subcommittee on Government Oversight and Reform," U.S. Congress (October 23).

Krainer, John. 2008. "Recent Changes in the Homeownership Rate," in *Synopses of Selected Research on Housing, Mortgages, and Foreclosures*, New York Federal Reserve (March 17).

Krugman, Paul. 2009. *The Return of Depression Economics and the Crisis of 2008.* New York: W.W. Norton and Company.

McDonald, Daniel J. and Daniel L. Thornton. 2008. "A Primer on the Mortgage Market and Mortgage Finance," *Federal Reserve Bank of St. Louis Review* 90 (January/February): 31-45.

Morris, Charles R. 2008. *The Two Trillion Dollar Meltdown.* New York: Public Affairs.

Murphy, Edward Vincent. 2007. "Subprime Mortgages: Primer on Current Lending and Foreclosure Issues," *CRS Report to Congress*, Congressional Research Service, RL33930 (February 19).

Nelson, Rebecca M., Paul Belkin and James K. Jackson. 2017. *The Greek Debt Crisis: Overview and Implications for the United States.* Congressional Research Service (April 24).

Rosen, Richard J. 2007. "The Role of Securitization in Mortgage Lending," *Chicago Fed Letter* 244 (November).

Toossi, Mitra. 2012. "Projections of the Labor Force to 2050: a Visual Essay," *Monthly Labor Review* (October).

Wilcox, James A. 2008. "House Price Dynamics," in *Synopses of Selected Research on Housing, Mortgages, and Foreclosures*, New York Federal Reserve (March 28).

Wilcox, James A. 2008. "Research Findings on House Prices and Fundamentals," in *Synopses of Selected Research on Housing, Mortgages, and Foreclosures*, New York Federal Reserve (March 28).

News Articles
Appelbaum, Binyamin, "Federal Reserve Chairman Sees Modest Growth," *New York Times*, February 29, 2012.

Bajaj, Vikas and David Leonhardt. "Tax Break May Have Helped Cause Housing Bubble," *New York Times*, December 19, 2008.

Barboza, David. "Changes in China Could Raise Prices," *New York Times*, June 7, 2010.

Bradsher, Keith. "China Slows Purchases of U.S. and Other Bonds," *New York Times*, April 13, 2009.

Bradsher, Keith. "China's Addiction to Debt Now Threatens Its Growth," *New York Times*, May 24, 2017.

Chan, Sewell. "Fed Ends Its Purchasing of Mortgage Securities," *New York Times*, March 31, 2010.

Duhigg, Charles. "Pressured to Take More Risk, Fannie Reached Tipping Point," *New York Times*, October 5, 2008.

Goodman, Peter S. and Gretchen Morgenson. "Saying Yes, WaMu Built Empire on Shaky Loans," *New York Times*, December 28, 2008

International Monetary Fund, "Ease off Spending Cuts to Boost U.S Recovery." *IMFSurvey Magazine: Countries and Regions*, June 14, 2013. [www.imf.org/external/pubs/ft/survey/so/2013/CAR061413A.htm]

Labaton, Stephen. "Agency's '04 Rule Let Banks Pile Up New Debt," *New York Times*, October 3, 2008.

Landler, Mark. "Chinese Savings Helped Inflate American Bubble," *New York Times*, December 26, 2008.

Lewitt, Michael. "Wall Street's Next Big Problem," *New York Times*, September 16, 2008.

Lowenstein, Roger. "See a Bubble?" *New York Times*, June 5, 2005.

Morgenson, Gretchen. "Behind Insurer's Crisis, Blind Eye to a Web of Risk," *New York Times*, September 28, 2008.

Nocera, Joe and Edmund L. Andrews. "Struggling to Keep Up as the Crisis Raced On," *New York Times*, October 23, 2008.

Pilling, David. "Japan's Fearless Women Speculators," *Financial Times*, February 20, 2009.

Sorkin, Andrew Ross. "JP Morgan Pays $2 a Share for Bear Stearns," *New York Times*, March 17, 2008.

Sullivan, Patricia. "Obituary: Fed Governor Edward M. Gramlich," *Washington Post*, September 6, 2007.

Appendix
How to Use the Macroeconomic Model

This appendix describes the whole model and illustrates how it works with an extended made up example. It shows how to use the model to turn a set of macroeconomic indicators into a story of what happened in the economy. Read it all at once, or use it for reference as you go.

The Goods Market

Start with a horizontal Q axis, a vertical P axis and the potential output line, Qp. Q stands for quantity of output, measured by real GDP. P stands for the change in prices, measured with the inflation rate. Qp is potential output, marking the level of output when all resources are used as their ordinarily are. That's Figure A-1. Forget the mess in the middle for now.

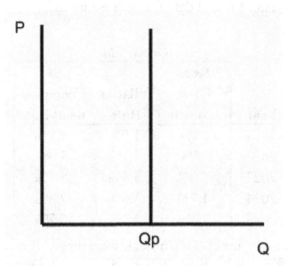

Figure A-1. Goods Market Axes.

Unemployment rates. Look at the first year's unemployment rate. If it is greater than 5%, then the first equilibrium is below potential output, to the left of the Qp line. If it is less than 5%, then the first equilibrium is above potential output, to the right of the Qp line. If the unemployment rate is 5%, or close, then the first equilibrium is on the Qp line. Do the same for the second year's unemployment rate. Is it to the right, the left, or on the Qp line?

Real GDP growth rate. Now look at the *second year's* GDP growth rate. This tells you how real GDP or real output changed from the first year to the second year. If the growth rate is positive, then output on the horizontal axis increased from the first to the second year. If the growth rate is negative, then output decreased from the first to the second year. If it zero or near zero, then output didn't change from the first to the second year.

Inflation rate. Compare the first and second year's inflation rates. If the inflation rate increased, then inflation on the vertical axis moved upward. If the inflation rate decreased, then inflation on the vertical axis moved downward. If the inflation rate did not change, or was nearly unchanged, then inflation on the vertical axis was nearly unchanged.

Draw the AD and AS lines. Draw the aggregate demand-aggregate supply "X" so that the intersection is to the left, right or on the Qp line, based on the position of the first year's output relative to potential output. That was defined by whether the unemployment rate was above, below or equal to 5%.

Now, look at how real GDP changed, which you based on the sign of the second year's real GDP growth rate. If it's positive, the second year's equilibrium "X" must be to the right of the first year's. If the second year's real GDP growth rate is negative, the second year's "X" must be to

337

the left of the first. Then check the inflation rate. If it increased from the first to the second year, the "X" intersection must be above the first. If the inflation rate decreased, the "X" must be below the first.

These two comparisons will show whether AD increased, or AD decreased, or AS increased, or AS decreased. It shows which line shifted, and in what direction.

Finally, check the second year's unemployment rate. If it is less than 5%, the new equilibrium must be to the right of Qp. If it is more than 5%, the new equilibrium must be to the left of Qp. If it is equal to or nearly equal to 5%, the new equilibrium must be at the Qp line. This shows how much the line shifted.

Here are some made-up data to illustrate data-model-story in the goods market. (If you're reading this in 2021 or after, don't be confused! This isn't the real data for your economy!)

2020-2021. The unemployment rate is 4.8% in 2021, which is near 5%. The 2021 equilibrium was close to potential output. In the left part of Figure A-2, the circle labeled 4.8% shows equilibrium output at potential. That's why the first "X" is right at Qp (point 1). Real GDP increased from 2021 to 2022, as shown by the positive real GDP growth rate of 3.1% in 2022. (Ignore the 2021 real GDP growth rate! That shows you the change in real GDP from 2019 to 2020.) The AD-AS equilibrium must have

Goods Market

Year	Real GDP Growth	Inflation Rate	Unemploy- ment Rate
2021	2.4%	1.9%	4.8%
2022	3.1%	4.1%	3.9%
2023	-0.3%	6.6%	5.1%
2024	-1.7%	3.5%	7.8%
2025	2.0%	3.4%	6.7%

moved to the right from 2021 to 2022. That's shown in Figure A-2 as the rightward arrow labeled "3.1%". The inflation rate increased from 1.9% to 4.1% from 2021 to 2022 shown by the upward arrow. The AD-AS equilibrium must have moved up from 2021 to 2022. The unemployment rate is 3.9% in 2022, less than 5%. The 2022 equilibrium was to the right of the Qp line, shown but the circle labeled 3.9%.

We have an increase in output, an increase in inflation, and a move from potential output to more than potential. The only possible single shift that could produce these results is an increase in aggregate demand, AD, which is a movement up and to the right (a). The first year equilibrium is at Qp; the second year equilibrium is right of Qp. The right part of Figure A-2 shows the result.

What's the story? Aggregate demand depends on spending, so you know that spending increased. Spending is consumption plus investment plus government purchases plus exports minus imports. Figure A-3 shows the list and the determinants of these five spending categories using shorthand symbols.

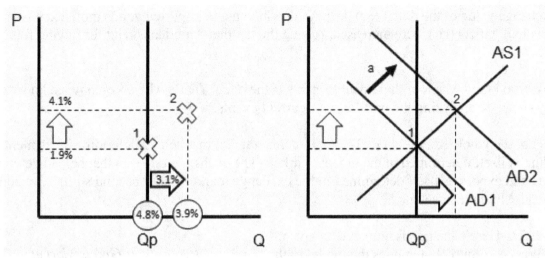

Figure A-2. Data and Model in the Goods Market, 2021-2022.

Determinants of Aggregate Demand

- Consumption = A + b (Y − T + R)
- Investment = I (r, exp)
- Government purchases = G
- Exports = X (xr, tar)
- Imports = M (xr, tar)

Figure A-3. Determinants of Aggregate Demand.

The determinants of consumption spending are shown in the consumption function. Perhaps consumers spent more because their incomes increased (Y), or their taxes were cut (T), or their transfer payments increased (R). Perhaps their wealth increased, or they finally paid off their debts (A).

The determinants of investment spending are shown in functional form, "I" followed by a list in parentheses. Perhaps businesses spent more on buildings, equipment or inventories, or consumers bought more new houses, because the real interest rate fell (r), which made borrowing for investment spending cheaper. Perhaps businesses became more confident, so their expected profits (exp) from investment increased.

We don't list any determinants for government purchases. We'll take that as the result of public policy. Perhaps government purchases increased. Maybe Congress decided to spend more on infrastructure. Maybe there was a war.

Export and import spending depends on the same determinants, but in opposite directions. Export spending may have increased—that is, maybe the rest of the world bought more goods made in the U.S. Maybe the exchange value of the dollar (xr) decreased, making exports cheaper. Maybe foreign tariffs (tar) were reduced, which would have reduced the tax foreigners had to pay on the U.S. goods they bought.

Maybe import spending *decreased*. When Americans buy fewer goods from other countries, they buy more from U.S. producers, and that increases spending and aggregate demand. Perhaps the exchange value of the dollar (xr) decreased, which made imported goods more expensive. Perhaps U.S. tariffs (tar) were increased, raising the tax that Americans paid for buying foreign goods.

How do you know which of these determinants is the one? That's where you have to know your history (if we're analyzing the past) or your current events.

That's not the whole story, either. The real interest rate (r) that helped determine investment spending is itself determined in the money market. The exchange rate (xr) that helped determine imports and exports is itself determined in the exchange market. The "second shifts" can add to the story. More on those later.

2022-2023. Here's the goods market data again, for reference. Figure A-4 applies the model to the (made up) data for 2022-2023. Unemployment is 3.9% in 2022, which is less than 5%, so the starting equilibrium is to the right of potential output. Real GDP growth in 2023 is negative, so output is falling. The new equilibrium will move left on the horizontal Q axis. The inflation rate went up from 4.1% to 6.6%, so the new equilibrium will move up on the vertical P axis. The unemployment rate for 2023 is 5.1%, close to 5%, so the new equilibrium will at potential output. The equilibrium must shift from point 2 to point 3 in Figure A-4.

	Goods Market		
	Real GDP	**Inflation**	**Unemploy-**
Year	**Growth**	**Rate**	**ment Rate**
2021	2.4%	1.9%	4.8%
2022	3.1%	4.1%	3.9%
2023	-0.3%	6.6%	5.1%
2024	-1.7%	3.5%	7.8%
2025	2.0%	3.4%	6.7%

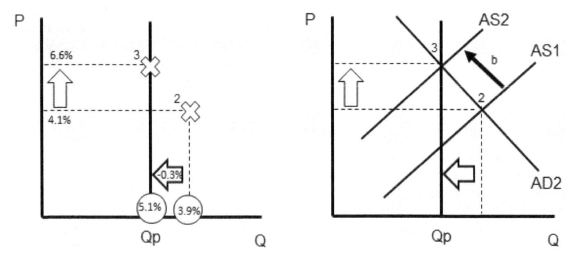

Figure A-4. Data and Model in the Goods Market, 2022-2023.

The only possible shift that can produce these results is a decrease in aggregate supply (b). There was a decrease in production, which is what aggregate supply represents. That's a shift upward and to the left of the aggregate supply curve, from AS1 to AS2 in Figure A-4.

What's the story now? That depends on what changed aggregate supply. Figure A-5 shows the list of aggregate supply determinants.

Perhaps input costs increased. A decrease in supply usually happens for one of two reasons. The price of oil might have increased. This was the reason for the supply shocks of the 1970's. Then there's second shift #1. Output was above potential, which means inputs were being used with extraordinary intensity. Unemployed inputs are scarce. Firms bid up the prices of inputs, which makes production less profitable. They scale back their plans. Wages in particular should rise with the unemployment rate less than 5%. This is second shift #1.

> **Determinants of Aggregate Supply**
> * Input costs (labor, machinery, materials)
> * Technology/Productivity
> * Natural conditions

Figure A-5. Determinants of Aggregate Supply.

We don't often think of technology deteriorating. Occasionally we outlaw a particular technology, like a pesticide or Freon in refrigerators. When we banned child labor we reduced aggregate supply. Perhaps productivity grew more slowly. We could represent that by a decrease of aggregate supply.

Maybe a freeze destroyed the fruit crop in Florida. Perhaps a hurricane in the Gulf of Mexico knocked out some oil refineries, or flooded a major city. Perhaps an earthquake wrecked an industrial center, or a plague killed a large part of the labor force. The story behind decreases in aggregate supply can get pretty dramatic.

2023-2024, 2024-2025. Figure A-6 shows the data and diagrams for 2023-2024. Real GDP decreased in 2024, so we move left on the Q axis. The inflation rate fell from 2023 to 2024, so

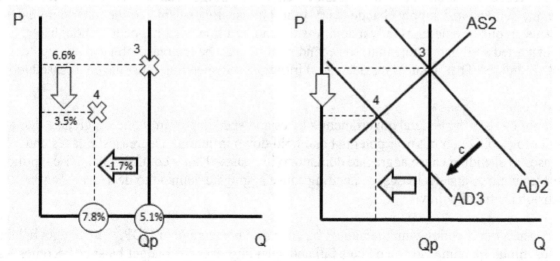

Figure A-6. Data and Model in the Goods Market, 2023-2024.

we move down on the P axis. The unemployment rate starts near 5% in 2023, then increases, so the 2024 equilibrium will be left of Qp.

The data imply a decrease in aggregate demand (c), the only shift that can produce a drop in real GDP and a fall in inflation. Spending must have decreased, and the determinants of aggregate demand and the second shifts would give clues as to why.

Figure A-7 shows the data and diagrams for 2024-2025. This one is different. Yes, real GDP increases by 2.0% in 2025, so we move right on the Q axis. We begin and end with unemployment above 5%, so the shift takes place to the left of Qp. But the inflation rate is nearly unchanged. If only one curve shifts, the inflation rate will move more decidedly up or down.

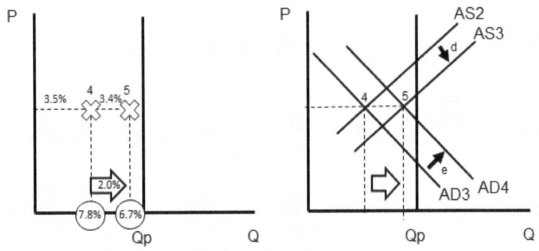

Figure A-7. Data and Model in the Goods Market, 2024-2025.

So two curves must have shifted. Both aggregate supply (d) and aggregate demand (e) must have increased, but about the same amount to leave the inflation rate unchanged. In reality, both aggregate demand and supply change every year, but usually one shift or the other dominates, so we focus on one. Sometimes only a double-shift can describe what happened, though. Output started well under potential, so second shift #1 may be the reason for the aggregate supply increase. That would have decreased inflation, but spending must have increased too.

Fiscal Policy
Fiscal policy uses the Federal government's taxes and spending to influence aggregate demand, in order to stabilize output near potential and hold down inflation. Decreases in taxes and increases in spending cause aggregate demand to increase. That's contractionary fiscal policy. Increases in taxes and decreases in spending cause aggregate demand to decrease. That's expansionary fiscal policy.

We measure fiscal policy with the budget balance as a percentage of GDP. The budget balance is taxes minus spending, so when taxes fall and spending rises the budget balance becomes less positive or more negative. That's an increase in the budget deficit. When taxes rise and spending falls the budget balance becomes more positive. That's a decrease in the budget deficit. If the balance turns positive that's a budget surplus. We can use the budget balance data to add fiscal policy to the story about the goods market.

The data table shows the goods market data again, with some (made up) budget balance data. From 2021 to 2022 the balance became much more negative, from -0.4% of GDP to -3.5% of GDP. Taxes decreased or spending increased, or both. Expansionary fiscal policy added to spending. Lower taxes (T) and higher transfer payments (R) could have raised disposable income, which stimulated consumer spending. Government purchases (G) could have increased, which would have added from spending directly.

	Goods Market			Policy
Year	Real GDP Growth	Inflation Rate	Unemploy-ment Rate	Budget Balance % GDP
2021	2.4%	1.9%	4.8%	-0.4%
2022	3.1%	4.1%	3.9%	-3.5%
2023	-0.3%	6.6%	5.1%	-3.7%
2024	-1.7%	3.5%	7.8%	-2.2%
2025	2.0%	3.4%	6.7%	-4.8%

Now we have a nice explanation for the increase in aggregate demand shown in Figure A-2. The government stimulated spending with tax cuts or spending increases. This is pro-cyclical policy. The economy was at potential output with low inflation in 2021, and the budget was close to balanced. The government disrupted this happy scene, destabilizing the economy. Perhaps it was a mistake. Perhaps the government had other priorities than stabilization.

Not much happened to the budget balance in 2023, but in 2024 it became less negative, moving towards balance (at zero). Again, we've got an explanation for the drop in aggregate demand in figure A-6. Government may have raised taxes and cut transfers, to decrease consumer spending, or cut purchases, which decreased aggregate demand directly. Again, this is pro-cyclical policy. Output was at potential, and the contractionary fiscal policy helped move it below potential. Perhaps, though, this was an intentional effort to create a recession to bring down inflation. Only knowledge of policy history or current events could tell.

In 2025 fiscal policy became more expansionary, which helps explain the increase in aggregate demand in figure A-7. The decrease in the budget balance (increase in the deficit) in 2025 is definitely counter-cyclical fiscal policy. Unemployment was high, output was well below potential, so expansionary fiscal policy increased spending. Output moved towards potential, which is a stabilizing policy.

Second Shifts

Second shifts are the term we use in this textbook (and nowhere else) when a shift of demand or supply in one market causes another shift in the same or another market. We focus on five second shifts, shown in Figure A-8.

Second Shifts

1. Goods to goods, through shifts in aggregate supply towards potential output.
2. Money to Goods, through real interest rate effects on investment.
3. Goods to Money, through income and price changes to money demand.
4. Exchange to Goods, through exchange rate effects on exports and imports.
5. Money to Exchange, through real interest rate effects on lender exchange demand.

Figure A-8. Five Second Shifts.

Second shift #1, which we've already mentioned, is the only one that happens entirely within one market. When equilibrium output is different from potential output, inputs costs change, which shifts aggregate supply back towards potential output. Costs rise and aggregate supply decreases when output exceeds potential. Costs fall and aggregate supply increases when output is less than potential.

Second shift #2 shows how changes in the money market affect the goods market. When money demand or money supply shift, the real interest rate changes, which affects investment spending in the goods market. Increases in money demand or decreases in money supply raise the real interest rate, which reduces investment spending and aggregate demand. Decreases in money demand or increases in money supply reduce the real interest rate, which raises investment spending and aggregate demand.

Second shift #3 shows how changes in the goods market affect the money market. Changes in aggregate demand or aggregate supply change output and inflation. Remember that output and income are the same in the aggregate. Changes in income and prices affect money demand, which changes the real interest rate. When income and inflation rise, money demand increases and the real interest rate rises. When income and inflation fall, money demand decreases and the real interest rate falls. When the two move in opposite directions, look at the relative size of the changes. It's always possible that the two cancel out and money demand doesn't change at all. Be careful—second shifts #2 and #3 can lead to an endless back-and-forth cycle. Generally, shift a curve in each market just once. The exception is "crowding out." More on that later.

Second shift #4 shows how changes in the exchange market affect the goods market. Shifts in the exchange demand for the dollar or exchange supply of the dollar change the exchange rate, which affects exports and imports, and so affects aggregate demand. If dollar demand rises and dollar supply falls, the exchange value of the dollar (exchange rate) rises, which reduces exports and raises imports. That decreases aggregate demand. If dollar demand falls and dollar supply rises, the exchange value of the dollar falls, which raises exports and reduces imports. That increases aggregate demand.

Second shift #5 shows how changes in the money market affect the exchange market. It's the only one that doesn't involve the goods market. If money demand or money supply shift, the real interest rate changes, and that affects dollar demand and dollar supply in the exchange market. If the real interest rate increases in the money market, lenders will want to lend more in the U.S. The demand for the dollar will increase, and the supply of the dollar will decrease. That will raise the exchange value of the dollar. If the real interest rate decreases in the money market, lenders will want to lend less in the U.S. The demand for the dollar will decrease, and the supply of the dollar will increase. That will reduce the exchange value of the dollar.

The Money Market

The money market has the quantity of money on the horizontal axis and the real interest rate on the vertical axis (Figure A-9). Our main interest is the real interest rate, which influences investment in the goods market (that's second shift #2). *Always start with money demand*, based on its determinants (Figure A-10). Then check the change in the interest rate spread, which we used to measure the real interest rate. If the shift in money demand is consistent with the change in the real interest rate, you may be done (check monetary policy though). If not, shift money supply as needed to change the real interest rate in the right direction.

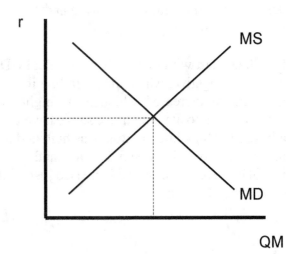

Figure A-9. The Money Market.

2021-2022, 2022-23. Start with money demand. The determinants of money demand are income and price (Figure A-10). In the aggregate economy, GDP and income are the same, so the positive real GDP growth in 2022 shows an increase in income. Inflation increased too. People needed more money in their checking accounts to handle the increased purchases they made with the higher income, and the increased prices on those purchases. Money demand increases.

We measure the real interest rate with the interest rate spread, the difference between the interest rate on more-risky corporate bonds and less-risky corporate bonds. The data table shows some (made up) interest rate spread data. The spread increased from 2021 to 2022.

The increase in money demand shown in Figure A-11 (left) can explain this change (shift a). There is no need to shift money supply. The real interest rate (and the spread) often increase when the economy expands, especially when output rises beyond potential output.

	Goods Market		Money Market
	Real		**Interest**
	GDP	**Inflation**	**Rate**
Year	**Growth**	**Rate**	**Spread**
2021	2.4%	1.9%	0.7%
2022	3.1%	4.1%	0.9%
2023	-0.3%	6.6%	1.0%
2024	-1.7%	3.5%	2.1%
2025	2.0%	3.4%	1.4%

Now we can add another element to our story. We think that aggregate demand increased because of expansionary fiscal policy. Money demand increased with rising incomes and inflation. That increased the interest rate spread, which would have decreased investment spending (second shift #2). That's crowding out! A bigger government budget deficit reduced business borrowing and investment spending.

For 2023, start with money demand. Real GDP growth is negative, which means falling income.

Determinants of Money Demand

- Income
- Prices/Inflation

Figure A-10. Determinants of Money Demand.

But inflation increased, which means higher prices. The two determinants are moving money demand in opposite directions, so we have to guess about money demand. Here, income fell just a little (-0.3%) while inflation was high and increasing (6.6%). Those higher prices probably mean that people increased their demand for money, which is shown in Figure A-11 (right, shift b). The interest rate spread increased just a little from 2022 to 2023, so the money demand shift explains that change.

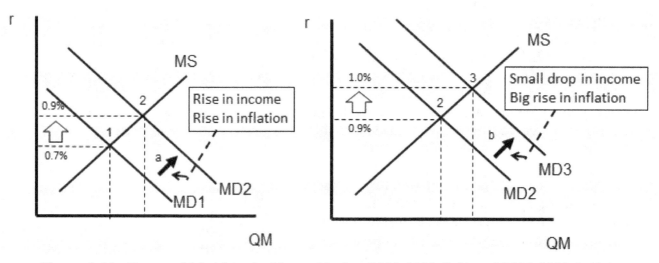

Figure A-11. Data and Model in the Money Market, 2021-2022 (left) and 2022-2023 (right).

2023-2024. Start with money demand. Real GDP growth was negative, so income falls. Inflation decreased. Both indicators point to decreased money demand. That's shown as (c) in Figure A-12. But look at the data—the interest rate spread increased! A lot! A decline in money demand should decrease the interest rate spread, but that didn't happen.

That means money supply must have decreased, but more than money demand. That's the only shift that can produce an increase in the interest rate spread when money demand is decreasing. The money supply shift is shown as (d).

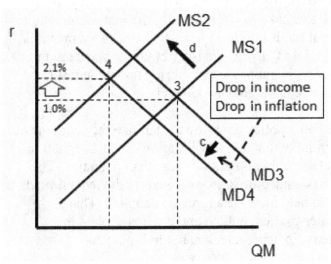

Figure A-12. Data and Model in the Money Market, 2023-2024.

Now we can add more to the story of 2023-2024 by consulting the determinants of money supply, shown in Figure A-13. We'll consider Federal Reserve policy soon. It didn't change in 2024. That means lenders must have turned pessimistic. They increased reserves, so the money multiplier decreased, and that decreased the money supply. Perhaps there was a panic in financial markets.

Aggregate demand decreased (Figure A-6). It looks like a panic in financial markets increased the interest rate spread, which cut off lending and borrowing by more-risky corporations. That's second shift #2. The decline in business investment would have decreased aggregate demand, and helped cause that recession.

2024-2025. Start with money demand (do you sense a theme here?). Inflation was almost unchanged, but income increased, so money demand must have increased, at least a little. That's shown as (e) in Figure A-14. But again, this is inconsistent with the data. The interest rate spread decreased in 2025. An increase in money demand would have increased the spread. Money supply must have increased by more than money demand. That's shown as (f) in Figure A-14. To tell the story of this shift, we need monetary policy.

> **Determinants of Money Supply**
> - Lender expectations
> - Federal Reserve policy

Figure A-13. Determinants of Money Demand.

Monetary Policy

The Federal Reserve uses monetary policy to try to stabilize the economy at potential output with low inflation. The federal funds rate is the main indicator of Federal Reserve policy. It's the interest rate that banks charge one another on overnight loans. An increase in the federal funds rate shows that the Fed is reducing the money supply. That's contractionary monetary policy. The Fed uses contractionary policy when output is above potential and inflation is high. A decrease in the federal funds rate shows that the Fed is increasing the money supply. That's expansionary monetary policy. The Fed uses expansionary policy when output is less than potential and inflation is low.

The (made up) federal funds rates in the data table show little change in monetary policy from 2021 to 2024. In 2025, though, the Fed decreased the federal funds rate from 4.0% to 1.6%. That means the Fed was buying Treasury bonds in an attempt to increase the money supply, bring down interest rates, and increase aggregate demand.

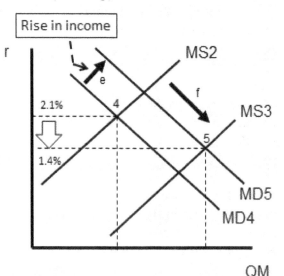

The Fed's policy goals are to stabilize the economy at potential output and low inflation. In 2024 inflation was falling, but output was less than potential. The Fed responded in 2025 with a cut in the federal funds rate to help increase aggregate demand. That's counter-cyclical policy, and it helps explain the increase in aggregate demand in Figure A-7.

Figure A-14. Data and Model in the Money Market, 2024-2025.

Let's not give this Federal Reserve too much credit, though. They sat on their hands in 2022 and 2023 as inflation was rising well above the 2% target. Counter-cyclical policy required an increase in the federal funds rate, to restrain aggregate demand and hold inflation down. The *real* federal funds rate is the nominal rate (shown in the table) minus the inflation rate, and it was falling in 2022 and 2023. In a sense, that was pro-cyclical policy, a lower real interest rate when a higher rate was needed. When evaluating Fed policy, remember to check unemployment, inflation, the federal funds rate and the *real* federal funds rate.

	Goods Market			*Money Market*	*Policy*
Year	**Real GDP Growth**	**Inflation Rate**	**Unemploy- ment Rate**	**Interest Rate Spread**	**Federal Funds Rate**
2021	2.4%	1.9%	4.8%	0.7%	4.0%
2022	3.1%	4.1%	3.9%	0.9%	3.8%
2023	-0.3%	6.6%	5.1%	1.0%	3.9%
2024	-1.7%	3.5%	7.8%	2.1%	4.0%
2025	2.0%	3.4%	6.7%	1.4%	1.6%

The Exchange Market

The exchange market in Figure A-15 has the quantity of dollars traded in international currency markets on the horizontal axis (Qex) and the exchange value of the dollar (the exchange rate) on the vertical axis ($ex). Our only interest is the exchange value of the dollar, which influences exports and imports in the goods market (that's second shift #4). Measure the exchange rate as

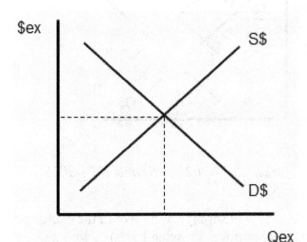

foreign currency units per dollar (like euros per dollar, yen per dollar, etc.). That's the price of the dollar as measured in another nation's currency. If the exchange value of the dollar goes up, then the demand for the dollar has increased and the supply of the dollar has decreased. If the exchange value of the dollar goes down, then the demand for the dollar has decreased and the supply of the dollar has increased. You can shift either curve or both, as you please, because the determinants of exchange demand and supply are symmetric.

Figure A-15. The Exchange Market.

The change in the number of dollars traded in currency markets would decide which curve to shift—but there are no data measuring that. That means you can choose which curve to shift. Use the shift that you understand the best. Get it right, and you'll have the right story to tell.

2021-2022. Here are all the data we've used, plus a (made up) exchange value of the dollar. Perhaps this is measured as European euros per dollar. The exchange value of the dollar increased from 2021 to 2022, from 0.96 euros per dollar to 1.07 euros per dollar. Figure A-16 (left) shows the shifts that must occur for the exchange value of the dollar to increase. The demand for the dollar must increase (a), and the supply of the dollar must decrease (b).

	Goods Market			Money Market	Exchange Market	Policy	
Year	Real GDP Growth	Inflation Rate	Unemploy-ment Rate	Interest Rate Spread	Exchange Value of Dollar	Federal Funds Rate	Budget Balance % GDP
2021	2.4%	1.9%	4.8%	0.7%	0.96	4.0%	-0.4%
2022	3.1%	4.1%	3.9%	0.9%	1.07	3.8%	-3.5%
2023	-0.3%	6.6%	5.1%	1.0%	1.06	3.9%	-3.7%
2024	-1.7%	3.5%	7.8%	2.1%	1.08	4.0%	-2.2%
2025	2.0%	3.4%	6.7%	1.4%	0.93	1.6%	-4.8%

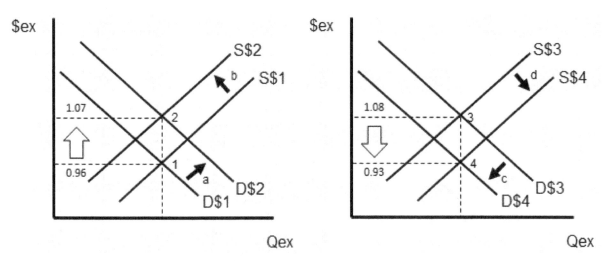

Figure A-16. Data and Model in the Exchange Market, 2021-2022 (left) and 2024-2025 (right).

Figure A-17 shows the determinants of exchange demand and supply. Why would the exchange value of the dollar rise? In 2022 the U.S. economy was booming, growing by 3.1% with a low unemployment rate. Profit expectations for U.S. businesses would be high, so foreign investors would demand dollars in order to buy U.S. land, businesses and stocks. That would increase the demand for the dollar. Likewise, Americans would want to invest in the U.S. too, and not in the rest of the world, so they would demand fewer foreign currencies. That means they would supply fewer dollars in exchange.

The interest rate spread is rising too, which means lenders can earn more interest on loans in the U.S. They'll demand more dollars in order to lend. Americans will want to lend in the U.S. too, and not in other countries, so they'll demand fewer foreign currencies and so supply fewer dollars. That's second shift #5—interest rate changes in the money market affect demand and supply in the exchange market.

Remember, in the exchange market, we look at the behavior of lenders. In the goods market, we look at the behavior of borrowers. So higher interest rates in the exchange market increase the demand for the dollar. Higher interest rates in the goods market decrease investment spending.
The higher exchange value of the dollar makes U.S. exports more expensive, and U.S. imports cheaper. That's second shift #4. This is another aspect of crowding out. The budget deficit increases the demand for money, which increases interest rates. That increased the exchange value of the dollar, which reduced exports. Imports would have increased. The rise in consumption and government purchases increases aggregate demand,

Determinants of Exchange Demand and Supply

- Income
- Quality
- Prices
- Interest Rates
- Expectations
- Government Policy

Figure A-17. Determinants of Exchange Demand and Supply.

but at a cost of declines in investment and exports, and a rise in imports.

2024-2025. Nothing much happened to the exchange value of the dollar from 2022 to 2024, but it dropped in 2025. The demand and supply shifts are shown in Figure A-15 (right). Exchange demand must have increased (c) and exchange supply must have increased (d). For a story, let's look at second shift #5 again. The Fed cut the federal funds rate and the interest rate spread came down. Lenders will look elsewhere than the U.S. for high returns. The demand for the dollar will fall. Americans will also want to lend abroad. They demand foreign currencies by supplying more dollars. The supply of the dollar will rise.

This is a second path for monetary policy. The Fed cuts interest rates, which makes lending in the U.S. less profitable. The value of the dollar falls, which increases exports and decreases imports. This raises aggregate demand, which was the counter-cyclical monetary policy result the Fed was looking for.

The Whole Story
The three-market macroeconomic model lets us interpret the data, to give us the outline of a story about what happened in the economy. So what happened? The economy was at potential with low inflation in 2021. But in 2022 the government cut taxes and increased spending. Maybe they had a good reason—defense spending for a war, or a response to a big natural disaster—or maybe it was a mistake. In any case, consumer and government spending increased, which raised the real interest rate and reduced investment spending. Export spending fell too, as the high interest rates caused an increase in the exchange value of the dollar.

Input costs began to rise as businesses bid for resources and workers began to expect inflation. That decreased aggregate supply, and created stagflation, rising inflation with declining output. The economy just moved back to potential in 2023, where it had been in 2021, but with a much higher inflation rate.

Then came a financial crisis in 2024. Banks became pessimistic and increased their reserves. That cut the money multiplier and caused the money supply to decrease. The real interest rate spiked, and investment spending dropped. The economy plunged into recession.

Policymakers responded in 2025. The Fed cut the federal funds rate, increasing the money supply. The real interest rate fell, and this encouraged businesses to resume investment spending. This also reduced the exchange value of the dollar, which encouraged exports. The federal government cut taxes and raised transfers to aid consumption spending, and increased government purchases. All this increased aggregate demand. Meanwhile, high unemployment held down input costs, and businesses found production more profitable. Production increased. The recession ended and recovery began.

Reality
This example was made up. The model works to build a story from these numbers. Real data will be more difficult. The model is simple (really!); the economy is complex.

There's a list at the very front of this book of the 16 data-model-story analyses throughout all 11 chapters. That's where to go to see the model in action, using actual data from actual events.

One piece of advice. When you apply the model to real data, don't be too mechanical.

- *Sometimes you have to look at changes or trends over three or four years to get a sense of what's happening.*
- *Sometimes (especially before 1955) you want to see actual deflation—negative inflation—when the price level declines on the vertical axis of the goods market, not just a decline in the inflation rate.*
- *Sometimes real interest rates explain more than the interest rate spread or the nominal federal funds rate. Check out the interest rates minus the inflation rate.*
- *Sometimes the economy is at potential output when the unemployment rate is a bit higher than 5%, or a bit lower than 5%.*
- *Sometimes it's important to remember that potential output is always increasing with population, the capital stock and advancing technology.*

Sometimes the model won't match the data very well at all.

What to do then? The best you can. Especially, learn the story. What did the people on Main Street and Wall Street think was happening? What did policymakers intend to happen when they applied their policies? What were reporters reporting? What have analysts figured out? All these apply to using the model with current events, too.

What you're seeking is an analysis of what's going on. The data and the model should help, but in the end what you want is the story.

Index